Teaching and Learning in the Elementary School

Teaching and Learning in the Elementary School

SECOND EDITION

John Jarolimek / Clifford D. Foster

University of Washington, Seattle

Macmillan Publishing Co., Inc.
New York

Collier Macmillan Publishers
London

Printed in the United States of America

Macmillan Publishing Co., Inc.
866 Third Avenue, New York, New York 10022

Collier Macmillan Canada, Ltd.

Library of Congress Cataloging in Publication Data

Jarolimek, John.
Teaching and learning in the elementary school.

Includes bibliographies and index.
1. Elementary school teaching. 2. Lesson planning. I. Foster, Clifford Donald (date) joint author. II. Title.
LB1555.J34 1981 372.11'02 80-12188
ISBN 0-02-360400-X

Printing: 1 2 3 4 5 6 7 8 Year: 1 2 3 4 5 6 7

PREFACE

We assume that an elementary school that does not help all children who attend it to become literate and numerate has a professional staff that is not doing its job properly. This text, however, is based on the additional assumption that the elementary school curriculum has responsibility for a broad range of educational goals. To embrace broad goals means that teaching in the elementary school concerns itself with the intellectual, social, emotional, and to some extent, the physical development of young people. Teaching to achieve broad goals is a process that has as its purpose the bringing of individual pupils to full growth as maturing persons.

A commitment to broad educational goals has many implications for the arrangement of the classroom environment and how teaching takes place in it. If one is concerned only with narrow goals, such as the mastery of basic skills, teachers can be quite successful by using direct instruction with fairly large groups of pupils on a whole-class basis. Concern for broad goals, however, necessitates a balance among configurations that include individual, one-on-one settings, small within-class groups, larger within-class groups, along with whole-class instruction.

The primary focus of this text is on *generic* teaching skills. Generic teaching skills are defined as those general, universal skills that can be applied in a wide range of subjects, skills, and instructional contexts. Once learned, they can be transferred to, and applied in, many different settings. They are not idiosyncratic fundaments of teaching such as those associated with performance-based teacher education programs. The generic teaching skills developed in this text can be inferred from the statements of competencies and related performance criteria found at the beginning of each chapter. The competencies and performance criteria have come, of course, from several sources, including current educational literature and research. Most importantly, they have been derived from our experience with the national award winning teacher education programs at the University of Washington. Many of the ideas and suggestions presented in the text have been field tested with hundreds of students in teacher education programs and related activities at the University of Washington.

Throughout the text, the reader will find vignettes of situations that a teacher might encounter in working in an elementary school. These are based on actual incidents we have observed in our work with students and teachers. This edition of the text also introduces "Photo Folios." These are problem situations based on photographs in the text. The vignettes and the Photo Folios are included for the purpose of stimulating thinking and discussion. In most cases there is not a single acceptable or "right" answer. Rather than attempting to find a single correct answer, students should be encouraged to explore alternative ways of dealing with the situation. They should be challenged to search out the consequences of each alternative they suggest. The text stresses that much of teaching involves decision making, and that good or effective teaching consists of making wise decisions at appropriate times.

We are instructed by an age-old legacy of conventional wisdom that the characteristics associated with an educated person, such as disciplined intelligence and skillful performance, are the result of the diligent application of the individual over a period of several years, to the successful attainment of training tasks related to educational achievements. An individual may be born with a predisposition for a particular talent, but, obviously, no one is born educated. To become educated the individual must be directly and personally involved in the successful performance of appropriate learning tasks. Parents, teachers, other adults, and peers assist in this process and often enhance it, but no one can *give* another person an education. In the final analysis, it is the individual person who must make the investment of time and effort in securing an education. We should not be surprised, therefore, that recent educational research has confirmed that "time on task" is an important variable related to pupil achievement. In other words, those pupils who spend their time doing the work assigned to them learn the material; those who for whatever reason fail to complete their tasks successfully do not learn as well. It could hardly be otherwise.

The position taken in this text is that it is the teacher's responsibility to provide a classroom environment—a learning "context"—that will facilitate pupils engaging in those tasks that are essential for them to perform if they are to learn what the school curriculum offers. This means that teachers will need to engage in thorough planning—including some teacher-pupil planning—in order to have a systematic, and in some sense, sequential program of instruction. It means, too, that the teacher has to be well grounded in such teaching skills as classroom management, lesson preparation and presentation, setting objectives, using various modes of teaching, selecting and using appropriate instructional materials, selecting and implementing learning activities, asking questions and responding to pupils' answers, and evaluating pupil learning. These and other similar teaching skills are treated in this book.

The authors are indebted to the following individuals who assisted in procuring photographs for the text, and we wish to express our sincere thanks and appreciation to them: Ann Avery, National Bilingual Training Resource Center, University of Washington; Dr. Robert Bernard, Concordia University, Montreal, Canada; Ella Colson, Elementary School Principal, Northshore Public Schools, Bothell, Washington; Gary Gerhard, Personnel Director, Battle Ground Public Schools, Battle Ground, Washington; Steven Koyama, graduate student, University of Washington; Ruth A. McReynolds, Secretary, Canyon Creek Elementary School, Bothell, Washington; Barbara Scott and Lowell R. Jackson, both of the Shoreline Public Schools, Seattle, Washington; Dr. Leighanne Harris, University of Washington. Our sincere thanks, too, are expressed to the many teachers and pupils who allowed us to come to their classrooms to take photographs. We very much appreciate their fine spirit of cooperation.

We wish again to express our gratitude to our wives, Mildred Fleming Jarolimek and Margie Osborn Foster, for their expert technical assistance with the preparation of the manuscript and for their thoughtful and constructive comments regarding the substance of the text.

John Jarolimek
Clifford D. Foster

CONTENTS

6

7

8

9

10

11

1

The Challenge of Teaching in the Elementary School

THE QUALIFIED AND COMPETENT TEACHER . . .

1. Is familiar with the social realities that confront the children he or she teaches.
2. Knows how his or her behavior impinges directly on the achievement and aspirations of children.
3. Is firmly committed to the idea of the improvability of the human condition.

Performance Criteria

As a result of the serious study of this chapter, the student should be able to . . .

1. Identify conditions in and out of school that profoundly relate to a pupil's success in school.
2. Identify conditions that stand in the way of achieving equality of educational opportunity.
3. Describe pupil behavior that would suggest educational disadvantage.
4. Provide examples of institutionalized racism and racial and sex-role stereotyping in schools.
5. Describe specific teacher behaviors that illustrate a caring, concerned, and humane approach to teaching.
6. Identify major purposes of elementary education.

THE CHALLENGE OF TEACHING IN THE ELEMENTARY SCHOOL

The March 1979 *Bulletin* of the Council for Basic Education carried the following announcement:

> Anchorage, Alaska, has opened an alternative fundamental school; Broward County, Florida, has closed one. Both happenings are signs of the times.

This excerpt calls attention to the great amount of uncertainty that surrounds much of education today. The innovations in curriculum and teaching of the recent past have had disappointingly little impact on school procedures. School leadership all over the nation finds itself confused as to how school programs should respond to the maelstrom of human events taking place at the local, national, and international levels. Locally, schools are being buffeted by pressure groups. On the one hand, Americans hold high expectations for their schools; on the other they perceive their schools with suspicion and with a lack of trust. Quite clearly there is widespread concern over the quality of education being provided the nation's children, even though such concern is not always carried to the point of providing needed financial resources that would ensure quality education. Whereas some seek order in all this confusion by insisting that schools return to fundamentals, others have gone that route and have found it wanting, as the foregoing excerpt illustrates.

In recent years some theorists have suggested that society be "de-schooled;" that schools should be eliminated entirely. But in a modern, complex, technologically-based society, such fanciful proposals cannot be considered as serious alternatives to organized schools. There is an overwhelming amount of scientific and anecdotal evidence that indicates that the elementary school experience is one of the most significant forces that shapes the lives of children. Of course, home background is of primary importance in this process, too, as are other environmental influences external to the school. But these out-of-school influences have to be very powerful and consistently positive to overcome deficiencies created by a weak elementary education. When one is identifying factors that contribute to success in school learning, there is simply no substitute for a good beginning, and even the most capable pupils can feel the effects of defective elementary education. It is nearly impossible to overstate the importance of a good elementary education in terms of building a foundation for a lifetime of school-related learning.

This becomes apparent as we examine what elementary education is supposed to achieve.

Purposes of Elementary Education—Then and Now

Literacy

Since colonial times, schools for young children have had responsibility to develop basic literacy in children. Often the colonial schools were little more than schools for reading, a skill that was taught mainly for religious purposes. Reading continued to be an important component of the elementary school curriculum through out the history of the nation, and remains so today. Indeed, at the early levels, more time is spent on the teaching of reading than on anything else, and some critics say that even today elementary schools are essentially reading schools.

The concern for literacy, of course, goes beyond the teaching of reading. During the late 1970's, there was a national outcry for schools to place a greater emphasis on "the basics." Used in this context, "the basics" refer to fundamental literacy skills—reading, writing, and arithmetical operations, in other words, the 3Rs. These learnings are judged to be *basic* in the sense that without them the individual would be handicapped in his or her ability to learn other things. These are the *tools* one uses in learning, and without them the individual is stymied in learning how to learn. Without having command of these basic skills, the individual would also be handicapped as an adult in conducting the activities of ordinary living in a society that relies so heavily on written communication and quantitative operations in carrying on its business.

There is no way that an elementary school can receive a high rating without doing a respectable job of teaching children the fundamental skills of literacy. (Specific suggestions as to how this can be done are provided in Chapter 9.) When parents are critical of elementary school practices, their concerns are most often with the teaching of basic skills. The reasons for poor skill achievement often can be found in the lack of conscientious and competent teaching. In almost any junior high school in the country, one can find pupils who have learning deficiencies, and each is an indictment of elementary education.

Although the 3Rs are obviously basic skills, being a literate person must include some additional learnings. We assume that when people have attended school in the last decades of the twentieth century, they have a general background of knowledge about the world and its people, that they are familiar with basic scientific information, and that they have a modicum of cultural awareness. Important beginnings in these fields must be made in the elementary school years. Basic education that is provided by the elementary school must include elements of the common culture that are presumed to be a part of the intellectual equipment of everyone. After all, one does not read reading or write writing. Skills that do not have an anchor in some kind of substantive knowledge are of little value to the individual.

Citizenship Education

A second purpose of elementary education, also having a long tradition in American schools, is citizenship education. Education for intelligent and loyal citizenship was introduced in the school curriculum early in the nation's history to ensure self-government at an enlightened level. Citizenship education was to take place through the formal study of such subjects as history, government (civics), and geography, and through the indoctrination of such values as freedom, human dignity, responsibility, independence, individualism, democracy, respect for others, love of country, and so on. Informally, citizenship education was promoted through an educational setting that included learners from a broad social and economic spectrum of the white society. Unlike its European counterparts, the American educational dream of the "common" school was to provide an institution that would serve all the children of all the people. Although that ideal has not been reached completely, it comes close to being realized in the elementary school. With the advent of court-ordered desegregation of schools in recent years, the mix of schoolchildren includes those of all racial and ethnic groups.

School policy regarding the teaching of citizenship has been far from clear or consistent. There is not consensus on the solution to many political issues. As a result, the teaching of controversial issues may be something of a no-man's land for the teacher who seeks to approach such topics in a conscientious and honest way. Regrettably, the tendency is to seek approaches to the presentation of political content in so-called safe ways. Citizenship education and social studies, in particular, often become formal, bookish, and not very stimulating.

Citizenship education in the elementary school must include the development of affective attachments to this nation and its democratic heritage. The pageants, plays, creative stories, poems, and creative dramatics, under the direction of an imaginative and stimulating teacher, can make the struggle for freedom and the history of this nation's development an unforgettable experience for young children. These are powerful tools in building appreciations, ideals, and values. The folklore and legends associated with the development of this nation are important and valuable vehicles for teaching citizenship when they are sensibly used. For young children, an intellectual approach to citizenship and history is often inappropriate, but they certainly can develop strong feelings of empathy, for example, with Francis Scott Key, who in 1814, when he witnessed the all-night shelling of Fort McHenry, experienced great joy and relief the following morning upon seeing that "our flag was still there." A certain amount of symbolism, such as saluting the flag and reciting the Pledge of Allegiance, is a necessary part of citizenship education of children, and if kept within reasonable limits, probably has some value in engendering feelings of fidelity. Teachers should be careful not to overuse such activities and should not substitute them for a more rational approach to citizenship education, as appropriate to the maturity of the pupils.

Personal Development

Personal development or self-actualization did not take on major significance as a goal of elementary education until the present century. Today the personal growth of individual children, concern for the maximizing of each individual's potential for development, and the broadening of school goals to include emotional, social, and physical growth as well as intellectual development are seen as major purposes of elementary education. The nation expects its elementary schools to be concerned about *individual* children, to help them develop a sense of self-identity, to help them get to feel good about themselves, to help them know what their individual talents are, and to help them set realistic goals for themselves. Out of necessity, schools must teach aggregates of children in what we call classes; but the teacher's concern is and must always be the individual human beings within those groups.

The dimension of personal development that *has* had a long tradition in elementary education is something that might be called character education or moral education. Elementary schools are not simply information supermarkets, they are shapers of human beings. The earliest schools in this country recognized this reality—schools for young children were to extend and reinforce moral and character education begun in the home and in the religious life of the family. As schools became public, secular institutions, moral and character education became separated from their religious orientation. Schools, nonetheless, were expected to continue to concern themselves with principles of right and wrong under the assumption that such knowledge would be used to serve the betterment of society. In recent years this has taken the form of values education. Teachers continue to develop classroom settings that encourage pupils to develop a sense of fair play, do what is right, live up to verbal commitments, show consideration for others, be trustworthy, and so on. The fact is that society cannot survive unless a high percentage of its people internalize these values and live their lives in accordance with them. This is why character education and moral education in some form will doubtless always be imporant concerns of elementary education.

THE SOCIAL WORLD OF CHILDHOOD: REALITIES OF THE REAL WORLD

In any historical period, there are social conditions, trends, or movements that impact directly on the work of the school. The broad goals of elementary education discussed in the preceding section are greatly influenced and conditioned by social realities external to the school. Two decades ago, the nation's anxiety over Russian successes in space technology resulted in crash programs in mathematics and science education. Similarly, an entire generation of Americans was taught that the Peoples Republic of China was enemy territory. Almost overnight, it seems, such teaching has been reversed, and today's schoolchildren in America are taught much more liberal attitudes toward China. In this section, we will examine a few trends and social realities that have direct relevance for teaching and learning in the elementary school.

A Pluralistic Society

In recent years, Americans have developed an increased awareness of, and appreciation for, the pluralistic nature of their nation. Doubtless this came about in part as a result of the increased militancy of minority groups, especially Blacks, during the decade of the sixties. Encouraged by the successes of the Blacks, other minority groups began to make themselves heard, and their influence felt. Chicanos, Puerto Ricans, Native Americans (Indians and Eskimos), and Asians pressed for the achievement of social goals unique to their own groups. By the early 1970's, there were clear signs that minority group membership no longer carried the stigma it once had.

The interest in ethnic identity has also moved beyond the generally recognized ethnic minority groups. There is a very strong interest in ethnic heritage being expressed by many groups. Descendants of European immigrants, who have by now been thoroughly socialized and assimilated by white America, are beginning to identify them-

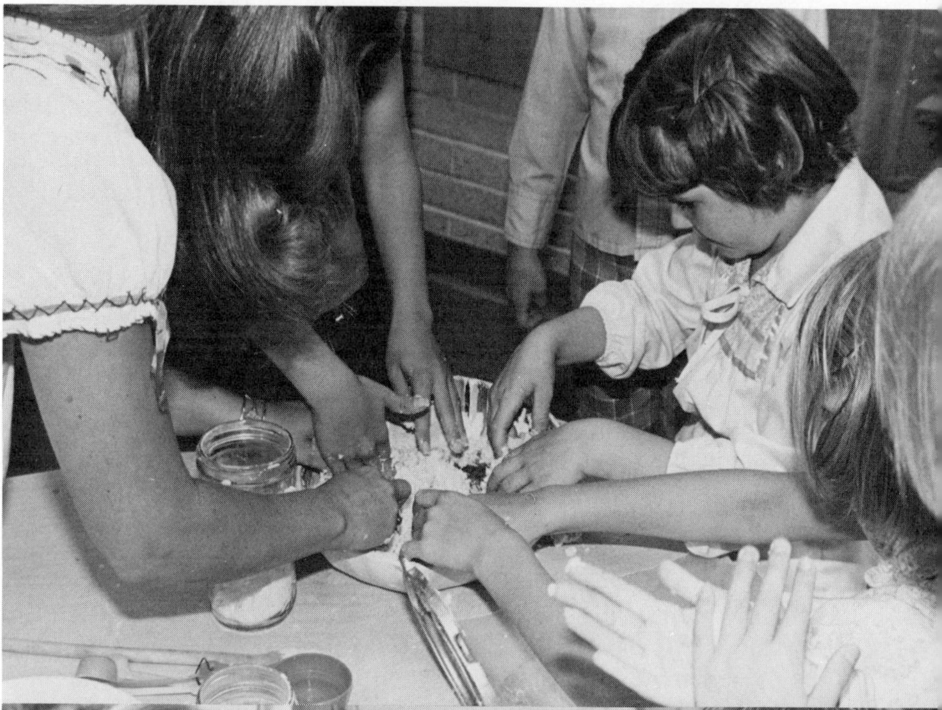

PHOTO FOLIO

Modern elementary school programs are designed to achieve a broad range of goals. It is taken for granted that elementary schools have a primary responsibility to help children develop basic literacy skills. But exemplary elementary schools are usually those that do considerably more than attend to "reading, writing, and arithmetic." Elementary schools that have earned high praise for their programs are ones that are activity oriented and pupil involving. They are schools in which one might see pupils doing what the children in these photographs are doing.

1. What educational goals or objectives are sought when children are involved in activities such as the ones shown in these two photographs?
2. How can an activity-oriented elementary school curriculum enhance the school's program in the basic skills?

selves with the culture of the homeland of their forebears. There is widespread recognition of the fact that this nation truly does represent a confluence of world cultures. It is apparent that a part of this nation's greatness comes from the fact that it has grown as a result of the contributions of many and diverse peoples of the world who brought a part of their homeland with them when they came to these shores.

The pluralistic quality of this nation is now generally accepted as a reality. It has been institutionalized in textbooks and other learning resources. Elementary school teachers are obligated professionally to recognize and respect the diversity of American life that has come about as a result of the diversity of our cultural origins. At the same time, they also have the responsibility to help all groups and all individuals, regardless of background, to become attached to those core values that hold us together as a nation, especially freedom, equality, and human dignity. We must be careful not to stress pluralism to the extent that it destroys any sense of common identity that we share as a people. Should that happen, it will lead to civil strife and conflict just as it has in every place in the world where pluralism, rather than unity, has been emphasized.

One of the implications of the greater acceptance of multiethnicity and pluralism is that teachers need to know much more about a variety of ethnic groups. Each ethnic group has its own unique history, problems, and concerns. Teachers need to know what these are for the various ethnic groups: Native Americans, Blacks, Chicanos, Asians, Jews, European whites, and others. Teachers need to have a great deal of information about the kinds of specific learning problems that children from particular ethnic environments are likely to have. What does a child's ethnic background really have to do with how he or she learns, adapts to school, and makes life choices? This is the relevant *educational* question that relates to ethnic identity.

Life Styles—Old and New

Prior to the time children have any formal contact with a teacher or with the school, they have, of course, been receiving early education from their families. There can be little doubt that these early experiences in the family are among the most powerful and pervasive influences on the development of the human being. A family that is doing its child-rearing job properly will help the child learn some of the most important and fundamental things he or she needs to know in life. It is in the home that language is learned and linguistic skills developed. Here, too, the child learns to give and receive emotional support. The family provides security and reassurance, thereby providing the psychological support needed to face life, and to function confidently and competently. In the process, the child develops feelings of personal worth and a positive self-concept. It is in the family that the child first learns what is right and wrong, what things are prized and valued, and what standards of conduct are expected. Lifetime ambitions and aspirations are planted and germinate in one's early family life. The family helps the child begin to form ideas about social roles, especially male and female roles. The extent to which the family has handled these responsibilities well, or poorly, will reflect itself in the child's life in school.

All societies have families, although there is considerable variation in their structures around the world. Most often they are relatively small, kinship-structured units that have as a major function the socialization of young children. A family consisting of the parents and their offspring functioning as an autonomous unit is described as a *nuclear* family. When this unit is augmented by grandparents, aunts, uncles, cousins, and other close relatives, it is said to be an *extended* family. There are numerous variations in these two structures.

The precise form and structure of a family at any point in time is related to a series of complex factors in a society. In early America, and indeed up until modern times in some rural sections of the country, the extended family was the usual pattern. More recently, because of economic and social conditions, some variation of the nuclear family has been the prevailing pattern in America.

In terms of the upbringing of children within the framework of expectations of a family, there are obvious advantages to an extended-family arrangement. The young child has more contact with closely related adults and consequently has a greater range of adult role models available. Similarly, child behavior can be more closely and constantly monitored by concerned and caring adults. There is also likely to be a more elaborate family culture or set of rituals that provide emotional stability and roots for the growing child, as for example, the gathering of the entire family for holidays, anniversaries, birthdays, and other special events. In arrangements of this type, the child is hardly ever out of range of the supervision of some member of the immediate family.

A variety of factors have contributed to changing the traditional extended-family pattern. People tend to move in the direction of increased economic opportunity. Thus, a young couple may locate hundreds of miles away from any of their relatives. Children growing up in nuclear families today may hardly know relatives other than their parents. They may see their grandparents a time or two each year; aunts, uncles, and cousins even less frequently. Baby sitters replace grandparents in part-time care of children. Neighbors and friends may assist with the supervision of children in the neighborhood. Often this does not work out well because many families change their places of residence so frequently that close bonds of friendship and confidence do not develop between and among neighbors.

In recent years we have also seen an increase in innovative marriage and family arrangements. The conventional sharp delineation of adult male-female roles within the family is changing to the extent that many couples share all responsibilities associated with maintaining the family. The wife and mother may be employed outside the household, along with the husband and father. Conversely, both may share in the care of the children, housekeeping chores, food preparation, and other household tasks. In some instances the wife and mother is the sole wager earner and the husband and father becomes the homemaker, known as the "house-husband."

Some couples have broken out of the traditional family structure altogether and have become part of a communal family. In these instances several couples share a common place of residence and share responsibility for the maintenance of the dwelling. They also share responsibility for the supervision of the children, and for providing emotional support for each other. In a sense, the communal family fills some of the psychological needs that were provided by extended families in an earlier time.

Undoubtedly, the most common exception to the conventional family arrangement today is the one-parent family. Death, separation, and, most commonly, divorce not only dissolve the marriage but leave one or the other of the partners with the responsibility of carrying on as a family. Because custody of children is usually given the mother in the case of divorce, the one-parent family for the most part means a mother and her children. Divorce rates in this country have continued to rise for the past century, peaking during the years immediately following World War II, receding during the fifties and early sixties, and rising sharply again in the seventies. Presently, for the nation as a whole, nearly one out of every two marriages ends in divorce. In some counties the rate is much higher, with the number of divorces equaling—or even exceeding—the number of marriages for any given year.

Through the years, teachers have found it convenient to blame home conditions for the poor achievement of children in school. The behavior problems or low achievement of children from one-parent families is explained away on the basis of their being products of "broken homes." This, of course, ignores the fact that many children from one-parent families achieve at extraordinarily high levels and present no behavior problems in school, although many from so-called intact families are low achievers and do present behavior problems. It also ignores the psychological and emotional damage to a young child that results from growing up in a family filled with conflict and hostility between parents where the marriage is maintained.

Whether we consider one-parent families, innovative family structures, or conventional intact marriages, great changes are occurring in the life styles of families. People move about a great deal. Approximately one-fourth to one-third of all Americans change their places of residence each year. With increasing numbers of parents employed outside the home, greater numbers of children are enrolled in day-care centers or are placed in the care of persons other than parents for several hours each day. Undoubtedly, parent guilt stemming from contemporary life styles often results in permissive child-rearing practices. The frustrations of contemporary life may also result in various forms of child abuse. Teachers of elementary-school-age children find themselves enmeshed in these complex life styles of modern families as they work with the children who are products of those homes.

SOCIAL-CLASS INFLUENCES ON TEACHING AND LEARNING

Social stratification occurs because individuals are ranked by others in the society as being higher or lower on some standard of preference. When a segment of the society is set apart as having characteristics different from the others, we have the beginning of a social class. In time, a hierarchy of groups develops in accordance with societal preferences, and a social-class structure emerges.

If a group of individuals has particular characteristics that are valued by a society, the group so identified will enjoy high status. The reverse also obtains. Thus, when speaking of upper or lower classes, we are referring to groups of individuals who either have or do not have qualities in common that are prized by the larger society. In America, upper classes are those groups that have wealth, advanced education, professional occupations, and relative freedom from worry concerning material needs. Conversely, lower classes are those groups that live in or on the edge of poverty, have poor educations, are irregularly employed or employed in jobs requiring little or no training, often require assistance from government welfare agencies, and are constantly concerned about meeting their basic needs of life.

There can be no question that one variable that separates the "haves" from the "have nots" in this or any other society is level of education. The people who are the decision makers, the people who have good jobs, those who contribute in significant ways to the health and welfare of their fellow citizens, those who have power and wealth, are almost always educated people. It is patently clear from research, as well as from the personal experiences of countless thousands of individuals, that limited education forecloses many social and economic options for the individual and thereby severely restricts opportunity for upward social mobility. It does not follow, of course, that improved education will alleviate all of the problems surrounding the poverty life styles of lower social classes in this society. Restricted or foreshortened education, for whatever reason, simply means limited opportunities to exercise alternatives and options for self-development.

Evidence that the largest number of educational casualties come from the lower social classes is overwhelming. These children come from environments that are educationally impoverished, and this conditions nearly every aspect of their lives. Most significantly it contributes to the perpetuation of educational deprivation. The traditional school program simply has not been able to deal successfully with the educational needs of these children. When schooling fails to educate, the usual assumption is that there is something wrong with the learner. We are likely to have large numbers of miseducated children until we commit ourselves to the idea that teachers and schools must accommodate learners, rather than the other way around.

Equality of Educational Opportunity

Equality of educational opportunity traditionally has been interpreted to mean *access* to education, and the nation has made a substantial effort to have schooling available to all of its children. No area of the country is so remote as to preclude the opportunity for children who live there to go to school. Children of all racial and ethnic groups; children of the migrants; children of the poor; children who are physically or mentally handicapped—all of these are not only encouraged, but required, to attend school. But does school attendance in itself ensure equality of educational opportunity? Many think not, because there are social, psychological, and economic inequities that condition both the quality of schooling provided from place to place and that affect the ability of the individual to take full advantage of what is offered.

It is apparent that tremendous inequities in educational opportunity exist in this country. Educational inequity is usually thought of in terms of differences in dollar amounts spent on education from one place to another. Because communities differ in their *ability* to support education and in their *willingness* to support it, the average amount of money spent per pupil to educate children varies from $1218.00 in one state to $3890.00 in another. Variations are even greater between school districts.

The amount of money spent on education does not, however, fully explain prevailing inequities in educational opportunity. The quality of education tends to follow the pattern of power and wealth in a community. Those parents who are reasonably well educated themselves, and who have average or above average incomes, select residences in areas that provide well for the education of their children. The poorly educated, low-income families tend to live in areas that provide less well for the education of children. It is not so much a matter of actual dollars spent on education in the more favored areas, but a combination of complex forces coalescing to produce better quality education.

The realities are that the teacher is confronted with a situation in which the children come from varying backgrounds and, consequently, are highly diverse in their capabilities for learning. Moreover, they are on their way to a wide variety of yet-to-be-determined stations in life. The teacher and the school provide intervention experiences that should help each child on his or her way to becoming a fully functioning human being, making maximum use of his or her potential for self-development and self-fulfillment.

Education, and most especially early education, must be concerned with the way it either opens or forecloses subsequent opportunities for learning. If a child does not learn to read, this should be a matter of great concern to the teacher and the school because this deficiency severely limits the options open to the child in later stages of education. Similarly, if a child grows to dislike school or to dislike particular subjects studied in school, this also imposes limiting conditions on continued educational growth. It can be said that *any* experience that a child has that discourages or terminates continued ability or motivation for further learning imposes a restriction on the equality of educational opportunity. This is an old idea in education, but it is one that continues to be important to teachers as they work with today's children.

WHAT'S IN A NAME?

Do you believe that some of the children listed below are less likely than others to secure a good education?

Karen Ann Johnson	Wendy Giles
Franklin Washington	Miya Nishimura
Robert Henderson	Jackie Runningbear
Carmelita Rodriguiz	Moses Hanks
Stanley Stanislaus	Olga Ouchennickov
Graham Priestley	Nanette Le Duc
Bernard Goldstein	Nels Johanson
Michael Papadapolis	Marie Novak
Gina Minoletti	Francisco Braga
Patricia O'Reilly	Jan Van Troost
Dat Vu	Mohammed Sadr

PHOTO FOLIO

These children are on their way to visit a museum in the downtown area of the city. Modern transportation has made learning resources of the entire community available to schoolchildren, and few persons object to the use of school buses for that purpose. Moreover, in rural areas schoolchildren are transported many miles each day in order to attend modern elementary schools. Yet when children in urban centers are bused from one area to another to achieve racial balance in schools, there often is considerable citizen objection.

1. Why is busing acceptable in some circumstances and objectionable in others? Is *busing* per se the real issue? Explain.
2. What are other ways in which the use of modern transportation has affected school policies and practices?

THE TEACHER AND THE CLASSROOM AS SELF-FULFILLING PROPHETS

The self-fulfilling prophecy, in one form or another, has been a part of folk wisdom for countless generations. Basically, this phenomenon has to do with the notion that one's mind-set, that is, what one believes to be true, whether consistent with reality or not, has a great deal to do with influencing contingencies that flow from such beliefs. For example, a man's wife may be quite plain in appearance, based on objective criteria, but he believes her to be a ravishing beauty. This belief conditions his relationship with her and, consequently, she tends to behave and act in accordance with her husband's perceptions of her. Golfers and bridge players report that they invariably play better games when their competitors are skillful, because they are then expected to perform at a higher level of proficiency.

In recent years, considerable attention has been given to the implications of the self-fulfilling prophecy for the education of children.

Just as a water glass may be perceived as being half empty or half full, so a teacher may regard a class as having a high or low potential for achievement. The same applies to the teacher's perception of individual pupils. Roy Sanders relates this interesting case of a teacher dealing with a pupil on the basis of erroneous information:

> The story is told of the new third grade teacher who was warned by the second grade teacher to keep a wary eye on Albert Erickson because he had caused trouble by his deviancy all year long. The third grade teacher took great precautions with young Erickson: she seated him in the front of the room; she kept a close eye on him; she darted accusing glances at him when the least unnecessary noise or commotion arose. At first, the teacher thought she detected hurt looks on the lad's face when she looked reprovingly at him, but she told herself that he was only pretending to look hurt as a cover-up for further deviancy. And the thought that the boy was feigning innocence made her redouble her efforts to keep him in line. Later in the school term, she and the second grade teacher were discussing behavioral problems they had encountered.
>
> "The Erickson boy turned out just as you told me he would," said the third grade teacher; "although at first he pretended to be ever so innocent."
>
> "The Erickson boy?" queried the second grade teacher. "Oh, I thought you knew. Albert's family moved away just before the term began. You must be thinking of his cousin, Alfred Erickson . . . But I have never heard of his causing any trouble!"[1]

The teacher obviously made an inaccurate assessment of the case, but nevertheless dealt with the child as though her appraisal was correct. Consequently, the child did not disappoint his teacher—he acted in accordance with her expectations, and the deviancy became real.

Most authors and researchers in education agree that the self-fulfilling prophecy needs additional study and further analysis. The literature on this subject, which is considerable, suggests strongly that the authors assume that predictions influence achievement levels, especially in the education of ethnic minorities and so-called disadvantaged youngsters. In most cases these assumptions stem from the application of common sense to observed relationships or from inferences based on what appear to be co-related conditions. There has not been a great amount of research to substantiate the hypothesis that teacher attitude and expectation influence the performance of pupils, but what there is tends to support such a relationship.

[1] Roy Sanders, "The Self-Fulfilling Prophecy and the Teacher," *School and Community*, 57:11 (January 1971).

How do teachers communicate these increased expectations to pupils, which thereby encourage pupils to expect more of themselves? Little is known about these processes. The authors of *Pygmalion in the Classroom*[2] suggest that it may be that teachers treat pupils in more pleasant, friendly, and enthusiastic ways when they expect them to perform at a high level. Teachers provide recognition for certain pupils by calling on them to respond more frequently than others. Undoubtedly there are a variety of nonverbal signals that subtly communicate feelings and attitudes of the teacher to the child. These might be facial expressions, gestures, physical contacts, or particular looks. The tone of voice and choice of words in verbal communication might also be significant.

There are clear implications in this, not only for teachers who work with children of ethnic minorities, gifted children, lower-social-class children, or exceptional children, but for all teachers. Many school practices need to be critically re-examined in light of what is coming to be known about the impact of the teacher's attitude and influence on children's learning. What is important is that procedures, such as those following, not be misused. Any practice that tends to stereotype or label a child must be suspected of influencing the child's expected performance. A few of the more common ones:

1. *Cumulative Records.* The school history of a child can obviously be of value to a teacher in planning a program of instruction. It can also condition the teacher's perception, resulting in the setting of inappropriate levels of expectations for the youngster. A single comment by a previous teacher may be very damaging to subsequent teachers' assessment of a pupil's learning capacity.
2. *Achievement Examinations.* Poor scores on achievement tests may indicate not only the present level of performance of a child but also set future levels of expectation.
3. *Homogeneous Ability Grouping.* No amount of contrived deception can prevent pupils, parents, and teachers from knowing which groups are the high, medium, and low-level achievers. Once placed in a group so labeled, the pupil is likely to perform in accordance with expectations set for that group. The infrequent movement of pupils from one ability group to another confirms this fact, teachers' claims of flexibility of such groups notwithstanding.

[2] Robert Rosenthal and Lenore Jacobson, *Pygmalion in the Classroom, Teacher Expectation and Pupils' Intellectual Development* (New York: Holt, Rinehart & Winston, Inc., 1968).

4. *Report Cards.* Through report cards pupils are labeled as A students or C or D students; these labels in turn provide an obvious level of expectation for the child, the parents, and the teachers, thereby affecting the child's level of performance.
5. *Nonpromotion Policies.* Nonpromotion from one grade to the next is perhaps the most devastating of all experiences in terms of lowering expectations for oneself. However such policies are rationalized, their long-term effects on the individuals involved are usually detrimental.

It is important to stress that the teachers who engage in the practices described are usually well-meaning, humane individuals. They often deal with children in kind and loving ways. Nonetheless, the *effects* of these procedures are so subtle that teachers may not be—and in most cases probably are not—aware of the power these practices have on their attitudes toward, and expectations of, individual children.

More malicious forms of teacher attitudes that affect pupil performance are various kinds of out-and-out prejudice. Here we get into such matters as the teacher believing that children of various ethnic groups cannot achieve as well as others simply because they are Black, Indian, Chicano, Puerto Rican, Filipino, and so on. It is often difficult for children of an ethnic minority to excel, because their teachers do not expect them to do very well. When such children do achieve at a high level, credit is often given grudgingly. One cannot be around schools very long and listen to informal teacher talk without realizing that, in one form or another, teacher prejudice toward pupils is fairly widespread. Considering the effects such prejudices have on learning, one can only speculate on the depressing effects these attitudes must have on schoolchildren.

HOW DID YOU GET THAT WAY?

Are you what your teachers, parents, and fellow students call an A student? B student? C student? What kind of a student do you perceive yourself to be? Are your perceptions of yourself the same as those of your teachers, parents, and friends? When did you first discover that you were an A, B, or C student? How did you get classified that way? Must you forever remain in the category in which you are now perceived?

Does this tell you anything about the self-fulfilling prophecy?

RACE AND RACISM

It is perfectly obvious that human beings differ in their physical characteristics. Some are fair skinned; others are dark. Some have curly hair and others have straight hair, which may be light or dark. Through the centuries, groups of people who have occupied certain geographical areas of the world and who have, more or less, physical traits in common, have been identified as subspecies of homo sapiens and have been called *races.* These physical traits are inherited qualities and are, therefore, innate and immutable. But because the differences within these groups are as great as they are, it is sometimes extremely difficult to assign an individual human being to any such group on the basis of unique characteristics. Consequently, anthropologists have not found the use of geographical races to be an altogether satisfactory way of grouping human beings. Be that as it may, the fact that groups of human beings have differing physical characteristics, and that we designate these groups as races, does not in itself give rise to social and educational problems.

There is nothing inherently wrong in defining human groups on the basis of innate and immutable physical characteristics. Problems of race arise when nonphysical, social, or cultural qualities are assigned to individuals simply and only because they are members of those groups. When this happens, race becomes defined socially, rather than on the basis of objective physical qualities. Racism inevitably follows the practice of associating significant cultural abilities and/or characteristics with groups that are defined socially as races. Racism becomes institutionalized when these associations, whether overt or subtle, are given legitimacy and social approval.

Racism, particularly institutionalized racism, is difficult to deal with because of the tendency to associate it with overt and conscious acts of prejudice. It has been referred to as the "disease of hate." Thus, individuals who generally have humanitarian attitudes toward others may be shocked and outraged to be accused of racist behavior. The practices may have become so thoroughly institutionalized that awareness of their racist dimensions has been hidden.

Institutionalized racism consists of practices that have been *legitimatized* by the society and that result in the *systematic* discrimination against members of specific groups. Practices that have been legitimatized are accepted. Few question them. Until recently, even those against whom the discrimination was directed have accepted these practices. The word *systematic* in this definition is also very important. This means that the discrimination is not a random occurrence; the discrimination is practiced with consistency and regularity, thus making it systematic rather than whimsical or capricious. It is directed against specific groups (perhaps not even by design), because members of those groups have certain characteristics or qualities.

What are examples of practices that would qualify as institutionalized racism? Here are a few:

1. Imposing height requirements for certain jobs, such as those held by police officers, fire fighters, bus drivers, and so forth. (This practice discriminates systematically against Asians, who tend to be physically of short stature.)
2. Literacy requirements for voting. (This discriminates against Blacks and other ethnic minorities, who are known to have lower literacy rates than the dominant group.)
3. High fees for filing for public office. (This practice discriminates against the low-income groups, many of whom are of ethnic minorities.)
4. Associating certain groups with specific positions. (This stereotyping discriminates against easily identifiable persons, such as ethnic minorities, because traditionally they have been in low-status occupations.)
5. Use of qualifying tests that require a high level of verbal behavior. (This discriminates against ethnic minorities.)

IN THE TEACHERS' LOUNGE

You are carrying on a conversation with a colleague, Miss Singletary, who perceives herself to be somewhat of a liberal when it comes to intergroup relations. The two of you teach in a school composed mainly of whites, but perhaps as many as a third of the school population consists of Blacks, Indians, Chicanos, and Asians. You are discussing the ethnic composition of the school. At one point in the conversation she suggests, "We make too damn much of this ethnic identity business. Lord knows, I'm no racist. As far as I am concerned, I am color-blind when it comes to race."

1. Does Miss Singletary's attitude ensure equality of treatment for all groups in the school?
2. Which groups have most to gain and which ones have most to lose when teachers adopt Miss Singletary's views?
3. Do you suppose Miss Singletary is a white teacher or a member of an ethnic minority? Why do you think so?

6. Segregated housing patterns. (This practice discriminates against individuals easily identified as members of certain groups, that is, ethnic minorities.)
7. Use of dual norms. (This discriminates against ethnic minorities because it implies inability to achieve as well as whites.)
8. Homogeneous grouping. (This discriminates against ethnic minorities because it often results in their being in low-achieving groups.)
9. Automation, technology, labor-reducing practices. (These absorb jobs of low-skilled persons, thus a high percentage of ethnic minorities.)
10. Specific racial quotas. (These quotas foreclose opportunities beyond the stated quota, regardless of availability of qualified personnel from those races.)
11. Curriculum content unrelated to the life of certain groups. (This discriminates against groups who are not represented in the subject matter of the school—again, ethnic minorities.)

SEX-ROLE STEREOTYPING

Just as racism is the practice of ascribing certain abilities and characteristics to individuals on the basis of their identification with groups socially defined as races, sexism does the same thing on the basis of one's sex. Female roles have tended to be stereotyped along the lines of domestic and child-rearing responsibilities, whereas male roles have been stereotyped in the world of work outside the home. Also, women have been portrayed frequently in roles subservient to men, for example, ones in which they serve, wait on, and pick up after men.

There can be little doubt that such stereotyping has worked to the disadvantage of women by restricting the range of significant opportunities for self-development. Additionally, this has led to discrimination against women that has been manifestly unfair. Changing attitudes, the growing independence of women, and legislative reforms have aided in combating the invidious distinctions between males and females that are the result of sex-role stereotyping.

Educational programs, and particularly the part teachers play in them, are vitally important in shaping the young child's image of sex roles. If the child always sees males rather than females in preferred, prestigious occupational and social roles, he or she is bound to conclude that the male is superior; because these positions are obviously not available to women, therefore women must not be sufficiently capable of holding them. It hardly seems necessary to add that when sex roles are presented this way, boys *and* girls come to believe in the superiority of the male. Girls may grow up believing that the vocational choices available to them are teaching, nursing, secretarial service, and airlines hostessing, although boys have literally the whole world of work from which to choose. This has not been far from the truth because women generally have been excluded from many of the professional, executive, and political vocations. Conversely, if boys always see females involved in domestic and child-rearing duties, they naturally conclude that it is improper for males to be involved in such responsibilities. The fact that this may have been true in the past does not make it right today, when increasing numbers of husbands and wives are sharing in the responsibilities of family life that have traditionally been handled by women.

It seems clear that a broader range of role models will need to be presented to young children as a part of their formal education than has been the case in the past. Boys and girls should encounter models of men and women in a variety of occupations. Children must learn that it is just as appropriate for a woman to be a physician, a business executive, a judge, a mayor, a senator, a scientist, a bus driver, a carpenter, or any of a variety of occupations as it is for a man. They must also learn that there is nothing wrong with a man's taking care of and feeding his young children, doing household duties, secretarial work, nursing in a hospital, or being engaged in any of several tasks and occupations that have traditionally been associated with women.

What is important is that sex-role models must be presented in ways that provide the individual with a maximum opportunity for choice. Certainly many men and women will want to conduct their lives along more or less traditional sex-role patterns. Some may wish to exercise other choices, and they should not be prevented from doing so or be handicapped in doing so because of prejudicial attitudes and ridicule. The opportunity for choice will not exist if children are taught that all men and women must conform to the sex-role stereotypes that have prevailed through the centuries.

CURRENT ISSUES AND TRENDS IN ELEMENTARY EDUCATION

Minimum Competency Testing

In 1975 and 1976, California, Florida, Oregon, and a few other states began to require what has come to be called "minimum competency testing." This means that certain minimum standards of proficiency are required for promotion from one grade to another and/or for graduation from elementary or secondary schools. By 1979, all the remaining states passed legislation requiring such testing, had legislation pending, or had state board studies underway. The number keeps changing, but at least sixteen states require minimum competency tests before grade seven, and some use the results in grade promotion decisions. A great deal of controversy surrounds this issue, with the major question being whether or not minimum competency testing contributes to the improvement of elementary and secondary education.

Minimum competency testing has come about in part because the public is not confident that the schools are doing an adequate job of teaching basic skills and basic school subjects. This lack of confidence seems to be the result of (1) general observation of academic skills of school graduates, (2) the poor showing of achievement on the National Assessment of Educational Progress, and (3) the declining scores of students on standardized tests. No doubt the publication, in 1976, of the Benjamin Bloom book *Human Characteristics and School Learning,*[3] encouraged the minimum competency testing movement. In this influential book by a respected and reputable scholar, the author states that based on more than ten years of research on mastery learning, he is convinced that it is possible for 95 per cent of the students to learn all that the school has to teach at or near the mastery level. Bloom identifies one per cent to three per cent at the low level who are not able to master the curriculum, and one per cent to two per cent at the top for whom the regular curriculum is not really appropriate because of their superior intellectual ability. The rest, according to Bloom, could master the curriculum when provided with favorable learning conditions.

Those who support minimum competency testing see it as a way of improving basic education, and as a way of making the educational enterprise accountable to its constituents. They claim that under minimum competency testing, educational objectives are more sharply defined, thus making teaching more precise. They also suggest that such testing will call attention to pupils who have difficulty and, therefore, will be given the additional help they need in order to master the material. They also see competency testing as a hedge against social promotion of pupils from one grade to the next. This policy, i.e. the elimination of social promotion, will presumably restore meaning to the high school diploma. Advocates indicate that the requirement of mastery level learning will ensure that

[3]Benjamin Bloom, *Human Characteristics and School Learning,* New York: McGraw Hill Book Co., Inc., 1976.

every high school graduate possesses certain skills at the required minimum level of proficiency.

These views, of course, are not shared by the opponents of minimum competency testing. They insist that such tests freeze the curriculum around the test content. Moreover, because teachers are evaluated on the basis of how well their pupils score on the tests, it is inevitable that teachers will "teach for the test." This means that other important areas of the school curriculum will be neglected or omitted altogether. Opponents say that in order to be workable, the minimum levels required must be low enough to be achievable by the slowest-learning pupils. When this happens, the standard becomes meaningless for average and above average achievers. There is the possibility, too, that minimum levels will be perceived as maximums, causing a plateau effect on the distribution of achievement test scores.

There is currently great variation in the implementation of minimum competency testing. Teachers will need to familiarize themselves with local policy. Some extremely difficult decisions confront the teacher in those areas where social promotion is not permitted, where teacher accountability is based on pupil test scores, and where minimum levels of attainment are required for graduation. At this writing, many issues surrounding minimum competency testing are unresolved.

Mainstreaming

The traditional approach to the education of handicapped children was to segregate them into what was, and still is called, "special education." Public schools, state departments of education, colleges and universities typically have departments or divisions of special education that concern themselves with educational programs for handicapped persons. But in recent years there has been a strong movement away from the segregation of the handicapped from the main stream of social life, whether this be in school or in the larger society. Increasingly, public accommodations are taking into account the need for "barrier free" environments that make it easier for orthopedically handicapped and/or blind persons to negotiate them. In schools this movement has taken the form of placing children in what is for them a "least restrictive environment," also called, although not altogether correctly, mainstreaming.

In 1975, Congress passed, and the President signed into law, the Education for All Handicapped Children Act, otherwise referred to as P.L. 94-142. This law stipulates the rights that must be extended to all handicapped pupils, including the right to a free and appropriate public education. It also details procedures that must be followed in implementing programs for the handicapped. But most important for the classroom teacher is the requirement that an Individualized Education Program be developed for each pupil and that each handicapped pupil be provided instruction in the least restrictive environment. The process of preparing the IEP must include (1) the teacher; (2) a representative of the school such as the principal or school counselor; and (3) the child's parent(s) or guardian(s). The IEP must indicate the pupil's present level of performance; a statement of annual goals as well as shorter-term objectives; the specific educational services to be provided; a statement of the extent to which the child will be able to participate in the regular curriculum of the school (mainstreamed); and objective assessment criteria and evaluation procedures and schedules.

A great deal of controversy and misunderstanding surrounds the "least restrictive environment" concept, i.e. mainstreaming. The law requires that states establish procedures that will assure that, *to the maximum extent appropriate,* handicapped children are educated with children who are not handicapped. It stipulates additionally that separate schooling or the removal of handicapped children from the regular educational environment should occur only when the educational service cannot be provided in the regular classroom. The qualification, "to the maximum extent appropriate," is an important one. This obviously means that handicapped children cannot simply be deposited on a massive scale in regular classrooms. The handicapped child is to be placed in the most beneficial environment for learning. In some cases this may mean special instruction, perhaps even tutoring on a one-to-one basis. In other cases, the most beneficial environment might be the regular classroom. In any case, the clear intent of the legislation, as well as public attitudes generally, is calling for the integration of handicapped children into the regular classroom, wherever possible.

The education of all handicapped children will become a reality during the decade of the 1980's because it is now the law of the land. This development will place new demands on regular classroom teachers in the area of diagnostic and prescriptive teaching. As the philosophy of *inclusion* (as opposed to *segregation*) of the handicapped becomes fully operational, most elementary school classrooms will have, for all or part of the day, one or more children who are in some degree handicapped. This means that elementary school teachers will need to know a great deal more than most of them know today about the nature of handicapping conditions and the technical and legal aspects of working with handicapped children, as well as the specific teaching strategies that are uniquely suitable to the education of handicapped children.

English as a Second Language (ESL) And Bilingual Education

From early Colonial America to the present time, the people of this nation have been multilingual. People from every ethnic and cultural group of the world came to these shores, and, of course, brought their language with them. Often they settled in communities inhabited by immigrants from the same part of the world. Consequently, throughout America there were, and still are, areas where people speak a language other than English on a more or less regular basis. Immigrant groups in large cities such as New York, Chicago, Cleveland, and Milwaukee, organized and maintained foreign language schools where elements of these immigrant languages and cultures could be maintained.

The use of languages other than English was so widespread that in some cases those languages were used for instructional purposes in public schools. All of this was changed, however, in the period during and after World War I, when adverse feelings toward immigrant groups in general, and German-speaking people in particular, were so great that several states passed legislation prohibiting instruction in languages other than English in public schools. At the federal level this repressive legislation took the form of severely restricting immigration from areas of southern and eastern Europe, and from Asia. The xenophobia that spawned suppressive legislation at the state and federal levels was destructive of foreign-language learning in America. The attitude was widespread that to speak in a language other than English was somehow unAmerican.

There have been some changes in these attitudes and practices since the 1960's, probably as a result of growing ethnic awareness and identity, and the increased militancy on the part of certain ethnic minority groups, particularly those who were Spanish speaking. The movement to legitimatize bilingual education as a part of the curriculum of the public schools has been partially successful. The enactment by Congress in 1965 of the Bilingual Education Act and Title VII of the Elementary and Secondary Education Act, along with the Educational Amendment Act of 1974, gave very substantial support to the concept of bilingual education. In 1974, the United States Supreme Court, in a now famous case known as *Lau v. Nichols,* ruled that the San Francisco schools had to provide bilingual education to non-English speaking pupils. Several states

IT'S THE LAW

Federal law P.L. 94-142, the Education for All Handicapped Children Act, requires that all handicapped children receive a "free and appropriate public education." Here are some of the highlights of the law:

1. "Handicapped children are defined as: 'mentally retarded, hard of hearing, deaf, speech impaired, visually handicapped, seriously emotionally disturbed, orthopedically impaired, or other health impaired, or children with specific learning disabilities, who by reason thereof require special education and related services.'" (Sec. 602)
2. Public schools must seek out, identify and evaluate handicapped students or those suspected of having a disability.
3. Handicapped children must be educated with their nonhandicapped peers "to the maximum extent possible." This does not mean all handicapped children must be in regular classes, but it does mean that children should not be in segregated institutions or even in separate wings of a building any more than is necessary.
4. Before placing a handicapped child, a professional evaluation team consisting of a principal, classroom teacher, special education teacher and a parent must evaluate the child and make a placement decision.
5. The regulations add that teachers should not "put undue reliance" on tests which may discriminate against those with lesser sensory, manual or visual skills.
6. Parents must be informed in advance of any placement decision and may appeal in a formal hearing.
7. A written, individualized program of instruction must be developed by professional staff members in consultation with the child's parents. The program must be evaluated periodically—again, in consultation with the child's parents.
8. The confidentiality of all data and information pertaining to the child must be assured, and access to all the child's records must always be immediately available to his or her parents.
9. The child must be given access to all aspects of the school program normally provided for nonhandicapped children, including art, music, physical education, library science and other special subjects or services.
10. All services to the handicapped child shall be provided at no cost to the parent.[4]

[4] *Your Public Schools* (March 31, 1980), Olympia, Wa.: Superintendent of Public Instruction, p. 10.

have passed laws in recent years requiring schools to provide special instruction for children who do not speak English, and have allocated additional funds for this purpose.

One of the central issues concerning bilingual education is whether these programs are to be transitional or maintenance oriented. That is, should the bilingual effort be undertaken for a relatively short period of time, such as three years, until the pupil learns English,

at which time English becomes the language of instruction? Such programs are *transitional* and are the most common. English as a Second Language (ESL) programs are obviously of this type. The child who speaks Samoan, for example, is taught English, but until English is learned, regular school instruction may be in Samoan. Bilingual *maintenance* programs are those in which the bilingual instruction continues for several years in an effort to maintain a

PHOTO FOLIO

This photograph illustrates vividly that the present-day emphasis on space technology extends well beyond the school's science and social studies curriculums. Children today have information available to them from sources outside the school that would not have been known, even by the most knowledgeable scholars only a few years ago. In addition, so much of what is known by children is taken for granted—"Doesn't *everyone* have a rocket on the school playground?" Some have suggested that the information transmission systems used by schools—largely books, pictures, and teacher talk—suffer by comparison with information transmission systems available to children outside of school.

1. Do you agree or disagree with the suggestion in the last sentence of the foregoing paragraph? Explain.
2. List five "profound ideas" with which most ten-year-olds have at least a familiarity that would have been unknown to the president of a university in 1900.

fluent command of the language. Militant advocates of bilingual education, who represent non-English speaking ethnics, often support maintenance rather than transitional programs. They argue that it makes no sense to allow the knowledge of an alternate language, already mastered, to deteriorate.

Many other controversies surround bilingual education. For example, should it also be bicultural? Often the two are linked as bilingual-bicultural, and advocates claim that language and culture cannot really be separated. Also, there is the question of the status to be accorded the non-English language. It may be true that one language can convey ideas as well as any other language, and, therefore, value judgments should not be made about language worthiness. The problem here is that ours is an English-speaking society, claims to the contrary by advocates of bilingualism notwithstanding. This country has *one* and only one official language, and that language is English. An individual who is not fluent in English is likely to be handicapped in conducting the affairs of ordinary living in this society. This suggests that schools should be cautious in entertaining alternates to the accepted use of the English language.

Organizational Structures of Elementary Schools

State compulsory school attendance laws require children to attend from about age six to age sixteen. These ages vary slightly from place to place—the beginning age may be as late as seven or eight for *required* attendance, and in some states the terminal age is eighteen. The kindergarten, typically a one-half day experience for five-year-old children, is not considered one of the required years of school attendance. Nonetheless, kindergartens are a well established part of the educational enterprise, especially in urban areas, and few persons question their value as a bridge between home and school. Thus, when one speaks of the elementary school, usually the reference is to children between the ages of five and eleven; converting these ages to grades, we get K–6. In some places the elementary school grade ranges are K–8. The K–6 elementary schools are usually followed by a three-year junior high school, followed by a three-year senior high school (K–6–3–3). The K–8 elementary schools ordinarily are followed by a four-year high school (K–8–4).

Schools in Colonial America and those of the early national period did not use an age-sorting system we call "grades." Children of varying ages were assigned to a single teacher who tutored the youngsters on an individual basis, or who taught them in small cross-age groups. It was not until the middle of the nineteenth century that the practice of grouping children according to age, i.e. age-grading, became widespread. This practice was developed in Germany in the eight-year *Volkschule.* It appealed to American educators as an efficient way of managing the teaching of a large number of children. Following the Civil War, there was rapid acceptance of the practice of grouping children who were of a similar age, and keeping those groups intact from one year to the next as children progressed through school. Schools were therefore "graded" by age, and communities and states used that term in curriculum documents, school regulations, and in naming their schools. Even today it is possible to find etched into the stonework of some of the remaining old school buildings such names as Frederic Graded School. The expression "grade school" is commonly used in ordinary parlance in speaking of the elementary school.

The graded concept has some genuine strengths, and that is why it is so well established in school systems around the world: (1) it does reduce *some* variability within instructional groups by keeping the age constant; (2) it attempts to equalize educational opportunity by exposing all children to the *same* curriculum; (3) textbooks, instructional materials, and achievement tests can be constructed on the basis of age-grade norms; (4) children's social development relates to age, therefore, age groups tend to be natural social groups; (5) it is an efficient way to accommodate a large number of children who are required to attend school; (6) it allows teachers to specialize their teaching skills in terms of the age children with whom they work best; (7) it is possible to require set standards of achievement for the various grades.

There are also a number of limitations associated with the graded idea, and its critics have been numerous. They say that (1) it is a lock-step program that encourages teachers to disregard individual differences; (2) it sets unrealistic standards for children and treats low-achieving children unfairly; (3) it encourages mechanical teaching, analogous to assembly-line production in industry; (4) it encourages traditional recitation-response teaching practices; (5) the curriculum becomes rigid and undifferentiated; (6) the competitive and comparative system of determining grades (marks of achievement) and promotion are often educationally and psychologically unsound; (7) it encourages an authoritarian classroom atmosphere.

There has been no shortage of suggested alternatives to the graded system. The proposed reforms, which, it must be said, have enjoyed only limited success, deal with some combination of the following variables:

1. cross-age grouping—use of nongraded classrooms; homogeneous ability grouping of children of varying ages for specific subjects, such as reading, arithmetic, or spelling.
2. differentiated staffing—team teaching; use of specialists; use of teacher aides, parents, and paraprofessionals; departmentalized arrangements.
3. flexibility—open classrooms; individually prescribed instruction; continuous progress education.
4. individualized instruction—individually guided instruction; pupil contracts; programmed instruction; individually prescribed instruction; teaching machines.
5. child-centeredness—combines several of those listed above.
6. societal needs—middle schools; magnet schools; year-around schools; storefront alternative schools.

The tendency of schools to experiment with innovative organizational structures seems to have slowed to some extent at the start of the decade of the 1980's. The flurry of activity that characterized the decades of the 1960's and the 1970's is not apparent today. In elementary schools today we find the self-contained classroom—that is, one teacher with a single group of similar-age pupils—to be the prevailing mode. Within this organizational pattern, we see incorporated many of the concepts generated through the efforts of innovators of the past: a concern for the individual child; flexible classroom arrangements; some use of specialists and teaming; use of teacher aides; some cross-age grouping; and so on. Most large school districts do offer some options to parents in the way of alternative classrooms or schools.

Overshadowing all of these developments is the continuing effort to build educational programs that will reach individual children—all children—in ways that will enhance their opportunities for self-development. The shared planning of educators, parents, and other lay persons for this purpose is on the increase. Although great strides have been made in reducing the inequalities and inequities in educational opportunity, American education has yet a long way to go in finding a satisfactory solution to this problem. The ideal is to produce individuals who are able to make wise decisions concerning their own lives, and who are able to relate to society in responsible ways.

DEVELOPING RELATED COMPETENCIES

Can You Top This?

Primary-grade teachers are often privy to highly personal information about the family lives of their pupils because of what children talk about during their "Sharing Time" or "Show and Tell." One student teacher found herself in difficulty because she was relating intimate information concerning the family of one of her pupils to her boyfriend. The conversation was overheard by a relative of the family, who happened to be sitting in an adjoining booth in the restaurant where the conversation took place. This, of course, was reported to the family, who in turn took the matter to the school principal.

1. What does this incident suggest about the need to handle in a professional manner confidential matters relating to school?
2. Do you see any ethical problems involved in a teacher violating the trust and confidence that young children, in their innocence, place in their teacher?

Jumping to Conclusions

Miss Evans noticed that fourth-grade Julie often appears tired in school. On three occasions in the past month Julie had fallen fast asleep at her desk. In a chance conversation one day, Julie said something to Miss Evans about seeing a performance on the "Tonight Show" on television. In that part of the country the "Tonight Show" was telecast at 11:30 P.M.

1. Can the teacher assume that this child's condition is the result of late television viewing?
2. What might Miss Evans do to look into this matter more thoroughly? Should it be a matter of concern to Miss Evans?

Where Have All the Children Gone?

Mr. Berg is completing his first year of teaching. In looking over his records, he sees that he had fifty-six children enrolled during the school year. Only fourteen children who started in September were in his class when the school year ended. At no time did he have more than thirty-two pupils in his class.

1. What does this tell you about the life styles of families who send their children to this school?
2. How would a teacher go about planning a program of instruction for a situation such as the one described?

Separate and Unequal

One of the realities not discussed in this chapter is the extent of separation of our adult population from our child population. When parents go out of an evening, children are left with baby sitters. Children are sent away to summer camp. There are matinees for children in movie houses. Some department stores provide a baby-sitting service. In school, children are removed from the adult world for several hours each day. Many adults still feel that "children should be seen and not heard."

1. Do you believe this is a desirable set of conditions for optimum child rearing? Why or why not?
2. Why is the separation of children from grownups as widespread as it is today?
3. What might be done to reverse the tendency to segregate children from adults?

FOR FURTHER PROFESSIONAL STUDY

Books

Bloom, Benjamin S. *Human Characteristics and School Learning.* New York: McGraw-Hill Book Company, Inc., 1976.

Good, Thomas L. and Jere E. Brophy. *Looking in Classrooms,* 2nd ed. New York: Harper and Row, Publishers, Inc., 1978.

Henderson, George. *Introduction to American Education: A Human Relations Approach.* Norman, Oklahoma: University of Oklahoma Press, 1978.

Jarolimek, John. *The Schools in Contemporary Society: An Analysis of Social Currents, Issues, and Forces.* New York: Macmillan Publishing Co., Inc., 1981.

Purkey, William Watson. *Inviting School Success.* Belmont, California: Wadsworth Publishing Co., Inc., 1978.

Periodicals

Banks, James A. "Shaping the Future of Multicultural Education." *Journal of Negro Education* (Summer 1979), 237-252.

Bloom, Benjamin S. "New Views of the Learner: Implications for Institutions and Curriculum." *Childhood Education* (October 1979), 4-11.

Brandt, Ronald S., Ed. "Mastery Learning." *Educational Leadership* (November 1979), 104-161. (Several articles)

Clark, David L., Linda S. Lotto and Martha M. McCarthy. "Factors Associated with Success in Urban Elementary Schools." *Phi Delta Kappan* (March 1980), 467-470.

Garcia, Jesus and Carol S. Woodrick. "The Treatment of White and Non-White Women in U.S. Textbooks." *The Clearing House* (September 1979), 17-22.

Ware, Martha L. and Dorothy Massie. "Educating the Handicapped: Opening the Schoolhouse Doors to a Newly Demanding Minority . . . and New Judicial Interventions." *Contemporary Education* (October 1977), 24E ff.

2

The Qualified and Competent Teacher

THE QUALIFIED AND COMPETENT TEACHER . . .

1. Performs in accordance with the characteristics of an effective teacher.
2. Perceives teacher education as an open-ended, career-long process.
3. Defines teaching as a conceptual process.
4. Analyzes the teaching process on a conceptual level.
5. Functions effectively in a variety of professional roles.

Performance Criteria

As a result of the serious study of this chapter, the student should be able to . . .

1. Provide examples of teacher behavior in a variety of psychological roles.
2. Describe teacher behaviors that are known to be correlates of pupil achievement.
3. State and defend an operational definition of teaching.
4. Define a model for the analysis of teaching.
5. Conduct a self-analysis to determine his or her own potential to become a "qualified and competent teacher."

Those who aspire to teach in the elementary school should be aware of its critical role in the development of citizens. Elementary school teachers have a unique opportunity to influence learners because pupils learn early to respect knowledge or to scorn it. They learn "how to learn" or to become "teacher dependent." At the elementary-school level pupils must master the rudiments of the basic skills in order to avoid an ever-increasing complexity of learning difficulties as they proceed through school. They also develop respect for themselves and for others, or they learn to reinforce existing prejudices. Too, the development of habits consistent with democratic processes must begin at this level. All of these are critical outcomes and are considered basic to effective citizenship.

The concept of a common school for the nation's children has been a foremost guiding factor in the development of education for over a century. This ideal has been realized most completely on the elementary level. The elementary school, free and open to all, is uniquely fitted to the democratic ideal. This status makes it extremely important that basic citizenship education, as discussed in Chapter 1, occurs at this level. At the same time, efforts to provide it have resulted in an overcrowded curriculum.

As a result of so many expectancies, the elementary school has become a "cognitive pressure cooker" for both teachers and children. Learning in such an atmosphere produces many questionable side effects. There are some children who learn to read but who, in the process, learn to dislike reading. There are others who learn basic mathematical concepts and skills but develop a fear of the subject. The overstressing of cognitive learning has been at the expense of pupil development in the affective and psychomotor areas. This is not to suggest that cognitive learning is unimportant—rather, it is to express a concern for the neglect of affective learning in citizenship education.

Psychologists have known for a long time that children's attitudes affect how they perceive learning tasks. A high-pressure learning environment does little to promote positive attitudes toward learning. The teacher who plans carefully can reduce the pressure to a degree, but more must be done to lighten the burden imposed by an overloaded program.

Elementary teachers often find it very difficult to provide instruction in such a large number of curricular areas. The problem is becoming increasingly complicated as a result of new programs in such fields as mathematics, science, social studies, and the language arts. During the past decade, elementary teachers have attempted to keep pace with new curriculum developments by attending late afternoon classes offered by colleges and universities, and through participation in workshops and in-service classes. These activities, added to an already crowded agenda for teachers, are very demanding of their time and energy. Teachers have little time left to plan a humanistic learning environment for children. The thrust to improve teaching in the cognitive area and its related skills has produced much that is good, but at the same time, it has created a curriculum with a heavy cognitive bias. The recent emphasis on competency testing has also reinforced attention being given to cognitive learning. Thus, balance needs to be restored in favor of the humanistic dimension of the curriculum if the elementary school is to familiarize the child with the full range of his/her cultural heritage. In any event, the elementary teacher must confront these realities as part of the everyday business of teaching.

Nevertheless, teaching in the elementary school offers many rewards for those who are qualified. For those who lack the necessary qualifications, frustrations and failures take the place of rewards. The elementary-school teacher must be many things to many people. At no other educational level is there a greater demand on the time and energy of the teacher to provide both personal and educational services for pupils.

In most instances, the same pupils are with the teacher all day, beginning with the opening exercises, continuing through the lunch period, until the ending of the school day. In this setting, the teacher gets to know each child very well indeed and therefore has an excellent opportunity to provide learning experiences that support the needs and interests of the individual. But superimposed on these personal relationships is the necessity to provide learning experiences in a broad area of subject fields. In addition, the teacher must be a record keeper of the child's progress, and also is responsible for disseminating this information to parents.

This setting requires a teacher who likes children. One who does not would lack the patience to work and live, day in and day out, with children in such a confined and highly personal setting. The psychological roles that the teacher performs are very important in setting the stage for motivating children to learn. We must emphasize that the personal interactions between the teacher and pupils in the elementary school are greater in number and extent than at any other level. These situations should be used as learning experiences because in many instances they are as important as the knowledge and skills that are taught to children in their school subjects. But to do so requires a teacher who likes children, and one who is endowed with an infinite capacity for patience.

The teacher must be a good student. Demands to know a wide range of subject matter assume that the teacher is interested in knowledge and learning. Teachers who possess this quality are open-minded. They are curious about the world around them and are able to reach out beyond a single field of knowledge to inquire about matters that span a continuum from simple to complex. The child's world is one of wide-ranging interests, a curiosity that needs only to be directed toward positive ends. The qualified teacher is able to capture this interest and to make the most of it. Elementary-school pupils should have teachers whose zest and interest in learning are contagious to those around them. The successful teacher is able to create a situation where children like and respect learning for learning's sake, and this requires that the teacher have this quality, too.

The ability to organize is an important qualification. Without it the teacher would be unable to navigate successfully through a normal school day, which contains numerous transitions from one activity to another. Organization presumes skill in planning. This skill is one not possessed by many people, but it is one that can be learned. Those who fail to learn it, or who do not respect it, frequently find teaching frustrating. A positive classroom environment is dependent on these skills; the necessity to enforce control occurs infrequently among teachers who are good organizers and planners.

Knowledge of the major teaching modes and strategies is a basic qualification. The typical teacher education program devotes much time to their development. The assumption is that these can be learned by the prospective teacher during the preparation program. Probably too much time is devoted to teaching modes, and not enough spent on the affective, psychological roles in teaching. Too frequently, teaching problems result from psychological, affective-type situations. Illustrations of these are failure to understand children's needs and interests, inability to get along with colleagues, and parental problems. Less frequently, problems seem to occur that are the result of a lack of knowledge of teaching modes and strategies. This observation may be misleading, however; a problem may be the result of a teacher using a teaching strategy inappropriate for the class, but the problem may surface in the form of classroom disorder, apathy, or parental criticism. The prior condition may well have been the result of the teacher's failure to provide children with the psychological support they need. When this is the case, no amount of skillful teaching can compensate for the psychological deficiencies. In other words, it is not enough that the teacher is knowledgeable and proficient in the area of teaching modes and strategies, per se. These operate successfully only when the teacher has diagnosed the needs and interests of the children beforehand, and subsequently determines the appropriate mode of teaching.

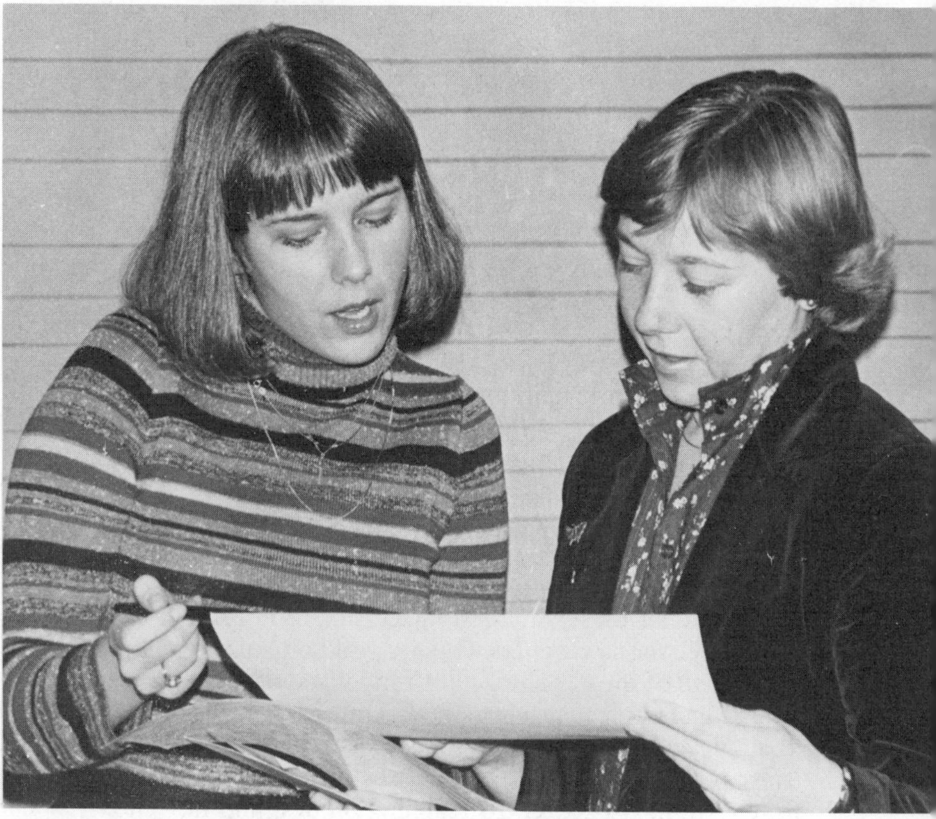

A firm understanding of teaching modes and strategies is necessary to enable the teacher to select a mode that best serves a particular need or interest of the group. Knowledge of modes should provide the teacher with a selection that ranges from highly teacher-directed to highly pupil-centered strategies of teaching. The teacher who is inflexible usually relies on the teaching strategy that best suits his or her needs, as opposed to serving the needs of the group. Such a practice is very unproductive and is generally associated with unsuccessful teachers.

The teacher must be able to adapt teaching strategies to the variables that influence the lesson. The variables take many shapes and forms: the nature of the subject matter, the characteristics of the learners, the learning outcomes sought, as well as numerous other considerations. Thus, the qualified teacher has a repertoire of strategies from which to select the one that fits the occasion.

Communication skills are essential. Contacts with parents are pro-

PHOTO FOLIO

In this photograph classroom teachers are cooperating in a lesson-planning activity. Team planning, such as this, requires an atmosphere of trust and respect. Teachers freely share techniques that have worked well and point out practices that have fallen short of success. The teachers will compare the results of their planning after the lessons have been taught.

1. What is there about the organization of the elementary school that encourages or discourages team planning?
2. How do you account for the fact that although most experts agree that team planning is a sound concept, it has not always worked well in actual practice?

ductive and pleasant experiences for teachers who possess these skills. Parent conferences require skills in communicating on a one-to-one basis, for the conference may be critical to a child's future. The teacher frequently must reassure a parent, assist in resolving conflicts that are essentially centered in the home, offer suggestions to enable the parent to provide support and guidance to the child in school subjects, and so forth. The teacher must also be proficient in group communication skills. These skills are obviously important in everyday teaching, and they are becoming increasingly important in adult groups where school topics are discussed. PTSA and "open house" type meetings frequently require presentations by the teacher relative to objectives and curriculum processes.

Basic to all these qualifications is a healthy self-concept. Teachers who possess it are positive, confident, accepting of others, intellectually curious, and usually have a sense of humor. Evidence suggests that the teacher is a powerful model of behavior for pupils. Children are very sensitive to the teacher's behavior as it relates to what the teacher values and rewards. The teacher who has a healthy self-concept is apt to reward children's behavior that is consistent with it. There are teachers who seem to need the constant assurance that others are dependent on them; such a feeling does little to encourage independence in children. Teachers who are pessimistic do little to encourage optimism and self-confidence in children. Those who are impatient with failures do little to reassure children with learning problems. And those who are deadly serious miss countless opportunities to experience the laughter and joy of the child's world.

Those who are anticipating a career of teaching in the elementary school would do well to assess themselves in terms of these qualifications for successful teaching. Experience has verified their importance over many years. An excellent way to do this is by working with children in many settings before applying for admission to a teacher education program. There are many opportunities available in community agencies, in tutoring experiences, as well as in numerous school-related activities. Additional data can be obtained by talking with teachers and other adults who work with children. School counselors have information relative to objective measures, such as tests and inventories designed for self-analysis. The final decision to become an elementary teacher should be based on a wide base of evidence, coupled with extensive self-analysis. Elementary-school teaching requires the best, and teacher candidates must possess the qualifications requisite for success.

PROFESSIONAL STATUS OF ELEMENTARY-SCHOOL TEACHERS

Teaching in the elementary school has come into its own in relatively recent times. Only during the past twenty-five years have the qualifications for teaching in the elementary school equalled those required for teaching in the secondary school. Equally recent is the provision for a single salary schedule for both elementary- and secondary-school teachers. Prior to this time, elementary teachers were paid less than their professional counterparts in the secondary school. And even today many citizens view teaching in the elementary school as a woman's job—a notion equally abhorrent to both sexes.

The status of the elementary-school teacher in this nation has paralleled the growth of public awareness of the elementary school as a critical institution in a democratic society. In Colonial times, the elementary teacher was perceived essentially as a mother figure,

THE NEWER TEACHER EDUCATION PROGRAMS ARE EMPHASIZING THE QUESTION

"Are you really sure you want to be a teacher?"

The time, expense, and effort required to complete certification requirements are very substantial in the newer programs. Many students underestimate this investment because an initial teaching certificate can be obtained along with a bachelor's degree. These same students would take a second look before entering law or medicine, because certification in those fields requires an extended preparatory program beyond the bachelor's degree before the individual can practice the specialty. Teaching is the only profession that certifies practitioners after only four years of preparation. This may well be a mistake; some students enter teacher education programs because they can get a degree and a teaching certificate at the same time.

But teacher education is becoming more rigorous every year. The newer programs require a full-time involvement during the last two years. Some programs even require a decision during the freshman year. They no longer make it possible for the student to get a degree and a teaching certificate "on the side." Professional associations are beginning to talk about controlling the number of students who enter teacher education. Thus, selection and admission procedures are also becoming more rigorous.

1. With the possibility that fewer students will be selected for teacher education programs in the future, what criteria would you suggest for screening applicants in order to get the best?
2. When did you decide you wanted to become a teacher? On what evidence did you base your decision?

one who had the maternal qualifications needed to work with young children. During that period, the Dame School, the dominant institution for the education of children, was conducted largely by mothers.

The male teacher was a rarity and was usually considered to be unfit for most manly duties. During the eighteenth century, with the expansion of schooling for children, the status of the elementary school changed very little. According to Otto,[1] teaching in many

[1]Henry J. Otto, "Historical Roots of Contemporary Elementary Education," *The Elementary School in the United States.* The Seventy-second Yearbook of the National Society for the Study of Education, Part II. (Chicago: University of Chicago Press, 1973), pp. 31–59.

ways was considered to be an auxiliary of the ministry. Thus, a knowledge of the Scriptures and membership in the dominant church were important qualifications, along with an unblemished character, a minimum knowledge of the subjects to be taught, and an unflinching ability to discipline children.

Nor did the elementary-school teacher enjoy an attractive image in early American literature. Washington Irving's Ichabod Crane[2] did little to portray the teacher as a hero figure. But with the frontier movement in the nineteenth century, the teacher emerged as a somewhat more heroic figure, depicted as one who needed sufficient physical strength to subdue the strongest boy in the school in order to establish order. Edward Eggleston's hero in *The Hoosier School Master*[3] contributed to this image. One might say that a substantial body of folklore surrounding the elementary-school teacher emerged during the development of the nation. Much of this did little to establish the elementary-school teacher on a sound professional footing. The consequence of these popular impressions of the teacher was to create a stereotype that has had many unfortunate connotations. Among these was the belief that those who taught in the elementary school were not qualified for a more demanding occupation. And certainly we have seen that the male teacher was viewed as being intellectually inferior to his counterpart in the secondary school. Thus, a popular notion was that the elementary-school teacher "did not need to know as much" as the secondary-school teacher. A combination of these and other similar notions did much to retard the development of elementary-school teaching as a high-level professional enterprise.

In the past few decades, a great deal has happened to change the status of elementary-school teaching. During the 1940's, the baby boom increased public awareness of the need for an adequate program (one that required a massive effort) to provide needed physical facilities. This increased visibility spotlighted the need for more stringent teacher qualifications if schools were to deliver the kind of program required in a society constantly becoming more sophisticated in its educational expectations. Other factors included ever-increasing attention to the importance of children and their nurture, in both the popular press and in low-cost paperbacks written for parents of young children. And last but not least, the expanding economy of the 1940–1970 era provided the public funding neces-

[2] Washington Irving, "Legend of Sleepy Hollow," modern printing (New York: Franklin Watts, Inc., 1966).

[3] Edward Eggleston, *The Hoosier School Master*, modern printing (Gloucester, Mass.: Peter Smith Press, 1959).

sary to develop and support the growing demands for elementary education.

Today, elementary education in this nation is a gigantic enterprise. During the 1978–79 school year there were approximately 1,170,357 elementary-school teachers[4] who were responsible for the instruction of approximately 24,403,027[5] children in the public elementary schools.

The magnitude is even more impressive when viewed from an economic perspective. Census data[6] show that in 1978, an estimated $76.3 billion was spent on public and private school elementary and secondary education. This represented nearly 7.5 per cent of the Gross National Product. Data on elementary-level costs are difficult to obtain because most school districts lump together elementary and secondary expenditures. The public has become increasingly sensitive to expenditures for all services, and this relatively substantial investment in education no doubt has contributed to a growing demand for accountability. In this atmosphere, teaching competence is becoming increasingly important. Attention to the qualifications of the elementary-school teacher has reached its highest level in the history of the enterprise, and there are signs that it will continue to be important.

Coupled with the emphasis on accountability, the instability of the teacher supply and demand situation during recent years has created additional problems for elementary-school teachers. In the face of a decreasing school enrollment, an inflationary economy, and strong demands from taxpayers to economize, school districts have reduced the number of elementary teachers. At the same time, the rate of teacher turnover has also decreased. Hence, the market for beginning teachers has shown an over-all drop during the past few years. For example, there were approximately 73,046 persons who completed degree and certification requirements for elementary teaching in 1978.[7] During that year the National Education Association Research Division predicted that approximately 34,100 beginning teachers would be hired in public elementary schools.[8] This estimate of over two applicants for each available position is probably conservative in terms of the supply-demand situation in the near

[4] *Estimates of School Statistics,* 1978–79, National Education Association, Research Memo, 1979, p. 8.

[5] *Loc. cit.*

[6] Bureau of the Census, U.S. Department of Commerce, *Statistical Abstracts of the United States* (Washington, D.C.: Government Printing Office, 1978), p. 135.

[7] *Teacher Supply and Demand in the Public Schools, 1978,* National Education Association, Research Memo, 1979. p. 4.

[8] *Ibid.*, p. 11.

future. In any case, many individuals are apt to view elementary education as a professional field that has little to offer in the way of career positions.

How long this situation will continue is a matter of pure conjecture because of the complex variables that affect it. It should be noted that trends in the demand for qualified teachers fluctuate yearly. This is because of changes in such factors as (1) major modifications in school programs; (2) receipt of federal grant monies; (3) change in pupil-teacher ratios as a result of federal or state funding for special programs; (4) change in rate of replacement of teachers with substandard qualifications; and (5) change in numbers of teacher turnover because of resignations, retirements, and leaves of absence for professional study or illness.

Data on supply-demand are usually presented according to prevailing conditions. The NEA Research Division, in addition to presenting data on this basis, predicts needs on the basis of a quality-criterion estimate. This is based on a consideration of the factors that were described earlier as variables that annually create a changing situation. The quality-criterion estimate, however, views needs in terms of desirable conditions that are necessary for quality education. The prediction for 1978–79, based on this criterion, was 373,050 needed positions.[9]

On the positive side, the future may well provide an increase of personnel needs in elementary education. With a decrease of the number of children to be educated and an attendant emphasis on accountability, there is an opportunity for elementary educators to give attention to quality programs. This could mean a greater diversity in the kinds of teachers that are needed for a quality elementary school. It could also mean an actual increase in the number of teachers required to perform the tasks necessary to prepare citizens who will spend most of their lives in the twenty-first century. Greater attention to special education, parent education, preschool education, community education, and the affective growth of children are examples of dimensions that have been tapped only on a surface level at the present time.

In short, there is always a demand for excellent teachers. Competition for positions is becoming very keen, and prospective teachers should carefully explore the qualifications required for elementary-school teaching before investing in it as a career.

[9] *Loc. cit.*

"IF I HAD ONLY KNOWN EARLY ENOUGH . . .

that jobs were this scarce I'd never have gone into teaching," remarked Mr. Andrews after his fifth visit to the University Teacher Placement Office for a job interview. His remark, like those made by a growing number of teacher education graduates, has a familiar ring.

1. Do you know where to go to obtain current data on teacher supply-demand on your campus?
2. Do you have a sufficient commitment of purpose to be an elementary-school teacher with no certainty of finding a position right away?
3. Have you considered an alternate, related vocation if a teaching position is not readily available when you graduate?

CHARACTERISTICS OF EFFECTIVE TEACHERS

Who should teach? The answer seems simple enough—only those who are qualified and competent. Yet, the profession has been unable to establish a data base that has sufficient validity to predict with certainty who will succeed and who will fail. There are many reasons why research efforts have failed to produce criterion instruments with adequate predictive validity. One reason is that teaching is a human process, requiring almost constant interactions between the teacher and pupils. In such a situation, the number of variables affecting the process is very great.

The absence of scientific data has not, however, deterred the profession from producing a vast amount of descriptive literature on the subject. Nor has the lack of definitive evidence seemed to stand in the way of certification agencies and teacher education institutions in their efforts to define and prescribe qualifications for teaching. Literally hundreds of textbooks dealing with the topic have also been written. In most of these efforts, the qualifications for teaching have been based on knowledge that has resulted from tradition, experience, and, to some extent, research data. This body of knowledge serves to guide the profession in establishing requirements for the certification of teachers.

Critics have asserted that the profession contains too many teachers who are neither qualified nor competent. On the other hand, supporters of the profession contend that, when the high level of

national educational attainment is considered, the record speaks for itself. Surely some recognition should be given to the quality of teaching that must have been necessary to produce a citizenry as well-educated as ours.

Regardless of the position one might take on the question, the profession must continue its efforts to identify the qualifications needed for competent teaching. The authors believe that the problem is larger than simply predicting failures. There is no solid line between success and failure, because one may be weak in certain qualifications but strong in others, to the point that a limited success is assured.

The identification of characteristics that describe the qualifications required for successful teaching is necessary in order to have some basis for screening applicants for teacher education programs. Agreement on qualifications is also needed for the evaluation of teachers once they enter the profession.

Experience and available research evidence underscore the fact

PHOTO FOLIO

In this photograph a principal-teacher conference is being conducted following a visit the principal has made to the teacher's classroom. The qualified and competent teacher recognizes the importance of the school principal as a source of professional support and assistance. Beginning teachers, however, sometimes have the impression they should not seek help from the school principal as they fear it may suggest weaknesses on their part.

1. As a prospective teacher how do you feel about the principal visiting your classroom when you know that his/her rating may affect your professional future?
2. What arrangements should be made to make the principal's visit to the classroom a productive experience for the teacher?
3. Does this photograph suggest anything about the affective atmosphere of this conference?

that teaching comprises numerous character traits. It is a mix of these rather than a single trait that appears to constitute the qualifications for successful teaching. Hamachek[10] identified traits that good teachers possess. His conclusions remain valid at the present writing and are summarized as follows:

1. They view teaching as basically—first and last—a human process. Such teachers have a sense of humor; they can empathize with students; they are fair; they are flexible; they are more democratic than autocratic; and they relate naturally and easily with pupils and peers. Their classrooms reflect an openness and a sense of mutual trust.
2. They feel good about themselves and they have a positive view of others.

[10] For an excellent review of the research of teacher qualifications and an elaboration of these characteristics, see Don Hamachek, "Characteristics of Good Teachers and Implications for Teacher Education," *Phi Delta Kappan* (February 1969) 341-345. Also reprinted in J. Michael Palardy, *Teaching Today: Tasks and Challenges* (New York: Macmillan Publishing Co., Inc., 1975), pp. 33-42.

Thus, they identify with people rather than withdrawing from them. They feel adequate; they feel wanted; they are trustworthy, and they feel worthy in what they believe to be a significant human service.

3. They are knowledgeable and well informed on a wide range of subjects. They have a respect for knowledge, and they believe strongly that their pupils must also learn to respect it as a vital force in a happy and a productive life.
4. They are able to communicate effectively. They understand that the communication process includes more than presentations—it also provides for discovery and interaction with others as it provides for the development of personal meanings. They employ a comprehensive repertoire of teaching modes that produce affective as well as cognitive gains in their pupils.[11]

Hamachek, after a careful review of the literature, concluded that "flexibility" was the single most repeated word used to describe good teachers. He provided an operational definition of the word in the following statement:

> In other words, the good teacher does not seem to be overwhelmed by a single point of view or approach to the point of intellectual myopia. A good teacher knows that he cannot be just one sort of person and use just one kind of approach if he intends to meet the multiple needs of his students. Good teachers are, in a sense, "Total Teachers." That is, they seem able to be what they have to be to meet the demands of the moment. They seem able to move with the shifting tides of their own needs, the student's, and do what has to be done to handle the situation. A total teacher can be firm when necessary (say 'no' and mean it) or permissive (say 'Why not try it your way?' and mean that, too) when appropriate. It depends on many things, and good teachers know the difference.[12]

There is a growing recognition of the fact that "good teaching" does not just happen. It is based on many qualifications. The selection and preparation of elementary teachers who possess these qualifications deserve the full support of the profession and public.

TEACHER ROLES

The teacher is the central force that shapes the behaviors of the individual child as well as those of children in groups. Even though there are many other factors that influence pupils' behavior in the

[11] Ibid., p. 343.

[12] *Loc. cit.* (For a reaffirmation of Hamachek's emphasis on "flexibility" as a primary characteristic of good teachers, see: Richard L. Turner, "The Value of Variety in Teaching Styles," *Educational Leadership* (January, 1979) pp. 257–258.

DO YOU KNOW THESE TEACHERS?

Ms. Acey and Mr. Bell Teach at Oaktree School.

Ms. Acey is pleasant and cheerful with everyone in a brief but courteous manner. Her day at school is completely organized. She brings papers to grade whenever she comes to the faculty lounge. Some of the teachers think she is "too professional" and feel uncomfortable around her, although she never criticizes anyone. Others say, "She makes me feel that I'm not working hard enough." The school principal considers her to be an excellent teacher. Parents comment on her efficiency. Her pupils tend to be quiet and aloof with children from other groups. Her close friends defend her when others accuse her of being a "high hat." One remarked that Ms. Acey believes school is serious business and that "fun and games" have no part in it.

Mr. Bell also is pleasant and cheerful with everyone. He spends his break time and after school time in the faculty lounge. His pupils are gregarious and highly visible in the lunch room or on the playground as a result of their propensity for visiting with others. Mr. Bell says, "Ms. Acey is just trying to make the rest of us look like loafers." The school principal would like to see Mr. Bell spend more time in his classroom and less time in the staff lounge. But he can hardly criticize Mr. Bell, because he does get at least minimal planning done. Parents are generally supportive of Mr. Bell. One parent remarked, "I think Jimmy learned more from other teachers, but Mr. Bell taught him to be kind and friendly with others." The other teachers consider him to be an average teacher and "one heck of a good guy."

1. Which teacher, Ms. Acey or Mr. Bell, would you rather have as your colleague? Why?
2. Based on these descriptions, which teacher better fits Hamachek's description of a good teacher? (Presented in a previous section.)
3. Where are each of these teacher's (1) strong and (2) weak points, with respect to the characteristics of a good teacher?

school setting, early experiments have shown that the way the teacher behaves with and toward children is a major determinant in shaping behavior. The teacher's behavior can be described according to specific roles that stem from the expectations of society, school, peers, colleagues, and the children themselves.

In this context, a role is a set of behaviors derived from the expectations demanded of it. It is simply a pattern of behavior recognizable in repeated performances. The effective performance of such behaviors is dependent on a body of knowledge and a set of skills consistent with the role expectation. Without these prerequisites, the teacher is greatly disadvantaged in performing the role in a competent manner. For example, a traditional role expectation of the teacher has been characterized as a "source of information." As such, the teacher is expected to possess a sufficient knowledge base of what is to be taught. Equally important is possession of those skills necessary for the communication of that knowledge to others. However, many educators would question "source of information" as an appropriate role for teachers in a world where knowledge changes its form and substance at so rapid a pace.

Teacher behaviors are primarily based on the performance of "psychological" and "instructional" roles. The qualified and competent teacher has mastered the knowledge and skills necessary for the performance of these roles. Although they are interrelated, they will be described separately for the purpose of clarity. The performance of psychological roles is very demanding on the teacher's energy. Even experienced teachers must frequently contend with role conflict in attempting to meet the psychological needs of pupils.[13]

Psychological Roles

A Social Model

This role is more difficult to perform than was the case a few years ago. Traditionally, the teacher was expected to represent the values that the community held dear. In performing this particular role, the teacher served as a model for the children. In the multicultural atmosphere of the present time, the teacher must recognize that values differ from one subculture to another, and that a group of children probably represents several sets of values, some of which may be contradictory. The teacher who attempts to be a model for a given value or a set of values is engaging in a risky venture. Thinking has recently shifted away from the importance of the teacher's modeling a value to that of providing instruction in value-setting as a process. Nevertheless, the teacher must be aware that certain communities still expect the teacher to be a model for the social values found therein. Thus the teacher is expected, through the use of precept and example, to inculcate those moral values, life styles, and career goals that have high priority in the community.

[13]See Susan Ketchin Edgerton, "Teachers in Role Conflict: The Hidden Dilemma," *Phi Delta Kappan*, October, 1977, pp. 120–122.

An Evaluator

The way the teacher performs this role can frequently determine how children view themselves. On countless occasions the elementary-school teacher is evaluating something about the child. Sometimes it concerns the way the child behaves in the hallway or lunch room; at other times it pertains to the manner in which classroom work is performed. But at still other times it is even more critical—when report cards or parent-conference time comes around. Because children are sensitive about all matters concerning success or failure, the way in which the teacher performs the evaluator role is often more critical than the evaluation itself. Children should be made to feel good about themselves and to have confidence in themselves; in short, to possess a strong, positive self-image. The elementary teacher who approaches the tasks that go along with the evaluator role in a positive, helpful manner is contributing to the healthy development of the child's personal and psychological makeup. Too many children lose confidence in themselves and learn to dislike school because they have been subjected to repeated failures, with a corresponding negative approach to the evaluation of their problems. The competent teacher plans ahead for evaluation by providing learning experiences that allow children the maximum opportunity to succeed.

A Walking Encyclopedia

This is probably the oldest teacher role. From the earliest elementary schools until well into the twentieth century the teacher was expected to be a walking mine of information. Even today the role is an important one, but its meaning has changed substantially from that of former times. The competent teacher recognizes that it is impossible to be an unfailing source of information for the vast number of questions children are prone to ask. It is more important to help children learn how to locate the information they are seeking. The traditional concept of the role frequently led to the teacher's dispensing the knowledge to children by lecturing, telling, or reading to them. These forms of instruction represent *passive* learning in its purest form.

To be sure, the teacher of today must be knowledgeable. Some teacher education programs require elementary teachers to study a field of knowledge in some depth. But more important than what the teacher actually knows is the teacher's respect for knowledge and the power it offers. The elementary teacher who is curious, always searching for answers to challenging questions—one who provides a positive model for acquiring and applying the tools that produce knowledge—is one who is performing the role in an exemplary manner.

A Moderator

The elementary-school teacher portrays the moderator role on many occasions. Especially in the area of personal conflicts, the role must be played with objectivity. Children are very sensitive to the fairness of the teacher's judgment calls when settling disputes. The pupil who is a perennial trouble maker presents a real challenge if the teacher is to handle the child in a consistently objective manner. The role of moderator affords the teacher a powerful opportunity for modeling behavior. In reconciling disputes, the fair, calm teacher can set examples for others to follow. The teacher who performs the role well is assured of the abiding respect of pupils.

An Investigator

Not always a pleasant role to perform, investigating requires the utmost discretion on the part of the teacher. Pupils frequently misplace their possessions; and on some occasions thefts occur. Problems for teachers sometimes result from confusion on the part of children as to what actually happened. More often than not, the object reappears and its disappearance can be attributed to carelessness on its owner's part. In any case, the investigator role is almost always performed best in a low-key manner. Too frequently the pupil who is the group scapegoat becomes the suspect when something is missing. Even though children are quick to accuse and equally quick to forgive, the victim may not recover so rapidly. Those pupils who already have emotional problems or a weak self-image are especially apt to develop scars that remain long after the incident seems to be forgotten.

When the teacher suspects a theft, and this turns out to be the case, the child who is involved probably should be referred for psychological assistance. Such a decision depends, of course, on the teacher's knowledge of the child's personal and school history.

It is generally agreed that mass punishment should be avoided. The teacher who takes away privileges from the whole group "until someone confesses" is doing children a great disservice. There are many pupils who have feelings of insecurity to begin with, and such a practice reinforces anxiety. When a theft is proven, equally devastating results accrue from information leaks concerning the guilty child. No good whatever comes from others knowing who did it. The real good comes from helping the child to overcome the need to steal.

The investigator role is one that is seldom discussed in literature and it deserves more attention than it receives. This role can be performed in a constructive way by an understanding teacher, or it can result in devastating trauma for children if it is performed in an insensitive manner.

An Ombudsman

Pupils sometimes develop anxiety in the process of learning to control their impulses. This is part of growing up. But the process must be understood by teachers. The role of an ombudsman is one too often overlooked by teachers who are preoccupied with teaching children to succeed in their school subjects.

Some children are afraid that, if given too much freedom, they are certain to do something wrong. Some worry about falling victim to imaginary dangers or threats; others worry about turning out to be like someone who is bad, or ill. The majority of children have these thoughts and feelings, and they look to the teacher as a source of reassurance. As such, the teacher who responds by listening to these needs of pupils in an understanding way is performing the role of an ombudsman. Teachers in whom children will usually confide are those who exude a confident and competent air; who set limits for permissible behavior, and who are consistent in enforcing them; who deal intelligently with negative behavior; and who understand that children worry about many things. The teacher who creates an atmosphere of rigidity, who is cold and unforgiving, who makes stern threats, and who believes that learning should be painful, is reinforcing and increasing the level of anxiety in children.

In the final analysis, this role provides the support and encouragement that many children need if they are to overcome difficulties in learning and personal-social matters. Without making the child or the group "teacher-dependent," the role provides a healthy psychological atmosphere, one that is conducive to the growth and development of children.

A Morale Builder

This role is important in the daily instructional program, especially where cognitive learning tasks are concerned. Unlike the role of ombudsman, the role of morale builder deals with learning situations that confront children. As children confront various learning tasks, they feel more secure about some than they do about others. When they feel inadequate, or experience an early failure, they look to the teacher to restore their morale. Teachers should plan carefully to insure a success pattern—no matter how limited—for the child. There is nothing more devastating to self-confidence than repeated

failure. On the other hand, there is a lot to be said for the cliché, "Nothing succeeds like success."

More will be said, in a later chapter, about planning a success pattern for children. But it is important to note here the significance of the teacher's attitude about the matter. The patient, reassuring teacher can do wonders for a child's ego. This is why it is essential that the prospective elementary teacher recognize the necessity of patience, especially toward those who learn slowly. If this character trait is weak, the prospective teacher should look carefully at his or her motivation for wanting to teach children.

A Leader of the Group

Many teachers are very effective with children in a one-to-one relationship but have difficulty interacting with pupils in a group. To be sure, twenty-five or thirty children in a group present a situation quite different from dealing with pupils singly. The phenomenon of a group personality and of group mentality can sometimes be frightening to teachers. Skills in group leadership lie in the area of classroom management and planning for instruction. Additional coverage is devoted to these skills later in the text. Suffice it to say

PHOTO FOLIO

The teacher in this photograph is helping the pupil learn to form letters correctly. Such individual attention creates a positive impression on pupils. The caring teacher makes every effort to insure each child does well. Obviously the child in this photograph is pleased with the attention she is receiving.

1. Which of the psychological roles described in this chapter do you think this teacher is performing?
2. Professor Paul Brandwein has drawn some criticism for his statement, "Above all, a teacher heals."*

What do you understand this statement to mean, and why do you believe some persons disagree with it?

*Greil Marcus, "Schoolbook Scandal: The Messy 'Truth,'" *Rolling Stone* (November 15, 1979), p. 33.

at this point that group leadership is a critical role for the teacher to perform.

A Substitute Parent

Teachers act as parents for many pupils. With little children, the role becomes one of serving as a parent during school hours. With very young children, the teacher frequently must assist the pupil with personal attire, as well as help to perform a number of other essentially psychomotor tasks. With older children, the teacher performs the role on a more subtle level, by shifting from physical to psychological support. The role may represent the teacher as a confidante, for those who have no parent or who come from one-parent families. The courts have ruled that in a limited, legal sense, the teacher may perform in *loco parentis,* that is, in the place of a parent during the time the child is in school.

A Target for Frustrations

Some children displace their emotional attitudes toward others onto their teachers. When this occurs, the teacher may become a target for their frustrations. Pupils experience many frustrations in their efforts to grow away from various kinds of adult domination. The role is sometimes made more difficult when the child displaces hostilities toward a parent onto the teacher. The intensity of resentment toward the adult world varies with circumstances. Those children who have positive relationships with adults are less apt to use the teacher as a target when venting their frustrations.

Even though the teacher probably would not choose the role, it is inescapable. The teacher should recognize the fact that a child's hostility frequently is a displaced frustration that originated elsewhere. In no case should the teacher take it personally, and develop hurt feelings. But many do. The important thing is to analyze the situation, talk to the child, and become familiar with his/her personal and school history. The origin of the child's frustrations will be identified sooner or later. There are too many responsibilities related to teaching for one to become personally hurt in such instances. Recognizing the role and performing it objectively are the wisest courses of action.

A Friend

Although this is more common among adolescents, younger children sometimes develop a strong friendship with teachers. This is a far more comfortable role than being a target for displaced frustrations, but if carried too far, it can have unproductive consequences. Probably too many beginning teachers are so overly concerned with "winning over" their pupils that they attempt to become close friends with them. This is not necessary. A friendly atmosphere can be established without developing a close relationship with each child. It must be remembered that teaching is a professional endeavor, one that is, to be sure, deeply human, but it should be based upon objectivity.

Teachers who become too friendly with their pupils frequently find it difficult to be objective with them. It is far better to strive for an open, trusting relationship on a group basis rather than on a close friendship with individual children. Objectivity in confronting a friend's problems is usually difficult to achieve. The teacher's perspective is apt to be more objective toward the pupil's behavior when it is viewed in terms of the consequences for a total group.

There are some children who seek a strong individual friendship with teachers as a result of an inadequate human relationship elsewhere. In these instances, the teacher must be understanding, but must attempt to alert those professional workers who have the expertise to work with the home in an effort to improve the situation. To produce the best results, the role of a friend should be exercised cautiously by the teacher.

Commentary

The foregoing examples certainly do not exhaust the list of possibilities. But enough have been identified to suggest that teachers have a critical responsibility for roles that are essentially psychological. Teachers might wish to concentrate on one or on only a few; but the fact is that at some time or another they will have to perform all of the roles. Each teacher is likely to feel more comfortable in some roles than in others, thus creating a tendency to stress some at the expense of others. Whether teachers recognize it or not, the children will cast them in all of these roles. And the children will expect that the roles be performed in a certain way.

Each role is a combination of variables, which will affect how the teacher performs it. First is the image of the child; second is the profession's position relative to it; third is the teacher's perception; and fourth is the community's expectations. The teacher must analyze each situation carefully, weighing the effects of each variable on the situation. Only then can the role be performed in a manner that will minimize counter-productive reactions.

The teacher has considerable freedom in determining the particular style for performing each role. The teacher may be more democratic in some instances, less so in others. The common denominator for success lies in the teacher's displaying a consistent feeling toward children in performing all of the roles. Pupils are quick to respond to teachers whom they trust and respect. Even in instances where sternness is employed, children respond better when they know that, underneath it all, the teacher has their best interests at heart.

Performance of these psychological roles can become complicated in a class because the group tends to take on a personality of its own. One group may be looking for a leader; another may be looking for a target for frustrations. Before attempting to provide assistance through role performance, a careful diagnosis is indicated.

The age group must also be considered. As elementary children mature, the power of the peer group becomes a factor the teacher must consider when selecting an appropriate psychological role.

Ethnic, religious, and economic factors also influence the performance of psychological roles. Each subculture has its own perceptions of the generic role of the teacher, and the selection and performance of roles should be carried out with these expectations in mind. For instance, the teacher may not be accepted as a model for the greater society, but may be expected to nurture the values of one particular subculture. In a multicultural group, these differences in perceptions of the teacher roles must be considered carefully. As we know, there is a substantial number of private religious schools, an illustration of the fact that parents have their own preferences for the roles of the school and the teacher, and wish their children to be in a school that emphasizes their religious choice.

Economic differences also have an impact on the way parents and teachers view the teacher's role. Because the majority of elementary teachers still come from middle-class America, a recognition of the points of view held by parents and children on other economic levels is extremely important. The competent teacher knows this and makes every effort to become acquainted with parents and the school community.

Several of the psychological roles bolster each other. Teachers who are successful in the role of evaluator may find it easy to perform the investigator role. On the other hand, roles may sometimes conflict with each other. Teachers who emphasize the ombudsman role, when faced with the role of an evaluator, may experience role conflict. *Consistency* in the way the teacher deals with the child usually is the important factor in reconciling the conflict.

This discussion of psychological roles has not been directed toward dealing with disturbed children who should be receiving therapy or special attention. Rather, we have attempted to emphasize the importance of psychological roles as they pertain to conditions found in conventional classrooms.

Instructional Roles

Although teaching may take many forms, the basic form is, of course, instruction. This aspect of teaching includes three generic roles: (1) planning for learning and instruction; (2) facilitation of learning and instruction; and (3) evaluation of learning and instruction. The validity of these roles is based on a review of the literature and on the authors' observations of teaching over a period of many years. Furthermore, reviews of research on instruction emphasize the critical importance of these roles for teaching and learning.

The manner in which these roles is performed will vary from teacher to teacher. This is as it should be, because teachers' styles vary considerably. But essentially, each role makes basic provisions that enhance learning.

Good teachers perform these instructional roles conscientiously, and they evaluate their own performance according to the criteria on behaviors for these roles. Self-evaluation makes teaching a challenging and rewarding activity. This process provides the means for

THE PSYCHOLOGICAL ROLES OF TEACHERS

Situation #1 Tommy comes from a "different" neighborhood.
Remark: "I'm sorry Tommy, but you should use correct English even though you say your parents and neighbors don't."

Situation #2 Mary just failed a reading test.
Remark: "That's all right, Mary. You'll do better next time. All of us fail now and then."

Situation #3 Mr. Wise explains that he isn't the fount of all knowledge.
Remark: "Yes, I can see that you are surprised that I couldn't answer your question. But I know where we can find the answer."

Situation #4 Jane Todd decided to teach fifth grade instead of kindergarten.
Remark: "I thought I wanted to teach kindergarten until I observed in a class for several weeks. You couldn't pay me enough to baby sit 25 kids all day."

Situation #5 Ms. Hunter introduces herself to her student teaching class of sixth graders.
Remark: "My name is Miss Hunter, but my friends call me Skippy. I want to be your friend, so why don't you call me Skippy, too?"

Situation #6 Mr. Parker decides to settle, once and for all, who took Edith's purse.
Remark: "I'm sorry, but you will all have to sit quietly in your seats until someone confesses."

Situation #7 Andrew, a fourth grader, confides in his teacher that he worries all the time about being kidnapped.
Remark: "Andy, you're too big to worry about imaginary things. Now go back to your desk and don't fret anymore."

1. Identify the psychological role in each of the above examples.
2. What do the teachers' remarks, in each instance, tell you about how well the teacher performed the role?

renewing enthusiasm and energy, because the teacher is constantly alert to possibilities for becoming a better planner, facilitator, and evaluator of learning.

These generic roles will be given attention throughout the book; the reader is well advised to develop a frame of mind about teaching that gives them top priority. The door to competent teaching cannot be opened until successful performance of these roles is assured.*

TEACHING BEHAVIORS THAT ENHANCE PUPIL ACHIEVEMENT

There are literally hundreds of prescriptions for effective teaching. Some of these are based on studies of teaching and others are simply the opinions of experts. Unfortunately, authorities are not always in agreement about the relationship of teaching behaviors and pupil successes in the classroom. Therefore, a great deal of teaching is essentially a trial and error process. Much more research needs to be done before a valid baseline of effective teaching behaviors can be identified.

Rosenshine and Furst[14] reviewed about fifty investigations that attempted to study the relationship between teaching behavior and pupil achievement. Their review provides an excellent starting point for the identification of certain teaching behaviors that seem to show a consistent relationship to pupil achievement. Out of the fifty studies reviewed, eleven teaching behaviors were identified as being related to achievement. The best results were obtained on the first five behaviors (variables) with less conclusive results on the last six. The behaviors described here are the five strongest variables identified by Rosenshine and Furst in their review of the fifty studies. The review constitutes a very useful source of information for the teacher who wishes to employ behaviors that have demonstrated a potential for producing pupil achievement.

1. *Clarity.* The studies that dealt with this variable defined it variously: "Clarity of presentation" . . . "whether the points the teacher made were clear and easy to understand" . . . "whether the teacher was able to explain concepts clearly" . . . "had facility with her material and enough background to answer her children's questions intelligently" . . . "whether the cognitive level of the teacher's lesson appeared to be 'just right most of the time'."[15]

*Evaluation of student teaching at the University of Washington, Seattle, is accomplished through a performance-based instrument that contains criteria classified according to these three generic instructional roles. This instrument was developed by Professor Norma M. Dimmitt and her colleagues.

[14] For a complete description of these studies see Barak Rosenshine and Norma Furst, "Research in Teacher Performance Criteria," *Research in Teacher Education: A Symposium,* ed. by B. Othanel Smith (Englewood Cliffs, N.J.: Prentice Hall, Inc., 1971), pp. 37–55.

[15] Ibid., p. 44.

Unfortunately, an operational definition of *clarity* still needs study. However, in those studies where specific behaviors were controlled and observed, the research indicated that the most effective teachers (1) spent less time answering pupil questions that called for an interpretation of what the teacher said; (2) phrased questions so they were answered the first time, without additional information or additional pupil questions before responding to the original question; (3) used fewer "vagueness" words such as *some, many, of course,* and *a little.*

Another variable, *organization,* although difficult to define, appeared to be closely related to clarity. This variable pertained to "coherence of the lesson" and appeared to focus on the degree of confusion encountered.

Even though more research is needed to identify the specific behaviors that comprise "clarity," enough evidence is present to suggest its importance in effective teaching and learning transactions in the classrooms.

2. *Variability.* Several studies dealt with the relationship of the teacher's use of variety or variability during the lesson. These studies demonstrated that pupil achievement is positively related to teaching-learning situations where a variety of instructional procedures and materials is utilized. Similar results were identified where the teacher varied the cognitive level of discussions and pupil tasks.

3. *Enthusiasm.* This variable was studied through three approaches: (1) observers rated the teacher as "stimulating vs. dull," "original vs. stereotyped," or "alert vs. apathetic"; (2) observers estimated the amount of vigor and power the teacher exhibited during presentations to the class; and (3) students rated the teacher's involvement, excitement, or interest in and for the subject matter. Significant results were obtained on the relationship between enthusiasm and pupil achievement.

More research is needed to identify additional specific behaviors that are included in the enthusiasm variable. Up to this point, the studies suggest that movement, gesture, and voice inflections are associated with it.

4. *Task-Oriented and/or Businesslike Behaviors.* In the studies that dealt with businesslike behaviors, a number of variables were studied. Among these were observer ratings of whether the teacher was "evading-responsible," "erratic-steady," "disorganized-systematic," "excitable-poised."[16] In two studies (at the first- and third-grade

[16] Ibid., p. 47.

levels) teachers were rated on whether they were concerned that pupils learn—rather than simply enjoy themselves. A sixth-grade study was based on the extent to which the teacher encouraged the class to work hard and to do such tasks as independent and creative work. Significant results were obtained relative to the relationship of businesslike behavior and pupil achievement in these studies.

Task-oriented teachers seem to be positively related to pupil achievement. Teachers who focused on the learning of cognitive tasks had better results than those who stressed other activities (hoping, presumably, that cognitive growth would occur indirectly).

5. *Pupil Opportunity to Learn Criterion Material.* Generally speaking, studies dealing with this variable reported a positive, significant, and consistent relationship between measures of opportunity to learn and pupil achievement. Teachers should recognize the importance of stressing cognitive classroom activities if their objective is to promote cognitive growth in pupils. This awareness suggests that careful planning is required to provide the time for children to study cognitive areas, with adequate time remaining to promote pupil growth in affective and psychomotor areas as well.

Rosenshine[17] has qualified the conclusions reported in the 1971 review. He stated that although clarity and teacher enthusiasm remain potent predictors of student gains on the college level, they have not appeared as significant contributors to pupil achievement in recent studies on the elementary level. They appear to be less important in the primary grades than on the intermediate level where more verbal teaching is encountered. Also, because of the shift away from teacher-led discussions, clarity and teacher enthusiasm have become less important as teacher behaviors in the direct instruction employed in those schools where these studies were conducted. We attribute this situation to the current thrust on accountability—the expectation that pupils should be kept on task, learning information that will be covered on achievement tests. Rosenshine supports this belief by his statement that pupil opportunity to learn criterion material and task-oriented and/or businesslike behavior remain as variables that produce pupil achievement. *Variability,* a variable reported as important in the earlier

[17] Barak V. Rosenshine, "Content, Time, and Direct Instruction," in *Research on Teaching: Concepts, Findings, and Implications,* Penelope L. Peterson and Herbert J. Walberg, eds. (Berkeley, McCutchan Publishing Corp.), 1979, pp. 28–57.

review, has been found to be dependent for its success on careful teacher supervision.

In the final analysis, it can be said that the five variables remain as important teacher behaviors in those situations where teacher-directed instruction is employed. We recommend these five teacher behaviors for mastery by beginning elementary teachers because they represent characteristics that have persisted in the literature on effective teaching, as well as having been long recognized for their importance by those who have responsibility for the supervision of teaching.

TEACHER BEHAVIORS THAT PRODUCE ACHIEVEMENT

To emphasize the importance of teacher behaviors on pupil achievement read the following sketches and identify the specific teacher behavior for each. Check your answers below.

1. Mr. Lund is able to generate a sense of excitement for learning in his pupils. His almost boundless store of energy and his positive approach to learning have a lot to do with his ability to make children like to learn.
2. No two lessons ever seem to be taught alike in Ms. Brown's room. She uses a wide range of teaching modes and assorted learning resources. Pupils like to be in her room, and their achievement is consistently good.
3. Ms. Allen's presentations are always well organized. She gives examples for each point she is trying to make. She knows her material well enough to handle questions intelligently, and uses words that have specific meanings. She doesn't have to spend time answering pupils' questions about what she has just said.
4. Mr. Carpenter organizes the school day to provide large blocks of time for cognitive learning. He believes that pupils need sufficient time for the accomplishment of learning tasks.
5. Mr. Martin is a no-nonsense teacher when it comes to insisting that pupils do their work thoroughly and punctually. He believes that "Learning is fun" is an old bromide that should be discarded. He insists that, "Learning can be fun when you work hard enough at it."

1. Enthusiasm
2. Variability
3. Clarity
4. Provides opportunity to learn assigned material
5. Task-oriented behavior

WHAT IS TEACHING?

The question, "What is teaching?" has yet to be answered to everyone's satisfaction. There are numerous definitions of the term, which have been generated from the way people actually teach. Other definitions are based on philosophical assumptions; still others are based on anthropological, psychological, or sociological premises. Even within the ranks of these disciplines, there are profound differences in the way teaching is defined. As a consequence, teachers and those who evaluate them do not always have a common frame of reference with which to approach their tasks.

The failure to achieve a consensus on a definition of teaching creates problems for educators who attempt to evaluate it. It is equally difficult for a teacher to practice self-evaluation when there is no conceptual frame of reference. Even though many teachers are aware of the "why and how" of teaching, some are not. When asked how they developed their particular, generalized teaching styles, some respond that they imitate former teachers whom they admired. Others reply that they have no consistent style, that they teach by intuition—whatever their "hunches" suggest is considered appropriate for the situation.

Imitation is a low-level method of learning how to teach. It works very well for the learning of simple skills and tasks, but few would agree that teaching is a simple task. Teaching is extremely complex, and for one to base his/her pattern of teaching behaviors on imitating someone else is grossly inadequate. For one thing, it is very difficult for a second person to imitate successfully the behavior of another, human nature being far too complicated to be reduced to such a process. Also imitation does not permit flexibility because the teacher would be unable to provide options for meeting the changing conditions of classrooms or for the wide variance found in the abilities, needs, and interests of children. The teacher who is an imitator is limited in his/her capacity to grow beyond the pattern of teaching behavior that has been copied from someone else. Yet a surprising number of teachers teach as they do as a result of imitation.

Teachers who say they teach according to their intuition have a highly unpredictable style. Even though intuition is a valuable resource in some instances, it certainly falls short of serving as a conceptual base for teaching. Intuition can serve the teacher well in making ad hoc modifications while a lesson is in progress. It may provide a useful resource in diagnosing children's interests and needs. But whenever intuition is used, it should be checked out with evidence. By itself, intuition is little more than a hunch or a guess. Competent teachers recognize the importance of collecting data before making a decision about a child's needs or problems. Intuition is mainly an extension of the perception of the person who employs it. Thus, it is subject to all of the weaknesses, as well as the strengths, of that person.

We believe that something more is needed to place the teaching process in a framework that lends itself to analysis. There are many ways to teach, but there should be a common thread that replicates itself throughout the teaching process, regardless of time and situation. The process must have recognizable characteristics, and these must be independent of time and place.

THE ANALYSIS OF TEACHING

There are numerous approaches used in the analysis of teaching. Some of these are complicated and require instruction in their application; others are easier to implement. Teachers can do much to improve their own teaching by merely being reflective about it. To encourage this approach, a simplistic model for the analysis of teaching is provided. The following assumption is basic to the model and should be read carefully:

> Analysis of teaching should focus on the interaction of (1) those behaviors and mediating conditions that were "planned" to produce desired learner outcomes with (2) those behaviors and mediating conditions that "occurred" during the teaching process.

When conceptualized in this way the analysis of teaching enables teachers to assess the quality of the process on the basis of the behaviors and mediating conditions that either facilitated or inhibited the realization of the desired learner outcomes. This model for analyzing the teaching process comprises a set of suggested questions designed for the teacher's use in evaluating the interaction of what was planned with what actually occurred.

Did the children respond with interest when I introduced the lesson?

Did the pupils seem to understand what was expected of them?

Did I organize the learning environment sufficiently to reduce distractions and interruptions?

Did I provide sufficient learning resources for the lesson?

Was there a high level of verbal and nonverbal interaction among the children and between them and me?

Did I pace the learning activities to permit pupils adequate time for the various activities in the lesson?

Did I provide pupils with an opportunity to evaluate what occurred and to make suggestions for the next lesson?

Were the objectives for the lesson appropriate to the needs and interests of the children?

Was my planning successful in anticipating the behaviors and mediating conditions?

Were the expected learner outcomes realistic?

Did I select a teaching mode that was appropriate for the accomplishment of the desired learner outcomes?

Do I need to follow up immediately with learning activities that will produce a greater degree of achievement of the desired learner outcomes, or should I go on with extended learning?

When the teacher asks such questions, the teaching process can be analyzed in a meaningful context, one that enables a sorting out of those variables that facilitate learning as well as those that inhibit it. This is the essence of diagnostic teaching. It enhances the quality of teaching and learning.

Teachers should analyze their performance on a consistent basis. It is the sure road to growth and maturity. And most importantly, it makes teaching a satisfying and self-rewarding activity throughout a career.

DEVELOPING RELATED COMPETENCIES

All Work and No Play . . .

Ms. Lane is considered to be a fine reading teacher. She is often called on to conduct workshops for other teachers. Her principal is concerned, however, because of frequent complaints from parents. It seems that Ms. Lane's pupils don't really like to come to school. They say Ms. Lane is cross when they fail to learn. The principal is also disturbed by the tenseness he observes in Ms. Lane's classroom. Sooner or later she may be identified as a teacher who never should have entered the elementary-teaching profession.

1. Evaluate Ms. Lane's potential for performing the psychological roles of teaching. Which ones do you believe she would fail completely?
2. Have you ever observed in a classroom taught by someone like Ms. Lane? If you have, what pupil behavior did you observe?

Mr. Arnold is considered to be a successful sixth-grade teacher and is well liked by his pupils. He is always well prepared and very organized in his school work. His pupils score high on achievement tests. Mr. Arnold is rarely seen in the community. His social life is almost nonexistent and he has few, if any, outside interests. His life is consumed by his classroom activities. Frequently he appears tired and is often noncommunicative with his colleagues. He appears to be an unhappy person when away from his classroom.

1. Do you think Mr. Arnold is a good social model for his pupils?
2. Because academic demands seem to be making such serious inroads on Mr. Arnold's personal life, is he apt to eventually become a cold and uninspiring teacher?

FOR FURTHER PROFESSIONAL STUDY

Books

Cooper, James M., ed. *Classroom Teaching Skills: A Handbook.* Lexington, Massachusetts: D. C. Heath and Company, 1977. Chap. 1.

Gage, N. L. *The Scientific Basis of the Art of Teaching.* New York: Teachers College Press, 1978.

Orlich, Donald C., *et al. Teaching Strategies: A Guide to Better Instruction.* Lexington, Massachusetts: D. C. Heath and Company, 1980. Chap. 1.

Weil, Marsha, Bruce Joyce, and Bridget Kluwin. *Personal Models of Teaching.* Englewood Cliffs, New Jersey: Prentice-Hall, Inc., 1978.

Periodicals

Fischer, Barbara Bree, and Louis Fischer. "Styles in Teaching and Learning." *Educational Leadership* (January 1979), 245-251, 254.

Gage, N. L. "The Yield of Research on Teaching." *Phi Delta Kappan* (November 1978), 229-235.

Good, Thomas L. "Teacher Effectiveness in the Elementary School." *Journal of Teacher Education* (March-April 1979), 52-64.

Pedersen, Eigil. "The Lifelong Impact of a First-Grade Teacher." *Instructor* (December 1979), 62, 63, 66.

Pine, Gerald P., and Angelo V. Boy. "Self-Enrichment through Teaching." *The Clearing House* (September 1979), 46–49.

Tschudin, Ruth. "The Secrets of A+ Teaching." *Instructor* (September 1978), 66-76.

3

Classroom Management Skills

THE QUALIFIED AND COMPETENT TEACHER . . .

1. Is able to manage a classroom in a way that promotes social, emotional, and intellectual development of pupils.
2. Is able to secure the willing cooperation of pupils in organizational and management aspects of teaching.
3. Perceives classroom management as an essential ingredient of teaching, but views it as a means rather than an end.

Performance Criteria

As a result of the serious study of this chapter, the student should be able to . . .

1. Describe the characteristics of a well-managed classroom and identify principles related to sound management.
2. Describe in terms of pupil behavior the consequences of specific inadequacies in management.
3. Differentiate among such concepts as management, control, discipline, and "keeping order."
4. Assess his or her own personal qualities in terms of their possible effects on classroom management.
5. Demonstrate his or her ability to exercise management skills by teaching a group of children in a classroom setting. (In a first-time experience this might be a small group, but at an advanced level of preparation, it would be an entire class.)

Each year, for more than a decade, the Gallup Poll has conducted a national survey to measure attitudes of Americans toward their public schools. When asked to respond to the question, "What do you think are the biggest problems with which the *public* schools of this country must deal?" Americans mentioned "lack of discipline" more frequently than any other problem in 10 out of the 11 years the survey was conducted.[1] Classroom management is popularly, but not altogether correctly, referred to as "control" or "discipline." It is the one component of teaching that worries beginning teachers more than anything else. It is also what experienced teachers often find most exhausting. New teachers want, above all, to be successful. They also want their pupils to like them. Yet they know that they cannot achieve either of these goals unless they are able to succeed in classroom management. They may recall experiences they had as pupils in a classroom where the children were unruly and boisterous. Perhaps the principal had to be called to quiet them. Maybe they remember that one or more teachers had to terminate during the year because of management problems. Now that they are beginning student teaching, or starting their first job as a teacher, they may recall very little from their teacher education program that prepared them for the complex challenges involved in managing a classroom. This worries them.

CLASSROOM MANAGEMENT AS RELATED TO TEACHING

There can be little doubt that skill in classroom management or "control" is a major factor contributing to the success of the teacher. More time is spent on it in student teaching supervisory conferences than on anything else. It is the one aspect of a teacher's credentials that principals are most interested in examining. It is the one part of a teacher's behavior that parents are most concerned about. When a teacher is in difficulty on the job, the chances are very good that the problem can be traced to classroom management.

The beginning teacher is likely to disassociate what is thought to be "teaching" from classroom management. Teaching is regarded as conducting reading, spelling, and mathematics lessons, developing concepts in social studies, doing science experiments, and so on. In an almost naïve way, the teacher may rely on the pupils to conduct themselves appropriately—to move about in an orderly fashion, to move quietly from one grouping arrangement to another, and to

[1] Reported in *Phi Delta Kappan*, 60, Number 1, September 1979, pp. 33–45.

treat each other courteously and respectfully. When they do not do so, the teacher regards their behavior as misconduct requiring disciplinary action. Classroom management is perceived primarily in the negative sense—correcting pupil misbehavior, keeping a watchful eye for evidence of mischief, and disciplining pupils. This approach, although fairly common, is likely to cause the teacher some difficulty because it neglects to take into account the important part that classroom management contributes to successful teaching.

When teaching is perceived as described in the foregoing paragraph, it should more appropriately be called *instruction.* Elementary-school teachers spend much of their time conducting instruction in the various subjects and skills that make up the curriculum. But *teaching* responsibilities go considerably beyond the conduct of instruction. This additional responsibility falls largely in the management realm. It involves the deployment of pupils and resources in ways that will make the conduct of instruction possible. It is clear, therefore, that management and instruction are two sides of the same coin we call teaching.

An example will clarify this distinction. Ms. Artiz is a fourth-grade teacher in a self-contained classroom. On three days each week, however, a special music teacher comes to the room at 11 o'clock. During the time the music teacher is in the room, Ms. Artiz gets the children seated in the way the music teacher wants them arranged, sees that the music books or other materials are distributed, and stays in the room supervising the pupils' behavior while the music teacher *instructs.* If Ms. Artiz left the room during the half-hour that the music teacher had the class, then the music teacher would have both instruction and management responsibilities; she would be truly teaching, rather than simply providing instruction. Similar examples could be cited in the use of television instruction, resource visitors to the class, or special demonstrations by outsiders.

We are describing teaching as a process involving the interaction of classroom management and instruction. It is clear that successful teaching cannot take place without both of these elements. The interaction of these two components of teaching means, also, that they affect each other. Skillful management facilitates the conduct of instruction. Inspired and interesting instruction reduces the likelihood of management problems.

We take the position here that classroom management must be perceived positively rather than negatively. The teacher needs to develop a management system that builds habits of responsible self-direction in children. Such a system also produces and maintains an environment in which teaching and learning are facilitated. Good classroom management procedures must be planned, just as the instructional components of teaching are planned. Through planning, a teacher can anticipate and avoid problems.

Let us now consider some of the characteristics of a well-managed classroom.

1. *Good classroom management enhances the mental and social development of pupils.*

Getting "control" of a class, in the sense of the teacher's ability to wield power over children, should not be much of a problem for an adult. A situation can be created where the teacher has absolute control over everything that takes place in the room. The teacher uses threats of low grades and failure, ridicule, punishment, rigid rules, and keeps pupil activity controlled to the point that children cannot move or talk without permission. This may be justified on the grounds that it is the only way the teacher can maintain order and therefore conduct instruction. But these repressive tactics can be detrimental to young children.

We are learning that a positive self-concept is not only important to learning but is vital to the total development of the individual. In the type of distrustful setting just described, pupils may not develop good images of themselves. Moreover, the pressures that build up in some children as a result of an authoritarian atmosphere in school erupt, either in or outside of school, in various forms of aggression, tears, withdrawal, bed-wetting, nail-biting, or other more serious forms of maladaptive behavior.

The elementary school should be a laboratory for the social growth of children. Here the child learns to give and to take, to share with others, to interact with peers, and to develop a degree of responsible independence. The child learns social skills partly through instruction, but mainly by having opportunities to participate with others in social situations. Programs that have children working continually on an individual basis do not provide adequately for the social dimension of a child's learning. One cannot learn social skills except in social settings.

Good management will reflect itself in a room where children are comfortable intellectually, emotionally, and socially. Here, the teacher as an authority figure is recognized and respected but is not feared by the pupils or perceived as a constant threat to their self-confidence. This room is a confidence-building place, where children grow in their competence as human beings.

2. *Good classroom management facilitates the achievement of goals of instruction.*

Mr. Campbell is working with a group of eight third-graders on phonetic skills in a reading lesson. Meanwhile, the remaining twenty-four third-graders are moving about the room, talking loudly; occasionally there is an altercation that necessitates Mr. Campbell's intervention. The noise level is high. The pupils in the reading group often ask to have things repeated because they cannot hear, or are not paying attention to what is being said.

This is a serious matter because the pupil behavior resulting from Mr. Campbell's poor management is interfering with the instructional program. Phonetic analysis depends on fine sound discrimination, and, therefore, pupils must be able to hear those sounds. This would obviously be difficult, perhaps even impossible, in the situation described. Moreover, Mr. Campbell himself cannot attend properly to the lesson because of the commotion in the room. And the pupils not in the reading group are reinforcing behavior patterns that contribute neither to good study habits nor to social skills. The pupils in the reading group are apt to report unfavorably to their

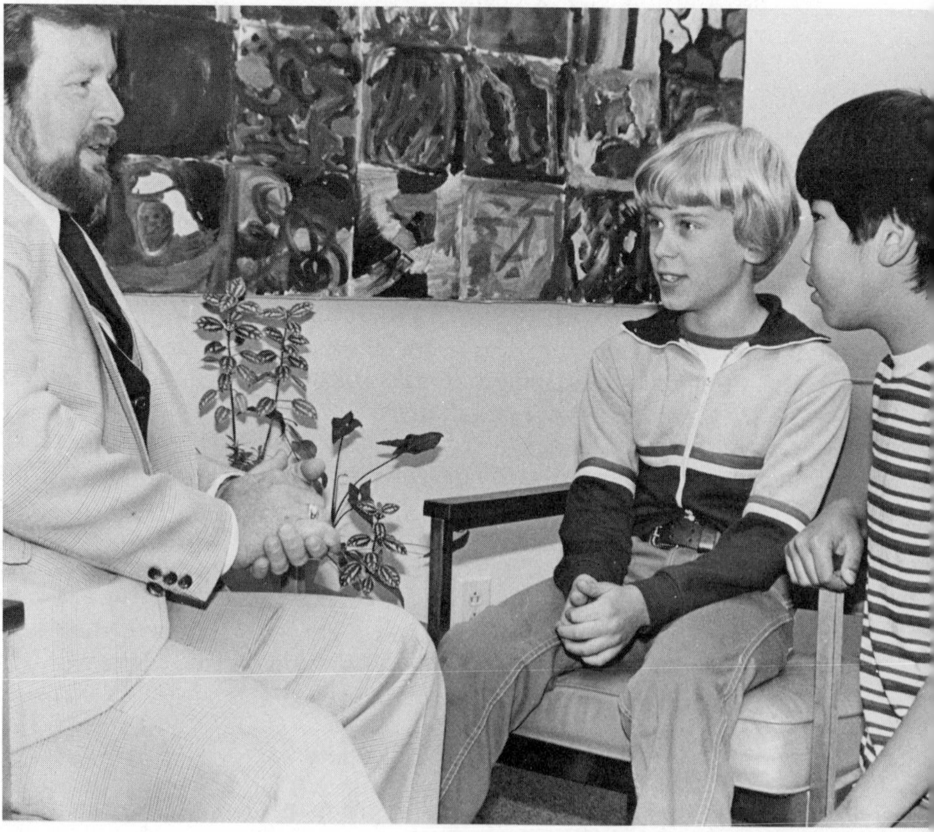

parents on Mr. Campbell's ability to create a situation where they can learn.

In order to establish conditions that make possible the conduct of instruction, it is necessary to develop a systematic method of organizing classroom activities. The teacher will need to steer a course somewhere between Mr. Campbell's lack of organization and the other end of the continuum, characterized by rigidity and teacher dominance. For most classrooms, a schedule of events of the day will be needed. These will probably not vary much from day to day. Children like this. They like to know when each of their classes is to take place. They know when there is to be quiet time and when there is activity time. This type of flexible, but planned, organization of the day makes it possible for the teacher to do his or her job and the pupils to do theirs, in order that the goals of instruction can be achieved.

PHOTO FOLIO

In this photograph we see a school principal talking with two boys. It is obvious from the expressions on their faces that the conversation is a friendly one. The principal has an important role to play in setting the emotional tone and psychological climate of the school. How the principal performs his or her job has a great deal to do with the management of classrooms by individual teachers. Poorly managed schools can and often do encourage disruptive behavior by pupils in the classroom.

1. Discuss the idea that a principal should be supportive of teachers in pupil-teacher conflicts from the perspective of teacher rights and pupil rights.
2. Cite specific examples from your own experience of leadership styles of school principals that enhanced the work of classroom teachers.
3. Why is it important not to stereotype "going to the principal's office" with disciplinary action?

3. *Good classroom management provides intellectual and physical freedom within known parameters.*

If children were to attend school knowing the subject matter and skills of the curriculum, and were completely socialized, well-mannered, and well-behaved, there would be no point in their attending. It is hard therefore to understand why teachers should be upset when pupils make mistakes, or why they are intolerant of the behavior of children when it is childlike. The school should be one place where a child can be as free as possible to try to do new things. Not only that, children should be encouraged to do so without having to fear, or be embarrassed by, making mistakes.

Although children should be as free as possible to explore intellectually and be allowed a great deal of physical freedom as well, they need also to learn that no one is totally free. All of us have rules to live by, and there should be no mystery about this fundamental fact of social life. There *are* rules and regulations that apply in every classroom, no matter what the teacher's personal philosophy may be on this issue. For example, the teacher cannot, and must not, allow children to do things that injure others, that are inhumane, or destroy the property of others. Such behavior is simply not permitted.

When teachers pretend there are no rules or fail to make them explicit, it can be predicted that they will have a stormy time of it with the pupils. When there are no rules, no one knows what is expected. Pupils may run wild, and in the process may injure themselves or each other. Even when there are explicit rules, pupils will test the outer edges of them. Pupils seem to need to search out the parameters of freedom, within which they then know they must function. In cases where the procedures are made known, the testing will be more focused. Where procedures and rules are not known, the testing takes the form of trial and error—to see what the teacher's tolerance level is.

4. *Good classroom management allows children to develop skills of self-direction and independence.*

This point is an extension of the previous one. It is a curious fact that teachers often expect children to develop self-direction and independence without permitting them to practice the skills needed to achieve these characteristics. It is not clear just how pupils are to gain self-direction and independence in classrooms that are almost wholly teacher-directed and teacher-dependent. What is needed is a good balance: providing sufficient guidance and direction, on the one hand, and allowing children to experiment with independence and self-direction, on the other. The tendency is either to be too highly teacher-directed or to be completely permissive. Neither provides an appropriate setting for pupil learning.

5. *Good classroom management allows pupils to share some responsibility for classroom management.*

In totalitarian countries, policies and decisions are made by the authorities in charge and are handed down to be carried out and/or obeyed. Americans do not take well to such highhanded procedures. Involving children in some aspects of the management of the classroom provides them with practical experiences in contributing to policy and decision making.

Such involvement also gives children a sense of identity with the classroom. Insofar as possible, the feeling should be generated that it is not only the teacher's room but the pupils' room as well. Of course, this will not be easy to do if the teacher makes all the rules, makes all the decisions, and makes no effort to involve pupils in the management aspects of classroom life.

This is not to suggest that the teacher can evade responsibility for the conduct of the classroom by turning the management over to the children. This has been tried many times, and it usually fails because children lack maturity for such responsibilities. It is asking more of them than can reasonably be expected. The teacher, being the most mature person in the classroom, must provide the leadership and guidance needed to make the operation function as an educationally viable unit. In point of fact, the teacher is legally accountable for what goes on in the classroom.

6. *Good classroom management works toward a warm, but firm, relationship between the teacher and pupils.*

Sometimes beginning teachers, especially in the middle and upper grades, believe they can develop a close "buddy" relationship between the pupils and themselves. Informality is encouraged by allowing the pupils to call the teacher by his or her first name or even a nickname. Social distance is removed by the teacher, who assumes somewhat of a peer relationship with the pupils. This rarely works well; it usually means that in the process the authority of the teacher is compromised.

The other extreme is represented by the teachers who feel they cannot "get too close" to the pupils—they must maintain an appropriate social distance. They talk in a stilted way in front of the pupils. They do not relax because they feel if they did the pupils might take advantage of them. They are careful never to reveal much of the informal aspects of their personality to the pupils. They develop and maintain the traditional stereotypic role of the teacher.

Good teachers extend their warmth and "human-ness" to children. They work with children in ways that show they enjoy young people. At the same time they maintain the basic firmness needed and, what is more, *wanted* by children. Children expect the teacher to behave in certain more or less conventional ways. When teacher behavior strays too far from this expectation, children do not know how to deal with it.

7. *Good classroom management results in positive pupil attitudes toward the class.*

When the school situation is what it should be, children like to go to school. They may complain some, but this is out of deference to a culturally institutionalized attitude that children are supposed to dislike school. Given a choice, however, most children would prefer to go to school rather than stay home. After all, their friends are there, and a child's natural curiosity does not make learning completely distasteful.

Also, children will usually develop a strong identity with the class, if conditions are right. There will be in-group and out-group alliances formed, but this is to be expected. In general, pupils will take pride in their class if all is going well.

If children genuinely dislike school, if there is a high level of unexplained absenteeism, or if there is a great deal of conflict and aggression in the classroom, one should suspect that there may be something wrong with management procedures. This does not mean that school experiences must in all cases be fun for children. It does mean that over-all, school is a pleasant rather than an unpleasant place to be.

BASIC CONCEPTS RELATING TO CLASSROOM MANAGEMENT

There are several concepts and terms associated with the process of classroom management. Sometimes these terms are used synonymously (or interchangeably, in the popular sense). As we shall see, however, there are important differences in what these terms mean and imply.

Management

When one speaks of management, one means that there is something to manage and that someone does the managing. To *manage* means that one person is in charge—the manager directs, administers, succeeds in getting a job done. In the context of the classroom, the

WHAT DO YOU THINK ABOUT THIS?

Long before the opening of school, Mrs. Badger had decided what behavior standards she wanted in her classroom, and had constructed a set of rules concerning pupil conduct. She felt uneasy about this, however, because she remembered what one of her professors had said about pupils being more willing to respect and accept rules and standards if they had a hand in the formulation of them. Mrs. Badger resolved her dilemma in the following way:

On the first day of school, she explained to the children that she was sure that all of them wanted to do their best work in the room. If this were to happen, there would need to be rules and standards. If everyone did anything he or she pleased at any time, without consideration for others, no one could do his or her work, and the room would not be a very pleasant place. The children, of course, understood and expected this. She went on to explain that because rules and standards affected everyone, she thought they should help her make the rules. This too, received a favorable reaction from the pupils. It was agreed that pupils would suggest rules and standards, and when they were accepted by the group, Mrs. Badger would write them on the chalkboard.

As pupils made suggestions, Mrs. Badger would involve the class in a discussion of each one. She was careful not to reject any suggestion, but when one surfaced that she had already decided was one she wanted, she would say something like "Mrs. Badger thinks that is a *good* idea." By the time the period was over, the rules and standards adopted by the pupils were those Mrs. Badger had decided on three weeks before the opening of school, but the pupils seemed pleased with "their" rules.

1. Do you find anything objectionable about Mrs. Badger's procedures?
2. What would you predict to be the lasting effect on pupil conduct of rules generated in this way?
3. Can you suggest an alternative procedure to that of Mrs. Badger's, that would legitimately provide for pupil input?

teacher is a classroom manager; he or she is directing, administering, and succeeding in getting the job of teaching accomplished, in accordance with recognized educational and psychological principles.

Teachers often deal with a class as if that conglomerate of individuals were a single individual. This is well documented. Consider the kinds of statements teachers make to class groups: "Now, class, I want you to turn to page 53." "The class should now pay close attention to what is being said." "If the class does not stop talking, we will be late for lunch." "I will need to have the attention of the class." These are just a few instances of the teacher's referring to a class of individuals as if they were a single individual. It is important to stress that a class is a *group,* and in successful group management, it is group psychology rather than individual psychology that is relevant. Groups develop their own characteristics, as *groups,* quite apart from the individuals who comprise them.

Because of the special characteristics of pupil groups, teachers must secure from pupils their implicit consent for the management procedures used. In other words, the pupils must be willing to cooperate with the teacher or the system cannot function. Without the willing cooperation of pupils, an adversary relationship develops between the class and the teacher. When this happens, the atmosphere is so tense that even the smallest issue can, and often does, become the cause of a major confrontation between the teacher and the class. If such relationships are prolonged, the teacher becomes totally ineffective and would probably be forced to terminate.

Control

The term *control* is often used as a convenient catch-all for what is more correctly called classroom management. Control implies restraint, regulation, regimentation, and the direct use of power. Popularly, it is sometimes referred to as "keeping the lid on,"– appropriately so, in those classrooms that operate as pressure cookers. "You have good control" is usually regarded as a compliment to a beginning teacher. One is never sure whether the meaning is intended in the broad sense (to cover all of classroom management), or in the literal sense, that of keeping pupil behavior so curbed that the classroom is totally teacher-dominated. If it is often used in the literal sense, the term *control* can easily be given unwarranted importance, becoming an end rather than a means.

Control should not, in itself, be a goal of teaching–nor should management, for that matter. These should be perceived as processes used to accomplish other more important tasks. A negative example is a third-grade teacher who has "perfect control" of a class: the class is quiet, individual pupils are immobile, no one speaks out of turn, and so on. In order to achieve this calm, the teacher has the children doing relatively meaningless "busywork" at their seats, while attending to other matters. These "other matters" may have to do with preparation of lessons and materials, teaching small groups or individuals, or taking care of business relating to pupil accounting, reporting, or the lunch program. To achieve this level of restraint, the teacher does indeed need to control most of the physical and intellectual activities of the pupils, and, in fact, pupil freedom needs to be reduced to nearly zero as often as possible. One must, of course, ask whether these kinds of training procedures are appropriate for present-day society.

An objectionable aspect of the control concept is the implication that it is the teacher who is wholly responsible for maintaining an orderly classroom environment. This runs counter to the idea that children need to learn responsible habits of self-direction. They need to learn to conduct themselves properly, not to please the teacher, but because in so doing they develop greater maturity and independence. Of course, children cannot do this entirely on their own. Left unguided they are likely to become unruly and mischievous. Learning to take care of oneself should be an important outcome of the school experience. It is not likely to be achieved if the behavior of the learner is always controlled by the teacher.

Discipline

The term *discipline,* like control, is often incorrectly used to mean various aspects of classroom management. "She has good discipline" usually means that the teacher maintains an orderly, probably a strict, classroom. Discipline also connotes punishment. "Strong discipline" is used to describe teacher behavior that is rigid, firm, unbending. There is an adversary quality to this meaning of discipline. When teachers say, "Anyone who leaves the room without permission will be disciplined," they mean that the offender will be punished in order to teach him or her not to do it again. In this sense, discipline means both punishment and corrective treatment.

A more acceptable use of the term would describe discipline as an imposition of controls on oneself in order to develop character, efficient habits of work, proper conduct, consideration for others, orderly living, or control of one's impulses and emotions, as when the teacher says, "We will need to discipline ourselves not to talk unnecessarily if we hope to finish this project by the end of the day." Discipline as internally imposed control, i.e., self-control, is, of course, a worthy objective. But in order to develop discipline, the learner must be given some independence; and in the process of experimenting with such independence, the teacher's guidance will be needed. Neither highly structured, teacher-dominated environments, nor those that are completely permissive, facilitate the development of self-control and self-discipline.

Classroom Climate

This term is not in as widespread popular use as are management, control, and discipline. Climate has to do with the emotional tone and quality of human relations that prevail in the classroom. Classroom climate may be described as being relaxed, pleasant, flexible, rigid, autocratic, democratic, repressive, or supportive, and so on. Classroom climate results from a composite of the interactions and transactions that take place in the room. Consequently, it is related to the management procedures used by the teacher.

The type of classroom climate sought is one that enhances the mental and physical health of children, that is conducive to good work, is consistent with the developmental level of children, and facilitates the overall goals of the program. It is a "caring" environment. Pupils and teacher feel good about themselves and about each other. The children like and respect their teacher. A good classroom climate is characterized by the absence of hostility, bitterness, and of destructive criticism of others.

Classroom climate is usually the result of classroom management procedures, rather than the cause of management problems, if they develop. Teacher-pupil transactions are critical in developing a wholesome classroom climate. What the teacher says and how it is said are also related in important ways to the quality of the classroom climate. If the teacher is continually giving directions in a tone suggesting hostility, the pupils will respond in like fashion. Moreover, they will treat each other in the same way. If the teacher approves or rewards the behavior of children who tattle on others, there will soon be a room full of tattletales. If the teacher creates anxiety by pacing the instruction too rapidly, the pupils will reflect a tenseness that will probably surface as aggressive behavior. If standards are unreasonably high, the teacher encourages dishonest behavior on the part of pupils. All of this suggests that the classroom climate is directly affected by most of what the teacher does and says when working with the class.

TYPICAL CLASSROOM PROBLEMS

It is a mistake to believe that the removal of certain children, so-called trouble-makers, will in itself solve problems of classroom management. Far from it. If the management procedure is unsound, there will be problems arising no matter what the composition of the group. This leads us to the conclusion that pupil disruptive behavior is often a function of the social dynamics of the class itself.

In the case of teachers assessing the emotional and psychological problems of pupils, two types of teacher attitudes prevail. On the one hand, there are teachers who see nothing disturbing about any behavior of any child. "There are no problem children, only children with problems." "No child's problem is so great that it can't do with some love and affection." "A wanted child is a loved child, and a

WHEN VIEWS COLLIDE

Mr. Watson, a beginning fourth-grade teacher, has a very "loose" classroom. He is much opposed to anything that suggests conformity behavior. In his classroom there are few rules, and there is nothing that even approximates a schedule. He believes that pupils need to grow up as independent, self-directed human beings, and that this can never be achieved when they learn to be blindly obedient to rules. "Our whole society is too regulated," he says. Mr. Watson is a sensitive and warm person, devoted to the children he teaches.

Mr. Watson is a constant source of problems for the principal. His attitudes run along more conventional lines than do Mr. Watson's, although he too is a sensitive and humane person. He is bothered by the "noise and confusion" in Watson's room. He is irritated by complaints from parents who are bothered by the laxness in "discipline and control" in Watson's classroom. The principal has urged Watson to "tighten up," to set some rules and standards of conduct and hold the pupils to them. He also wants Watson to prepare a daily schedule and follow it. "For heaven's sake, Mike, get some control in that room," he says. Watson resists all of these suggestions, and three months into his first year of teaching, it is clear that he is on a collision course with his principal.

1. What are your views as to the goals Mr. Watson has set for his class?
2. What are your views as to the effect of rules and standards on the development of overconformity, something Mr. Watson was very concerned about?
3. Does the principal have a legitimate concern in this situation?
4. Speculate on various ways this problem might be resolved. (One way, obviously, is that Mr. Watson be dismissed, but provide other alternatives.)

loved child is a happy child." These are only a few of a bag full of clichés that have been generated regarding the handling of behavior problems of children. Although the clichés contain valuable kernels of conventional wisdom, they do not serve as well as plans of action for working with children who have deeply rooted psychological problems. The attitude that all that is needed is "plenty of love and affection" is a naive approach to a complex problem. Love and affection are important, of course; most of us can do with more of both. But there is considerably more to psychotherapy than love and affection.

The second teacher attitude that prevails vis-à-vis the behavior of children is one of total suspicion. The smallest infraction of a rule of conduct is interpreted as psychological imbalance. There is a low tolerance for anything except the most straitlaced behavior.

This attitude is especially unfortunate because it may create problems where there are none. Children who are in good mental and physical health can be expected to be lively and active. They naturally find the classroom environment restraining, even under the best of conditions. As part of the growing-up process, they have to test the system from time to time to assure themselves that it is still working—whether the rules are enforced, whether anyone really cares what they do. There will be conflicts between children and groups of children. All of this and more is to be expected, and to interpret as emotional disturbance such normal expressions of child behavior is not a professionally sound judgment.

Teachers are neither psychologists nor psychotherapists, and it is a mistake for teachers to behave as though they are. Some teachers tend to "over-psychologize" the problems of children in their classroom. The story is told of the teacher who made various ominous interpretations of a child's black-crayon drawing. The truth of the matter was that the child had no other crayon except a black one; and as far as he was concerned, black would do the job as well as green, orange, or any other color.

As a part of their professional preparation, teachers need to be able to make some assessment, in a general way, of the potential seriousness of the behavior of children with whom they work. No single checklist of behaviors is sufficient for this purpose. Through training and the careful observation of children, teachers will begin to detect signals warning of possible danger. They will learn to discern what can be ignored and what deserves further careful watching. Once a problem is suspected, it should be discussed with the school psychologist, counselor, or guidance officer, if there is one. A parent conference may help the teacher learn what the child's behavior is like at home and how consistent the in-school and out-of-school behavior is. Often it is wise for a child to have a thorough physical examination when there are unexplained changes in behavior. In any case, the teacher needs to know enough about the development of children to be able to assess the seriousness of behavior patterns. A child should not be sent to the school psychologist for minor infractions of rules of conduct, but neither should serious signs of maladaptive behavior be ignored.

Management problems in the classroom are usually a result of the collective behavior of the children, rather than the result of the actions of one or of a few. Individual children may engage in disruptive behavior, but when this happens repeatedly, it means that the behavior is approved or even encouraged by the group. For various types of management problems to persist, there must be covert, or even overt, reinforcement feedback from the group. In other words, there is consensus in the group that supports the behavior. This, of course, is rarely expressed openly.

What kind of management problems are most common in classrooms? Lois V. Johnson and Mary A. Bany collected hundreds of descriptions of incidents of classroom problems over several years. These incidents, according to the authors, are very similar—year after year, teachers describe the same troublesome behavior. "Children talk at inappropriate times, they delay work processes, engage in disputes and conflicts, react with indifference and lack of interest, and fail to follow prescribed procedures. They quarrel, fight, resist, protest, and fail to cooperate."[2] In order to deal with these problems in terms of analysis and remediation, Johnson and Bany classify classroom management problems as shown in Table 1.[3]

This table deserves careful study. It will help the teacher recognize symptoms of problems developing in the management of the class, and, consequently, will be helpful in doing something about them. There are specific strategies, to be discussed later in this chapter, that can be used to avoid or correct specific problems.

ORGANIZATIONAL ASPECTS OF MANAGEMENT

The way a classroom is organized will not, of course, eliminate management problems. But actions can be taken that will move the teacher a long way down the road toward preventing problems and toward resolving them when they arise. In this regard, there are two principles that are so important that they need to precede all else that is said on this subject:

1. The first few days of the school year are critical in setting the behavior pattern of pupils in a class,

and

2. Preventing problems from arising is always easier than correcting them once they have occurred.

The first day of school and the ones that immediately follow it are the times when the teacher must set the pleasantly firm tone of the classroom. Whatever happens during these few days will establish the "set" for pupil conduct for the remainder of the year. If the

[2] Lois V. Johnson and Mary A. Bany, *Classroom Management: Theory and Skill Training* (New York: Macmillan Publishing Co., Inc., 1970), p. 45.
[3] Ibid., pp. 46–47.

TABLE 1
Classroom Management Problems in Terms of Behavioral Descriptions*

Distinguishing Characteristics	*Behavior Descriptions*
1. *Lack of unity*	The class lacks unity, and conflicts occur between individuals and subgroups, as: when groups split; argumentative over competitive situations such as games; boys against girls; when groups split by cliques, minority groups; when group takes sides on issues or breaks into subgroups; when hostility and conflict continually arise among members and create an unpleasant atmosphere.
2. *Nonadherence to behavioral standards and work procedures*	The class responds with noisy, talkative, disorderly behavior to situations that have established standards for behavior, as: when group is entering or leaving room or changing activities; lining up; cleaning up; going to auditorium; when group is working in ability groups; engaging in committee work; when group is completing study assignments; receiving assignments; correcting papers; handling work materials; when group is engaged in discussion, sharing, planning.
3. *Negative reactions to individual members*	The class becomes vocal or actively hostile toward one or more class members, as: when group does not accept individuals and derides, ignores, or ridicules children who are different; when group reacts negatively to members who deviate from group code; to those who thwart group's progress; or when a member's behavior upsets or puzzles members of the class.
4. *Class approval of misbehavior*	The class approves and supports individuals, as: when they talk out of turn; act in ways that disrupt the normal work procedures; engage in clowning or rebellious activities.
5. *Easily distracted; prone to work stoppage and imitative behavior*	The group reacts with upset, excited, or disorderly behavior to interruptions, distractions, or continual grievances, as: when group is interrupted by monitors, visitors, a change in weather; when members continually have grievances relating to others, lessons, rules, policies, or practices they believe are unfair; and when settlements are demanded before work proceeds.
6. *Low morale and hostile, resistant, or aggressive reactions*	The class members engage in subtle, hostile, aggressive behavior that creates slowdowns and work stoppages, as: when materials are misplaced, pencils break, chairs upset; when books, money, lunches are temporarily lost; when there are continual requests for assignments to be repeated and explained;

TABLE 1
Continued

Distinguishing Characteristics	*Behavior Descriptions*
	when children continually complain about behavior of others with no apparent loss of friendship; when children accuse authority figures of unfair practices and delay classwork by making claims.
7. *Inability to adjust to environmental change*	The class reacts inappropriately to such situations, as: when a substitute takes over; when normal routines are changed; when new members transfer into the class; when stress situations cause inappropriate reactions.

*Reprinted by permission.

teacher is lax in establishing standards of conduct during these first few critical days, it will be almost impossible to do so later in the year. Experienced teachers know that it is easy to become more permissive as the school year progresses without compromising standards of conduct expected, but that it is enormously difficult to become more strict once a permissive pattern has been set. Because beginning teachers want pupils to like them, they are reluctant to take a firm stand on pupil conduct in the room for fear they will offend the children. This form of indulgence is almost always a mistake. The time for firm, strict, and formal—but always, of course, fair—teacher action is during the first few days of the school year.

Several suggestions are presented in the remainder of this chapter that deal with the prevention of behavior problems. In a way, the firmness being suggested as appropriate at the beginning of the school year is a prevention strategy. An interesting, stimulating, instructional program, combined with the rewarding of expected behavior, is a much more effective deterrent to disruptive pupil behavior than is punishment, or the threat of punishment, of misbehavior. When pupils know clearly what is expected, when teachers follow through on pupil expectations, and when they do not permit a gradual erosion of standards of conduct, the behavior of pupils can usually be kept within manageable levels. Of course, no class is totally free of behavior problems all of the time.

Schedule

Teachers create all sorts of management problems for themselves simply by not planning and observing a daily schedule of events in

WHAT'S WRONG HERE?

Miss Fox knows that if she is to succeed as a beginning teacher she must have good "control" in her classroom. She is determined, therefore, not to allow the slightest infraction of room conduct to go unnoticed. When children enter the room, she is usually seen standing at the door, where she can monitor the behavior of children in the hallway and in the classroom at the same time. She likes to think of herself as a "no nonsense" teacher who will not put up with any "monkey business and foolishness" from her fifth graders. Many of her comments to the pupils during the day run along this line:

"Stop running in the hall, boys."
"Now settle down quickly, boys and girls."
"Karen, what are you doing over there? Please take your seat."
"I want it quiet in here—What are you two talking about over there? Is that Billy's book you have, Cindy? Give it back to him and get on with your own work."
"Everyone listen carefully to the directions, because I will give them only once."
"Clear everything from the top of your desks except the book we will be using. (Pause.) Mark, put that ruler away. Sally—the pencil inside your desk! Jim, the waste paper goes in the basket."

Although the pupils have nicknamed her "Hawkeye," they really do not dislike Miss Fox. But they often talk about the good times they had with Miss James the year before, and this bothers Miss Fox.

The classroom gives the outward appearance of orderliness, yet one senses an unnatural tenseness about the room. There is more carping and petty bickering among pupils than one would expect. Pupils are complying with Miss Fox's expectations, but there is little evidence of cooperation among the pupils or between them and Miss Fox. When the principal visited her classroom, she advised Miss Fox to try to develop a more positive approach to room management but did not provide examples of what this entailed.

1. If you were Miss Fox, what would you do to implement the principal's recommendation?
2. What pupil behavior can one expect if teacher talk is mainly directive, negative in content, and perhaps hostile in tone?
3. Do you think Miss Fox likes being a teacher?

the classroom. It is probably true that classrooms of the past have been too tightly scheduled. Part of the rigidity of classrooms comes about because of too close adherence to a time schedule. "Schools are run by bells and ditto machines," the critics say, and to a degree the criticism is well-taken. The inflexibility created by clinging slavishly to a minute-by-minute schedule can hardly be condoned; however, this is not the same as saying there should be no schedule.

Because of the ordinary requirements imposed on the teacher to attend to various areas of the curriculum, it is possible to block out large periods of time to be devoted to reading, social studies, science, language arts, and so on. The schedule can be tentative, to be changed from time to time during the year, if this seems necessary. Also, the schedule can be perceived as reasonably flexible. If on some days a few more minutes of time are needed to complete an important task, obviously such time should be taken. If, however, every lesson exceeds the budgeted time, or does not require the amount of time allotted, this is evidence of weak planning, poor pacing of the lesson, or an inaccurate estimate of the time needed, and should be corrected.

When a teacher has a schedule and observes it reasonably closely, this ensures that all of the children and all areas of the curriculum will receive the attention they deserve. When teachers are careless about scheduling classroom events, days may go by without finding time for some subjects. What usually happens is that favorite subject areas of the teacher get the lion's share of time; those the teacher is less fond of, or those in which the teacher is not particularly strong, get shortchanged. Also, if the teacher works with subgroups within the class, some groups may not get an adequate amount of the teacher's time. If this happens once in awhile, it is not a serious matter, but if it occurs regularly, it cannot help but be detrimental to a well-balanced instructional program, and will therefore contribute to management problems.

Routines

Closely related to the setting of a schedule is the establishment of routines that regularize activities that occur day after day in a classroom. Included are entering and leaving the classroom, taking roll, collecting lunch money, moving from one grouping configuration to another, going to the restroom, getting books and supplies, coming to order after recess, checking out athletic equipment, and so on. There should be routine ways of doing these routine activities, and others like them, simply to avoid altercations, bickerings, and conflicts that are inevitable when they are handled on an ad hoc basis each day.

As with scheduling, there has been some criticism of the use of routines. This criticism is not without justification. Traditional classrooms were undoubtedly overroutinized. For example, in old-fashioned dismissal procedures, the teacher might expect all children to be seated upright, with hands folded and resting on top of the desk. With a series of taps on the desk with a ruler, the teacher would signal that the children were to turn, stand, and pass in rows. It is against antiquated procedures of this kind that criticism of routines is leveled. Routines should approximate ways of behaving and acting that are normal and natural for children. They should not require stilted and regimented behavior, such as one would expect in a military or prison environment.

When routines are reasonable and are implemented sensibly, the children do not find them objectionable. As a matter of fact, they get some security from knowing what is to be done and how they are expected to do it. Almost invariably, substitute teachers are reminded by the pupils as to how things are done in their classroom; they object strongly when alternative ways are suggested.

PHOTO FOLIO

A variety of creative learning activities can contribute to effective classroom management by stimulating pupil interest and providing an outlet for their emotional and physical energy. If such activities are to serve those purposes, however, the teacher needs to plan them carefully and must anticipate potential problems that might contribute to pupil disruptive behavior.

1. Examine this photograph carefully and then list the specific things the teacher would have had to do in advance in order to have the children engage in this activity. Keep in mind that there are at least another twenty children in the classroom.
2. Good classroom management involves providing a balance between periods of quiet time and concentration with periods of physical movement and activity. Try your hand at organizing a daily schedule for a grade in which you are interested. Then discuss your ideas with a practicing teacher of that grade.

Clarity of Directions and Goals

Human beings find it annoying to be asked to do things without knowing the reasons for doing them. Children in school often are assigned tasks without the least idea as to how the specific activity fits into the larger framework that serves as a long-range goal. Time taken to explain what is to be done and where the activities lead is usually time well spent.

Management problems can also be reduced by the giving of clear directions to pupils. When specific directions are carelessly given, or are ambiguous, pupils will not know what they are to do and consequently will ask to have directions clarified or repeated, sometimes several times. This annoys the teacher, and it is a great temptation to establish a rule that directions will be given only once. This is generally not a good idea, because it is patently unfair. Besides, there are times when, for obvious reasons, directions will need to be repeated. The teacher is then placed in the position of having to violate one of the classroom rules. If the teacher is careful about having the attention of the class before directions are given, and is skillful in giving directions clearly and completely, it is not likely that directions will be misunderstood. It is helpful for teachers to tape-record themselves in order to evaluate how clearly they give directions or make explanations to their pupils.

Physical Arrangements

There is much in the arrangement of a classroom that can either contribute to or alleviate management problems. Most authorities on modern methodology advise against straight-row seating of pupils. There are good reasons for this, chief among them being the formality and rigidity that such arrangements suggest. Unfortunately, a completely satisfactory alternative to the traditional arrangement has never been suggested. There is no one "best way" to arrange pupil stations in a classroom. Most would agree that the arrangement should be kept flexible, and that pupils be deployed in ways most suitable for accomplishing specific tasks.

Because teachers often form subgroups within their classrooms, and because these smaller groups might, to some extent, represent ability levels, the teacher may be tempted to cluster pupils from the same group. The teacher might reason that there will be less shuffling around when moving from one subgroup to another. (In a sense, it is the teacher who moves from group to group, rather than the pupils who move in the direction of the teacher.) And on the surface, this seems to make good sense; however, there are other values at stake in this situation. Three strong reasons argue against this arrangement. First, it is apt to create problems in trying to build unity in the total class group. Second, although the teacher probably cannot disguise the fact that the groups represent high-, middle-, and low-achievement levels, seating children accordingly is to them a constant reminder of their position in the class. Third, from what is known about self-expectation and self-image, it is reasonable to assume that such an arrangement does not work to the advantage of slower-achieving pupils.

Teachers are often bothered by pupils interacting with each other at times when this distracts from what others in the classroom are doing. Constant whispering, talking, and visiting are encouraged by some seating arrangements. If a teacher has a low tolerance for pupil interaction, he or she should obviously not arrange to have pupils seated close to each other. When children are seated side by side, it is perfectly natural for them to talk to each other. Therefore, if the purpose is to encourage social interaction, they should be seated close together; if the reverse is wanted, pupils should be separated. But the teacher cannot have it both ways.

Perhaps it is best not to have *a* single room arrangement but to move seats from one configuration to another, depending on what the nature of the task is. For independent study it is certainly better for a child to sit and work alone, in order not to be distracted by others. For group discussion or other group activity, pupils obviously will have to be seated close to others. It is unreasonable for teachers to place children in situations that encourage a maximum amount of interaction, then admonish or berate them for whispering and talking.

The teacher should not be seated much of the time during the day, therefore it matters little where the teacher's desk is located. The elementary teacher will be moving about, helping pupils, supervising their work, providing individual instruction, and so on. In conducting instruction with small subgroups, in working with individual pupils, or in supervising the work of pupils at their seats, the teacher should habitually be positioned in such a way to monitor easily the behavior of the class. The pupils should be aware of the teacher's presence.

PERSONAL DIMENSIONS OF MANAGEMENT

Just as the physical arrangements of the classroom may facilitate or obstruct classroom management, so may the personal characteristics of the teacher. Teachers, like everyone else, have their personal strengths and liabilities, assets and peculiarities. Although there doubtless is value in modeling one's behavior after that of an outstanding teacher, or even role playing in early experiences in teaching, the teacher must be his or her own person. The greatest contribution the teacher makes lies in what is brought to the classroom in one's own unique personality. Therefore, what is said here should not be construed to mean that all teachers need to fit into a type of prescribed or established mold that is supposed to represent teacher behavior.

The concepts of *with-it-ness* and *overlapping* are often used in discussing the subject of classroom management. These concepts were identified and so labeled by Jacob S. Kounin and his associates as a result of their research and are described in Kounin's book, *Discipline and Group Management in Classrooms.*[4] With-it-ness has to do with the teacher's intuitive sense of knowing what is going on in the classroom. When the teacher is "with it," he or she is especially skillful in monitoring the behavior of the entire class and in

[4] Jacob S. Kounin, *Discipline and Group Management in Classrooms.* New York: Holt, Rinehart and Winston, 1970, p. 79.

WHAT WOULD YOU HAVE DONE?

It was the first really warm, spring day that Middleton had had that year. In fact, it was downright hot. And the school children loved it! After a long cold winter and a damp and rainy spring, it seemed as though summer had arrived with one big burst of sunshine, and energy that had welled up during the many dreary months seemed to have released itself like a mountain of water flowing through a broken dam! During the noon hour the children played hard, ran and yelled and had a glorious time in the welcomed spring sunshine. Now the "first" bell had rung and several hundred very reluctant children found their way into the building and to their respective classrooms, still talking loudly, perspiring profusely, and with flushed faces.

Mr. Gardner scheduled his math immediately following the lunch hour. Today the children wandered into the classroom, talking loudly, highly stimulated and hardly ready for the concentration needed for a math lesson. Mr. Gardner saw the hopelessness of the situation confronting him and immediately decided to alter his schedule for the day.

1. Do you think this was a wise decision on the part of Mr. Gardner?
2. If you were in Mr. Gardner's position, what would you have done?
3. Can Mr. Gardner forget about math each time the area has a beautiful day?
4. If this is a persistent problem, what might Mr. Gardner do to deal with it on a long-term basis?

processing feedback signals from members of the class that indicate when intervention is needed. In this way it is possible to stay on top of things and defuse potential trouble spots before they become serious problems. As has already been noted, preventing behavior problems is much more critical to successful classroom management than is correcting disruptions once they occur.

The concept of *overlapping* means that the teacher is able to do more than one teaching task at the same time. For example, while Mr. Trimble is conducting a reading lesson with one group of third graders, he notices that there is some confusion about a seatwork assignment that another group is supposed to be completing, and in yet another part of the classroom a child is raising her hand for permission to go to the bathroom. The teacher nods his head to the girl and then moves to the group having trouble with its seatwork. A clarifying statement from Mr. Trimble gets the group back on track, and he returns to the reading group he is teaching to find that they are ready to discuss the passage. All of this happens in about two minutes. Much of teaching is like this because of the dynamic character of elementary school classrooms. The teacher must be able to do more than one thing at a time and must also have eyes that scan all pupil activity in the room all of the time. Obviously, Kounin's concepts of *with-it-ness* and *overlapping* are closely related.

Verbal Behavior of the Teacher

Professional literature on teaching is generously sprinkled with statements such as "teaching is not telling" and "teaching is more than talking." In spite of this, there is a considerable amount of evidence, based on observations in countless numbers of classrooms, that teachers do a lot of talking. Some estimates indicate that almost 70 per cent of classroom instructional time is spent in talk by the teacher or pupils. Teachers evidently have a low tolerance for silence.

Not only do teachers do a lot of talking, but what they say and how they say it often contributes to rather than reduces management problems. Much of what the teacher says has to do with directing pupils' work and behavior, relating his or her own opinion or ideas about content and procedures, criticizing pupil behavior, reminding pupils of the teacher's authority, and using that authority. It is well known that utterances of this type strengthen the domination of the teacher over the pupils, consequently *increasing* the dependence of pupils on the teacher. This, of course, leads in a direction away from building self-direction and responsible independence on the part of the pupils. It makes the teacher *more* responsible for the conduct of the pupils in the classroom and the pupils *less.* For good classroom management, the situation should be reversed. That is, the teacher should do as much as possible to make pupils self-directed and responsible for their own conduct.

In order to move away from domination of pupils and toward a more independent relationship between pupils and teacher, the teacher needs to be aware of the effect of his or her own verbal behavior on the pupils. As this awareness deepens, the teacher will be likely to encourage and praise more appropriately. Rather than evaluating every pupil response, the teacher will be more inclined to accept what is said, clarify if necessary, and restate pupils' responses. Support will be given to the ideas and feelings of pupils. Research on the reaction of learners to teacher verbal behavior, spanning the past fifty years, shows clearly that both the learning potential of pupils and their classroom conduct is greatly influenced by the statements made by the teacher.

Quite apart from the *content* of the teacher's utterances, the tone, modulation, and volume of the teacher's voice itself bears on classroom management. Children are quick to detect impatience or insincerity in the tone of the teacher's voice and are likely to react negatively. Similarly, shouting at a class to get attention or to give directions works as a deterrent to good management. Making a tape recording of one's teaching from time to time helps correct problems of this type.

Appearance

There can be no question that a teacher's appearance and bearing have much to do with success in classroom management. Successful teachers project an appearance of quiet confidence that communicates security and competence. When the teacher's behavior is such that it appears as though there is some uncertainty about what to do next, pupils are sure to sense this quickly and will take advantage of the teacher's insecurity. It is paradoxical that often rather small, slight teachers have little difficulty managing classes and maintaining control whereas large, athletic-type males may find themselves in unmanageable circumstances, even with young children. The teacher's "commanding presence," in the benign sense, helps explain these differences.

No doubt there are wide individual differences in personality traits among teachers that make it easier for some and more difficult for others to develop a secure, competent demeanor. Nevertheless, any teacher can work toward the improvement of this characteristic. Professional competence can be strengthened through sound scholarship and thorough planning and preparation. Part of the teacher's insecurity may come from fear of being unprepared to handle ideas or questions that may come up. Confidence in one's own competence, and preparation, will do much to dispel such fears. Also, the beginner can model the behavior of a successful, fully competent inservice teacher. In this connection, role-playing strategies may be helpful in establishing an appropriate presence with a class.

Warmth in Interaction

The teacher in the elementary school is without question the most influential and powerful personality in the classroom. The teacher's behavior will set the qualitative pattern of interactions in the group. If the teacher is warm and caring, the chances are that these traits will be modeled by the pupils. Conversely, if the teacher is domineering, arbitrary, carping, and critical, pupils are likely to reflect those behaviors, too.

Wholesome classroom management procedures cannot be developed in an environment lacking in trust and respect. Because control problems loom so large in teaching success, the beginner may take a mistrusting and suspicious attitude toward children. Such mistrust is apparent when the teacher is constantly casting his or her eyes about the classroom, looking for children who may be up to mischief; is quick to reprimand the slightest infraction, to be sure no one "gets away with anything." There is an exaggerated fear that misbehavior, if left unattended, will undermine the teacher's authority. When teachers assume such distrustful attitudes, children will usually not disappoint them. If the teacher goes to a class expecting trouble at every turn, he or she is likely to find it. In such settings it is reasonable to assume that events come under the influence of the self-fulfilling prophecy.

Nonverbal Communication

Educators are beginning to appreciate the powerful influence of unspoken cues provided by the teacher in communicating with children in the classroom. Sometimes overt, but more often quite subtle, these nonverbal cues may range from a gesture to a facial expression, to simply the expression of a mood. For example, a restless child may be calmed by the reassuring smile of an understanding teacher. Or a teacher may place a hand on the shoulder of a child who seems to need emotional support. Or a teacher will show enthusiasm in his or her eyes as the child is relating what is considered to have been an exciting experience. Some authors have referred to this system of communication as "the silent language."

It may be that teachers communicate more profoundly through such nonverbal cues than in any other way. Words are always manipulated to come out the way the teacher thinks is most appropriate. But true feelings and attitudes are laid bare by those unspoken messages that flow between human beings, and which children, in their innocence, are so skillful in decoding. It is these signals that tell the child whether or not the teacher is, indeed, a concerned and caring adult. It is this unspoken message that will have much to do with the management of the teacher's classroom, and will, in the long run, be the deciding factor in whether or not the classroom is to be a fertile seedbed for the growth of an enlightened and sensitive humanity.

DEVELOPING RELATED COMPETENCIES

The Teaching Profession?

Anita Jenkins is an attractive, pleasant, gentle young woman who loves young children and is determined to be a good primary-grade teacher. She is looking forward to student teaching the next quarter.

Her roommate, who is now teaching, is having problems with room management and this is a frequent subject of conversation between them. "You really have to know how to give them the old evil eye," her roommate tells her. "You have to look stern and give them the 'I really mean it' look." This is a difficult role for Anita to assume because it is not consistent with her nature. She has an easy smile, and in the past has been able to relate well to young children. So each morning she practices frowning and glaring in front of her bathroom mirror, in order to develop a threatening, menacing, commanding "look."

1. In terms of the ideas discussed in this chapter, what is your assessment of this approach to classroom management?
2. Is it possible that although her roommate was having management problems, Anita might have little or no trouble in this regard? Why or why not?

And Miss Swanson Said . . .

Assume that you are Miss Swanson in the following situation, and complete the last line.

"May I go to the bathroom, Miss Swanson?" asks eight-year-old Heidi, a third grader.

"Not now, dear. We had recess not more than 10 minutes ago and you should have taken care of it then," replies Miss Swanson.

"But I *have* to go, Miss Swanson."

And Miss Swanson said, "____________________."

What's Going On Here?

When you report for your student-teaching assignment, Miss Wetherfield, the principal, tells you, "Mrs. Johnson is a primary teacher of several years experience and has never been known to have any problems of classroom management and control. You can learn a lot from her." During the first few days of your assignment, you spend most of your time observing Mrs. Johnson. You notice that she frequently uses such expressions as these, often stated in the third person:

"Mrs. Johnson knows when all the boys and girls are ready because she can see *all* their eyes."

"Mrs. Johnson likes the way Louise is sitting up nice and straight."

"Mrs. Johnson was not pleased with the way her boys and girls came into the room today."

"Jennie, will you be a dear and help Mrs. Johnson pass out the books?"

"Who would like to do something nice for Mrs. Johnson, by taking a note to the Office?"

"Mrs. Johnson likes to see all the boys and girls doing their work so well."

1. Does this aspect of Mrs. Johnson's behavior help explain why she "has never been known to have any problems of classroom management and control?"
2. What is there about this procedure that gives Mrs. Johnson so much power over the behavior of the pupils?
3. In terms of the ideas discussed in this chapter, what is your assessment of this approach to classroom management?

Out of Sight, Out of Mind

Mr. Wilkinson enjoyed the academic aspects of his job as a sixth-grade teacher, but he had no patience with children who were uncooperative, disruptive, or who engaged in minor horseplay during class time. He refused to "waste my time and the time of pupils who *really* wanted to learn something on those who haven't yet learned why they come to school." His solution to disciplinary problems was a simple one. He removed disruptive children from the group. Almost always one could see a child seated all by himself behind the piano, another in a remote corner of the room, and another one or two in the hallway just outside his classroom. He frequently sent children to the school office, not to see the principal but to sit there, out of the way, where they would not disturb the work of the class. He rarely did any follow-up with these children. They would simply re-enter the group, only to be removed again the next time a problem arose. As the school year progressed, Mr. Wilkinson noticed that more and more of the children were becoming involved in behavior that necessitated their isolation.

1. What is your assessment of Mr. Wilkinson's approach to classroom management?
2. What risks are there in removing a child from the classroom, such as in a hallway or the school office, outside the reach of a teacher's direct supervision?
3. What alternatives can you suggest for dealing with a situation such as the one faced by Mr. Wilkinson?

FOR FURTHER PROFESSIONAL STUDY

Books

Kounin, Jacob S. *Discipline and Group Management in Classrooms.* New York: Holt, Rinehart and Winston, Inc., 1970.

Lovitt, Thomas C. *Managing Inappropriate Behavior in the Classroom.* Reston, Virginia: Council for Exceptional Children, 1978. (44 pages)

Long, James D. and Virginia H. Frye. *Making It Till Friday: A Guide to Successful Classroom Management.* Princeton, New Jersey: Princeton Book Company, 1977.

Sloane, Howard N. *Classroom Management: Remediation and Prevention.* New York: John Wiley & Sons, Inc., 1976.

Tanner, Laurel N. *Classroom Discipline for Effective Teaching and Learning.* New York: Holt, Rinehart and Winston, Inc., 1978.

Periodicals

Brandt, Ronald S., ed. "Discipline Strategies," *Educational Leadership* (March 1980), 457–476. (Four articles)

Canter, Lee. "Discipline! You Can Do It!" *Instructor* (September 1979), 109–112.

Carberry, Hugh H. "Behavioral Blockbusters." *Instructor* (March 1979), 72–78.

Glasser, William. "10 Steps to Good Discipline." *Today's Education* (November-December 1977), 60–63.

Hipple, Marjorie L. "Classroom Discipline Problems? Fifteen Humane Solutions." *Childhood Education* (February 1978), 183–187.

Leverte, Marcia, Arden Smith, and JoAnn Cooper. "How to Have A Responsible Classroom." *Instructor* (October 1978), 71–73+.

Simms, Richard L. and David Boger. "Classroom Management That Works in Inner-City Schools." *Contemporary Education* (Fall 1978), 24–28.

4

Modes of Teaching

THE QUALIFIED AND COMPETENT TEACHER . . .

1. Is familiar with the assumptions, major purposes, role of the teacher, role of the learner, role of learning resources, and methods of evaluation for each of the four modes of teaching.
2. Knows when and how best to use various modes of teaching.
3. Is skillful in using specific teaching methods associated with each of the four modes.

Performance Criteria

As a result of the serious study of this chapter, the student should be able to . . .

1. Describe, behaviorally, the role of the teacher and the role of the learner in the expository, inquiry, demonstration, and activity modes.
2. Provide a specific example of applications of different modes of teaching from at least two areas of the school curriculum.
3. Demonstrate his or her ability to use the expository, inquiry, and demonstration modes by teaching a group of children or a peer group.
4. Provide a detailed description of how he or she would organize a classroom in the activity mode, or, where circumstances will allow, actually demonstrate his or her ability to use the activity mode by teaching a group of pupils.

Human beings have been teaching other human beings for a long, long time; perhaps even from the beginning of their tenure on earth many millions of years ago. Having been doing it for such a long time, one might assume that a great deal is known about the teaching process. One might think that there may have evolved, over these countless generations, at least some principles of teaching on which there is general agreement. Regrettably, this is not the case. There is a great deal of disagreement, even among well-informed persons, about what constitutes good teaching and how teaching should take place. Perhaps this will always be so, because teaching involves not only the conduct of instruction; it reflects one's social philosophy regarding how children should be treated, what the ultimate values of education are, how the results of learning are to be demonstrated, how teachers and children should interact, and a host of similar issues. Outside of the teaching profession, much of what we think we know about teaching and learning is a distillation of folk wisdom that has come down through the ages, and that is unacceptable today in terms of present social values. Examples are "Spare the rod and spoil the child"; "Children should be seen but not heard." In this century, the profession of teaching has moved steadily away from a total reliance on folk wisdom and has sought to base more of its decision making on the findings from research. Needless to say, in the research on teaching, the surface has hardly been scratched.

It is undoubtedly true that much of good teaching is the application of common-sense principles. For example, when one is interested in something, one is more likely to want to learn than if one is not interested in it. Consequently, anything the teacher can do to create interest would be beneficial to learning. Young children have difficulty sitting quietly for long periods of time; therefore, on a common-sense basis, the teacher would provide a balance among activities calling for quiet time and those requiring movement. Children obviously learn at differing rates, and it therefore follows that slower-learning pupils are likely to need more time and teacher assistance than faster-learning ones. There is nothing wrong with the application of common sense to teaching. Indeed, the problem is quite the contrary. As has been noted by many observers, it is unfortunate that common sense is such an uncommon commodity.

The act of teaching is so complex that it is very nearly impossible to demonstrate that a specific way of teaching is superior to other ways for all purposes, with all teachers, with all pupils, for all times, and in all circumstances. Time and again, those who supervise the work of teachers report remarkable exceptions to standard practice. Certain procedures, teaching styles, and techniques that are generally not recommended seem to work well for a specific teacher. We are forced to conclude that there are many good ways to teach. Although there are professionally sound guidelines in terms of the research now available, individual teachers need to adapt what they do to their own personality styles and to the idiosyncrasies of the situations in which they find themselves. The dynamics and flow of day to day work with children call for teacher behavior that is flexible and fluid, accommodating and adjusting to the constant unfolding of classroom circumstances. This means that the teacher is continually making decisions—when to negotiate, when to hold firm, when to intervene, when to let events play themselves out. The decision-making ability and the judgment factor that goes with it undoubtedly have much to do with the success of the teacher.

In our discussion of classroom management in the previous chapter, we stressed the interactive relationship between management and instruction. It is important for the reader to be mindful of that relationship as we move into an analysis of modes or ways of teaching. Some modes of teaching make pupil behavior more manageable simply because children are not placed in situations where it is easy for them to become disruptive. Other teaching modes are an invitation to management challenges because of the permissive environment in which children work.

CONTRASTING THE TEACHING MODES

Each of the four modes of teaching to be discussed here have value in achieving specific purposes. The teacher may develop a preference for one or another of these modes but the competent teacher must be skillful in using more than a single mode appropriately. In order to do so, the teacher will have to understand the basic theory that underlies each, and must also be able to use specific teaching skills associated with each. The chart on pages 131–132 identifies specific methods of teaching usually associated with each of these modes. It is important to note that some methods, such as discussion, can be used effectively with any mode. We now turn to an examination of the four modes of teaching in terms of (1) the assumptions underlying each, (2) the purposes to be served, (3) the role of the teacher, (4) the role of the learner, (5) the use of instructional materials, and (6) the methods of evaluation to be used by each.

THE EXPOSITORY MODE

The term expository mode is derived from the concept *exposition,* which means, most simply, to provide an explanation. In the context of teaching, exposition has to do with the teacher's providing facts, ideas, and other essential information to the learners. Expository strategies are *telling* or *explaining* strategies. Suppose, for example, that a teacher was about to present the concept "boundary line" in a social studies lesson, using an expository strategy. Displayed about the room might be maps of the local village or city, a home-state map showing counties, a map of the United States showing the states, and one of North America showing the countries. There might also be photographs showing stateline markers, border crossings between countries, and a photograph of the sign at the edge of the village or city. Perhaps the teacher would begin the explanation by citing an analogous situation familiar to the pupils, such as the areas assigned to different groups on the playground. Visual devices would be used to explain the meaning of the concept "boundary line." Pupils would be provided not one but many examples of the concept in a variety of settings. After this explanation, there would probably be some discussion, along with follow-up work calling for the application of the concept to new situations. The reader will recognize this as a very familiar mode of teaching.

In the example cited, it was the teacher who was doing the explaining; but other sources of information and data are often used in expository teaching. The most frequently used resource other than the teacher is, of course, the textbook. Any of the standard learning resources such as films, filmstrips, pictures, encyclopedias, the library, and community resources can be, and frequently are, used in expository teaching.

Expository teaching is the primary object of criticism by those who favor inquiry strategies. Often it is claimed that exposition concerns itself with the "*mere* transmission of information," as if there were something objectionable about learners becoming well-informed. We do not share this point of view. Exposition, if well done, can be a very effective teaching strategy, even with young children. Some of the most interesting and long-remembered experiences of elementary-school children are short and exciting explanations provided by an animated teacher. The problem is that teachers often do too much expository teaching; too much talking and explaining, with a corresponding reduction in the use of other, more pupil-involving strategies. It is doubtless true that schools have relied too heavily on expository teaching. This does not mean that it should be eliminated; rather, it should be appropriately balanced with other strategies.

Because of the overuse of expository strategies, serious efforts have been made to redress the balance in favor of inquiry. In this process, the contrast between the two modes of teaching is often overdrawn. That is to say, exposition is often associated with the worst practices in teaching—unimaginative use of textbooks, rigidity, emphasis on factual learning and memorization, misuse of lecture methods, and so on. In contrast, inquiry is associated with all that is good in teaching—a warm and friendly teacher, flexibility, concern for higher-level thought processes, and highly motivated pupils searching out data to test hypotheses they themselves have proposed. Such exaggerated criticisms of exposition and acclaim for inquiry actually misrepresent both modes of teaching. The expository mode often is not as bad as is suggested. Similarly, the inquiry mode is not necessarily as productive in terms of pupil learning as its most enthusiastic supporters would have us believe.

Research studies that compare the effects of inquiry and expository teaching do not suggest consistent superiority of one method over the other. In spite of the great values attributed to inquiry teaching, the research data leave an objective observer unconvinced of its demonstrable advantage in terms of pupil achievement. It might be argued that inquiry makes its contribution in the development of specific problem-solving, reflective-intellectual skills, rather than in terms of measurable pupil achievement. This can be accepted as a hypothesis, but the evidence to support the idea has yet to be gathered. On a common sense basis, this would seem to be the case. In reference to this point, Manson and Williams write:

> Instruction based on the pupil as a knowledge seeker is generally posed as the antitheses of expository teaching in which the learner is to be a knowledge recipient. Learning may occur in either situation, but proponents of inquiry maintain that the nature of the learning is likely to differ. This is to be expected since the purposes for which the methods were designed are quite different. Exposition may be better suited to transmitting knowledge while investigation may be more effective in developing thinking; however, the paucity of research does not permit a final conclusion about such a claim. What can be asserted is that learning resulting from expository teaching need not be meaningless, and the learning resulting from inquiry teaching need not be meaningful. Lecture is not inherently bad nor is inquiry necessarily good. "Problem solving can be just as deadening, just as formalistic, just as mechanical, just as passive, and just as rote as the worst form of exposition."[1] The instructional format should not be mistaken as adequate assurance of desirable learning.[2]

[1] David P. Ausubel, *Educational Psychology: A Cognitive View* (New York: Holt, Rinehart & Winston, Inc., 1968), p. 470.

[2] Gary A. Manson and Elmer D. Williams, "Inquiry: Does It Teach How or What to Think?" *Social Education* 34 (January 1970), 78–81.

Assumptions

The expository mode assumes there is an essential body of content, skills, and values to be learned. It is assumed, further, that this learning has been pulled together into courses of study, textbooks, and other curriculum documents that form the core learning of the school curriculum. Teachers are prepared to teach this essential learning to pupils. Teaching is assumed to be basically a transmission process. The teacher and the learning resources serve as conduits for moving information, skills, and values from their sources to the learner. Teaching, therefore, is a variation of telling; learning is the receiving of information that has already been processed in terms of its importance and "learnability." Information and information-gathering skills are deemed to be important. Consequently, pupil achievement is measured in terms of either the amount of information that can be recalled or how effectively information-gathering skills can be used.

Major Purposes

The major purpose of expository teaching is, clearly, to transmit knowledge and skills to the learner. If it is deemed important to get across to pupils particular information relating to science, mathematics, social studies, health, safety, and so on, this can often be done efficiently and effectively through an expository mode. Exposition does not necessarily concern itself with the social values of the learning experience. Its purpose is purely and simply getting across to the learner that which is specified by the curriculum requirements. For example, a teacher may want to teach a group of fourth graders that the major land masses and water bodies of the earth consist of seven continents and four oceans. The teacher displays a world map, points out relevant information, names and labels the continents and oceans, explains that the earth's surface is divided between water and land, and that these land and water bodies have names. Pupils are not necessarily involved in discovering anything for themselves; the essential information to be learned is presented to them.

Role of the Teacher

In the expository mode, the teacher directs the learning program. The teacher *is* the programmer. He or she must see to it that the prescribed learning is covered and that the pupils have mastered it. The teacher is an important data source and is an important component of the transmission line between instructional resources and the learners. The teacher decides what books and other instructional materials will be used. His or her role is to guide the pupils to get the right answers—those that are a part of the required curriculum. In the expository mode, the teacher's directions and explanations must be crystal clear to the pupils. Ambiguous questions and confusing explanations are a deterrent to pupil learning.

Role of the Learner

In the expository mode, the learner is expected to meet requirements of learning that are established by the teacher. This usually includes reading required material, answering assigned questions, discussing topics or problems presented by the teacher, and demonstrating skills deemed to be important. The pupil is not required to exercise the same degree of self-direction as would be expected in the inquiry mode. The learner is not necessarily encouraged to go beyond the tasks outlined by the teacher, although this sometimes happens by means of "extra credit."

The role of the learner in the expository mode is often described as "passive." This is probably an inaccurate description, because it carries a negative connotation. The learner can be and often is very active in the expository mode, but the learning activity is directed toward achieving predetermined outcomes.

Use of Learning Resources

In contrast to the inquiry mode, the expository mode does require that the pupil get certain prescribed information and skills from the instructional resources used. Typically, learning materials will be used to respond to questions framed by someone *other* than the learner, i.e., the teacher, the textbook authors, and so forth. Rather than seeking data in order to make their own interpretations, pupils will be looking for and learning the interpretations and summaries presented by the information sources. Learning resources are best used to *summarize* learnings for pupils in the expository mode. There can be no question that the expository mode relies heavily on learning resources that stress verbal learning as opposed to direct pupil experience. The mode also uses learning resources that are compartmentalized along conventional subject matter lines—reading, mathematics, social studies, science, and so forth.

Method of Evaluation

The achievement of pupils in the expository mode is represented by the extent to which they have acquired the prescribed learning that was transmitted to them. Instruments that assess knowledge of informational content covered in the curriculum are appropriate, as are those that measure use of skills. Conventional standardized tests are a good example of evaluative instruments based on the expository mode of teaching. Teacher-made tests designed to find out whether or not pupils can reproduce correct answers are also consistent with the expository mode. The expository mode operates on the premise that there is a predetermined curriculum that pupils are supposed to learn. It follows, therefore, that the method of evaluation will be one that assesses the extent to which this learning has been achieved by the pupils.

BUT HOW DO YOU DO IT, REALLY?

The National Council for the Social Studies was holding its annual convention in a nearby city and Miss Simmons, a first year second-grade teacher, decided to attend. She found the experience both inspiring and instructive. She listened to some great speakers but was confused about some of the things she heard. One speaker emphasized that "Teaching is not telling. Pupils have to experience on a firsthand basis the cultural world that surrounds them. They need to find things out for themselves. Pupils need to inquire and to discover."

The next day Miss Simmons attended another general session where the speaker was just as eloquent, just as distinguished, and just as convincing as the first one was. He told the audience, "You must consider how a culture is passed on from one generation to another. Is it likely or even reasonable to expect that the whole of culture will be rediscovered by each individual as a part of the growing process? I think not. Not even with the best schools and the most creative teachers could we reasonably expect that a child would discover all that he needs to know. We cannot rely on discovery as the means of transmitting the culture to children and youth. Culture cannot be discovered; it must be passed on or it is forgotten."*

1. How can Miss Simmons reconcile these two points of view?
2. Are the speakers necessarily in disagreement?
3. Do these sketches tell you anything about the importance of being able to use more than one mode of teaching?

**See* Jerome S. Bruner, "Some Elements of Discovery," in Lee S. Shulman and Evan R. Keislar, eds., *Learning by Discovery: A Critical Appraisal* (Chicago: Rand McNally & Co.), 1966, pp. 101–14.

THE INQUIRY MODE

To *inquire* means that one is involved in asking questions, seeking information, and carrying on an investigation. Inquiry strategies in teaching and learning, therefore, are those that involve learners in these operations. To a large extent, the pupil is responsible for providing ideas and questions to be explored, proposing hypotheses to be tested, accumulating and organizing data to test hypotheses, and coming to tentative conclusions. Inquiry can take many forms, but the problem-solving format, suggested by John Dewey near the turn of the century, is one that is commonly used. This process involves five steps. The learner confronts a problem situation; what Dewey called a "felt need." The learner moves to resolve this need by searching for a solution. In the process, possible solutions or hypotheses are proposed and then a search is conducted for evidence that will support or reject them. On the basis of data and the testing of proposed solutions, the learner either comes to a tentatively held conclusion or rejects the hypothesis and continues the search until a satisfactory resolution of the problem is found. These five steps, e.g., (1) defining a problem, (2) proposing hypotheses, (3) collecting data, (4) evaluating evidence, and (5) making a conclusion, have become institutionalized in the so-called scientific method of problem solving.

Often overlooked is the fact that the procedure, as proposed by Dewey, includes two thought processes. The defining of the problem and proposing the hypotheses involve *inductive discovery.* In gathering data, applying and testing solutions, one engages in *deductive proof.* It is clear that problem solving of this type makes use of both inductive and deductive thought processes, even though it is commonly assumed that inquiry involves inductive processes only.

When inquiry is conducted in such a way that pupils find out the meanings of concepts and form conclusions and generalizations from data they themselves have gathered, we may refer to such an inquiry as a "discovery experience." For example, in a science experiment dealing with the effect of light on a growing plant, the pupils may have two plants of the same variety, of similar size, and grown under the same environmental conditions. One is left to grow as usual in sunlight, and the other is covered. All other conditions of heat, moisture, and exposure are the same for the two plants. In a few days noticeable changes occur in the plants. From these observations, children conclude that sunlight is an essential component of plant growth. Throughout this process the teacher neither told the pupils what would happen, nor what to expect. The teacher might have asked reflective questions along the way in order to guide the inquiry, but the pupils themselves discovered the relationship. When educators refer to inquiry, they are usually referring to this kind of discovery learning. It is important to note that *discovery* used in this sense does not mean that pupils are uncovering new knowledge; they are discovering knowledge hitherto unknown to *them.*

Inquiry teaching and problem-solving procedures have suffered through the years because of their susceptibility to ritualism. Numerous workshops have been conducted throughout the country, ostensibly designed to teach teachers how to "do inquiry." Often, the result of such experiences is a knowledge of some of the procedures but little knowledge of the rationale. Nor is there any basic commitment to the philosophy underlying inquiry teaching. As a result, teachers go through the five steps of problem solving in a more or less routine and mechanical way, which bears no resemblance to genuine reflective inquiry. Some teachers are taught inquiry through the use of a questioning procedure; in this case, questions asked by the pupils must be answered by the teacher with a yes or no. This activity is not unlike the game of "Twenty Questions." Teachers may proceed through inquiry tasks as though these were ends in themselves, rather than learning experiences designed to develop intellectual processes. To be effective, inquiry procedures must be based on a teacher's willingness to involve learners in questioning, hypothesizing, data collecting, and concluding—activities in which the pupils find out things for themselves. The precise format used to achieve such purposes can be devised by the teacher to meet requirements of particular circumstances.

Assumptions

Inquiry assumes that the school serves the child best by facilitating the self-development of human beings. Therefore, inquiry is largely pupil-centered, requiring that the pupil be actively involved in learning. Inquiry involves a search-surprise element, and this characteristic makes it highly motivating to learners. There is no fixed body of knowledge and skills that all must learn. The *process* of learning is perceived to be at least as important an outcome as is the product, e.g., what is learned. Learning should be kept openended—the achievement of goals being simply an intermediate step to additional investigation. Learners are therefore encouraged to wonder and imagine, and this curiosity leads to further inquiry. Learning, for the most part, is applied as it is acquired, not stored only for future use. Learners have individual learning styles, and these can best be accommodated when the pupil is responsible for his or her own learning. There is less need to focus on a search for "right" answers, because conclusions are tentative in terms of the data available at the time.

Major Purposes

The major purpose of inquiry teaching is to provide a means for the learner to develop intellectual skills related to reflective thought processes. If thinking is to be the central purpose of American education, as many believe it should be, then ways must be devised to help individuals develop that capability. Inquiry is intended to do this by focusing on the development of such mental processes as identifying and analyzing problems, stating hypotheses, collecting and classifying relevant data, interpreting and verifying data, testing hypotheses, and coming to conclusions. It seeks to develop independence on the part of pupils; they are encouraged to find things out for themselves by applying principles of the scientific method of inquiry. Through inquiry, pupils should *learn how to learn.* Inquiry stresses discovering things for oneself, because things learned in this way tend to be retained longer than if they are presented in other ways. Helen McCracken Carpenter puts it this way, "Inquiry is considered to be the process by which a child, more or less independently, comes to perceive relationships among factors in his environment or between ideas that previously had no meaningful connection."[3]

Travel agencies advertise that "getting there is half the fun." This is analogous to the inquiry process in that the inquiry or the search is both the means and the end. Inquiry carries its own reward, quite apart from what is learned in the way of content and skills. It is important to understand this aspect of the inquiry mode, particularly if one is concerned that certain subject matter be covered at certain grade levels. The purpose of inquiry is to provide training in the development of specific intellectual skills; not to cover specified elements of subject matter.

Role of the Teacher

Because inquiry is highly learner-centered, the role of the teacher is that of guide-stimulator; a facilitator who challenges pupils by helping them identify questions and problems, and guides their inquiry. The teacher provides an atmosphere that ensures freedom of exploration, good human relations, along with needed psychological support. Insofar as possible, the teacher tries to encourage in-

[3] Helen McCracken Carpenter, "The Role of Skills in Elementary Social Studies," *Social Education* **31** (March 1967), 220.

dependent habits of work. As needed, the teacher helps pupils find appropriate sources of information and is responsible for seeing that an adequate amount of appropriate instructional resources is available. The teacher restates and clarifies pupil responses; suggests alternative interpretations of data. The situation is structured to the extent that inquiry can actually take place. That is, pupils are not wholly free to wander about on their own "doing inquiry." The teacher does not stress seeking *the* right answer but helps pupils find and validate appropriate answers. The teacher must be particularly skillful in asking the kinds of questions that encourage inquiry.

Role of the Learner

The inquiry mode places pupils in a role that requires considerable initiative in finding things out for themselves. They must be actively engaged in their own learning. Naturally it is not expected that they will be left unguided by the teacher in inquiry searches, but it is expected that the pupils will be encouraged to ask questions, to challenge what is presented to them, and to think about alternatives. Within limits, the learners, with the help of the teacher, set their own goals for learning. Learners are free to explore broadly and are provided many opportunities for choice making. Learners are encouraged to range widely in their search for information. The role of the learner is not one of responding to questions posed by the teacher, but of asking questions and discovering answers to those questions through quests and searches. Carpenter, cited earlier, describes the role of the learner:

> Thus the inquiry approach views the learner as an active thinker—seeking, probing, processing data from his environment toward a variety of destinations along paths best suited to his own mental characteristics. It rejects passiveness as an ingredient of effective learning and the concept of the mind as a reservoir for the storage of knowledge presented through expository instruction directed toward a predetermined, closed end. The inquiry method seeks to avoid the dangers of rote memorization and verbalization as well as the hazard of fostering dependency in citizens as learners and thinkers. . . . The measure of ultimate success in education through inquiry lies in the degree to which the teacher becomes unnecessary as a guide.[4]

Use of Learning Resources

Contrary to what is often assumed, the inquiry mode does not require the use of specially designed instructional material. Any of the conventional resources, i.e., textbooks, supplementary books,

[4] Ibid., p. 220.

films, pictures, fieldtrips, resource persons, the library, can be used effectively for inquiry searches by the pupil. Indeed, the pupil is encouraged to use a broad range of data sources. In the inquiry mode, as in the case of the other modes as well, the question is not so much *what* learning resources are used as it is one of *how* the pupils make use of them. Inquiry necessitates the pupil's getting data in order to make interpretations. Presumably prior to the data search, the pupils and their teacher have raised questions and suggested hypotheses concerning the topic under study. The instructional resources are used to shed light on these queries. This suggests that there is no requirement that any particular learning resource, such as the textbook, for example, be "covered" in the traditional sense. Also, there is no prohibition against the use of the textbook as a data source in conducting inquiries.

Method of Evaluation

Evaluation of pupil learning in the inquiry mode focuses on the extent to which the learner is able to use the intellectual skills associated with this mode. Because the major purpose of inquiry is to generate and verify propositions, the pupil should not be evaluated on the ability to recall and reproduce known information. Often when an inquiry mode is used in teaching, the evaluation is based on the extent to which knowledge has been transmitted to the pupil. This is an obvious confusion of purposes in the instructional and evaluation phases of the learning process.

THE DEMONSTRATION MODE

Miss Krasny is introducing cursive writing to a third-grade class. She finds that a wholly verbal explanation of what is involved is an inadequate way to present this skill. Therefore, she makes use of the chalkboard. As she writes the letters on the board, she explains how each letter is formed. She points out to the children how they are to make specific curves, and how best to overcome any difficulties they might encounter. Miss Krasny says, "Now watch carefully how I make the top part of the letter. I will do it a few more times." This teacher is *showing, doing* and *telling.* These are the essential components of a demonstration mode of teaching.

Often demonstrations are developed on the spur of the moment when the teacher discovers the limitations of an explanation. Suddenly chalkboard erasers become ships in a harbor to clarify a social studies concept; pencils are grouped to illustrate a mathematics concept; a handkerchief is used to show a particular stitch. Such

DOES IT MATTER WHAT YOU CALL IT?

From the time of her first brush with the classroom as a student teacher, it was clear that Miss Marsh had a knack for asking questions that sparked the thinking of pupils. And they loved it! She would rarely come right out and tell the pupils much of anything. She would rephrase and clarify what they said and in the process provided a cue or two that led them in the direction of what they wanted and needed to know. Now in her seventh month as a contracted teacher, her classroom was something of a science laboratory, a museum, a "fixit" shop, an art gallery, and a learning resources center all wrapped into one. Her pupils seemed always to be talking interestedly about what was going on in the classroom, and would often ask each other questions about projects and activities. A colleague told her one day, "How lucky you are to have such a curious and interested group of children. They've changed so this past year."

"Yes, they do seem interested in what we are doing, and they learn a great deal on their own. But I must get back to school this summer and learn how to do inquiry," replied Miss Marsh.

1. What is there about this sketch that suggests that Miss Marsh is already making very effective use of the inquiry mode?
2. Why do you suppose Miss Marsh did not recognize as the inquiry mode that which she is doing?
3. What do you think of the comment of her colleague, to the effect that she is "lucky to have such a curious and interested group of children"?

improvised demonstrations are common in teaching. Whether they are preplanned or improvised, demonstrations can be very effective in communicating to learners.

It is, of course, obvious that demonstrations can be an important part of inquiry or expository strategies. That is, they may be and often are combined with other modes of teaching. For example, a teacher may be conducting an experiment on magnetism in a science lesson. The use of magnets and iron filings are used to illustrate certain magnetic principles. The teacher may conduct the experiment by asking inquiry-type questions of the pupils. "If I place this magnet under the glass with the iron filings on it, what, if anything, will happen to the iron filings? Why do you think so? Shall we try it and see?"

"Now then, why do the filings take this particular shape? What would happen if I turned the magnet around?"

Here we see the teacher demonstrating while conducting a lesson that is basically inquiry-oriented. The pupils are hypothesizing, applying prior knowledge to the present inquiry, and are testing their hunches through the demonstration procedure.

The same demonstration setting could be used in an expository mode. In this case, instead of asking questions the teacher would be telling the pupils what to expect, what to look for, what is likely to happen, and why things happened as they did. Such demonstrations are usually used with more mature learners. With young learners, most educators would prefer a more inquiry-oriented procedure, with greater direct pupil involvement.

Demonstration modes, therefore, can be used to serve at least two educational purposes. The first is that they can be used to illustrate and dramatically present ideas, concepts, and principles in an engaging way to learners. It is more interesting and provocative to see something happening than to listen to a verbal explanation alone.

PHOTO FOLIO

This teacher is using the demonstration mode to teach these youngsters how to operate a ditto machine. This is an excellent example of a situation in which a demonstration is especially effective. Imagine how complicated his explanation would necessarily be if he tried to teach this process through the use of a lecture mode! Or think of the damage that might be caused to the machine if pupils were expected to learn how to operate it through inquiry or discovery!

1. Identify three or four other learnings in the school curriculum that are best taught through the use of a demonstration mode.
2. Can you identify any disadvantages of demonstration, or "hands-on" teaching modes?

Even professional actors depend on props and staging to get their ideas across to their audiences. The chances of misunderstanding are minimized if the learner can see as well as hear what is being explained. Verbal explanations used alone are necessarily more abstract than when they are combined with a relevant demonstration.

But demonstrations provide values in addition to their facilitation of the learning of subject matter and content-related skills. Their second purpose is that they can develop the intellectual skills of the learner. This is especially the case in some aspects of science and social studies. The demonstration provides an opportunity for the learner to speculate on what will happen, how it will happen, and why it happens as it does. This is undoubtedly the greatest value in having young learners participate directly in demonstrations. By involving themselves in the demonstration, they are applying and practicing important reflective capabilities that become a permanent part of their intellectual equipment.

Assumptions

The demonstration mode may accept either portions of, or all of, the assumptions that apply to the inquiry or expository modes. Good teaching is perceived in part as good communication, and demonstration facilitates communication. It assumes that learning will be enhanced if the pupil is exposed to a functioning model or guide. This exposure will shape the learner's future behavior or attitudes, because he or she will imitate the demonstration model. Through observing a demonstration, the learner engages in sympathetic behavior by visualizing and observing, perhaps even verbalizing subvocally, what is happening, and this strengthens the achievement of the desired behavior. Even when the teacher is conducting the demonstration alone, without direct pupil involvement, the pupil may be participating intellectually. The learner conducts the demonstration mentally, following along with what the teacher is doing. Learning is further facilitated through demonstration by focusing the pupil's attention on the most critical aspects of what is to be learned. That is, a well-conducted demonstration is one in which the key ideas stand out clearly to the learner.

Major Purposes

The purpose of the demonstration mode is to show how something is to be done, how something happens or works, or how something should not be done. Demonstrations are used to improve communication. Many demonstrations are extensions of exposition; the only difference being that the demonstration stresses seeing in addition to hearing. Where there is the expectation of a failure to understand a verbal explanation, where there are frequent errors in learning, where the possibility of misunderstanding is high, the demonstration mode can help overcome these difficulties.

Role of the Teacher

The role of the teacher in the demonstration mode is to plan, organize, and execute the demonstration in such a way that the key ideas to be learned are made clear to the pupils. The demonstration must be factually and technically correct, and presented in a step by step sequence. The teacher must be able to show, by his or her own behavior in conducting the demonstration, what it is that is to be learned. If demonstrating a skill, the teacher must be able to perform it skillfully. If equipment is involved, such as a motion picture projector, maps and globes, or science laboratory materials, the teacher must of course have those ready, and know how to use them for the demonstration purposes. It is the teacher's responsibility to see that all pupils are able to see and hear the demonstration. In order for the demonstration mode to be used effectively, the teacher must be able to make the presentation in a dramatic way.

Role of the Learner
In this mode the role of the learner is obviously to observe, listen, and follow the demonstration carefully and attentively in order to understand what is being communicated. In some instances the learner may be required to participate in the demonstration, or to replicate it, using duplicate materials or equipment. Pupils may be asked to respond to questions at critical points in the demonstration, to provide feedback to the teacher regarding the extent of their understanding.

Use of Learning Resources
Instructional resources for this mode consist of whatever materials and equipment are needed to conduct the demonstration. The pupil may or may not use materials in addition to those used in the demonstration. Ordinarily there would be some type of follow-up to a demonstration, and for this purpose the conventional learning resources can be used. Appropriate use of these materials would be similar to uses described in the sections on expository or inquiry modes, depending on which the teacher prefers.

Method of Evaluation
Any evaluative procedure that measures the extent to which the purposes of the demonstration have been achieved will usually be satisfactory. A written test may be used, but discussion will often be more useful in detecting understanding or misconceptions. The learner may also be required to replicate the demonstration and explain it to someone else. The teacher should be observing pupil behavior, noting whether important points have been omitted, whether there is misunderstanding and confusion, whether the proper sequence has been followed, or whether any other deficiency in the pupil's learning will require further clarification or re-teaching.

THE ACTIVITY MODE

The activity mode is different from the other three teaching modes discussed in this chapter because it encompasses many aspects of living and learning in the classroom. It requires a commitment on the part of the teacher not only to a unique style of instructional presentation, but to a particular philosophy of education as well.

HOW WOULD YOU DO IT?

Mr. Wills is considered to be a very good first year teacher, but demonstrations rarely work well for him. Right in the middle of things he always discovers that he is missing some important piece of equipment or material needed to complete the demonstration. Once, he was going to demonstrate how a candle extinguishes itself when covered with a glass jar. He had the candles and the jars all right, but he forgot to bring matches to light the candles. Another time, he planned to use an overhead projector in his demonstration, only to find at the last minute that the electrical cord was not long enough to reach the outlet, and he did not have an extension cord. On another occasion he wanted to use slides in his demonstration and found that he had placed the slides in the carousel upside down and backwards. The same thing happened once when he was to show a filmstrip. Things like that always seemed to pop up at the last moment to surprise Mr. Wills and spoil his demonstration.

1. If you were Mr. Wills, what action would you take to avoid such unexpected contingencies?
2. How can this carelessness result in other more serious problems for Mr. Wills?

When the teacher decides to use the activity mode, the entire classroom life will need to be planned in accordance with the philosophy that undergirds this method of teaching.

With the apparent interest in open education and the attraction of the informal procedures of the British primary school to American educators, the activity mode of teaching experienced something of a comeback in recent years. The activity mode had its beginnings in some of the writings of John Dewey, but was operationalized by William H. Kilpatrick under the title "Project Method." Later, these ideas were incorporated in the "Unit Method" of teaching. The book, *Unit Teaching in the Elementary School,* by Hanna, Potter, and Hagaman, provides an excellent explication of the methodology associated with unit teaching.[5]

Procedures associated with unit teaching had been under heavy criticism for several years following World War II. Critics of educa-

[5] Lavone A. Hanna, Gladys L. Potter, and Neva Hagaman, *Unit Teaching in the Elementary School,* Rev. Ed. (New York: Holt, Rinehart & Winston, Inc., 1963). Published as a third edition as Lavone A. Hanna, Gladys L. Potter, and Robert W. Reynolds, *Dynamic Elementary Social Studies* (New York: Holt, Rinehart & Winston, Inc., 1973).

tion were unconvinced of the educational values of having pupils engage in activities such as building a boat or a model farm, presenting a play, simulating a legislative body, or role-playing community service personnel. These looked too much like play schools, and the European (especially Soviet) schools, with which American schools were often compared, were work schools. Then came the curriculum reform movements of the 1960's; these brought a more fundamental approach to education and an increased emphasis on teaching the disciplines *qua* disciplines. As a result of the educational climate of the times, the activity mode lay dormant for a fifteen-year period extending from the late 1950's into the 1970's. Today there is renewed interest in this methodology.

The activity mode can best be described as a set of strategies that involve pupils in learning by doing things that are, for the pupils, meaningfully related to the topic under study. To a large extent, pupils can initiate such activities themselves and assume much of the responsibility for their own learning. The activity mode is a counterbalance to the "book learnin'" stereotype that has dominated formal education for generations. Because it involves the pupils actively and intensely in doing-type projects, it gives the appearance to an outsider as being nonintellectual, and as attributing a low priority to fundamental learning and skills that have been traditionally viewed as important to elementary education.

Misuse of the activity mode may indeed occur in those cases where the teacher does not conduct it properly. It should be stressed, however, that those who support activity strategies claim that fundamental skills and abilities are learned *more* effectively than with traditional strategies, because they are presented and taught in settings that are meaningful and functional to the learners. That is, the child *needs* to read in order to find out something of importance. A pupil *has* to write because what he or she is doing needs a label or an explanation. The following example illustrates how learning from various areas of the curriculum are incorporated in the activity mode:

A group of nine- and ten-year-old-children in Fargo, North Dakota, turned a story they read together into a house-building experience. The story, about a class which built a clubhouse, prompted a similar idea—the class would build one of its own. Children greeted the idea with such enthusiasm that some visited a lumber yard and arranged to get some old plywood. They developed rather elaborate plans which involved measurement and geometry. An architect demonstrated model making, which the children then tried. They viewed a variety of films on house building. A tape-recorded lesson taught them about tools—the lever, plane, and gear. Retired carpenters in the community provided additional demonstrations. Individual children pursued many different interests in relation to the house-building project. They wrote letters telling others of their experiences. They engaged in individual projects involving Indian homes, termites, trees, creatures who live in trees, homes around the world, workers who build homes, old and modern tools, skyscrapers, doll houses, and, of course, they built the 10′ × 8′ × 6′ clubhouse. They gave a party to thank parents and others who had helped, and presented their construction to the younger children in the school for use during recess.

Students not only have chances to structure their own learning experiences through this type of approach, but they are also able to approach learning in a more unified way, without the narrow and sometimes artificial categories of mathematics, science, English, and social studies impinging on the breadth of their possible learning experience.

Another example of the breadth of experience inherent in a seemingly inconsequential experience involved a junk motor from a Renault automobile. The motor was brought into a fourth- and fifth-grade classroom, and several boys began to take it apart. Before they were through, they learned not only the principle of the internal combustion engine, but also developed a vocabulary of key words like piston, head, cylinder, carburetor, etc. (spelling); wrote several letters requesting information on the motor (language arts); had read parts of several repair manuals (reading); had learned about fractions, the metric system, and cubic measure (mathematics); had learned something about levers and gears, power, and gases (science); and had learned certain things about France, its people, and the Renault Automobile Company, which had developed a car that set an auto speed record (social studies). These boys were "turned on" to learning, and as John Lubbock has said: "The important thing is not so much that every child should be taught, as that every child should be given the wish to learn."[6]

Assumptions

Like the demonstration mode, the activity mode may accept portions of, or all of, the assumptions that apply to the inquiry or expository modes. Theoretically and philosophically, it is tied most closely to the inquiry mode. It assumes that children have certain natural drives, urges, and interests, and that they bring these to school with them. Rather than teaching a predetermined curriculum, the teacher explores the backgrounds and interests of the pupils, and out of this interaction, significant activities emerge. The activities selected should capitalize on these natural interests and inclinations of pupils. A rigid time schedule and the compartmentalizing of curriculum components are rejected because they run counter to the natural exploration of children. A rich and stimulating

[6]Vito Perrone and Lowell Thompson, "Social Studies in the Open Classroom," *Social Education* 36 (April 1972), 463. Reprinted with permission of the National Council for the Social Studies and the authors.

learning environment is essential in order that the child may have many opportunities to explore interests and to learn from direct experience. The teacher serves as more of a guide, advisor, and expeditor than as a director of learning. Learning takes place best in settings that encourage social interaction and cooperation—children working with each other. Cross-age grouping is encouraged because children learn from each other, thus older children can help younger ones to learn.

Major Purposes

The purpose of the activity mode is to teach pupils to become self-reliant, independent problem solvers, consistent with what is known about the nature of childhood. As such it involves the child directly and purposefully in learning. It is designed to create a high level of interest in learning that will become personalized and individualized for the learner. It seeks to construct situations in which the child can learn what he or she wants to know, rather than what the curriculum specifies. Like inquiry, the purpose of the activity mode is to stress the process of learning as opposed to specific subject matter and skills. Moreover, it is designed to capitalize on the social values of learning in school. Another of its purposes is to help pupils understand and appreciate the extent to which school learning is integrated, rather than separated into a variety of discrete subjects and skills, as is the case with the traditional curriculum.

Role of the Teacher

In the activity mode, the teacher's role can be described as that of setting the stage and providing the environment within which children can engage in learning activities in terms of their own interests, needs, capabilities, personalities, and motivations. This requires a warm and stress-free atmosphere. The teacher needs to structure and guide the explorations of pupils, but should do so without stifling the initiative of the learners. The teacher must be skillful and resourceful in being able to capitalize on the interests of children, and to convert such leads into viable learning activities. Also, the teacher must be imaginative in seeing the possibilities for school-related learnings in the activities that interest children. The teacher must provide a carefully selected assortment of learning materials for pupils to handle, use for construction, manipulate, experiment with, explore, and puzzle over. The teacher should guide and provide; he or she should not direct, require, or mandate. The teacher's role should be that of a catalyst to stimulate children's learning. In this environment, the teacher should be a learner, along with the pupils.

Role of the Learner

Here, more than in any of the other modes, we find the pupils centrally involved in the learning process. It is expected that the pupils will initiate activities and that they will assume responsibility for their own learning. The pupil's exercise of *initiative* and *responsibility* are basic to the role of the learner in the activity mode. Emphasis is on cooperation; therefore, pupils are expected to work harmoniously with others on their learning activities. The pupils are not expected to be seated at their desks completing assignments that have been prepared by the teacher. They will, instead, be working on a project or activity in which they are interested, and will be searching for answers to questions they themselves have raised. This necessitates a mind-set of curiosity and wonderment about the environment. Pupils are given great intellectual and physical freedom. They may move about, ask any question they choose, and consult whatever data sources would seem to be appropriate.

Use of Learning Resources

The activity mode necessitates a wide variety of assorted learning materials. These should include the conventional ones—books, films, pictures, maps, and so on; but also included should be others, such as electric motors, branding irons, animal pelts, traps, science equipment, carpenter's tools, historical artifacts, construction kits, art supplies, musical instruments, and so on. Indeed, anything at all that allows children to construct, explore, and manipulate might be a legitimate learning resource. A rich and responsive environment is essential to the success of the activity mode. Because much of the learning is self-directed, these resources will be used to satisfy pupil needs rather than to respond to requirements established by the teacher.

Method of Evaluation

Evaluation of pupil learning in the activity mode is more difficult than in the other modes because it may bear little similarity to traditional evaluative procedures. As in all cases, evaluation must be conducted in accord with the major purposes of the program. Therefore, in the activity mode the teacher would be looking for such things as the extent to which the children are involving themselves in their own learning; how well they are sharing, cooperating, and assuming responsibility; how well they are able to attack and puzzle through problems as they confront them; how well they are able to use the tools of learning, i.e., reading, writing, spelling, and speaking, in solving problems and meeting their needs; the extent to which their work products show evidence of growth and increasing maturity over time; and the extent to which they are overcoming their learning deficiencies. Because these programs are highly individualized, emphasis will be placed on progress in terms of prior status, rather than in terms of comparing pupil achievement with classmates or with nationally derived norms.

IT WON'T WORK IN MY SCHOOL

The elementary school in which Miss Blackwell teaches is in a low-income area, and many children come to school with obvious limitations in language development, life experience, work-study skills, and social skills. The school qualifies for additional funding beyond what would be allowed by the regular budget because it has been identified as one serving educationally disadvantaged children. Miss Blackwell is taking a late afternoon class in Curriculum and Teaching at a local university in order to fulfill her fifth-year requirements. The class is discussing open, informal approaches to teaching and has discussed in some detail the activity mode.

"As I see it," volunteers Miss Blackwell, "such procedures might work well in places where pupils have well-developed work-study skills and are socially responsible. They have to be able to be reasonably self-directed in their studies. The pupils I teach have none of those characteristics. It simply would not work in my school."

1. Criticize or defend Miss Blackwell's point of view.
2. Might it be argued that such an approach is precisely what is needed with such children?
3. What would be needed to ensure the success of the activity mode with such (or any) children?

SPECIFIC METHODS ASSOCIATED WITH VARIOUS MODES OF TEACHING

Inquiry Mode

asking questions	interpreting	testing hypotheses
stating hypotheses	classifying	observing
coming to conclusions	self-directed study	synthesizing

Expository Mode

lecture	explanation	audio recording
telling	panels	motion pictures
sound film strip	recitation	discussion

Demonstration Mode

experiments	simulation and games	fieldtrips
exhibits	modeling	

Activity Mode

role playing	preparing exhibits	processing
construction	dramatizing	group work

DEVELOPING RELATED COMPETENCIES

How Would You Do It?

In each of the following situations, what would be the appropriate teaching mode?

1. To show children clearly how to do something.
2. To involve children extensively in projects in an informal setting.
3. To stress the social values of education.
4. To get across specific knowledge or skills in the shortest amount of time.
5. To have children develop independent habits of investigation.
6. To transmit important elements of subject matter.

"The Longest Journey Begins with the First Step . . ."

Miss Jewel is a conscientious and competent beginning teacher who enjoys a reciprocal, good working relationship with her pupils. She is aware that she relies too heavily on expository teaching and would genuinely like to incorporate other modes of teaching in her work. But she is secure in what she is now doing, and things are going very well for her. Yet she would like to involve the children more directly and actively in classroom work, and would like to have them do more inquiring. Because of her personality and disposition, she will probably never be comfortable with the activity mode on a steady day-to-day basis. Nonetheless, she would like to break the formality associated with expository teaching. She is worried, however, that if she changes her teaching style, she will upset the rather comfortable and orderly pattern she has established in the room.

1. What might Miss Jewel do to preserve the security she feels presently and, at the same time, move toward the use of more varied approaches to her teaching?
2. What danger is there in Miss Jewel's foreclosing possibilities for continued professional growth if she does *not* modify her teaching?

Where Do YOU Fit into the Picture?

Imagine teacher behavior spread over a continuum ranging from the most traditional, formal, textbook-bound teacher at one end, to the most creative, imaginative, "open" teacher at the other. Few teachers would be placed at either end of this continuum. Most position themselves somewhere in between these extremes. Think about such a continuum in relationship to yourself and respond to the following questions:

1. Where do you think your teaching behavior belongs on this continuum?
2. Should a teacher's position on the continuum change with each year of teaching experience? If so, in what direction should it change?

FOR FURTHER PROFESSIONAL STUDY

Books

Hanna, Lavone A., Gladys L. Potter and Robert W. Reynolds. *Dynamic Elementary Social Studies.* New York: Holt, Rinehart and Winston, Inc., 1973.

Klingele, William E. *Teaching in Middle Schools.* Boston: Allyn & Bacon Books, Inc., 1979.

Petreshene, Susan S. *The Complete Guide To Learning Centers.* Palo Alto, California: Pendragon House, 1978.

Wlodkowski, Raymond J. *Motivation and Teaching: A Practical Guide.* Washington, D.C.: National Education Association, 1978.

Periodicals

Kounin, Jacob S. and Lawrence W. Sherman. "School Environments As Behavior Settings." *Theory Into Practice* (June 1979), 145–151.

Learning (December 1979). *Learning* magazine's third "Annual Idea Bonanza." This issue contains a great many practical classroom ideas, teaching activities, learning games, and construction models from several curriculum areas, and suggestions include all modes of teaching.

5

Instructional Objectives

THE QUALIFIED AND COMPETENT TEACHER . . .

1. Understands the role of educational goals and instructional objectives in the learning and instruction process.
2. Is familiar with various types of instructional objectives and their purposes.
3. Is able to write behavioral objectives.
4. Understands the nature and interdependence of cognitive, affective, and psychomotor learner outcomes.
5. Recognizes the importance of sequencing instructional objectives according to sound educational principles.
6. Is sensitive to the need to select goals and objectives that are related and relevant to the needs, abilities, and interests of pupils.

Performance Criteria

As a result of the serious study of this chapter, the student should be able to . . .

1. Distinguish between educational goals and instructional objectives.
2. Cite examples of the major types of instructional objectives.
3. Recognize the three elements of a behavioral objective.
4. Write a behavioral objective.
5. Identify and prepare examples of instructional objectives in the cognitive, affective, and psychomotor areas.
6. Recognize and prepare a list of instructional objectives based on a psychological sequence.

Educational research has established the fact that achievement is enhanced in classrooms where children can perceive a sense of direction for learning. These classrooms are characterized by purposeful teaching that establishes the learner outcomes ahead of time. Such teaching is based on directional statements that identify the expected learner outcomes, establish purposes, and stipulate levels of achievement. Failure to provide these directions reduces the productivity of the learning environment for pupils. Classroom management and teaching blend together as a unified process when instructional objectives provide goal clarity for children. The qualified and competent teacher provides for this in the form of directional statements expressed as either educational or instructional objectives.

An educational goal* is a general statement of a desired educational outcome for pupils. "To develop an understanding and appreciation of our cultural heritage," "To develop literacy in oral and written English," "To appreciate the value of literature, music, and art," are examples. They state a goal—a desired outcome, in the broadest sense of these words. Educational goals are achieved through learning activities that result from the more specific directional statements contained in instructional objectives.

An instructional objective describes the specific learner outcome, the behavior required to perform it, and determines the means for measuring or evaluating it. The level of specificity of the language is dependent on the type of objective that is used as a directional statement. Instructional objectives may be classified in various ways. These will be described later in this chapter.

The relationship of educational goals and instructional objectives can be explained further: the former tend to identify generalized outcomes that are to be realized over an extended period of time. For example, a goal designed to enable children "to develop literacy in oral and written English" is one that requires years of learning before it is fully achieved, because the skill(s) are developmental. The educational goal, "to acquire an understanding and appreciation of our cultural heritage," also requires an extended period of time to understand the significance of its meaning.

Instructional objectives have an immediate intent. They also specify the learning outcome more sharply than do educational goals. Thus, the educational goal, "to develop literacy in oral and written English," when translated into an instructional objective for children at the second grade level, might be stated: "Children will increase their awareness of sentence structure by using the

*Sometimes referred to as an "educational objective" in the literature.

subject, verb, and object correctly in oral and written forms of expressions."

Even though the terms *goals* and *objectives* are sometimes used interchangeably in educational literature, this practice fails to acknowledge the proper relationship between educational goals and instructional objectives. Educational goals ordinarily reflect a synthesis of the expressed ideas or values of a given society or cultural group. They are usually normative in this respect, in that they reflect the prevailing ideas and values considered to be the most desirable by the society or cultural group. As such, they do not account for the variability that teachers encounter in specific classroom situations. To be made operational, these broad general statements must be translated into instructional objectives that are relevant to the specific situation. Both types of statements serve the critical purpose of providing the means for teachers to conceptualize the direction and shape of learning activities for pupils.

RATIONALE FOR USING INSTRUCTIONAL OBJECTIVES

Teachers who understand the relationship of instructional objectives and quality instruction recognize the need to:

1. Identify the learner outcome.
2. Establish purposes.
3. Provide direction for learner achievement.
4. Determine means to assess outcomes.

It is important that the teacher prepare instructional objectives that reflect the underlying educational goals. The latter are usually found in a variety of sources such as (1) state and local curriculum guides, (2) teacher's manuals that accompany children's textbooks in the various subject fields, and (3) statements by national professional groups. The beginning teacher should be aware of these sources. At the present time there is a movement to collect, collate, and disseminate instructional objectives on a national basis. This practice is designed to encourage teachers to make greater use of instructional objectives that contain sufficient specificity to permit the measurement of the desired learner outcomes. The movement is a reflection of the thrust for accountability in education. It is based in part on the assumption that the best criterion for evaluating the teacher's performance is to determine whether or not the pupils are learning. Educational literature frequently contains references to the "evaluation of the product," another way of describing this approach to accountability.

The accountability movement, with its stress on "evaluating the product," has placed a high priority on the use of instructional objectives that, stated in behavioral terms, permit measurement of learner outcomes.* As a result, this type of instructional objective has been given high visibility in educational circles. However, experienced teachers realize the importance of providing children with a variety of learning experiences. If instructional objectives are limited to those that restrict learning to "what can be measured," the richness which a variety of learning activities brings to children would be lost. Further, if classroom teachers develop the habit of selecting instructional objectives from a ready-made list, composed in another setting, the spontaneity and the capacity to meet the needs, abilities, and interests of a particular group of pupils would be greatly reduced.

We believe that instructional objectives should be prepared by the classroom teacher. Referring to other sources containing examples of instructional objectives may well be desirable when it is done to provide variety and enrichment. But when a ready-made list is followed exclusively, teaching and learning might become a "cook book" activity. The popularity of behavioral objectives is based on assumptions other than the need to evaluate teaching performance. These assumptions will be described in the section dealing with this type of objectives.

Purposes of Objectives

Teachers prepare objectives to serve a variety of purposes in education. They are essential to:

1. The development of unit plans and daily lessons based on learner outcomes.
2. The individualization of instruction based on expected learner outcomes that are specific to particular children.
3. The development of effective study habits.
4. The development of group socialization skills.
5. Evaluation of pupil growth and development.
6. Self-evaluation by the teacher.

Each of these purposes contributes to the development of a program of learning and instruction that is based on significant rather

*These objectives are commonly referred to as *behavioral objectives*.

than trivial learner outcomes. The preparation, implementation, and evaluation of objectives constitute a "sorting out" process that results in the continual improvement of the quality of learning and instruction.

Types of Instructional Objectives

There are several ways to classify instructional objectives. One way is to refer to them as "general" or "specific" statements of expected learner outcomes. This particular dualism has prompted the recent emphasis on so-called behavioral objectives. Proponents of specificity contend that statements of specific, concrete, and measurable learner outcomes are necessary to provide quality learning and instruction. Advocates of generality insist that specific statements reduce the range of possible learner outcomes to those that lend themselves to measurement. They conclude that learner outcomes based on higher-order learning are likely to be eliminated because they frequently do not lend themselves to precise measurement.

A second classification is based on "behavioral" and "nonbehavioral" types of instructional objectives. The first, a "behavioral" objective, is focused on specific, observable or measurable gains in pupil learning. A behavioral objective also establishes a minimal level of attainment for deciding whether or not the desired learning has been achieved. Nonbehavioral objectives, on the other hand, do not contain this specificity.

A behavioral objective may describe the mediating conditions under which the behavior is to be achieved, as well as provide the techniques or procedures for determining whether or not a certain level of attainment has occurred. Thus, the criteria of generality and specificity of the particular language used in the statement of objectives is imposed on this classification system. An example of each type follows.

EXAMPLE 1. A BEHAVIORAL OBJECTIVE

Given a worksheet following a lesson on subtraction, pupils will be able to rename and subtract numbers named by three-place numerals at the rate of two problems a minute with 80 per cent accuracy.

EXAMPLE 2. A NONBEHAVIORAL OBJECTIVE

Following a lesson on subtraction, the pupil will know how to rename and subtract numbers named by three-place numerals.

The use of the term *behavioral* is confusing to many beginners because they tend to view any statement of an expected learner outcome to be based on one form of behavior or another. The behavior may be somewhat vague, as in the case of the objective designed to enable the pupil to "know how to rename and subtract numbers named by three-place numerals." Nevertheless, the infinitive "to know" certainly implies a behavior. The essence of the distinction between a nonbehavioral and a behavioral objective seems to require a more careful examination in order to determine the difference.

Many teachers strongly oppose the use of behavioral objectives because they believe they are an expression of behaviorism. They insist there is much learning that does not result in overt pupil behavior. These are the more subtle forms of learning that stem from feelings and appreciations, and are referred to as *affective* learning. On a philosophical level, a conceptual dualism has resulted from the attention to behavioral objectives. This may be described as a behavioristic-humanistic dualism. Humanistic educators argue that the more important learning behaviors—those on the higher cognitive levels, and especially those that reside in the area of feelings and attitudes—cannot be stated behaviorally.

On the other side of the debate are those educators who subscribe to E. L. Thorndike's statement, made over sixty years ago, to the effect that:

> Whatever exists at all exists in some amount. To know it thoroughly involves knowing its quantity as well as its quality. Education is concerned with changes in human beings; a change is a difference between two conditions; each of these conditions is known to us only by the products produced by it—things made, words spoken, acts performed, and the like. To measure any of these products means to define its amount in some way so that competent persons will know how large it is, better than they would without measurement.[1]

Thorndike, a pioneer in educational psychology, insisted that objectives must be validated through the measurement of learner outcomes. His views were based on a theory of learning that regarded the learning process as the forming of bonds between specific stimuli and observable responses. This theory has often been refined and re-adapted since Thorndike's time. The most recent adaptation has resulted from a combination of several forces: instructional technology and programmed instruction; the accountability movement;

[1] E. L. Thorndike, "The Nature, Purposes, and General Methods of Measurements of Educational Products." The Seventeenth Yearbook of the National Society for the Study of Education, Part II, *The Measurement of Educational Products* (Bloomington, Ill.: Public School Publishing Company, 1918), Chap. 2, p. 16.

and the operant conditioning theory supported by B. F. Skinner's assumptions about learning. Skinner defines teaching "as an arrangement of contingencies of reinforcement under which behavior changes."[2] Learning, then, becomes divided into a sufficient number of very small steps, where reinforcement is dependent upon the accomplishment of each small step. Skinner has a wide following. There are educators who believe his theory is highly appropriate in the field of special education devoted to children who have problems or disabilities that impede learning. There are other educators who insist his theory is inappropriate for the instruction of all children. They argue that many pupils are capable of learning without the need for reinforcement at every step of the way.

Still other educators criticize Skinner's assumptions about learning on the grounds that they are based on an atomistic and dehumanized interpretation of human nature.

It seems unfortunate that this movement, which could result in a sharpening of the educational process through more precise attention to its outcomes, finds authorities polarized in their views concerning it. We believe there is a place for both the humanistic and behavioristic approaches to goal setting. It can be argued that learning has taken place when there is, on the part of the learner, a change in personal meaning. This change in personal meaning may or may not be reflected in a change in observable behavior. Whenever practicable, of course, an observable change in behavior should be sought. Circumstances may dictate the particular approach best suited to enhance learning. Because instructional objectives provide the directional statements necessary to facilitate and to assess learning, it follows that they must reflect variety and balance. This is best accomplished by giving priority to the nature of the expected learning prior to making a decision as to which type of instructional objective would be most appropriate.

WRITING BEHAVIORAL OBJECTIVES

A behavioral objective does not necessarily possess an inherent quality that makes it better than a nonbehavioral objective. What actually makes the difference is the purpose each is supposed to serve. Because this may best be determined by the nature of the desired learner outcome, the argument about which type of objective is superior is, at best, an unproductive exercise. Learner outcomes, even though interrelated, are usually classified according

[2] B. F. Skinner, *The Technology of Teaching* (New York: Appleton-Century-Crofts, 1968), p. 113.

to three broad areas of knowledge and skills: (1) cognitive, (2) affective, and (3) psychomotor.

Instructional objectives, written in behavioral language, specify learner outcomes for a lesson to the point that the teacher is able to determine quickly whether to:

1. reteach the lesson, or to
2. extend the learning from the lesson through additional practice activities, or to
3. progress to more difficult learning tasks.

Because objectives, written behaviorally, provide the means for assessing selected learner outcomes, the teacher uses them when the need arises. There are many learner outcomes, however, that do not lend themselves to this approach because some are too abstract, and therefore unmeasurable.

What Is a Behavioral Objective?

The three elements included in behavioral objectives are (1) the expected learner behavior is identified; (2) the condition under which the behavior is to occur is described; and (3) the acceptable level or standard for the expected learner behavior is specified.

The following is an example of a behavioral objective containing these three elements:

On a science quiz containing 20 examples, pupils will differentiate between descriptions of physical and chemical changes, with 80 per cent accuracy.

DEVELOPING RELATED COMPETENCIES*

Exercise One

From the above example, write the parts of this objective that contain (1) the expected learner behavior, (2) the condition, (3) the acceptable level of achievement.

1. ______________________________
2. ______________________________
3. ______________________________

---

*Because of the nature of the subject matter of this chapter, "Related Competencies" are interspersed rather than placed at the end of the chapter.

LET'S CHECK YOUR RESPONSES TO EXERCISE ONE

Here Are the Answers

1. pupils will differentiate between physical and chemical changes
2. On a science quiz containing 20 examples
3. with 80 per cent accuracy

The following statements are additional examples of behavioral objectives. Please read each carefully.

1. Given a spelling list of 20 words, pupils will correctly spell 80 per cent of the words.
2. After reading the story, "The Tallest Tree," pupils will write the story in their own words, including a minimum of five events.
3. During class discussion, pupils will ask permission before speaking by raising their hands.
4. In response to a lesson on creative writing, children will produce a written product of their own choosing and design.
5. After a demonstration of manuscript writing, pupils will write the letter *a* in conformance with the specifications presented by the teacher.

DEVELOPING RELATED COMPETENCIES

Exercise Two

Analyze each of the preceding examples by UNDERLINING the part of each statement that contains (1) the expected learner behavior with a single line, and (2) the acceptable level of achievement with *a double line.*

HOW WELL DID YOU DO WITH EXERCISE TWO?

Here Are the Correct Responses.

1. will correctly spell 80 *per cent of the words*
2. will write the story in their own words, *including a minimum of five events*
3. will ask permission before speaking *by raising their hands*
4. will produce a written product *of their own choosing and design*
5. will write the letter a *in conformance with the specifications presented by the teacher*

The conditions under which the expected learner behaviors were to be achieved in the five examples also deserve attention because they provide the frame of reference in which measurement occurs. Note that in number 1, it is a spelling list of twenty words; in 2, the behavior is to occur after reading a story; in 3, it is to occur during a class discussion; in 4, the expected behavior is in response to a lesson on creative writing; in 5, it follows a demonstration of manuscript writing.

Frequently the condition begins with the word "given." For example:

Given a spelling list of 20 words, pupils will . . .
Given a class dictionary, the pupil will . . .
Given a physical map of North America, the child . . .
Given a small-group activity, pupils will . . .
Given a bar graph of the population of the states in the Intermontane region, pupils will . . .

The condition can also set parameters that are either precise or general. For example:

. . . recite from memory . . .
. . . recite from an open book . . .
. . . use an encyclopedia . . .
. . . use any available reference . . .
. . . within a ten minute time period . . .
. . . within no set time limit . . .

The condition, as an element of a behavioral objective, states the limits within which children are to demonstrate their achievement of the desired learning.

DEVELOPING RELATED COMPETENCIES

Exercise Three

Let's see how good you are at identifying the missing elements in the following statements:

1. After reading the chapter, "The Planet Earth," the pupil will summarize it in writing.
2. Pupils will use the dictionary.
3. Following a science lesson, the pupil will demonstrate that a current-carrying wire acts like a magnet.
4. The child gives evidence of his/her ability to solve correctly the following equations:

$$m + 13 = 46$$
$$27 + m = 50$$
$$m - 20 = 50$$
$$40 - m = 16$$

5. Pupils will demonstrate their acceptance of other ethnic groups.

Behavioral objectives take on their precision mainly through the use of language that describes overt, observable behavior. For this reason the verbs used in writing behavioral objectives are often referred to as *action* verbs.

The description of the expected learner behavior is so clearly stated that whether or not the learner has achieved the objective can easily be determined by a qualified observer. A behavioral objective is made even more precise, of course, by adding the acceptable level or standard for the expected behavior. The teacher should have available a list of action verbs that have proven useful in writing behavioral objectives.

CHECK YOUR RESPONSES TO EXERCISE THREE

Missing Elements:

1. acceptable level of behavior
2. condition, acceptable level of behavior
3. acceptable level of behavior
4. condition
5. condition, acceptable level of behavior

DEVELOPING RELATED COMPETENCIES

Exercise Four

A verb is a verb is a verb, or is it?

Which of the words in the following list meets the criteria of denoting an observable behavior?

To understand	To solve
To locate	To read
To appreciate	To fully appreciate
To write	To compare
To listen	To believe
To recall	To list
To know	To use

(You've got the idea, so check your own answers.)

Exercise Five

Now that you have the idea, practice it by writing five behavioral objectives that contain the three essential elements.

(Compare your statements with those written by your colleagues.)

Because there are learner outcomes that do not lend themselves to the precise format used for behavioral objectives, the following sections will provide the reader with other forms of instructional objectives.

IMPORTANT

If you wish to learn more about how to write behavioral objectives, consult the references listed at the end of this chapter.

INSTRUCTIONAL OBJECTIVES IN THE BROAD AREAS OF LEARNER OUTCOMES

The best known of several efforts to classify instructional objectives according to the nature of expected learner outcomes is that of Bloom, Krathwohl, and their associates who have provided educators with two taxonomies of educational objectives.[3] The taxonomies have given educators a system that provides a frame of reference for communicating about learner outcomes. Bloom, Krathwohl, and their colleagues originally classified instructional objectives according to three basic domains: (1) the cognitive domain, based on the recall or recognition of knowledge and the development of intellectual skills; (2) the affective domain, based on a hierarchy of interests, attitudes, appreciations, and values; and (3) the psychomotor domain, based on a variety of learning activities that are dependent on the acquisition of attendant manipulative or motor skills.

Two of the three taxonomies—the cognitive and the affective domains—have been widely used since their publication. A taxonomy for the psychomotor domain was authored by Harrow at a later date.[4] Bloom, Krathwohl, and associates discovered in their early research that the preponderance of instructional objectives reflected in the literature was based on cognitive and affective behaviors, but only a few dealt with psychomotor learner outcomes. Priority was placed on the development of the first two—the cognitive and the affective domains.

The developers of the taxonomies acknowledged that it is difficult to separate cognitive and affective behaviors. Their decision to classify the behaviors according to two separate domains was based on the assumption that educators do make distinctions between the two in developing instructional objectives. They assumed, therefore,

[3]Benjamin S. Bloom, ed., *Taxonomy of Educational Objectives, Handbook I: Cognitive Domain* (New York: David McKay Co., Inc., 1956). Also David R. Krathwohl, Benjamin S. Bloom, and Bertram B. Masia, *Taxonomy of Educational Objectives, Handbook II: Affective Domain* (New York: David McKay Co., Inc., 1964).

[4]Anita J. Harrow, *A Taxonomy of the Psychomotor Domain* (New York: David McKay Co., Inc., 1972).

that the applicability of the taxonomies would be greater by separating them.

In using the taxonomies to develop learner outcomes, the teacher should be very careful to avoid isolating cognitive, affective, and psychomotor behaviors from each other. It is perhaps unfortunate that the term *domain* is used, because it implies a separation of spheres of activity. But these separate classifications are very useful for the development of a broad range of learner behaviors in each. As such, the taxonomies are excellent tools for curriculum development and evaluation.

On the classroom level, the teacher must remember that planning for learning and instruction should be based on the recognition that these domains are interdependent in terms of the learner's needs, abilities, and interests. The pupil who is asked to reproduce a picture or a map is performing a psychomotor task; however, the quality of performance is dependent on cognitive and affective behaviors as well—knowledge of maps and the extent of interest. Children who have poor muscular coordination may learn a particular psychomotor activity but their attitude toward it may remain forever negative unless they have a teacher who understands the interdependence of these areas of learning. Many adults seem to have a fear of mathematics, which originated early in their school life. Evidently their teachers did not sufficiently understand the importance of the interdependence of the affective and cognitive areas of learning to build their confidence and self-esteem in learning mathematics. There are hundreds of examples that could be cited to illustrate the interdependence of the three so-called domains. Suffice it to say that instructional objectives should reflect a balance of the three.

Developing Objectives for Cognitive Learner Outcomes

Bloom's taxonomy of cognitive objectives serves a very useful purpose in enabling teachers to have children develop a wide range of behavior.[5] The taxonomy includes six major categories of behavior, proceeding from low to high in terms of complexity. The system is based on the assumption that the development of the pupil's intellectual skills and abilities is dependent on a firm knowledge base. For example, the domain begins with simple knowledge outcomes and then proceeds through the increasingly complex levels of comprehension, application, analysis, synthesis, and evaluation.

Even without knowledge of this theoretical work, classroom

[5] For a comprehensive application of the taxonomy, the reader should consult: Benjamin S. Bloom, op. cit.

teachers, on a commonsense or intuitive level, prepare objectives designed to enable pupils to develop the ability to gain, apply, analyze, and evaluate information.

The following instructional objectives are cited as examples of how a wide range of cognitive behaviors can be developed.

EXAMPLES

Gaining Information

1. After reading a chapter on why European settlers came to the English colonies, pupils will recall four of the five major reasons given.

Ability to Apply

2. The pupil can apply the rules developed by the class for good citizenship by following them on the playground during free activities.

Ability to Analyze

3. On a science quiz containing 20 examples, pupils will differentiate between descriptions of physical and chemical changes, with 80 per cent accuracy.

Ability to Evaluate

4. Pupils will view a television program based on a book by Laura Ingalls Wilder and judge it according to criteria established by the class as to its authenticity in the portrayal of characters and its consistency of plot.

In the broad area of cognitive behaviors, the most important thing for the beginning teacher to remember in planning for learner outcomes is to provide pupils with opportunities to acquire intellectual skills and abilities that extend beyond the acquisition of knowledge. One of the perennial criticisms of teaching is based on the assertion that children are bored with spending their time in memorizing and recalling facts. This is unfortunate, because the teacher has countless opportunities to provide children with learning activities that are intellectually challenging and interesting to them. The careful development and sequencing of questions, and the use of the inquiry and activity modes of teaching, are admirably suited to the development of these higher-order levels of cognitive behaviors. The interdependence of the cognitive and affective areas of learner outcomes is actualized by the teacher who, during the course of the school year, prepares instructional objectives that include a sampling of various dimensions of cognitive behaviors. It is obvious that not all pupils will be capable of acquiring cognitive behaviors on the higher levels at the same time. There may even be a few children in the typical classroom who will not get beyond the literal level of comprehension during the year. But certainly the majority of children are capable of doing so when the teacher is skillful in varying instruction to accommodate pupil differences.

DEVELOPING RELATED COMPETENCIES

Exercise Six

Practice what you have just learned by . . . writing instructional objectives designed to enable pupils to develop ability in gaining, applying, analyzing, and evaluating information. If you are teaching, select a subject field or a topic you can use in the classroom.

Developing Objectives for Affective Behaviors

Krathwohl, et al., in the introduction to the *Taxonomy of Educational Objectives* for the affective domain write, ". . . there still persists an implicit belief that if cognitive objectives are developed, there will be a corresponding development of appropriate affective behaviors."[6]

They hasten to say that research evidence does not support such a belief. On the contrary:

> The evidence suggests that affective behaviors develop when appropriate learning experiences are provided for students much the same as cognitive behaviors develop from appropriate learning experiences.[7]

The recent emphasis on cognitive learning at the expense of other learner outcomes gives current credibility to these statements. Even though cognitive, affective, and psychomotor behaviors are interdependent, they have not been treated as such in many elementary schools in this nation. During the period commencing with the Russian successes in outer space in the late 1950's, the national preoccupation has been with the cultivation of cognitive development—particularly in mathematics and science. The social studies programs during this period began to shift from what was an overemphasis on cognitive behaviors to an increased attention on affective growth and development in pupils. More recently, increased attention is being given to moral education and the attendant skills of valuing. The following discussion is based on the assumption that beginning teachers need to be competent in developing instructional objectives that promote affective growth and development in children. Krathwohl has identified five major categories of affective behaviors: re-

[6] Krathwohl, et al., op. cit., p. 20.
[7] Loc. cit.

ceiving, responding, valuing, organizing, and characterization by a value or a value complex.[8] These, with their subcategories, constitute a hierarchical ordering, as was the case with the cognitive domain.

Teachers in the elementary school are primarily concerned with the first two levels of affective behavior in the learning and instruction of children as they can be developed over a relatively short

[8] For a comprehensive application of the taxonomy, the reader should consult: Krathwohl, et al., op. cit.

PHOTO FOLIO

In this photograph a child is shown checking out a book to another pupil. The school librarian believes that educational goals should foster the development of responsibility in pupils. Elementary schools that encourage pupils to develop responsibility for themselves and others are making important contributions to citizenship education. The opportunity to be a library helper has probably been earned by this pupil. Children respond positively to the idea that school-helper assignments are privileges and eagerly work to deserve them.

1. Develop an educational goal statement that is based on some aspect of citizenship education.
2. In your school observations, identify the kinds of school-helper assignments that are performed by pupils.
3. Suggest other possibilities for school-helper assignments.

period of time. Receiving and responding are interwoven so closely with cognitive and psychomotor outcomes that they ought to be given constant attention by the teacher. The remaining three behaviors—valuing, organization, and characterization—require a longer time for development.

The following statements provide examples of instructional objectives designed to promote affective behaviors:

EXAMPLES

1. Following the teacher's discussion about the need for assistance

in taking care of the classroom materials and room equipment, pupils will volunteer to assist.

2. Following a dramatization of a problem created by children arguing over who the best pupil is, the child will volunteer that it was a foolish thing to do, and will suggest ways to settle it rationally.
3. As a result of teacher-pupil discussions on behavior in the school cafeteria, pupils will voluntarily demonstrate positive behavior during the lunch hour.
4. As a result of role-playing episodes based on the use of the classroom learning centers, pupils will respond by exhibiting the demonstrated behavior.

DEVELOPING RELATED COMPETENCIES

Exercise Seven

Write examples of instructional objectives designed to promote affective behaviors. Discuss your product with a colleague.

Affective education is not intended to indoctrinate pupils with a single point of view on the "correct belief." Rather, it is intended to produce enlightened citizens who have an open mind about controversial issues. Instructional objectives that promote affective behaviors are necessary to provide learning activities that nurture their development. Learning and instruction based on the examination of attitudes, beliefs, and values is an exciting adventure for pupils. Knowledge and skill in strategies for affective growth are prerequisites for qualified and competent teaching.

Developing Objectives for Psychomotor Behaviors

Psychomotor objectives are those that emphasize a muscular or motor skill. They frequently include the manipulation of objects or materials that require psychomotor coordination. They ordinarily contain concomitant aspects of cognitive and affective learning, because a psychomotor behavior that is intended as a learner outcome would include knowledge and feeling about what is to be accomplished. The following instructional objective illustrates this relationship:

After a demonstration of manuscript writing, pupils will write the letter "*a*" in conformity with the specifications presented by the teacher.

Certainly the successful achievement of the expected learner behavior in this objective is based on the pupil's neuromuscular coordination. At the same time, the outcome is based on the pupil's knowledge of the process (cognitive) and the willingness to receive instructions and attend to the writing of the letter "*a*" (an affective behavior).

Instructional objectives that have psychomotor skills as expected learner behaviors are frequently used in the elementary-school program. The areas of music, art, physical education, and writing are examples where psychomotor development is critical to achievement. Because considerable attention has already been given to the classification and writing of instructional objectives, exercises based on the psychomotor areas will not be included. The interdependence of the three domains is nowhere more clearly evident than in psychomotor development. Experienced teachers recognize when to plan for learner outcomes that emphasize essentially psychomotor development. They develop this skill by carefully observing the behavior of their pupils. This is a skill that should be acquired early, to enable the teacher to vary more equitably the expected learner outcomes across the three broad areas of cognitive, affective, and psychomotor development.

SEQUENCING INSTRUCTIONAL OBJECTIVES

So far we have emphasized that teachers should (1) be able to distinguish between educational goals and instructional objectives, (2) know the major types of instructional objectives, (3) be able to write behavioral objectives, and (4) understand the nature and interdependence of cognitive, affective, and psychomotor learner outcomes.

An equally important competence consists of effectively sequencing instructional objectives.

Sequencing As Related to Educational Goals and Instructional Objectives

As noted at the beginning of this chapter, there are two ways of stating objectives as expected learner outcomes. One is to provide an educational goal to identify a learner outcome that requires an extended period of time to accomplish. The second is to state an instructional objective that specifies a behavior to be achieved on a short-time basis—at the end of a single lesson or the conclusion of a unit of work. Sequencing requires that there be a relationship between these two types of statements, one that provides direction and continuity leading to the long-range achievement of expected learner outcomes.

Rationale for Sequencing Instructional Objectives

There are several ways to sequence instructional objectives. Those most commonly used are designed to order objectives according to (1) areas of the curriculum, (2) broad areas of learner behaviors—cognitive, affective, psychomotor, and (3) levels of skill development. The basic rationale for the sequencing of instructional objectives lies in the assumption that pupils learn better when they are given a psychological set that provides a structure for what they are expected to achieve. Once the general set has been established, instructional objectives follow that sequence the learner outcomes on a simple-to-complex continuum, culminating in the expectation that the child can perform the expected behavior on a sophisticated level. This is referred to as a *psychological approach.* Its meaning is amplified in the following section.

Sequencing Objectives According to a Curricular Area

The following study guide contains an example of an educational goal with a psychological sequence of seven instructional objectives related to it.

A STUDY GUIDE BASED ON AN EXAMPLE OF . . .

an educational goal for pupils in the language arts, with related instructional objectives.

Educational Goal:	"To understand the structure of a sentence."
Related Instructional Objectives:	The child will develop an awareness of the importance of the sentence by telling a story using complete sentences.

(Objectives have been abbreviated to include only the expected learner-outcome element.)

The pupil will demonstrate awareness of sentence structure by writing a complete sentence.

The pupil will identify the subject, verb, and object in sentence form.

The child will use the subject, verb, and object correctly, in written sentence form.

The pupil will identify simple adjectives, adverbs, and prepositional phrases in sentence form.

The child will use simple adjectives, adverbs, and prepositional phrases in sentence form.

The pupil will independently use correct sentence structure in daily oral and written work.

Let us analyze the characteristics of the preceding example from the language arts:

1. Instructional objectives are sequenced within a curricular area.
2. The educational goal and its related instructional objectives are shown.
3. The instructional objectives begin with expected learner outcomes that provide a psychological set for sentence structure, by having pupils become aware of sentences in their daily usage.
4. The instructional objectives follow a "simple to complex" ordering of learner outcomes.
5. The final expected learner outcome is based on the pupils' using correct sentence structure in their daily work.

No doubt there would be numerous lessons dealing with each of the expected learner outcomes before they would be achieved. At the end of the primary grades, pupil achievement would range across the entire spectrum of expected learner outcomes included in the foregoing example. Most of the children, however, would have achieved, on all of them, at the minimal level of acceptable performance.

Sequencing Objectives According to a Broad Area of Learner Outcomes

The following examples of instructional objectives are related to the educational goal, "To develop an understanding of the major varieties of evergreen trees in the Pacific Northwest, and why they are native to this area." They are based on developing learner outcomes from a broad area of cognitive learning, encompassing science, geography, and history, and are presented here in a "scrambled" sequence.[9]

1. The pupil will be able to draw a simple illustration showing the basic differences between a Douglas fir and a pine tree.
2. The pupil will write a report comparing the prehistoric vegetation and the present-day vegetation of the Northwest, in order to deduce why changes occurred.
3. Following a teacher-directed discussion of the major varieties of evergreen trees in the Northwest and why they are native to this area, the child will name six varieties.
4. The child will propose an original theory of how the first Douglas fir tree came to this area. The theory must stand the tests of (a) feasibility and (b) scientific analysis.
5. The child will judge the theory based on criteria provided by the teacher and a reference book on the topic.
6. The pupil will write a paper explaining why the palm tree does not thrive naturally in the Pacific Northwest. At least three scientific explanations will be given and documented.

DEVELOPING RELATED COMPETENCIES

Exercise Eight

By referring to the preceding six instructional objectives, unscramble them by ordering them in a psychological sequence. This is a good opportunity for you to see how much you remember about levels of complexity of intellectual skills and abilities in cognitive learner outcomes.

CHECK YOUR RESPONSES TO . . .

Exercise Eight

Objective 1.	Second	Objective 4.	Fifth
Objective 2.	Fourth	Objective 5.	Sixth
Objective 3.	First	Objective 6.	Third

[9] From a Learning Module, *Using Instructional Objectives in the Language Arts*, prepared by Dr. Eunice Schmidt for the Teacher Corps Project at the University of Washington. Reprinted by permission.

The sequencing of instructional objectives according to a broad area of learner outcomes—such as the cognitive realm, illustrated by the preceding six examples—also provides the teacher with the opportunity to individualize learning and instruction. Refer to these examples and note how it would be possible to differentiate levels of learning and instruction for a group of children by allocating objectives 1 and 3 to a subgroup of pupils who are experiencing learning difficulties in the cognitive area. The expected learner outcomes contained in objectives 2 and 6 could be assigned to a second group that is achieving on a higher level. Objectives 4 and 5 would be expected only of those children capable of achieving them. On the other hand, all the pupils might proceed through the entire sequence, providing they have the prerequisite skills.

It should be stressed again that the pupils who were attempting to achieve the learner outcomes based on synthesis and evaluation skills would need the knowledge base and the skills of comprehension, application, and analysis in order to achieve the higher-order cognitive tasks expected of them. Differentiation of instruction by subgroups or individual children is accomplished more readily when instructional objectives follow a psychological sequence.

Sequencing Objectives According to Levels of Skill Development

The ability to use and interpret maps is a study skill frequently taught on the elementary-school level. The development of good study habits often is dependent on the pupil's possessing the technical knowledge and skills needed for various tasks. An educational goal based on intermediate pupils having "to acquire skills needed for the use and interpretation of maps" could be developed through such expected learner outcomes as the ones in the following examples.

Pupils will develop skills for . . .

1. reading map keys and symbols
2. finding and using directions
3. using map scales to compute distance
4. locating places on maps and globes by means of the grid system
5. comparing different maps in order to understand relationships and make inferences[10]

[10] From Allen Y. King, Ida Dennis, and Florence Potter, *Teacher's Annotated Edition, The United States and the Other Americas* (New York: MacMillan Publishing Co., Inc., 1980), "Teachers Manual," p. 8.

DEVELOPING RELATED COMPETENCIES

Exercise Nine

1. Are the five expected learner outcomes for developing map skills ordered in a psychological sequence?
2. What possibilities do these learner outcomes offer for differentiating instruction?

The beginning teacher should examine expected learner behaviors in the broad area of skill development to insure that they follow a psychological sequence. The qualified and competent teacher recognizes that classroom management is enhanced when pupils are competent in the study skills. Good study habits are very dependent on pupils' having the skills needed for achieving assigned tasks. Children acquire skills through a developmental learning process that requires careful sequencing from the simple to the complex. When this provision is lacking, pupils become frustrated by skill tasks that are too difficult for them. When this occurs, problems in classroom management are sure to result.

CHECK YOUR RESPONSES TO . . .

Exercise Nine

1. You are correct in concluding that the five expected learner outcomes are ordered in a psychological sequence.
2. Subgroups of pupils could be organized according to the levels of difficulty in the learner outcomes.

FOR FURTHER PROFESSIONAL STUDY

Books

Cooper, James M., ed. *Classroom Teaching Skills: A Handbook.* Lexington, Massachusetts: D. C. Heath and Company, 1977. Chaps. 2, 3, 4.

——, *Classroom Teaching Skills: A Workbook.* Lexington, Massachusetts: D. C. Heath and Company, 1977. Chaps. 2, 3, 4.
Gronlund, Norman E. *Stating Objectives for Classroom Instruction,* 2nd ed. New York: Macmillan Publishing Co., Inc., 1978.
Orlich, Donald C., *et al. Teaching Strategies: A Guide to Better Instruction.* Lexington, Massachusetts: D. C. Heath and Company, 1980. Chaps. 2, 3, 4.
Ragan, William B., and Gene D. Shepherd. *Modern Elementary Curriculum,* 5th ed. New York: Holt, Rinehart and Winston, 1977. Chap. 2.
Thompson, Duane G. *Writing Long-Term and Short-Term Objectives.* Champaign, Illinois: Research Press Company, 1977.

Periodicals

Jones, John A. "How to Write Better Tests." *Instructor* (October 1979), 66–71.
Melton, Reginald F. "Resolution of Conflicting Claims Concerning the Effect of Behavioral Objectives on Student Learning." *Review of Educational Research* (Spring 1978), 291-302.
Seddon, G. M. "The Properties of Bloom's Taxonomy of Educational Objectives for the Cognitive Domain." *Review of Educational Research* (Spring 1978), 303–323.
Thornell, John G. "Reconciling Humanistic and Basic Education." *The Clearing House* (September 1979), 23–24.

6

Planning for Teaching and Learning

THE QUALIFIED AND COMPETENT TEACHER . . .

1. Understands that the planning process consists of a continuing cycle of teacher-pupil behaviors.
2. Appreciates the importance of getting thoroughly acquainted with a new school and community.
3. Understands the nature of critical planning times.

Performance Criteria

As a result of the serious study of this chapter, the student should be able to . . .

1. Organize the first few days of instruction.
2. Plan a good learning atmosphere.
3. Select learner outcomes for the year in the various curriculum areas.
4. Plan for getting instruction underway.
5. Develop a sketch plan for several days of learning and instruction.
6. Develop a daily lesson plan.

The elementary-school teacher must be a good planner in order to succeed. The demands of teaching in an elementary classroom are extremely diverse, and the teacher who is a poor planner usually finds the task overwhelming. Teachers who are recognized as "having good classroom control" usually are those who see the relationship of instruction and classroom management and who plan accordingly. In the final analysis, good teaching results from good planning; thus the prospective teacher should become thoroughly familiar with the Why? What? and How? of planning.

The importance of planning is generally recognized by experienced teachers. But sometimes planning is done on a rather simplistic basis, resulting in mediocre teaching and learning transactions in the classroom. There are even a few instances where planning is entirely opportunistic.

In many cases there are philosophical factors that impose restraints on planning. In a structured setting, the beginning teacher may discover that textbooks are considered to be the major source of knowledge. In such cases, planning must be based on the assurance that the content of the textbook will be covered. But even so, the good planner recognizes alternatives that can provide the children with numerous learning activities.

In an open setting, the beginning teacher may be presented with the challenge of translating a vast number of learning opportunities into those that make a viable teaching situation. The problem in this instance becomes one of orchestrating a diverse array of possible activities into a meaningful learning sequence.

In any situation, the task of planning for classroom teaching and learning transactions becomes simpler and easier when the teacher understands the planning process and values it as an inherent property of competent instruction. The process requires a knowledge of planning procedures and skills in decision making. Planning in any walk of life requires the individual to make choices and to select alternatives that are consistent with one's goals and the realities of the situation. When planning is done in a sequential and orderly manner, the end result is more apt to be realistic in terms of the goals desired and the reality of the situation. To achieve such results, decisions need to be made at several points in the process. Each point of decision making requires sorting out and establishing priorities for the variables at hand. The process, when applied intelligently, is problem solving at its best. But decision making becomes very difficult when there is no provision for processing the data that bear on the situation. The teacher who plans effectively follows a sequence that flows through a number of planning phases. Each phase provides an opportunity to sort out data in order to make realistic decisions before proceeding to the next phase. Experience has shown that many teachers employ a planning design that consists of the following phases:

The teacher . . .

1. diagnoses learner characteristics.
2. conducts a reality assessment.
3. determines instructional objectives.
4. organizes for instruction.
5. facilitates learning and instruction.
6. evaluates achievement of objectives.
7. utilizes evaluative feedback for subsequent instruction.

THE PLANNING PROCESS

Beginning teachers sometimes have the mistaken idea that planning for instruction ends when the lesson begins. But the competent teacher realizes that planning is a continuous process. It occurs throughout the seven phases that were presented in the preceding paragraph. The process is depicted in the following schematic.

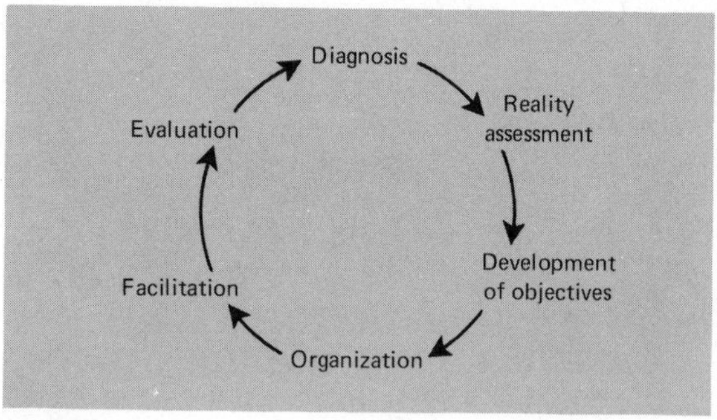

A Continuing Cycle

The teacher's *diagnosis of learner characteristics* provides information about the cognitive, affective, and psychomotor traits of the pupils. This is obtained from a variety of sources, such as (1) cumulative files containing test data, anecdotal records, pupil-progress reports, samples of school work, and so forth, (2) observations, (3) interviews, and (4) pre-tests. Next, and equally important is the *reality assessment* of the group's characteristics. The teacher is able to ascertain the extent of the group's cohesiveness, the readiness of the group to participate in activities that require cooperative behavior, the children who are leaders, and the pupils who seem to have difficulty with task-oriented activities. These data enable the teacher to make a reality assessment of the characteristics of the children and to plan instruction on the basis of where the pupils are in terms of their needs and interests.

The reality assessment also provides the teacher with information needed to make plans consistent with the human and material resources at hand. Beginning teachers sometimes fail to give adequate attention to this consideration and discover, too late, that their teaching strategies cannot be used because of the absence of needed resources.

Once the teacher has carefully analyzed the abilities, needs, and interests of pupils and has carefully assessed the available resources, *instructional objectives* can be stated in the form of expected learner outcomes. This is a critical decision-making point in the planning process that initiates the phase of the planning cycle where the teacher makes decisions on *organizing for instruction.* The lesson plan, developed by the teacher, ultimately contains the organizing elements that will be included in the lesson. But, first, alternatives for reaching certain learner outcomes may have to be considered. As stated earlier, in a situation where the textbook is the major learning resource, the teacher may have to center instruction on it. But other modes of teaching should also be provided. Sometimes this task may be difficult. If the teacher believes the activity mode would be valuable for the development of certain skills needed by the group, but finds that the school principal discourages noise and movement in the classroom, an alternative may have to be found.

The *facilitation* phase provides numerous opportunities for evaluation. The elementary-school teacher soon learns to develop the capacity for being "all eyes and ears." In the event the lesson is not proceeding smoothly, modifications are made at that point, not later on. For instance, a teacher may plan to have the class work in small groups to accomplish a learning task, but finds the pupils are not able to use their time well. The teacher should assess the situation with the children at that point, and perhaps make a decision to change over to large-group instruction to accomplish the task.

The *evaluation* phase is the appropriate time to conduct a comprehensive assessment. An examination is made of the learning outcomes as compared to those stated in the objectives. Decisions are reached as to what aspects of the lesson need reinforcement, which need re-teaching, and which can be set aside. Thus, the diagnostic phase has begun all over again, this time with the recently completed trial-learning experiences an additional data source. Subsequent instruction is planned accordingly; thus, the planning cycle begins anew.

WHEN A
YOUNG BIR
LEAVES THE N

The planning process also provides information that enables teachers to evaluate themselves. A lesson may succeed or fail depending on the suitability of the teaching mode selected. Or the teacher's employment of a classroom management procedure may

PHOTO FOLIO

The joy of teaching is never more real than when a child expresses wonderment or excitement about learning. Good teachers recognize that the world of nature offers an abundant source of possibilities for planning lessons that are interesting to children. They know that children are curious about their natural environment and enjoy exploring it. The teacher in this photograph is providing the child an opportunity to express her curiosity about how birds build their nests.

1. What does this photograph suggest about the teacher's views on teaching and learning?
2. Identify four or five lesson topics that would give pupils the kind of learning experience shown in this photograph.

or may not have been appropriate for the teaching mode used in the lesson. Skillful teachers use the planning process to analyze their behavior as it relates to the success of the lesson.

PLANNING FOR CRITICAL INSTRUCTIONAL EPISODES

This chapter is based on an application of the planning process to selected instructional episodes that occur during the school year, and will deal with the planning process for the following examples:

1. Getting acquainted with a new school.
2. Organizing the first few days of instruction.
3. Selecting learner outcomes for the school year.
4. Planning for getting instruction underway.

These critical instructional episodes will be presented as vignettes based on examples selected from a primary and an intermediate classroom taught by Miss Ellen Baxter and Mr. Jim Bond, respectively, who are fictitious teachers. The reader should approach the following vignettes with the purpose of analyzing the narratives with respect to the ideas presented. The narratives are not intended as light reading but rather as life-like situations that teachers actually face. Thus, Ellen Baxter and Jim Bond are prototypes of numerous beginning teachers throughout the nation. They are faced with situations that, when modified to fit a specific locality, are typical of those found in most school districts today.

Ellen Baxter and Jim Bond respond to their teaching situations with approaches we believe are appropriate to current ideas about effective teaching. This is not to suggest, however, that the specifics of each approach are those the reader may choose to follow as a beginning teacher. Rather, each approach exemplifies a general strategy that includes elements of the planning process presented at the beginning of this chapter. The successful teacher selects specific techniques appropriate to the given situation. The successful application of specific teaching techniques, however, is dependent on the teacher's having selected and followed an appropriate planning approach in the first place.

Getting Acquainted with a New School

Miss Baxter was hired to teach at East Elementary School in Middleton, a city of 50,000 people. Most of the children were from lower-middle-class homes, with a few from well-to-do families. There was also a mix of ethnic minorities in the school. She looked forward eagerly to reporting to her first assignment—a self-contained primary-level classroom.

Mr. Bond was delighted to accept a teaching position in an intermediate-level self-contained classroom. West Elementary School was located in a section of a city similar to the one in which Miss Baxter had secured a teaching position. Similar socio-economic conditions prevailed in both East and West Schools. Mr. Bond, too, eagerly awaited his first day on the job.

Miss Baxter and Mr. Bond were fully aware of the challenge teachers face in organizing for a new school year. Their challenge was even greater because they were beginning teachers, facing a new school year in a new school assignment.

Both teachers had been provided with ample instruction in their teacher education programs to appreciate the importance of:

1. getting acquainted with the school community by discovering resources for the enrichment of school learning, and determining the cultural and recreational activities enjoyed by its patrons.
2. attending orientation meetings conducted by the school district, in order to determine district philosophy; becoming acquainted with available curriculum materials and other learning resources; and identifying human resources available in supportive and consultant areas.
3. getting an early appointment with the school principal to determine the principal's philosophy of teaching and learning, and discovering the do's and don'ts of playground and building routines, especially those related to safety matters and emergencies.
4. obtaining the cumulative records that provide information about the children to be taught.
5. ascertaining learning resources immediately available in the building, and obtaining those to be used to develop an interesting room environment for the first few days of school.

NOTE TO READER

In the following account Miss Baxter and Mr. Bond arrive at their new schools and begin to acquaint themselves with their assignments.

As you read these vignettes, list your observations relative to the things they did in becoming acquainted with their new schools.

What Miss Baxter Found

Miss Baxter drove through the school neighborhood noting several possibilities for supplementing learning activities. The traffic flow was light and the school was located away from heavily traveled streets and approaches to the freeway. This discovery pleased her because it meant she could take the children on walks to various community agencies, businesses, and industries. She noted that there was apparently a community effort to keep the environment clean. Many houses and businesses had been painted recently, and several were being renovated. She also noted that there was still room for improvement, especially where the care of vacant lots and unoccupied buildings was concerned. All in all she was pleased with what she saw.

Miss Baxter's first impression of her appointment was a positive one. She felt good when she saw the school building. Roomy and attractive, with an open court, the one-story structure had a warm atmosphere. She immediately thought, "What a nice place to work." When she saw her classroom, the initial impression was reinforced. The room was large and the furniture consisted of small tables and chairs that could be arranged flexibly. There were ample work spaces, a sink, and much wall space that could be used for displays. She immediately realized that she could arrange the room in whatever way would best suit the children's needs as well as her own. She noticed, too, that the wall adjoining the next room was constructed to be opened, permitting the two rooms to become one large open space. There was also a door opening out to a patio in the court.

Shortly after receiving her teaching contract, Miss Baxter had received a letter of welcome from Mrs. Ginsburg, the school principal. She congratulated her on her appointment and assured her that she would be warmly welcomed at East School. Mrs. Ginsburg had closed the letter by suggesting that Miss Baxter come in for a conference with her when she arrived in town.

The visit with Mrs. Ginsburg had been a rewarding one. She was welcomed enthusiastically and was introduced to Miss Johnson, the school secretary. Miss Baxter was impressed with the secretary's offer to assist her in any way she could. She was pleased to learn that the principal was well acquainted with her background and teacher-preparation experiences. Mrs. Ginsburg made several references to the fact that Miss Baxter's teacher education program was a good one, especially so because of the substantial amount of actual experience in the classroom it had provided.

The principal explained that she liked to see classes where children went about their school work with a sense of purpose and a feeling of happiness and belonging. Miss Baxter noted that Mrs. Ginsburg emphasized the importance of good planning and the relationship it seemed to have to effective classroom management. She concluded that the principal would look for a high level of participation by the children in planning activities.

Mrs. Ginsburg provided her with an attractive "Teacher's Guide to East School," containing many helpful suggestions as well as explanations of policies and procedures. She suggested that Miss Baxter consult her if she had any questions or concerns about it, once she had finished reading it. She assured her that the other primary teachers would be most helpful in assisting her to get established. Mrs. Ginsburg explained that teachers at East School did a considerable amount of "cooperative teaching;" thus, she would have many opportunities to work closely with several of them.

Mrs. Ginsburg took her on a tour of the building and pointed out the location of various facilities, such as the learning resources center, the lunchroom, and playground areas.

What Mr. Bond Found

On driving to West School, Mr. Bond found it to be located in a rather congested area that was slowly being rezoned for business and light industry. He assumed that some of the children had to ride a bus to school because the residential area had receded some distance from it. He concluded that opportunities for informal excursions with the children would probably be limited.

West School was traditional in appearance—a large, two-story brick building, built in 1939. It was durable, to be sure, and had been maintained with care. It was clean and well furnished insofar as conventional equipment was concerned. Mr. Bond's classroom was located on the second floor. The room had a bank of windows overlooking a narrow front lawn. There were storage cabinets under the windows, with a countertop that extended along the length of the windows. A chalkboard was located along the length of the opposite wall, and there were bulletin board spaces on the wall behind the teacher's desk at the front of the room. A map rack was suspended from the wall. The rear wall provided coat hooks and storage spaces for the children's coats. Mr. Bond was struck by the fact that the pupils' desks were in rows facing the teacher's desk. He suddenly became aware of the ticking sound of a large clock on the front wall. Mr. Bond was impressed with the solidness of the atmosphere. It suggested strength and durability, if nothing else, and he reflected on the fact that teaching and learning had been occurring in this room for many years. As he stood behind the teacher's desk, idly spinning the world globe in its cradle, he felt that if he had the freedom to do so, he could provide the children with learning experiences that would interest and challenge them.

During the meeting with Mr. Park, the school principal, Mr. Bond concluded early that there would be a few constraints on his selection of learning experiences. Mr. Park stressed his concern about "accountability," a notion he said was receiving overwhelming support in the community. He explained that it really meant only one thing—that the school provide evidence that the children were learning the basic skills. He explained to Mr. Bond that, so long as the children learned according to their potential, he did not expect to receive any criticism from their parents.

Mr. Bond reflected on this point but did not ask Mr. Park to elaborate on it, although later that morning he wished he had done so. The principal stressed the importance of the fact that the school district had very carefully selected the textbooks for the various subjects. He asked Mr. Bond if he had any objections to basing his planning on the expected learner outcomes as stated by textbook authors. Mr. Bond replied that he had none, although he did believe that the books should be interpreted in a flexible manner and applied in terms of children's needs, abilities, and interests. Mr. Park "allowed" that that was fine, so long as the children learned the "basics" to the "best of their abilities." He added, "Whatever else they do, within reason, is up to you." Mr. Bond saw immediately that the principal believed firmly in having children follow a structured scope of learning.

Mr. Bond was aware, then, that cognitive learning and related skills were stressed at West School. He also concluded that Mr. Park was a "no nonsense" administrator who expected his teachers to concentrate on getting their children to learn. In one sense, Mr. Bond felt somewhat relieved that this was the case, because he would not be expected to do a lot of "creative teaching," at least in the beginning.

Mr. Park accompanied Mr. Bond on a tour of the building. Mr. Bond was repeatedly impressed with the principal's choice of words during their walk—"rules and regulations," "being responsible," "establishing routines," and "respect for property." He was also introduced to Mr. Martin, the school custodian, during the tour.

At the end of the tour, Mr. Park told Mr. Bond that if he needed any help in getting started, to call on him. He also reminded him that building policies were clearly described in the manual in the middle drawer in the teacher's desk.

Mr. Bond decided he had better get to work immediately to find out what those "policies" were. He also decided to plan carefully for the first week of school, in order to make a good beginning.

WHAT'S ALL THIS FUSS ABOUT ACCOUNTABILITY?

Mr. Park actually stressed only one aspect of accountability with Mr. Bond. He talked about the parents wanting assurance that their children were learning. That's rather basic to the concept, but there is more to it than just that. The idea of accountability is highly controversial in the professional and private sectors. It is being applied across the board to public servants on the local, state, and national levels.

The concept of accountability is no stranger to business and industry, where success has always been measured by the product—it is a different matter in education, where the product is people rather than things. Few would argue that a teacher should be held responsible for what he or she does, but they do question whether the teacher can be held responsible for what the pupil does or fails to do. Some say the teacher can no more be held responsible for a pupil's unwillingness to do school work than a physician can be held responsible for the health of a patient who refuses to follow orders.

The present concern for accountability in education stresses pupil outputs. Mr. Park is right—these are usually recognized as achievement or nonachievement. The public is demanding a return on its tax dollar. As a prospective teacher, you're going to hear a lot more about accountability in the future.

1. What are your views about accountability in education?
2. Should the responsibility for accountability be left to the integrity of the teacher, rather than imposed from the outside?

Organizing The First Few Days of Instruction

The opening of school is a critical planning time. The psychological impact of the first day on children is tremendous, as it is on a beginning teacher. A good first day, like a good opening night in the theater, goes a long way toward promoting a successful engagement. Experienced teachers have learned that they can anticipate many characteristics of a new group of children prior to their first encounter with them. By perusing the children's cumulative folders, they discover many important facts. By doing this, much can be learned about the children's abilities, needs, and interests. If the group has the same children as it had during the former year, the previous teacher's anecdotal notes concerning group traits and behavioral patterns are very helpful. The teacher's prior knowledge of goals and objectives for the instructional program is also important in planning meaningful learning activities. In the same way, the teacher's knowledge of available human and material resources is necessary for effective planning. Basic to all of this is the fact that decisions made relative to planning for the first few days of school are very important. The following assumptions are intended to provide a rationale for planning activities.

Assumptions

First and foremost, the children must feel that the teacher is a warm and friendly person. This should be accomplished in an atmosphere that also convinces the pupils they are there for a purpose, and that the teacher has specific expectations for them. The teacher should include the children in helping to develop needed routines. A tentative schedule of activities for the day should be developed. Helping children to organize and pace their time is dependent on this provision. Pupils can be introduced to the major types of learning resources they will use in the various curriculum fields during the year. Activities designed to teach study skills can also be included. Many activities begun during the first few days of school may extend over a long period of time before they are completed.

How Miss Baxter Went About It

She Establishes Her Priorities

Miss Baxter decided to divide her efforts three ways: (1) to get acquainted with her children as quickly as possible; (2) to prepare a room environment that would be attractive and interesting; (3) to develop tentative plans for the first few days of instruction. Miss Baxter jotted down the following priorities for the first week of school:

1. Observe the children as they work independently and as they relate to others in the group.
2. Establish classroom management procedures by introducing routines and expected behaviors.
3. Provide a stimulating and provocative learning atmosphere.
4. Provide incentives for pupils to practice responsibility and industry in a group setting.
5. Help the children develop a sense of purpose for the school year.

She Plans a Daily Schedule

With her priorities for the first few days in mind, Miss Baxter decided to establish a tentative schedule for the children and her to follow. She knew that, as the children became more efficient in helping her to plan the day, modifications could easily be made. She decided to stress this point with the children from the start. During her student teaching experiences, she had made notes of daily schedules in various classrooms, and she had also examined the schedule left in the previous teacher's notebook. With these resources at hand, she planned her schedule to allow as much flexibility as possible, permitting her to unify learning from various school subjects. She decided on the following schedule and printed it on a large chart for the children:

Our Daily Schedule

Opening Activities
Planning the Day
Language Arts (to include Reading)
Social Studies
Lunch
Mathematics
Creative Experiences
Health and Physical Education (alternate days)
Closing Activities

Miss Baxter decided that the length of each learning experience should be left flexible.* Later, teacher-pupil planning would determine the actual length, but she decided that probably a 30- to 90-minute range would provide a reasonable beginning frame of reference.

She Plans a Good Learning Atmosphere

Miss Baxter's classroom provided numerous possibilities for organizing the physical aspects of it in a cheerful, positive manner. A door opened onto a patio in the courtyard; the movable furniture enabled flexibility in room arrangement. She decided to organize the room according to various learning centers. With the subject areas in mind, she decided to establish a science center that would be built around a large aquarium (a terrarium could be added later). On the wall behind the aquarium were various pictures of marine life, with captions such as, "What is my name?" For social studies, she used a community map with the caption, "Can you find East School?" Photographs of occupations and industries were arranged

*Generally, state education codes stipulate minimum requirements of time to be spent on the various school subjects. Miss Baxter was not unmindful of the fact that she would need to adhere to those requirements.

around the map. Books on community life were also placed on the study table at this center. A third center contained puzzles and other manipulative materials designed to illustrate mathematics. There was a center on reading and language arts as well, complete with an attractive display of poetry, fiction, and factual books. She also prepared an attractive bulletin board display. On it were scenes of the local community, with the caption, "How many of these places have you visited?"

Because the children would be grouped for various purposes during the year, Miss Baxter prepared name tags and made a tentative seating chart, based on a more or less random selection of children. She knew that quite early in the week the children themselves would demonstrate the feasibility of her choices. Her basic concern was to work toward a positive group feeling. Groupings for specific learning would soon follow.

She Plans Learner Activities for the First Few Days

Miss Baxter organized the first few days of school with the following activities in mind: (1) introduce the various school subjects; (2) diagnose the needs, abilities, and interests of children; (3) determine the pupils' readiness for independent, small- and large-group activities; (4) diagnose their level of responsibility; and (5) determine the amount of teaching necessary to establish study, work, and social skills. Her planning for the first week resulted in the following arrangements.

LANGUAGE ARTS

Use informal discussion activities to establish rules for speaking and listening. Use the social studies "Our Community" theme to provide children with writing activities to produce samples of their handwriting, spelling, and composition skills. Read to the children on a daily basis to further determine listening skills,

---

PHOTO FOLIO

Learning centers provide excellent opportunities for pupils to extend and enrich their learning. The pupils in this photograph are participating in a small-group activity at a science learning center. They are working independently from their classmates who are involved in a reading assignment in the textbook. The teacher is observing the three children as they perform activities important to a class-wide experiment on the conditions necessary for plants to live and grow. Tomorrow, another group of pupils will work at the learning center. Activities such as the one shown here, enable pupils to develop social skills as well as to acquire knowledge.

1. Four major teaching modes were described in Chapter 4. Which of these teaching modes lends itself to the activity shown in this photograph?
2. Classroom management skills were discussed in Chapter 3. Seven characteristics of a well managed classroom were presented. Describe the learning situation in this photograph in terms of those characteristics.

---

and also to ascertain critical thinking skills. From the children's cumulative folders, use reading-test scores to determine tentative assignments of textbooks for reading instruction. Determine tentative groupings for reading instruction purposes according to test scores in the folders. Regrouping will be done later on the basis of specific needs or interests, and on results of the fall testing program. Plan to correlate the spelling program with reading by extending word-attack skills into the study of spelling. Make maximum use of sharing and planning activities to establish guidelines for effective speaking habits.

MATHEMATICS

Identify skill levels of children from the cumulative folders. Administer tests to determine their present level of reasoning and computational skills. Provide reinforcement activities for those who have regressed since last spring. Anticipate opportunities to correlate mathematics with the social studies unit.

SCIENCE

Have discussions based on the learning center, organized around the aquarium. Record children's questions. Summarize discussions by sorting out children's questions, recording them, and determining relevant sources of data to provide information on questions. Correlate science, where possible, with study of marine life as it relates to the social studies unit on community life.

CREATIVE EXPERIENCES

Encourage children to suggest songs they like to sing. Have children discuss their interest and involvement in music. Provide children with listening experiences based on records that highlight both instrumental and vocal selections.

Keep art activities uncomplicated until more is known about the group's ability to work with various media. Provide opportunities for self-selection of the form of expression. Help the children develop good work habits and a concern for the proper care and use of materials.

HEALTH AND PHYSICAL EDUCATION

Review good health habits learned the previous year. Use the warm fall weather to take short walks around the neighborhood. Provide opportunities for group play and make use of them to observe children's behavior. Note the leaders, the subgroups, the very active, and the retiring children. Introduce a simple group game. Relate health to the study of the community in the social studies program.

ROOM CITIZENSHIP

Plan the day's program with the children each morning. Begin immediately to determine with them a few simple rules for good citizenship as an individual and as a group member. Record these on a chart or on the chalkboard and have the children write them in their own notebook. Refer to these from time to time to evaluate behavior and to reinforce their importance. During the first few days, teach for the mastery of routines pertaining to the playground, cafeteria, lavatories, and the like. Conduct discussions with the children on "How well we did today" in observing good playgound habits, etc. Use every occasion to comment on good behavior by citing examples that prompted it.

Take time during the beginning and ending of the learning experiences associated with each subject area to discuss the work habits necessary for effective learning. Close each day with a brief discussion of the day's activities, and solicit suggestions from the children about "What I really liked today."

With these notes in mind, Miss Baxter felt more confident. At least she had developed a general plan of action. From it she could plan more specifically for a given learning experience.

How Mr. Bond Went About It

Mr. Bond followed procedures very similar to Miss Baxter's. Even though he was concerned about the principal's emphasis on "accountability," Mr. Bond knew that very little would be accomplished if he failed to get the children interested in what they were supposed to do. He decided that he should give priority to the basic skills, but in doing so he wanted them to be associated in a meaningful context. He developed a tentative daily schedule and wrote it on the chalkboard for the children.

Daily Schedule

Opening Activities
Planning the Day
Social Studies and Literature
Break
Basic Skills Block (Math, Reading, Language Arts)
Lunch
Basic Skills Block (continued)
Science
Creative Experiences on alternate days with Health and Physical Education
Closing Activities

He selected the social studies for the beginning period of instruction because it would permit him to utilize the periods that followed to extend learning or to develop learning included as basic skills (reading, spelling, arithmetic, spoken and written language). This would also provide enrichment activities during the creative learning activities.

Mr. Bond's classroom presented limitations on what he could develop. He did the best he could, however, and was able to equip one corner of the room as a reading center, with supplementary books on science, literature, and social studies, which he displayed on a table. He also arranged an attractive map and picture display on the bulletin board. It was designed to generate discussion on the social studies topic, "American People and Lands." He also located a table, which he arranged as a science center, with materials and equipment that would be used in the study of "Electricity and Magnetism." Although his teacher education activities in arranging a learning environment had been limited to a single student teaching experience, Mr. Bond felt he had done pretty well, nevertheless.

He consulted several sources to help him determine possible learner activities for the first week of school. The teacher's guides to the various children's textbooks had numerous suggestions for introducing the subjects. In the basic skills areas, Mr. Bond had been given a supply of inventory tests by Mr. Park to be administered during the first two weeks of school. These were largely survey and diagnostic tests and were accompanied by practice exercises. Mr. Elliot, the teacher next door, had advised Mr. Bond to provide learning activities that would relieve the monotony of the test program, if he could possibly do so. Mr. Bond inquired if the principal would approve of activities that were somewhat noisier than the usual study types. Mr. Elliot responded with the remark, "Mr. Park's bark is worse than his bite." He added that so long as Mr. Bond could show that the children were mastering the basic skills, he could include what Mr. Park sometimes called "fads and frills." Heartened by Mr. Elliot's encouragement, Mr. Bond decided to unify the social studies, language arts, and creative arts learning in an approach to the study of America. His supervising teacher last year had used a similar approach very successfully, and when Mr. Bond had taken over the teaching responsibilities for it, he had been favorably impressed with the approach. (Later we will see how Mr. Bond planned to accomplish his purpose.) He next turned his attention to the selection of expected learner outcomes for the school year.

Selecting Learner Outcomes

The teacher who plans on a weekly or daily basis, with knowledge of the scope of major learning for the school year, has a clear sense of purpose and direction. This is because the teacher is aware of the major understandings, skills, and attitudes basic to each subject field. The following days and weeks of instruction can then be planned within this general framework. In many school subjects, the major learner outcomes to be achieved are already stated—

NOTE TO READER

Now that you have seen how Miss Baxter and Mr. Bond went about the task of organizing for the first few days of instruction, you should make an effort to . . .

1. Talk with an experienced teacher about how to organize for the first few days.
2. Begin collecting ideas about the kinds of room environment—bulletin boards, learning centers charts, displays—that would be useful in orienting pupils to the first few days of school.

sometimes in the teacher's manual accompanying the children's textbook, or in a "curriculum guide." In any event, the beginning teacher should take the time necessary to "preview" the various subject fields to ascertain learning expectations.

Assumptions

Determining learner outcomes is an activity basic to good teaching. It results in a general framework that is used to provide direction for the teacher throughout the school year. Also, this enables the teacher to pace learning over a lengthy period of time, ensuring that continuity and a balance of learning will result. Statements of major expected learner outcomes that come "ready made" in teacher's manuals or curriculum guides can be very useful. But experienced teachers have learned that these usually need to be modified in order to serve best their particular group of children, and in order to be compatible with local curriculum requirements and the availability of teaching and learning resources. Used in a meaningful way, statements of expected learner outcomes are excellent foundations for planning. In a structured situation, the teacher may follow predetermined learner outcomes more closely than would be the case in an open atmosphere. In either case, competent teachers respect the value of such planning resources and use them regularly. Planning on a weekly or daily basis is expedited when the teacher is aware of the scope of the major learner outcomes for the school year. The actual sequencing of these is determined by the weekly and daily planning done by the teacher and the children to serve best their own situation.

Mr. Bond Identifies Learner Outcomes for the Social Studies

Recalling the principal's emphasis on having the children follow the scope of learning contained in their textbooks, Mr. Bond decided to become thoroughly acquainted with what lay ahead for the pupils. Because the first several days of school would be devoted to testing and review exercises in the basic skills, he decided to preview the social studies to determine the framework for the expected learner outcomes.

The children's textbook, *The United States and the Other Americas,*[1] had been selected by a committee of intermediate-level teachers as the basic text. Mr. Bond immediately consulted the teacher's manual contained in the *Teacher's Annotated Edition.* He was favorably impressed by the authors' statement of the purpose of the social studies.

> Our young people must understand and appreciate the principles and ideals on which our nation was founded. They must be willing to fulfill the great promises that have arisen from our increased ability to restructure the physical world that surrounds us. No school subject plays as great a role in preparing pupils for the responsibilities of citizenship as does the interrelated group of disciplines known as the social studies.[2]

Mr. Bond felt that he could easily adapt the textbook to the conditions that Mr. Park had stressed, at the same time permitting himself adequate leeway for improvisation. The text was organized according to six chief objectives.[3]

1. To give a basic introduction to geography and geographic principles that will contribute to the understanding of human life and problems in a global context.
2. To provide an acquaintance with the nations of the world, with emphasis on their geography, history, resources, peoples, and their varied contributions to world culture.
3. To give a background of historical information about the growth and development of the United States of America, together with a realistic picture of life in our nation today.
4. To develop an understanding and appreciation of our American heritage and of the responsibilities of American citizenship.
5. To develop the critical-thinking abilities of pupils through a variety of

[1] See Allen Y. King, Ida Dennis, and Florence Potter, *Teacher's Annotated Edition, The United States and the Other Americas* (New York: Macmillan Publishing Co., Inc., 1980).
[2] *Ibid.*, p. 4.
[3] *Ibid., Teachers Manual,* pp. 4–5.

activities that help them to see relationships, draw conclusions, and arrive at understandings.

6. To instill in pupils a sense of social responsibility and a respect for good human relationships.

The unit objectives for a study of "American People and Lands" were stated on page 22 of the *Teachers Manual.* Mr. Bond modified these to provide for specific learning activities for his pupils during the first two weeks of school.

The *Teachers Manual* also contained a statement of "Major Concepts and Generalizations Developed in This Series." These were grouped according to the parent disciplines from the social sciences—geography, history, economics, political science, sociology, and anthropology. He decided to use these statements throughout the school year to insure that each learning unit would contribute to the pupils' understanding of the contributions made by the parent disciplines.

Mr. Bond also discovered that an even more specific framework for expected learner outcomes was provided. These expected learner outcomes were grouped according to the statements of objectives for the skills and attitudes to be emphasized for each unit of study.

Miss Baxter Identifies Learner Outcomes for the Social Studies

Miss Baxter selected the social studies area for a major unit of study with which to begin the school year. She selected the social studies area because it offered so many possibilities for unifying learning from the various school subjects. She had considered the possibility of scheduling the social studies first thing in the morning, but decided against it. Her decision was based mainly on the fact that, on the primary level, the language arts usually are scheduled first. She recalled a conversation with one of her professors during the past year, about the justification for scheduling language arts at the beginning of the school day. She had explained that it was largely because of tradition—a very powerful influence in education—and also because of the assumption that children are rested and fresh at the beginning of the day, and are better prepared to learn the complex skills included in reading and language instruction. Miss Baxter concluded that she could still relate learning from the social studies with the other subjects by scheduling it immediately after recess.

The social studies theme for the year was based on a study of "Communities." Miss Baxter discovered that Unit One in the social studies textbook was a good starting point for the pupils as it offered numerous possibilities for knowledge acquisition and skill building activities that could draw from a variety of curriculum areas. This textbook,[4] based on the same statement of objectives for the social studies and also containing the same organization as the one Mr. Bond was using, provided excellent statements of learner outcomes. Miss Baxter selected the following learner outcomes from the list of objectives for the unit based on "Moving to a New Community."[5]

EXPECTED LEARNER OUTCOMES FOR A UNIT OF STUDY ON "MOVING TO A NEW COMMUNITY"

Major Understandings that Should Emerge

- . . . All people, no matter where they live, need water, food, clothing, and some kind of shelter
- . . . A community is a place where people live and work together

Skills to be Stressed

- . . . Specific reading skills in culling social studies information from subject matter, such as skimming to locate specific information, reading for detail, and reading for main ideas
- . . . Using early steps in reading maps, globes, and charts
- . . . Gaining information from pictures
- . . . Organizing, and beginning to carry out, effective group work

Attitudes for Special Emphasis

- . . . Realization that the necessities of life are food, water, clothing, shelter
- . . . Appreciation of the community as an organization for providing basic needs

Planning for Instruction Based on Expected Learner Outcomes

Determination of expected learner outcomes is a major accomplishment for the classroom teacher. It is only one step, however, in the continuous planning process. Once the expected learner outcomes have been determined, the teacher must select learning activities that promote them. Many experienced classroom teachers have found it very useful to identify, in the form of a "sketch plan," a variety of learning activities that can be developed over a period of several days. By doing this, the teacher is also able to anticipate the necessary learning resources for the activities. Beginning teachers, especially, should be prepared to engage in this type of planning, because school principals frequently ask them to do so. But competent teachers also do "daily lesson planning," designed to implement

[4]See Mae Knight Clark, *et. al., Teacher's Annotated Edition, Communities: Today and Yesterday* (New York: Macmillan Publishing Co., Inc., 1980).

[5]*Ibid., Teachers Manual*, pp. 23–24.

IF YOU DON'T KNOW HOW TO DO IT . . .

sometimes the identification of major learner outcomes can be as difficult as trying to locate the proverbial "needle in a haystack."

Now that Ellen Baxter and Jim Bond have shared their experiences in this activity with you, it would be timely for you to . . .

1. select a curriculum area, such as science, language arts, social studies, or mathematics, and see if you can identify the major learner outcomes that are suggested for development over the school year; consult a teacher's guide to a children's textbook series or a curriculum guide, to assist you.
2. plan a course of action to initiate instruction. That's what the next section of the chapter is all about.

the learning activities contained in the "sketch plan." Skill in this form of planning provides a margin of confidence that goes a long way toward insuring a good lesson. The teacher who begins a lesson by having anticipated a probable course of action for it has made progress toward removing barriers to learning for pupils. Skill in preparing sketch plans for a period of several days, as well as skill in developing a daily lesson plan, is prerequisite for the competent and qualified teacher.

Sketch Plan

The sketch plan provides an outline of suggestions for the teacher and children to draw on over the course of several days. It provides flexibility for teacher-pupil planning, because it is not locked into a day-by-day prescription of what is to be done. A complete realiza-

NOTE TO READER

Ellen Baxter's sketch plan and daily lesson plan are included in the following sections to serve as examples of format and activities that are appropriate to each type of plan.

Even though complete examples of Mr. Bond's sketch and daily lesson plans are not provided, references to their content will be made in the following chapter.

tion of each expected learner outcome is unrealistic for many children; thus, the teacher must evaluate carefully the extent to which individual pupils are succeeding. The plan should provide activities designed to implement the evaluation process.

Miss Baxter's Sketch Plan

Miss Baxter decided to select several learning activities that would initiate instruction emanating from the first two major understandings contained in the selected learner outcomes. She developed the following sketch plan to accomplish these learner outcomes and to help pupils acquire the attendant skills and attitudes.

A SKETCH PLAN FOR THE FIRST TEN TO TWELVE DAYS OF INSTRUCTION ON UNIT OF STUDY ON 'MOVING TO A NEW COMMUNITY"

LEARNER OUTCOMES

Major Understandings that Should Emerge

... All people, no matter where they live, need water, food, clothing, and some kind of shelter

... A community is a place where people live and work together

Skills to be Stressed

... Specific reading skills in culling social studies information from subject matter, such as skimming to locate specific information, reading for detail, and reading for main ideas

... Using early steps in reading maps, globes, and charts

... Gaining information from pictures

... Organizing, and beginning to carry out, effective group work

Attitudes for Special Emphasis

... Realization that the necessities of life are food, water, clothing, shelter

... Appreciation of the community as an organization for providing basic needs

LEARNING ACTIVITIES BASED ON EXPECTED LEARNER OUTCOMES

Introductory Activities

1. Before beginning the unit of study have the pupils leaf through the book to become aware of pictures, maps, charts.
2. Discuss general organization of the book as outlined in the Table of Contents.
3. Have pupils examine the title page and ask questions about the title, "Moving to a New Community." Note that the textbook has two chapters devoted to the unit of study.
4. Introduce new words and terms presented in the unit.
5. Relate new words to pupils' own experiences, current events, and topics previously studied.

6. Discuss photographs of the two communities shown on pp. 8-9.
7. Discuss the importance of the globe and the map of the United States as a learning resource for pupils in their study of communities.

DEVELOPING THE UNIT–"WHAT IS A COMMUNITY?" PP. 10-32

1. To reinforce map and globe skills, it may be necessary to:
   . . . reteach "Our States and Their Capitals"
   . . . teach (or review) directions north, south, east, and west on maps
   . . . teach intermediate directions, e.g. "southwest" on maps
   . . . teach location of United States on classroom globe
   . . . teach locational skills and cardinal and intermediate directions on globe
2. During daily silent and oral reading assignments in textbook, include tasks that will prepare children to:
   . . . skim to locate specific information
   . . . read for detail
   . . . read pictures
3. Plan activities that extend the pupils' learning through working with others in small groups or on an individual basis to:
   . . . relate their own travel experiences along the route discussed in the textbook
   . . . interview others about their experiences
   . . . prepare a bulletin board on current events along the route travelled by the texbook family
   . . . begin a list of questions they would like to explore about their own community.

CONCLUDING ACTIVITIES

1. Presentation of a bulletin board display entitled "Our Community."
2. Discussion of pupils' oral and written reports on trips they have made.
3. Presentation of art activities designed by the pupils to depict activities that provide for "basic needs" in a community.
4. Evaluation of pupils' understanding of "What is a community?" "What basic needs must be provided by a community?" "How communities differ in the way they satisfy basic needs," and "Why families sometimes move to other communities."
5. As a transition activity for the pupils, begin discussion on the latter half of the unit to be devoted to "Early Communities of the Woodlands."

Daily Lesson Plan

The daily lesson plan contains specific provisions for teaching and learning. These provisions make possible the successful interaction of instruction and management.

Every lesson should have a purpose which is understood by the children. In the daily lesson plan, the purpose is usually stated in the form of objectives that explain "what" pupils are to learn. The pupils should also understand the "why." Lessons that do not provide sufficient goal clarity for the children tend, more often than not, to fail. The daily lesson plan should also include the learning resources necessary for the conduct of the lesson. The competent teacher appreciates the necessity of having identified, located, and made available the learning resources needed in the lesson. When this provision is lacking, the lesson often degenerates as a result of management problems. The sequence of the daily lesson plan provides for building readiness for what is to be done, delineates the learning activities, and provides for a summary and evaluation of the lesson.

There is no one best form for a lesson plan, nor is there a consensus on the level of specificity that should be included. As a general rule, teachers use brief, directional statements rather than detailed sentences that include what the teacher will actually say. The importance of the daily lesson plan is based on the teacher's having planned for the components, as identified in the following format.

COMPONENTS OF A DAILY LESSON PLAN

1. Purpose
   Contains a statement of instructional objectives that include the specific learner outcomes that should result from the lesson.
2. Learning Resources
   Provides a list of the learning materials or media needed to teach the lesson.
3. Sequence of Lesson
   Describes the work-study activities that will occur during the lesson.
4. Summary and Evaluation
   Describes the closing activities designed for the lesson.

Experienced teachers do not always write out in detail the specifics for each and every lesson during the day. This would be an awesome task. They often rely on the sketch plan to provide direction for many ongoing activities. They do appreciate the need, however, to plan specifically for those lessons that introduce new skills, as well as those that require children to participate in a variety of activities. They realize that lessons which do not require careful planning are those that restrict children to a single learning activity—usually an assign-read-recite procedure. To reduce learning to this level would deprive pupils of acquiring the work-study and social skills they need in order to become productive citizens. The qualified and competent teacher accepts the fact that good teaching is hard work, and the habit of daily lesson planning can make it more enjoyable.

DAILY LESSON PLAN FOR BEGINNING THE UNIT OF STUDY "MOVING TO A NEW COMMUNITY"

1. Purpose of Lesson
   ... During a teacher-directed introduction to the textbook, pupils will demonstrate their readiness to use the textbook, wall map, and classroom globe
   ... During group discussion of the photographs on pp. 8–9 in the textbook, pupils will be able to respond orally to questions about the likenesses and differences between the two communities shown on these pages
   ... At the close of the directed-reading assignments, pupils will be able to respond orally to questions included in the lesson plan
   ... During group discussion pupils will participate in making suggestions for additional study about their own community
2. Learning Resources
   ... Pupils' textbook, *Communities: Today and Yesterday,* pp. 8–20
   ... Wall map of the United States
   ... Classroom globe
3. Sequence of Lesson
   ... Prepare pupils for the lesson by asking them to have their textbooks available on the top of their desks
   ... Explain that the class is beginning their social studies class this year with an interesting study of communities that are new to them
   ... Explain that pupils will need to follow the teacher's directions carefully
   ... Ask the class to open their textbooks to pages 8–9. Call their attention to the pictures shown and ask them:
      ... Which one is most like the place you would like to live?
      ... Which one is most like the place where you live?
      ... What places do the other two pictures show?
      ... Which picture shows something from the past?
      ... What might you see today in its place?
   ... Explain that they will soon become acquainted with the Roberts family which is planning to move away from its home community
   ... Ask them to turn to page 10 where they will meet the Roberts family.
   ... Ask them to describe what they think the Roberts family is like, based on the pictures
   ... Ask pupils to read silently pages 10–14 (skimming skill) to determine where the Roberts family now lives and where it will be moving
   ... Ask pupils to locate each place on the map on page 10
   ... Ask for a volunteer to locate each place on the wall map
   ... Ask designated pupils to name the states in which these places are located. Ask them to name the country in which these states are located
   ... Using the classroom globe, show pupils the location of the United States
   ... Ask "Why do people live together in communities?"
   ... Refer pupils to page 18 and ask them to identify the main idea. Ask a pupil to read it aloud

. . . Ask pupils to silently read page 18 and identify the four basic needs that communities provide for people

4. Summary and Evaluation

. . . Close the lesson by asking pupils to make suggestions about how the class can discover how their own community provides for basic needs of its own families

. . . Ask for pupil evaluation of how well the lesson went today

. . . Explain that tomorrow the class will read more about the Roberts family and its plans for moving to a new community

Completing the First Week of School

With their planning for the first few days of instruction completed, Miss Baxter and Mr. Bond were ready to begin formal group instruction. They were now faced with the challenge of managing children in groups. Miss Baxter had had many more opportunities than Mr. Bond to see how this is done, because her teacher educa-

tion program provided a year-long assignment in primary classrooms. Mr. Bond had had only a single semester assignment in a classroom where the teacher was managing pupils in groups.

Despite the disparity in their actual classroom experiences, both beginning teachers appreciated the importance of providing children with learning experiences in differentiated groups. Chapter 7 will give an opportunity to see how well they succeeded.

DEVELOPING RELATED COMPETENCIES

Here's One Way to Do It . . .

Mrs. Wilson believes that teaching should be creative. She views planning as a restrictive process that prevents her and the children from doing the kinds of activities that are truly creative. She begins each day by asking her second-grade class, "What would you like

---

PHOTO FOLIO

Qualified and competent teachers use a variety of learning resources in their instruction. Good planning includes careful examination of learning resources before they are presented to pupils. The teachers in this photograph have previewed a film and are discussing its possibilities for inclusion in a social studies unit.

1. Most local school districts have curriculum material libraries that provide teachers with an abundance of learning resources. Plan to visit one of these libraries and explore its materials.
2. Classroom teachers are usually expected to operate learning resources equipment. In the event you have not learned to operate such simple machines as the film projector, overhead projector, or tape recorder, you should arrange to learn the mechanics of their operation before beginning student teaching.

---

to do today?" From this point on, learning activities are based essentially on the pupils' interests.

1. In terms of the ideas discussed in this chapter, what is your assessment of this approach to planning for learning and instruction?
2. Would you consider the approach as being one you would feel comfortable in using?

Here's Another Way to Do It . . .

Mr. Moore believes that instruction should be based on the textbook. He insists that he cannot improve on the work of the authors who, after all, are experts. Thus, he follows an assign-read-recite approach. He makes assignments to his fifth-grade class by asking the children to, "Read pages 42–45 in the textbook and be prepared to discuss the questions on page 45."

1. Analyze this approach in terms of the ideas presented in this chapter.
2. What suggestions can you offer Mrs. Wilson and Mr. Moore to improve their teaching?

FOR FURTHER PROFESSIONAL STUDY

Books

Banks, James A. *Teaching Strategies for Ethnic Studies,* 2nd ed. Boston: Allyn and Bacon, Inc., 1979.

Bloom, Benjamin S. *Human Characteristics and School Learning.* New York: McGraw-Hill, 1976.

Good, Thomas L., and Jere E. Brophy. *Looking in Classrooms,* 2nd ed. New York: Harper and Row Publishers, 1978. Chap. 4.

Orlich, Donald C., *et al. Teaching Strategies: A Guide to Better Instruction.* Lexington, Massachusetts: D. C. Heath and Company, 1980. Chap. 5.

Ragan, William B., and Gene D. Shepherd. *Modern Elementary Curriculum,* 5th ed. New York: Holt, Rinehart and Winston, 1977. Chap. 5.

Periodicals

deVoss, Gary G. "The Structure of Major Lessons and Collective Student Activity." *The Elementary School Journal* (September 1979), 8-18.

Hunter, Madeline. "Diagnostic Teaching." *The Elementary School Journal* (September 1979), 41–46.

Leverte, Marcia, Arden Smith, and JoAnn Cooper. "How to Have a Responsible Classroom." *Instructor* (October 1978), 70-73, 76, 78.

Soloway, Rhoda Kahn. "Making Those First Days Count." *Teacher* (September 1979), 69-70.

Yinger, Robert. "Routines in Teacher Planning." *Theory Into Practice* (June 1979), 163-169.

7

Teaching Individuals in Groups

THE QUALIFIED AND COMPETENT TEACHER . . .

1. Understands criteria for organizing pupils in groups.
2. Has knowledge of PL 94-142: *The Education for All Handicapped Children Act* and its implications for providing the least restrictive environment for handicapped pupils.
3. Recognizes the importance of providing a balance of large-group, small-group, and individualized instruction.
4. Is sensitive to the importance of developing a group management plan.
5. Appreciates the importance of a two-way communication between home and school.
6. Is knowledgeable about procedures for closing the school year.

Performance Criteria

As a result of the serious study of this chapter, the student should be able to . . .

1. Develop a group management plan to provide for large-group, small-group, and individualized instruction—based on the abilities, needs, and interests of children.
2. Provide for pupil-progress reporting through report forms and parent conferences.
3. Perform closing of school activities.

The self-contained classroom is the dominant organizational pattern of instruction in the elementary schools of this nation. In its purest form it represents a "one teacher-one classroom" organization for teaching and learning. Various modifications of it have appeared in one form or another. In one instance, a teacher may have the responsibility for the instruction of a group and another, who has a specialty in music, provides instruction for the group in that curriculum area. Another group of pupils may receive instruction in reading from a specialist teacher, but is taught the remaining subjects in the curriculum by a teacher in a self-contained classroom.*

Team-teaching arrangements change the self-contained classroom into an organizational pattern in which two or three teachers share instruction for a group that is two to three times larger than the conventional classroom of 25 to 30 pupils. Team teaching in a setting such as this requires accommodations for a large number of pupils; many school buildings, however, are neither constructed nor equipped to handle this arrangement.

Other modifications are based on the premise that quality education can occur only when instruction is individualized. Teaching machines and programmed texts were very popular formats for individualized instruction during the 1960's. These did not meet with widespread acceptance for various reasons, some of which were philosophic and others economic. The development of learning programs for the machines and for programmed textbooks proved to be a costly venture, and there was a reluctance to invest in this approach which was yet to gain widespread favor. During the 1970's individualized instruction gained renewed vigor, largely because of the competency-based education movement. Born of a growing acceptance of "accountability" in the professional and public sectors, programmed instruction became a popular concept once again. It took the form of the "learning module" or "instructional package" containing carefully prescribed behavioral objectives enabling the pupil to master learning tasks in a "low-risk environment" and requiring only a minimum of teacher guidance. Individualized learning, accomplished through independent study, can promote the development of self-direction and self-reliance in pupils. Independent study activities, based on prepackaged materials that contain a high degree of direction, usually do not provide the child opportunity for decision making and, therefore, do little to promote these abilities.

*These variations weaken the "self-contained" concept in the absolute sense, but they bear, nevertheless, a closer resemblance to the self-contained pattern than they do to any other organizational format.

The computer is gaining recognition as an important tool in providing individualized instruction. Its major limitation is that it is so costly. This form of technology, however, seems to hold promise for improving the preciseness of the diagnosis of learner strengths and deficiencies, and in matching these with appropriate instruction. The impact that computerized instruction may have on the nature and size of instructional groups remains to be seen. More than likely, learning would be individualized rather than remain primarily as large-group instruction. This has been the case with the other forms of programmed instruction. In using these media, the setting for learning becomes one in which pupils participate mainly in independent studies or in a tutorial arrangement. As a result, there would be fewer groups that include the entire class or that provide for small-group activities. If this were to occur on a wide scale, the benefits of the group process in the development of the child would also be lessened.

Recently, large-group or total-class instruction has been promoted by advocates of *direct instruction* who believe it to be an effective approach for producing pupil achievement. Direct instruction usually occurs in those instances where the teacher uses factual questions and controlled practice to teach a large group of pupils. This approach, of course, represents a sharp contrast to individualized and/or small-group instruction.

We wish to emphasize the importance of pupils interacting with one another in the interests of their academic, personal, and social development. Teachers who share this point of view plan teaching and learning activities that provide a balance of individualized instruction, small-group lessons, and total-class experiences. Because group life remains the foundation of our society, children need experiences that prepare them to live and work in social groups. Teachers need to be skillful in organizing instruction that accommodates the pupils in both large and small groups.

Experienced teachers have learned that subgroup instruction also provides opportunities to reach individual children. They strive, therefore, to challenge each pupil by planning a balance of learning activities that occur in large groups or subgroups as well as in individualized settings.

In the final analysis, group instruction enables the teacher to:

1. Provide pupils with opportunities to acquire socialization skills needed for participation in a democratic society.
2. Make efficient use of teacher time and effort.
3. Utilize modes of instruction that require pupil interaction.

4. Provide for individualized learning that occurs in a group rather than in an isolated setting.

Because the majority of beginning teachers will find themselves in a self-contained classroom, with or without modification, they should be prepared to plan and to instruct pupils in both large and small groups. The following section will provide criteria that can be used to select pupils for a particular group.

CRITERIA FOR ORGANIZING PUPILS IN GROUPS

The prevailing practice of teaching pupils in groups did not come about by chance alone. The adoption of the graded-school model from Western Europe, in the nineteenth century, provided a convenient pattern for organizing children in groups on the basis of a common age. Thus, pupils who were six years of age were grouped together to form a first-grade class. Similarly, eleven-year-olds were grouped together to form a sixth-grade class, and so on throughout the grades that constituted the elementary-school organization. The pattern is now over one hundred years old. This is rather remarkable, considering that research evidence and experience over many years have shown that grouping based on age alone—when the age range is no more than a year or two—does not appreciably reduce the variability of individual differences in such attributes as ability and achievement.

Age As a Criterion

In a typical first-grade class, where pupils are grouped on the basis of age alone, test data have shown that there is likely to be a range of approximately four years in the mental ages of the children. The same range of variability would ordinarily be found in the achievement of the children in such traits as reading readiness and experience with numbers. At the end of the sixth grade, the range of the pupils' variability in intelligence and achievement in most school subjects has probably doubled to between seven and eight years.

Educators have persistently used the criterion of age as a convenient way to group children in the graded elementary school. Assigning pupils to a grade on the basis of age also made possible a convenient system for assigning teachers. Even today teachers are frequently assigned to teach the "first" or "third" grade. Textbooks also were graded, and children were promoted or failed on whether they could master the content of the textbooks assigned for their grade level. Unfortunately, this practice still persists in many instances.

Ability and Achievement As Criteria

During the 1920's, the testing movement provided educators with a ready access to group intelligence and achievement tests. Ability and achievement soon became widely used criteria for grouping children. Homogeneous grouping, based on general ability (IQ) as the criterion, was widely advocated as a panacea for reducing the range of variability among children. Educators soon learned, however, that grouping on the basis of general ability did not reduce variability to the extent they thought it would, because the same children differed so widely in their achievement levels in various individual school subjects.

Homogeneous grouping is based on the assumption that a pupil who scores high, average, or low on a general intelligence test will also be high, average, or low in the subjects that are taught in the elementary school. Evidence does not support this assumption. Pupils grouped together on the basis of a single factor such as IQ present the teacher with a wide range of abilities in the various school subjects. The teacher in this situation is still faced with the problem of providing differentiated instruction necessary to accommodate varying levels of pupil needs.

Currently, homogeneous grouping on the basis of a general factor such as intelligence is not widely favored as a procedure for assigning pupils to separate classes. There are various reasons for its decline. Probably the most powerful of these is a growing recognition that the practice does not provide the homogeneity required for mass instruction. Tests that purport to measure IQ or mental age have been criticized because they are not reliable predictors of children's school achievement. Moreover, there is no full agreement on what intelligence is; some insist that there are many types of intelligence, some of which cannot be measured. Hence, these tests cannot be relied on as a dependable means for grouping pupils. It is also well known that many tests are culture-biased and therefore reward children who come from homes that value and foster the factors measured by those tests. As a result the widespread use of intelligence testing, as well as homogeneous ability grouping, are regarded less favorably than they once were.

On the philosophical level, some contend that ability grouping that segregates children into high, average, and low groups prevents pupils from interacting with others who may be more or less able than themselves. Thus, the more able pupils do not have an opportunity for social contact with others who are less capable. The criticism strikes at the failure of intellectual ability as a criterion to provide pupils with a group experience that is consistent with society itself, where there is a mix of abilities in many groups.

It is important to stress here that grouping and testing are ways of improving education. Problems occur when grouping and testing are employed to determine the status of a learner in ways that are detrimental to individual and social growth.

Historically, ability and achievement have been the two common criteria that teachers have used in organizing children in groups for teaching and learning. Today, teachers frequently assign pupils to subgroups within the classroom on the basis of their achievement levels. This practice is usually followed in teaching the basic skills to children. But these groups should not remain static. There are other important factors that should also be considered in determining the setting for pupils' learning. These include (1) psychomotor development, (2) cultural background, (3) personal and social adjustment, and (4) interest.

Psychomotor Development As a Criterion

Even though grouping based on the psychomotor development of children is seldom used outside of physical and special education classes, this aspect of child development merits the teacher's careful attention. Frequently the pupil's physical status affects his or her acceptance by other children. Certainly the child who is strong academically but who has poor muscular coordination is not apt to be a popular choice for activities that require physical dexterity. This deficiency may well carry over into the child's academic activities as well, because no amount of academic prowess can compensate in a group that values physical skill.

In a more subtle sense, pupils who have poor eye-hand coordination are not apt to produce the quality of art or written work that other children are capable of producing. Their participation in a group activity based on this skill is apt to be less than satisfactory for them.

Pupils with auditory, visual, and speech problems, as well as those with illnesses that impair their psychomotor conditions, require the careful attention of the teacher when group membership is considered. Such children need to be in the group that provides them with empathetic—not sympathetic support. When a careful selection is made, a mutually educative and human experience accrues to all pupils who are involved.

Sheer physical size is frequently a determiner of whom the leaders and followers are in the classroom. The teacher should be aware of this human tendency to follow the "biggest" and make certain that the status of leadership is deserved on qualities that are more enduring. Even so, teachers sometimes set higher expectations for large children. When this happens they are prone to use the expression, "A big boy or girl like you should have known better than to do that."

Each of these factors is important for determining group members as well as for selecting children for membership in classroom settings. Social adjustment is strongly conditioned by the degree to which the group accepts and values the psychomotor differences of its individual members.

PHOTO FOLIO

Good planning takes into account the needs of learners. In this photograph the teacher is following up on a diagnostic assessment of pupil needs. The subgroup is a very effective organization for this kind of teacher-pupil activity. The group is small enough for the teacher to provide direct instruction of the pupils' specific learning needs as well as to closely supervise their efforts to strengthen a particular concept or skill.

1. In your classroom observations, identify the provisions the teacher makes for follow-up instruction based on specific needs of pupils.
2. Identify three or four additional learning experiences that are suitable for subgroup instruction.

Cultural Background As a Criterion

Children who come from a cultural background that values and rewards academic ability usually feel quite at home in the elementary school. This is because the typical school stresses knowledge, and even skills, that are essentially academic. The setting also puts the highest priority on learning to read and to speak middle-class English. Pupils who can learn to read and converse with one another according to the norms of acceptable English usage have a decided advantage over those children who cannot. The qualified and competent teacher recognizes the importance of getting to know the effects of the pupil's cultural background with respect to the way the home views and even practices the literary priorities of the school. Even more importantly, the teacher must provide groupings that enable pupils with limited English proficiency to have learning experiences that are rewarding to them. Also, as the children learn to read, speak, and write, all of the pupils should have learning experiences that share the cultural wealth contained in the various spoken and written language patterns represented by pupils from non-English speaking backgrounds.

Bilingual education, for example, has as its goal, not merely enabling pupils who speak a different language at home to learn English at school, but also to have all of the children understand and appreciate the contributions of others with a different heritage. This kind of learning should occur regularly at every level in the elementary school. It should not be reserved for a particular school year when a certain national group is scheduled for study. Experienced teachers who are sensitive to the importance of various cultures represented in a classroom find many ways for pupils to feel proud of their heritage, and to enrich the school program with their contributions.

Personal and Social Adjustment As a Criterion

Groups are profoundly influenced by the degree and extent of the personal and social adjustment of their members. A class with only a few pupils who show evidence of maladaptive behavior is apt to be a happier group than one that has a preponderance of children with these problems. Even experienced teachers are sometimes heard to remark, "We had a good day because Jane and Tom were absent." It is quite obvious that Jane and Tom are children with problems in their personal and social adjustment in the classroom.

Because elementary-school teachers are not trained to be psychologists or psychiatrists, they should not attempt to be diagnosticians who prescribe remedies for pupils' psychological and emotional problems. The majority of elementary schools today provide referral services for pupils with such problems. The teacher needs to become acquainted with these services and with the school procedures established for referral purposes.

The teacher can contribute to the personal and social adjustment of children by understanding the dynamics of group interaction and the importance of keeping group membership flexible. Children develop images of themselves in part from the groups with which they are identified. Static group membership (a particular pupil remains, day in and day out in the same reading or mathematics group) may be detrimental to a child's personal and social adjustment.

Interest As a Criterion

Children's interest in learning is affected to a great extent by the degree to which they appreciate the intrinsic value of what they are expected to learn. It is also affected by the learning atmosphere in the classroom. Pupils who are kept together consistently in a total-class grouping do not have the opportunity to interact with one another and to participate in a wide variety of modes of teaching and learning. In classrooms where children are provided with a variety of teaching modes, the learning atmosphere is apt to be more interesting.

Teachers who are skillful in group management frequently plan within-class groupings, or subgroups, which provide pupils with a variety of learning activities. It follows that forming class groupings, based on subgroups of children engaged in different learning activities, necessitates careful planning on the part of the teacher.

To be able to provide pupils with a variety of teaching and learning modes, the teacher should have available a wide repertoire of activities and should systematically introduce them to the group. The expected outcome is that pupils will become increasingly self-selective in matching activities with their particular interests. A helpful way for teachers to classify activities for ready reference is to organize them as follows.

SUGGESTED ACTIVITIES FOR WITHIN-CLASS SUBGROUPS

Activities Based on Gathering Information	Reading; interviewing; map and chart study; computing; field trips; observing; viewing television, films, and slides; listening; experimenting.
Activities Based on Presenting Information	Oral and written reporting; creative expression through art, music, and drama; demonstrating; exhibiting.
Activities Based on Evaluating Information	Experimenting; valuing; questioning; role playing.

Teachers should recognize that most pupils like to participate in activities in which they feel successful. All children, however, should develop an appreciation for a diversity of modes of learning. They should see the importance of these in helping them to learn their school subjects. Within-class groupings can offer the means for organizing pupils in task-groups that provide a variety of learning activities for children. The child who does only a few things well should have an opportunity to develop additional skills. When the teacher provides within-class groupings based on this criterion, there is little doubt that pupils' interest in learning is enhanced.

TEACHING THE MILDLY HANDICAPPED CHILD IN THE REGULAR CLASSROOM

Historically, the accepted way of educating handicapped pupils was to provide special education in an instructional setting removed from the regular classroom. Such separation of the handicapped was deemed necessary to meet the unique needs of these learners. As was explained in Chapter 1, the isolation of handicapped pupils from the mainstream of public education is no longer permitted since the enactment of Public Law 94–142: *The Education for all Handicapped Children Act* of 1975. Although the education of all handicapped children in regular schools is not yet a reality, the nation's schools are moving in the direction of implementing practices that *include* rather than *exclude* handicapped children from the mainstream of education.

PL 94-142

Many believe that this landmark act is the most important educational legislation in the history of this country. The law is intended to benefit an estimated eight million handicapped persons. Its rationale is based on the extension of civil rights to the handicapped. The Act also reinforces the 1954 Supreme Court decision in the *Brown v Board of Education* case in its premise that segregation has harmful effects on those who enforce the practice as well as on those who are segregated. Federal support of the Act in grants to the various states already approaches a billion dollar figure.

PL 94-142 requires that handicapped pupils be placed in the "least restrictive environment" for their instruction. This is identified as the regular classroom unless a different setting is more suitable for meeting the child's needs. If another placement is made it must be justified on evidence that it is expected to be more beneficial to the child than the regular classroom. The need is great for the professional development of teachers who can accommodate—in the regular classroom—children who are handicapped in one or more categories:[1] hearing impairments, orthopedic impairments,

[1] For definitions of the various categories of the handicapped and for an explication of the discussion in this section, see:

J. Affleck, S. Lowenbraun, and A. Archer, *Teaching the Mildly Handicapped in the Regular Classroom*, 2nd ed. (Columbus, Ohio: Charles E. Merrill, 1980).

mental retardation, visual deficiencies, speech impairments, other health disabilities, serious emotional disturbances, and specific learning disabilities.

The teaching profession must attract teachers who have an accepting attitude toward handicapped persons. The entire school setting provides the mainstream for the pupil's learning environment. The teacher must be able to influence all school personnel in the positive acceptance of handicapped pupils. PL 94–142 promises to end the practice of providing special education in segregated settings. Each teacher must now assume some responsibility for the enrichment of the lives of handicapped pupils. No doubt there are persons who will be unable or unwilling to accept the challenge. The realities of the legislation must be faced in order to select prospective teachers who can meet the task successfully.

Implications for Teachers

There are several aspects of PL 94–142 that every elementary teacher should understand and be prepared to implement. These may be summarized as follows.

1. *Provision of the Least Restrictive Environment for the Handicapped Child.*

The concept of a "least restrictive environment" is not generally well understood because of the use of "mainstreaming," which has been mistakenly taken to mean that all handicapped pupils are to be placed in a regular classroom. The wholesale "dumping" of handicapped children in regular classrooms does great disservice to them and to other learners in the regular classroom. PL 94–142 does not require that all handicapped pupils, regardless of their disabilities, be placed in the regular classroom as an appropriate environment. There are many handicapped pupils, however, who are capable of benefiting from instruction for the entire day in a regular classroom setting. For them, the regular classroom *is* the least restrictive environment for the realization of their potential for learning. Assignment to the regular classroom for a part of the school day and to a resource room for the remainder of time, a common practice, may be the least restrictive environment for other handicapped pupils. And, for those who are profoundly handicapped, a full-time assignment to a special room or even to a custodial setting may represent the least restrictive environment.

Maynard C. Reynolds and Jack W. Birch, *Teaching Exceptional Children in All America's Schools* (Reston, Virginia: The Council for Exceptional Children, 1977).

Ann P. Turnbull and Jane B. Schulz, *Mainstreaming Handicapped Students: A Guide for the Classroom Teacher* (Boston: Allyn and Bacon, Inc., 1979).

The goal, of course, is to move all those handicapped pupils who qualify into a regular classroom—the mainstream of public education.

2. *The Individualized Education Program.*

An Individualized Education Program (IEP) is required for each handicapped pupil. The IEP is to be prepared cooperatively by parents, educators, and other specialized personnel. It is a written document that contains statements about the educational objectives, instructional procedures, and evaluation of the pupil's progress.

The IEP may be initiated by parents and/or school personnel. It is developed through planning sessions that may, on occasion, include the pupil.

In the final analysis, the IEP provides the teacher with a framework for planning the daily instructional program for the pupil. Because it also includes the expected learner outcomes, it enables the teacher to assess the pupil's learning program on a long-range basis.

3. *Safeguards for Participants.*

Teachers should be aware of the provisions that are afforded by PL 94-142 for "due process" for the child, parent, teacher, or others who are involved in the screening and diagnosis of the pupil and in the preparation and evaluation of the IEP. The child and the parent are especially protected in such matters as confidentiality of the child's records (with parental access assured) and in the screening, placement, and evaluation of the child. All participants are provided with formal arrangements for the presentation of grievances concerning decisions or procedures. Such cases are reviewed to insure equity has been provided. Appeals can be made to state and federal agencies if satisfaction is not reached on a lower level.

Provision for the least restrictive environment under PL 94-142 will require the elementary teacher to take on new roles in teaching children and in working with parents. The prospective teacher should take every opportunity to acquire knowledge and attendant skills that are necessary for the successful implementation of *The Education for All Handicapped Children Act.*

MANAGEMENT OF GROUPS IN THE CLASSROOM

Experienced teachers realize that a class is not necessarily a group. To be a group, pupils must have a psychological identity with one another. They must also have a group spirit that binds them together. A class does not necessarily have these characteristics. We have already seen that a class of pupils, selected on the basis of age alone, or general intelligence, or on the ability to read, contains a wide variability in skills, achievement, psychomotor development, cultural background, personal and social adjustment, and interest.

LAUGHTER AND LOVE IN THE CLASSROOM . . .

Pupils should frequently have an opportunity to work in groups that are organized on the basis of criteria other than reading ability. They need to get acquainted with children they would not get to know very well at all, if groupings were based entirely on success in reading. Such groups are usually happy and productive.

Teachers who make provision for multibased groupings for their pupils experience the rewards that come from hearing and seeing laughter and love in the classroom. This is because children are free to accept each other on new terms. They begin to appreciate one another because they are free from the pressure of having always to compete.

1. After you have read the following vignettes on "Management of Groups in the Classroom," decide whether Ellen Baxter and Jim Bond provided their pupils with this kind of atmosphere.
2. Also determine what provisions, other than those made by Miss Baxter and Mr. Bond, you would make to create an atmosphere where laughter and love would be encouraged.

The teacher should make the necessary provisions for the class to become a group. These provisions are based primarily on (1) the establishment of a group atmosphere in the classroom; (2) making

NOTE TO THE READER

1. As you read the following vignettes identify the techniques Miss Baxter and Mr. Bond employed in teaching pupils in small groups.
2. Identify the learner outcomes that resulted from the pupils' being taught in subgroups that would have been difficult to achieve if they had been taught in a total class setting.
3. List the ideas you have gained from these vignettes about group management.

provisions for individual differences; and (3) teaching the skills needed for effective group participation.

Miss Baxter's Experiences with Teaching Children in Groups

Pupils need to develop effective group skills early in their school life. Many teachers assume that within-class groupings, where children work in subgroups, are more appropriate on the intermediate level. Miss Baxter believed otherwise because she had seen numerous examples of successful subgroup activities in her student teaching. She also knew the importance of teaching the skills that are basic to effective group participation. Her professors had stressed the importance of preparing pupils for subgroup work by making certain they possessed the skills necessary for the performance of group tasks, and that they were ready for the level of social behavior necessary for the achievement of the tasks in subgroups. Her teacher education and primary-classroom experiences had also taught her to begin subgroup work slowly, by first building group spirit and effective social behavior on a total-class basis.

Miss Baxter began on the first day of school to include pupils in the performance of certain duties related to the upkeep of the room. She wanted them to acquire a feeling of responsibility for the development and maintenance of the learning environment. She had also spent considerable time during the planning period each morning in helping pupils establish good speaking and listening habits, and in accepting each other's points of view. These experiences had convinced her that the children were capable of beginning to work in subgroups if situations arose that suggested the need for them to do so. During the first several days of instruction, the following situations occurred in the social studies (see sketch plan for the social studies), providing her with opportunities to plan and manage various types of groups.

Her First Group Discussion

Miss Baxter discovered during the first lesson, designed to introduce the unit of study, "Moving to a New Community," that the variability in the pupils' ability to carry on a group discussion was far greater than she had anticipated. When she attempted to have a discussion of the pictures shown on pages 8 and 9 of their basic textbook,[2] she found that many children insisted on talking at the

[2] See Mae Knight Clark, *et. al.*, *Teacher's Annotated Edition, Communities: Today and Yesterday* (New York: Macmillan Publishing Co., Inc., 1980).

same time, that their responses to her questions were inclined to be irrelevant, and that many pupils were more interested in relating their personal experiences than they were in answering her questions. She realized that the group discussion process would have to be structured more carefully to enable pupils to accomplish planned objectives relative to the topic under study. When she asked questions based on the material on page 10 of their textbook she was more successful. The children were better able to respond to her questions this time and their social behavior also improved. Miss Baxter concluded that this group had the potential for participating in group discussion when the topic was more limited in scope. She closed the lesson by having them suggest ways in which their discussion could be improved. The following rules were agreed on and written on the class chart.

Our Discussion Rules

Talk in turn
Speak clearly
Stay on the topic
Listen carefully
Respect the speaker

Miss Baxter decided to ask the more mature children to respond on how well the class had observed their rules. The idea worked very well, and she felt that she would continue having individual pupils assist in the evaluation. It seemed to be a very sound strategy.

Making Provisions for Variability in Reading Levels

Miss Baxter, during the first lesson, followed the picture-study activity by asking the pupils to read silently pages 10–14 to determine where the Roberts family now lived and where it would be moving. In doing so she discovered that the pupils differed widely in their skimming skills in reading. She realized that these differences would need to be considered carefully in the very near future, when pupils would be expected to gather information from other sources relative to the unit of study. In a second lesson Miss Baxter decided she would provide some variety in the way pupils could gather additional information, and at the same time vary the level of conceptualization required. She planned two types of activities to accomplish this goal—one based on reading and another on picture study. A search of the school library produced several copies of a reference textbook containing a section on "Community Life." She decided to make an assignment from it for one subgroup; this would have a teacher-directed learning activity based on picture study, followed by an art activity designed to produce illustrations. Pupils would discuss pictures of community life and then draw their own pictures of community activities. Another subgroup, comprising pupils who were capable of reading independently, would be given a silent reading assignment in the textbook based on "How Communities Satisfy Basic Needs." These children would be provided with a short list of study questions to guide their reading. They would be called on to share their answers with the class at the close of the information-gathering period. She was somewhat nervous about attempting the lesson because Stephanie's mother had come to visit her room that morning. But she decided to go ahead and carry out her plans to work with subgroups, anyway.

Miss Baxter learned a lot about group management skills as a result of the lesson. She had suggested that the subgroup which was given an independent reading assignment spend fifteen minutes on it. In her concern that they develop habits of self-direction, she had reminded them to observe the time by referring to the clock and pacing their reading by it. But she had become so engrossed with the picture-study activity in the second subgroup that she herself had failed to watch the time. She suddenly became aware that the children in the other subgroup had either completed their reading assignment or had completely lost interest in it. Tom, who was a good reader but nevertheless had a very short attention span,

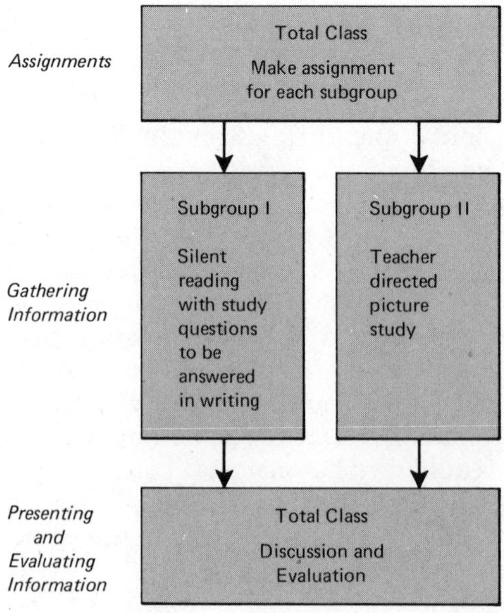

was in another corner of the room, bouncing a basketball. The other pupils were obviously visiting about matters unrelated to their reading assignment. How could she have been unaware of the noise and confusion? And what would Stephanie's mother think about it all? She managed to get the reading group together again, and they sat quietly. But by that time several of the pupils in the subgroup she had spent her time with had also become noisy and restless. It was obvious that many of them had not prepared the illustration which had been assigned. She decided against having the children present their information. She simply asked them to get ready for recess, and told them that tomorrow they would determine whether or not they were ready to present their information.

Later that evening, Miss Baxter reflected on what had happened. She realized that she was at fault. In the first place, she had not provided adequate supervision for the subgroup of independent readers. She had also failed to pace the lesson well. She wrote the following in her notebook:

> The lesson did not go well. Next time remember to provide each group with adequate supervision. The children just weren't ready to be left on their own in an independent reading activity. It's back to the "drawing board" for me.

Miss Baxter was able to rescue the situation on the following day. She had a good evaluation session with the class concerning yesterday's lesson. She was pleased with herself that she had not scolded Tom, because his personal and social behavior needed positive reinforcement. She noticed that he had had great difficulty in sitting still and listening to others during class discussion; she determined to find ways to get better acquainted with him and, if possible, to reduce those learning tasks that seemed to create tension for him. She was also pleased that Mrs. Ginsburg had come in and had observed the lesson when it had been going so well. Mrs. Ginsburg invited Miss Baxter to come to her office later, and they would discuss "group management in general."

Her Concluding Activities

After several days of work-study activities, Miss Baxter decided to plan with the pupils for creative learning activities that would conclude the first phase of the unit of study, "Moving to a New Community." She decided to schedule 40–50 minutes for these lessons as more time would be needed to organize and supervise the various subgroups of pupils that would be involved in these activities. Having the total class engage in each creative activity

would be too time consuming and would fall short of enabling pupils to concentrate on activities that most appealed to their interests and abilities. Miss Baxter recognized the challenge of managing several subgroups, all of which would be working at the same time. But she recognized that this approach would permit her to evaluate individual pupils on such criteria as psychomotor development and personal-social adjustment as they participated in small-group activities. It would also give her an opportunity to observe which children worked well together.

She referred to her sketch plan (as presented in the previous chapter) for the concluding activities she had anticipated using. With these ideas as guidelines, Miss Baxter and the pupils planned the following activities as a conclusion to the first phase of the unit.

1. Prepare a bulletin board display of "Communities Across Our Country."

PHOTO FOLIO

This teacher is directing the type of small-group instruction that is frequently employed in the teaching of reading and social studies. The teacher must plan carefully in order to provide at least two groups of pupils with independent learning activities while working with only one group at a time. Careful directions must be given at the beginning of the lesson in order that the group working independently will not distract the teacher while he/she is working with the other group.

1. Identify several teaching skills that are necessary for successful small-group instruction.
2. Identify several pupil behaviors that are necessary for the child's successful participation in small-group instruction.

2. Prepare illustrated stories of a family's experience in moving to another community.
3. Prepare a mural showing how our community provides for the four basic needs of its citizens.
4. Prepare wall charts with short explanatory statements on major inventions that have changed the communities studied in the unit.
5. Prepare dramatizations about a family preparing to move to a new community.
6. Plan a TV Quiz Program that would be based on answering the following questions:

   What is a community?

   How do communities differ in the way they satisfy basic needs?

   What are some reasons why families sometimes move to a new community?

Miss Baxter's management plan for the lessons based on concluding activities for the unit of study is presented in the following chart.

Miss Baxter's Management Plan

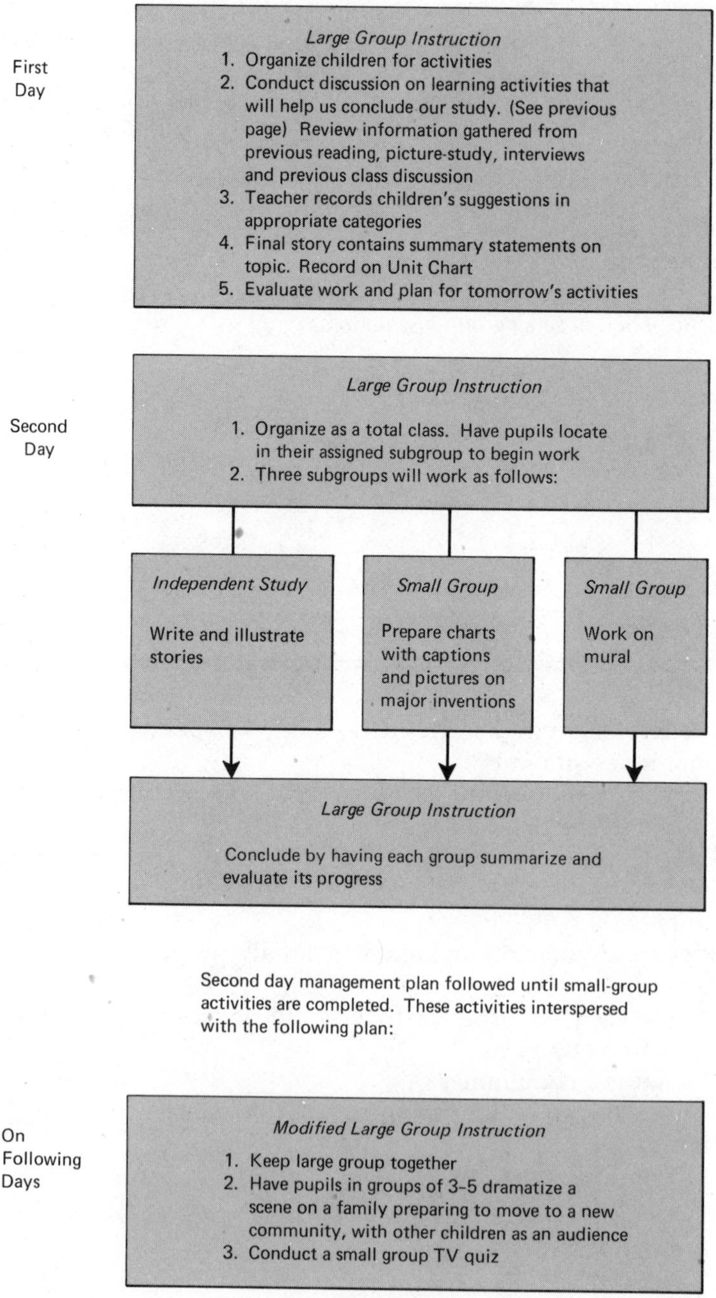

First Day
Large Group Instruction
1. Organize children for activities
2. Conduct discussion on learning activities that will help us conclude our study. (See previous page) Review information gathered from previous reading, picture-study, interviews and previous class discussion
3. Teacher records children's suggestions in appropriate categories
4. Final story contains summary statements on topic. Record on Unit Chart
5. Evaluate work and plan for tomorrow's activities
Second Day
Large Group Instruction
1. Organize as a total class. Have pupils locate in their assigned subgroup to begin work
2. Three subgroups will work as follows:
Independent Study
Write and illustrate stories
Small Group
Prepare charts with captions and pictures on major inventions
Small Group
Work on mural
Large Group Instruction
Conclude by having each group summarize and evaluate its progress
Second day management plan followed until small-group activities are completed. These activities interspersed with the following plan:
On Following Days
Modified Large Group Instruction
1. Keep large group together
2. Have pupils in groups of 3–5 dramatize a scene on a family preparing to move to a new community, with other children as an audience
3. Conduct a small group TV quiz

Miss Baxter's Strategy in Retrospect

On the first day Miss Baxter provided total teacher guidance and supervision for the entire class. Her purpose was to provide a review of the major learning by having pupils make statements that were essentially generalizations of what they had learned. By skillful questioning, a probing technique, and a cue here and there, she and the children were successful in stating several conclusions. Once stated, the pupils wrote their conclusions in their notebooks, and Miss Baxter later placed them on the unit chart. She told the children, "We now have a story that is based on facts we have learned. These statements will be helpful to us in planning ways to express what we have learned during the last several days."

Miss Baxter then conducted her teacher-pupil planning, resulting in the identification of the six concluding activities that were identified in the previous section of this chapter.

On the second and ensuing days, Miss Baxter rotated her supervision from group to group. She discovered that from time to time she had to call the entire class to attention in order to review what a particular subgroup had agreed to do. She found that having two or three pupils in each subgroup describe what the group had agreed to do before starting their work gave her more assurance that the children really understood what they were supposed to do.

Miss Baxter also began increasingly to depend on children to monitor, to distribute materials, and to supervise clean-up activities. What pleased her most was the progressive development of "group spirit" among the pupils. After all, they had participated directly in the planning of the activities, and they were especially pleased when, a few days later, Miss Baxter asked them if they would like to share what they had learned with Mrs. Juarez's class next door. Of course they would!

Miss Baxter's first attempt at dramatization also succeeded beyond her expectations. She attributed her success to the fact that she had conducted the activity on a total-class basis in the beginning. She had begun by asking a small group of children to dramatize a simple situation: depicting a family discussing moving to a new community. The other pupils were instructed to listen carefully and to provide positive suggestions during the evaluation. The children agreed not to criticize each other on the basis of acting ability, but to look for what was said and how well it agreed with the information they had gathered on the topic. This activity was carried on for several days, for a short period of time during each lesson. Miss Baxter knew that pupils would become inattentive and restless were she to continue it for an entire class period. The children gained experience in evaluation and became more spontaneous in their dramatizations as time went by. Miss Baxter was very pleased that Tom did well, and that the children had responded to his dramatizations as "being very real."

On the day the children presented their unit, Mrs. Juarez's class proved to be a responsive audience. The movable partition between the rooms was removed and Miss Baxter's children made their presentations in small groups. Each pupil had responsibility for some aspect of the presentation. The children had selected individuals who made short oral reports. Other pupils simply displayed chart stories; others participated in dramatizations. Mrs. Ginsburg, the school principal, also attended. At the conclusion, she complimented Miss Baxter's class on their performance, and told Mrs. Juarez's pupils that they had been an excellent audience. She suggested that Miss Baxter and Mrs. Juarez might very well plan together for other combined classroom activities. Mrs. Juarez seemed very interested and noted that her group had benefited from the presentation in many ways. She commented on the preparation she had given her group on good audience behavior prior to the presentation. Miss Baxter said that she would especially appreciate Mrs. Juarez's contributions in music and science. They agreed to begin immediately to plan for some cooperative teaching of their two groups.

Miss Baxter had achieved other significant outcomes from these experiences in the unit of study. She had observed the varied interpretations of family and school life that had appeared in the pupils' stories, dramatizations, and art work. They had reflected the divergence in the cultural backgrounds represented among the children. And these were now included as examples of local community life. Each had been accepted on its own merits. She also had assembled valuable data on each pupil's performance that would be important later when she held parent conferences. She kept a folder for each child, and samples of the children's stories and art work from the unit were added to the pupil's products from other school subjects. (Small-group activities had also given Tom an opportunity to express himself in ways acceptable to the principal and to children in another class.) Miss Baxter could only conclude that the time and effort required to provide a balance of individualized, small, and large group-learning activities had paid off well.

Mr. Bond's Efforts to Teach Children in Groups

On the intermediate-grade level, pupils should be somewhat accustomed to working in subgroups in the pursuit of various learning

HOW CAN SHE EVER TEACH THEM THAT WAY?

. . . asked Mrs. Thompson, Stephanie's mother. She had lost no time in going to the principal's office following her departure from Miss Baxter's classroom.

Mrs. Thompson continued, "The lesson finally ended in chaos." Mrs. Ginsburg asked the parent several questions and concluded that Mrs. Thompson didn't really understand what Ellen Baxter had been trying to do.

Mrs. Thompson asserted, "A new teacher like Miss Baxter ought not to attempt complicated teaching of that sort until she gets her feet on the ground."

Mrs. Ginsburg promised to talk to Miss Baxter about it, but she explained to Mrs. Thompson that she was probably attempting to provide pupils with a chance to locate information according to their reading levels. Thus, she had organized them into two groups—one with materials that were more difficult than the other. She invited Mrs. Thompson to come back later, when Miss Baxter had worked out the rough spots.

1. Do you recall what Ellen Baxter decided had gone wrong with the lesson?
2. Do you believe that Mrs. Ginsburg handled the parent criticism effectively?
3. Would you have wanted Mrs. Ginsburg to tell you about Mrs. Thompson's complaint if you had been in Miss Baxter's situation?

outcomes. The teacher cannot take this assumption for granted, however. Before attempting subgroup work, teachers should carefully evaluate the readiness of the class. They should recognize the wide range of differences in ability and achievement among pupils in the class. They should also make every effort to determine the pupils' variability in other major aspects of school life, described earlier—psychomotor development, cultural and language backgrounds, personal and social development, and interest.

Instruction on the intermediate level is highly oriented to textbook learning. Pupils enter this level with a wide range of reading abilities, but textbooks are geared for the average reader. Furthermore, there is a heavier reliance on printed material as a means of learning the cognitive skills in social studies, literature, science, and mathematics than in the primary grades. Thus, the child must be able to read in order to learn. It is fair to say that reading is the predominant learning mode for pupils at this level. This is a grave concern to those educators who know that children's interest in school begins to decline appreciably on the intermediate level. We return to an earlier observation: pupil interest is directly related to the teacher's skill in providing variety in learning activities. The teacher who relies entirely on reading as a learning mode is restricting the avenues of learning available to pupils.

Mr. Bond knew all of this, and therefore was determined to provide his class with a variety of learning activities, even in the face of Mr. Park's admonition that the children must learn the essentials set forth in their textbooks. He also appreciated the difficulty that would be encountered because the problems, topics, and themes presented in the intermediate-level curriculum are far more abstract than those on the primary level. This, he knew, is as typical in mathematics as it is in the social studies. He concluded that, under these constraints, the best way for him to proceed would be to base his program on cognitive learning, and attempt to provide pupils with extended learning activities in the language arts and creative experiences—activities offering concrete, personalized learning opportunities. Let us return to his earlier planning for the social studies, to learn how well he succeeded.

Mr. Bond's First Social Studies Lesson

Mr. Bond began by explaining to the children that he was interested in learning about their experiences in social studies during the previous year. He then proceeded with the questions he had planned for this assessment. He learned several important facts as a result of the discussion:

1. Pupils were fairly skilled in group discussion. They talked in turn, listened attentively, and seemed to respect each other's responses. He concluded that part of this might be because, almost without exception, the class was intact from last year. He also surmised that their teacher had been somewhat successful in building a feeling of group spirit.
2. He concluded that the children had been largely restricted to a read-discuss-write mode of learning. Some of them said they enjoyed reading about the history and geography of their region, but they disliked "always having to discuss it and then write it out." Several others said they "got tired of taking so many tests" on it. Others said they were "tired of always having to read something."
3. When he asked them to identify the topic they would be studying this year, he was surprised that they already knew. (He had asked them to write their guess on a slip of paper before he called on anyone to respond.) Almost without exception, they were accurate.
4. Their responses to his question, "Why do you think it is im-

portant for us to study the United States and the other Americas?" were highly diversified, but most of the pupils had a strong degree of interest in the topic. Mr. Bond considered this to be a positive factor. It would be largely up to him to find ways to sustain their interest.

Mr. Bond randomly selected several pupils to locate the Western Hemisphere on the globe. He noticed that he had to assist some of them before they could do so. He encouraged others to try; the fact that almost every pupil's hand was raised convinced him that they wanted to be called on and were not afraid of being ridiculed if they failed. Only one or two were able to find the approximate location of their city. Again, almost every child seemed to want to try. Mr. Bond sensed that the group, as a whole, needed to develop map and globe study skills, and that this learning outcome would receive early priority.

The activities he planned for introducing pupils to the basic textbook[3] convinced him that the children had received very little instruction in study skills. Very likely their former teachers had made teacher-directed study assignments. Their reference skills seemed to be poor. There were, however, five or six children who always had the correct responses to his directions and questions. The majority of the group made serious efforts to respond, and seemed to be interested in what he was asking them to do. He observed an unresponsive group of four pupils who, interestingly, had asked him if they could sit near each other. They appeared not only uninterested in the exploration of the textbook, but were very restless, and at times turned to whisper to one another. He made a mental note of this.

Mr. Bond learned that he had planned too many activities for a single lesson. He did not have time for the last part of the lesson, when he had hoped to ask the class to match pictures of landforms with their probable locations on the regional map. Nor did he arrive at the place in the lesson where he had planned an assignment for the next day. Instead, he asked the children for their comments about their book. He concluded they were impressed with its colorful layout and study aids. He decided to continue tomorrow where he had left off in the plan. During the next few days he would assess the pupils' ability to read the social studies, a content field that would introduce many new terms and concepts and require them to develop a number of map and study skills.

[3]See Allen Y. King, Ida Dennis, and Florence Potter, *Teacher's Annotated Edition, The United States and the Other Americas* (New York: Macmillan Publishing Co., 1980).

Making Provisions for Variability in Reading Levels

Mr. Bond had received excellent preparation in teaching children to read. His professor had stressed the importance of teaching reading in the content fields. Mr. Bond had been impressed with the soundness of this approach, and he had been somewhat critical of his supervising teacher's neglect of teaching reading in the social studies. The supervising teacher had done a good job providing pupils with extended learning activities in art, music, language, and drama, but he sometimes questioned whether the children actually related what they were doing with the cognitive learning in the social studies. He believed he could do a better job than had been done in teaching children to do research through reading. His plan developed as follows.

1. Continue with total class reading in their textbook *The United States and the Other Americas, pages 1–13.* The thrust in this part was aimed at having pupils acquire selected map and study skills while they were also being introduced to a few major concepts about the geography, climate, and resources of the Americas.
2. Pupils who had reading skills needed for independent study in the basic textbook would be assigned to a single reading group. This arrangement included three-fourths of the class. He would follow the excellent suggestions contained in the Teacher's Manual for helping children to read effectively. The remainder of the class would be assigned to a second group, which would, on some occasions, do directed reading in the basic textbook, and on other occasions would read in selected reference books. These books would treat parallel topics, written on a less sophisticated conceptual level and with a simpler vocabulary. Because the range of reading ability in the second group clustered around a beginning-second to a late-third-grade level, he would need to change his approach and adjust materials for them.

His grouping arrangement is shown on page 225.

Because Mr. Bond had limited experience in the actual management of children in subgroups, he determined to proceed carefully and to avoid a larger number of subgroupings, at least until he had the management of the total class well established. With this model in mind, Mr. Bond tentatively identified other approaches to provide

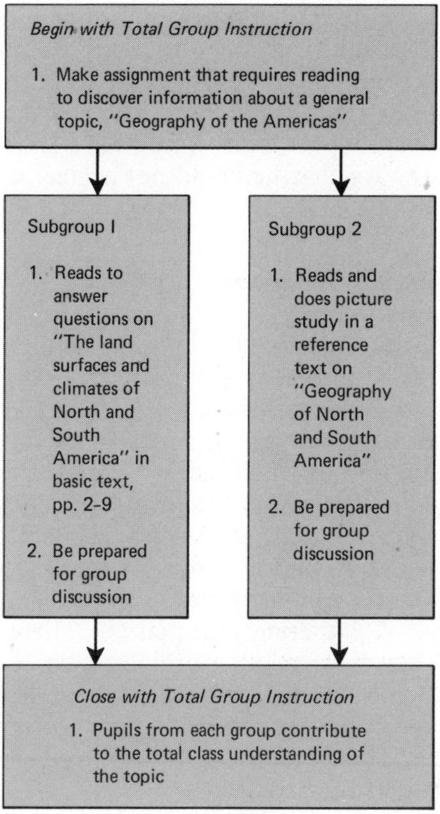

meaningful reading experiences for the class. Here are examples of these.

For Subgroup 1	*For Subgroup 2*
To individualize learning:	To provide variety in learning:
1. Research references, encyclopedia, *National Geographic.* Use to enrich reading in *The United States and the Other Americas.*	1. Directed oral reading with teacher in *The United States and the Other Americas.*
2. Picture study by individual children.	2. Picture study on a group basis.
3. Read selected fiction related to topic.	3. Silent reading in references that contain suitable concept and vocabulary load.
4. Read newspapers and other journals.	4. Teacher reads orally to group.

Mr. Bond felt the need to provide individualized reading experiences for pupils in subgroup one especially, because their reading differences ranged from a late-fourth-grade level to a few who could read material on the tenth-grade level. The amount of teacher guidance during the reading activities would have to focus on subgroup two, but he was aware that he could not neglect the other subgroup in this respect.

Providing Additional Opportunities to Gather Information

Too frequently, intermediate-level teachers tend to equate research with reading. This is unfortunate because there are numerous other ways for pupils to gather information. Field trips, films, filmstrips, video tapes, interviews, television, and a study of photographs are examples of media that can be used in the gathering of information. On the intermediate level, where the variability of children's ability to read is much greater than at the primary level, these additional learning resources offer children from the lowest to the highest level of reading achievement opportunities to work together in a subgroup that has the task of gathering information. There are many pupils who, although they have reading problems, are exceptionally able to interpret and make inferences on a very high level, when they are given the opportunity to use media that do not require a high level of reading ability. These pupils need every opportunity to become contributing members of the group.

Mr. Bond planned to vary the membership of subgroups one and two by mixing the children when the opportunity arose to gather information through learning resources that were not dependent on reading ability for interpretation. His basic model for group management could still be applied—only the membership of the subgroups would need to be changed.

This provision is very important for the psychological support of the poor reader and contributes to positive personal and social development of pupils.

Extended Learning Through Creative Activities

Mr. Bond's sketch plan included activities that were to occur in the language arts and creative arts classes. They were intended to personalize instruction and to make social studies more meaningful to pupils. To summarize briefly, Mr. Bond had planned to have the children engage in a variety of extended learnings that included the following activities.

1. Visit the school library to locate information (reading materials and other media) on the geography of the Americas.
2. Prepare art work to illustrate landforms and vegetation types that are characteristic of the natural regions of the Americas.
3. Prepare oral reports to present basic learnings. These are to include results of interviews on how physical features affect how people live and work in the community.
4. Use art work to illustrate the major learning, including illustrations and maps of the regions studied.

The children participated in several of these activities during the first week of formal instruction. Some were more successful than others. The following section discusses what occurred.

Mr. Bond's Strategy in Retrospect

1. Mr. Bond learned that planning activities for pupils to gather information through reading activities was worthwhile. He could devote the major portion of his time during the reading activities to the less able readers. He learned to make assignments very clearly and then walk around the room until he was certain that everyone was progressing satisfactorily. At first, pupils in subgroup one were distracted when he met with the other children, who read orally or else discussed their reading. But this tendency soon disappeared and pupils from each group seemed to recognize that each group had its own purpose and its own learning tasks. He was also pleased with the way the total class accepted the contributions from each other, regardless of the particular reading group to which they had been assigned. He looked forward to the mixing of subgroups to view the film on natural resources of North and South America.

2. The visit to the school library did not go very well. First, the children seemed ill at ease with the librarian, and she seemed somewhat perturbed that they had not been better prepared for library work. Mr. Bond realized that many of the pupils had never really been on their own in the school library. They were noisy and seemed at a loss as to where to look for the references they were seeking. Most likely their earlier experiences had been limited to "story telling" activities and checking out books under direct supervision. The librarian suggested that they could go ahead and select a book to their liking and, "perhaps your teacher will bring you back soon for a lesson on how to use the library."

Mr. Bond felt embarrassed, but he knew that she was right. He had expected too much of the children. They were not ready to do

reference work. He rescheduled another session for them, at which time the librarian would provide an orientation on how to use the library.

3. Encouraged by the success he had experienced with small-group activities for the pupils in their social studies reading assignment, he found an interesting way to differentiate their endeavors in the creative arts. The pupils would assemble pictures and illustrations of landforms, vegetation types, and occupations that were found in selected natural regions in the Americas. Through teacher-pupil planning, the group decided to develop individual notebooks in which they would include maps and visual materials. He discovered that some children preferred to draw and crayon-color their illustrations, but others preferred to paint watercolor scenes. The majority of the pupils wanted to search through magazines and newspapers for illustrations. During the art period he organized subgroups on the basis of their preferences. The identification of these subgroups

PHOTO FOLIO

Teaching pupils in groups sometimes falls short of providing the attention needed by an individual pupil. The teacher in this photograph recognizes the importance of a one-to-one relationship between teacher and pupil. She has provided this child with an opportunity to receive individual attention while the other pupils are working on their own. Teachers who are good planners and who are skillful in classroom management find little difficulty in providing their pupils with the individual attention they all need at one time or another.

1. Studies show that reducing class size does not necessarily promote the kind of individual attention shown in this picture. How do you account for this?
2. Suggest a classwide learning situation that would offer possibilities for the teacher to give individual attention to selected pupils.

enabled Mr. Bond to consolidate the supervision of activities more efficiently. He asked pupils who were painting to group themselves in one section of the room; those who were drawing and making color illustrations to group in another section, and those who were searching magazines and other printed matter to locate in another corner. This arrangement gave the children an opportunity to regroup themselves; it also made it easier to distribute and use materials. These tasks were assigned to individual pupils and he found that they handled them very well. At the beginning of each period, the children discussed what they planned to accomplish, and at the close of the period, a pupil in each subgroup was asked to give an oral progress report on what had been accomplished. The activities were somewhat noisier than the customary study type, because the children frequently talked when comparing efforts, making suggestions, and assisting each other. Mr. Bond saw a great deal of progress in their ability to work together. He had made certain that the four children who had been inattentive earlier were in separate subgroups. He reasoned that they needed to make new friends and learn to work with others. This form of task-oriented subgrouping seemed to be contributing to the personal and social development of the children.

On one occasion, Mr. Park came into the room with a report form for Mr. Bond. He seemed somewhat uncomfortable with the noise level in the room, but became reassured when Mr. Bond explained that this was their art period. Mr. Bond wondered what Mr. Park's reaction would have been had the same type of activities been going on during the social studies period. He guessed that Mr. Park might have been rather critical.

4. Mr. Bond knew that the quality of pupil oral reports frequently left much to be desired. Thus he planned to have a general group discussion on the progress the children had made toward interviewing various adults about how the physical features of the region had affected their occupations. He discovered that much haphazard fact-finding had resulted from most of the pupils' efforts. He realized he needed to teach children skills in conducting interviews. He was glad that he had not planned for the children to make oral reports on the results of their interviews. He assisted the pupils in summarizing the main ideas that had been collected. He decided to postpone any expectation of formal reports until the children had an opportunity to learn how to present a report orally. This could be scheduled for later language arts lessons.

5. All in all, the first several days of formal social studies instruction had been successful. Mr. Bond believed he had made several key decisions along the way that had kept the class on the track toward achieving the learning outcomes that had been established earlier. He was pleased with the pupils' map work and with their notebooks containing short descriptions and illustrations. The bulletin boards also contained examples of their work. He was even more pleased when he discovered that the children were able to provide examples of the generalization that "Geographical (physical features) influence where and how people live and what they do." These generalizations were obtained in the form of verbal and written responses to his questions, as well as from pupils' interpretations of their extended learning in the language and creative arts.

The fact that his sketch plan had undergone considerable modification as the actual learning activities got underway, did not trouble Mr. Bond. He remembered reading somewhere that good planning is tenative, and that the good teacher is flexible and knows when to modify and change the best of plans.

Mr. Bond wished that he had been able to gain additional student-teaching experiences in planning and managing such extended learning activities as construction, dramatization, and music. But he had made a good beginning, and he could add these to his repertoire later.

LEARNING FROM MISS BAXTER'S AND MR. BOND'S EXPERIENCES . . .

1. Why did these two teachers convert their classes from whole group to small group instruction gradually, over a period of several days, rather than doing it abruptly on a single day?
2. For what reasons did these teachers intersperse whole class with small group instruction?
3. What classroom activities are particularly well suited to a whole class configuration and which ones to small groups?
4. What criteria did these two teachers apply in evaluating the effectiveness of their small group instructional endeavors?
5. Give examples of how these two teachers made use of subgroups to help individualize learning.
6. What ill effects might flow from unwise within-class grouping of pupils? What would you consider "unwise grouping of pupils" to mean?
7. Why are grouping policies particularly relevant in light of the current emphasis on mainstreaming of mildly handicapped children?

PREPARING FOR THE FIRST PUPIL-PROGRESS REPORTING PERIOD

Having barely gotten the school year underway, Miss Baxter and Mr. Bond were confronted with the task of preparing pupil-progress reports. They were aware that elementary teachers across the nation were also involved in a process that has become almost a ritual during the early part of November. Because a considerable amount of emphasis had been placed on its importance in their teacher education programs, they were fully aware of its major purposes:

1. To inform the child of his/her progress.
2. To provide parents with an assessment of the pupil's strengths and weaknesses.
3. To serve as a two-way mode of communication between home and school.

They were also aware that there are several basic types of pupil-progress reports used in elementary schools. The most common are (1) numerical or alphabetical ratings, (2) written narratives, (3) check lists, and (4) parent conferences. In actual practice, some schools use a combination of (1), (2), and (3), as well as parent conferences.

Miss Baxter Prepares Her First Parent Conference

The parent conference is more prevalent on the primary level than in the intermediate grades. This is partly because progress in beginning reading is easier to interpret in a conference setting than on a report card. The teacher can do a better job in explaining to the parent what the pupil is actually doing, what the needs are, and what the home can do to assist. The conference also enables the teacher to become aware of the parent's attitudes about the child, the home, and the school. This information is very useful to the teacher in establishing the best possible learning climate for the child, and in selecting appropriate materials for an individual.

Many primary teachers conduct parent conferences during the first pupil-progress reporting period and write narrative reports during the remainder of the school year. Some teachers alternate parent conferences and written reports throughout the year. Frequently, the first parent conference follows an "Open House," when parents are invited to attend school, meet the teacher, and listen to an explanation of the school program. This was the procedure at East Elementary School. Mrs. Ginsburg, the school principal, began planning with her teachers early in September for the November "Open House" and the parent conferences. Mrs. Ginsburg stressed the following points:

1. Fill a folder with samples of the pupil's school work. Include for each subject representative products that show progress or the lack of it over a period of time.
2. Write anedcotes that reflect an objective description of the pupil's behavior.
3. Interpret the child's performance on readiness and achievement tests. Be sure to specify the pupil's level of performance in terms of his/her potential to achieve.

The principal also gave some helpful hints on conducting a good parent conference:

1. Begin on a positive note.
2. Accept the parent's feelings.

3. Emphasize the child's strengths.
4. Be specific about the pupil's learning difficulties.
5. Be receptive to the parent's suggestions.
6. Close on a positive note, and with a plan of action.

Miss Baxter discovered that the parent conferences were very rewarding. Mrs. Ginsburg's suggestions had proved very useful. The conferences were scheduled over a period of two weeks, during which the children were dismissed an hour early. The "Open House" had really tested her ability to describe for parents the type of work the pupils would be doing that year. She began to appreciate the time she had spent in determining outcomes for the school year and in getting acquainted with the textbooks and other learning resources the children would be using. These early planning activities had provided her with a frame of reference that made the pupil-reporting tasks much easier.

Mr. Bond Prepares His First Pupil-Progress Report

Mr. Park also distributed pupil-progress report forms to the teachers early in September. He emphasized that teachers should keep a work folder for every pupil. He also suggested that in certain instances the teacher might find it useful to schedule a parent conference in order to communicate better to the parents the status of the pupil's performance. The work samples would be very worthwhile to have in such instances.

Mr. Bond was disappointed that the form did not provide for pupil self-evaluation. He made the decision to improvise his own system for this purpose. He developed a simple report form that would allow pupils to evaluate their "School Habits." He began discussing it with the children as soon as the class had demonstrated they could work together as a group. He told them he would discuss

My School Habits

	Always	Usually	Seldom	Never
I assume responsibility				
I contribute to the group				
I work well with others				
I play well with others				
I do my best in my studies				
I take care of materials				
I follow school rules				

the form with each of them personally, at which time they would be asked to complete it. He prepared a large-scale version of it for a wall chart. Each pupil was given a copy for his/her notebook.

When he began to confer with the children about their self-evaluations, he learned that some of them were realistic in their ratings, others were not. In each instance he was able to have a candid discussion with the pupil about behavior that is very important to personal, social, and academic development. He felt much closer to each child following the discussion. He also spent a few minutes each day discussing the pupil-progress report form with them. He wanted them to know ahead of time what they were being evaluated on.

Because there were to be no school-wide parent conferences scheduled for the first pupil-progress reporting period, Mr. Bond would have little opportunity to meet parents early in the year. In thinking about the matter, he decided to telephone each home and introduce himself. He began each conversation with, "Hello, this is Jim Bond, ________'s new teacher. I'm just calling to say hello." During the course of the conversation, he extended an invitation to parents to visit his classroom during the year. He encouraged them to call him if they were ever concerned about any matter pertaining to the child's school life. By giving each parent his home telephone number, he convinced them of his sincerity. The parents seemed to appreciate his calling, and he did have a few visitors and several telephone calls during the course of the year. Mr. Bond concluded that his idea was really a pretty good way to establish a two-way mode of communication between himself and the parents.

Mr. Bond found the planning he had done at the beginning of the year had been of great value to him in completing the pupil-progress reports. He followed the advice of Miss Ward, a teacher down the hall from his room, in beginning the task of completing the reports a couple of weeks before they were due. He was very glad he had listened to her instead of waiting until the last minute to complete them.

Mr. Bond sent the pupil-progress reports home on schedule, and was pleasantly surprised to learn that many parents were pleased with their child's performance. He made this conclusion on the basis of their written remarks when the forms were returned. Two parents requested follow-up conferences; Mr. Bond scheduled them during after-school hours. One went very well, but the second one was far less successful than Mr. Bond would have liked. The parent was critical of the school, the principal, and Mr. Bond himself. Mr. Bond felt he should have challenged what the parent had alleged, and that he may have given the parent the impression that he agreed with him. He concluded that he needed to learn more about what to do in such instances.

SHARING EXPERIENCES AT A PROFESSIONAL MEETING

During February, the regional professional teacher education conference was held at a nearby university. Just by chance Miss Baxter and Mr. Bond chose the same section meeting, devoted to problems faced by beginning teachers. They began to share experiences, and found that although their teacher preparation, their present assignments, and their teaching levels were different, they shared many similar ideas and experiences. Mr. Bond was very impressed with the physical environment in Miss Baxter's school. He also was somewhat envious of the leadership Miss Baxter received from her principal. He was also impressed with the learning activities that Miss Baxter was able to provide her children in a unit of work. He especially liked the dramatic and creative activities she provided in small groups.

Miss Baxter was impressed with Mr. Bond's determination to make the most of what she imagined to be a rather rigid atmosphere. She liked his approach to providing differentiated learning activities through within-class groupings. She marvelled at his ingenuity in such matters.

Miss Baxter and Mr. Bond both agreed that careful attention to planning and organization had enabled them to get off to a good start. Mr. Bond described his plans to go to summer school in order to extend his professional development. He hoped to take courses in creative activities for children. Miss Baxter described her plans for travel during the coming summer. She said she hoped to return with a renewed professional commitment to do an even better job in teaching.

The teachers attending the meeting made several recommendations for the improvement of teacher education. These suggestions centered on many aspects of the type of teacher education program that Miss Baxter had experienced: (1) integrating theory and practice in a program that provides classroom experiences concurrently with methods courses; (2) providing contacts in classrooms that cover the significant events throughout the school year, from opening through closing practices; and (3) providing experiences with classroom teachers on different levels. Mr. Bond heartily concurred with these recommendations, because his teacher education program had provided none of them.

They also agreed on another important point made by the closing speaker—that learning to teach is a career-long process. Every teacher is, in one sense of the word, a beginner, every year—even every day, because no two days are alike. The qualified and competent teacher never ceases to learn, or at least, should not cease to learn.

Mr. Bond left the meeting thinking that he didn't have such a bad situation after all. It wasn't as good, perhaps, as Miss Baxter's, but it certainly was a lot better than many that he had heard described during informal conversations with others. Mr. Park wasn't the best principal, but certainly he wasn't the worst in the world. He could now appreciate that he had been given more freedom than he thought. Never once had he been discouraged from doing what he thought Mr. Park might consider to be a "fad" or a "frill."

Miss Baxter departed with a sense of appreciation for the quality of her teacher preparation program, and with a feeling of gratitude that she had been assigned to East School, where Mrs. Ginsburg was the principal.

Both had gained a greater perspective on their teaching situations. They agreed that the meeting had been well worth the time, effort, and expense. Even more important was their realization that participation in professional meetings is an excellent medium for professional growth.

CLOSING THE SCHOOL YEAR

The final two weeks of the school year are very hectic for teachers. The preparation of final pupil-progress reports, last-minute parent conferences, supervision of children during a field day, completion of final records, participation in a final conference with the school principal—all of this, in addition to the daily management of the classroom—contributes to making the closing of the school year a hectic experience.

Promotion and Retention of Pupils

Although the procedure for determining if a child is to be retained begins much earlier, the final decision ordinarily takes place during the last few weeks of the school year. Educators are very cautious about retaining pupils a second year on the same grade level. There is ample research evidence that retention does not usually result in improvement in the child's achievement. The majority of research findings also support what experience has indicated—failure contributes negatively to the pupil's self-concept. Thus, when a child is being considered for nonpromotion, the teacher usually does not make a unilateral decision. Rather, a group of educators, including the school psychologist, principal, and teacher, as well as the parents, arrive at the decision. As a result, few children are retained at the same level for a second year.

Neither Miss Baxter nor Mr. Bond recommended any children for retention. Had they done so, they were aware of the fact that their recommendation would have been reviewed and a final decision made based on group study and conferences.

Final Record Keeping

Miss Baxter and Mr. Bond discovered that final processing of the pupils' cumulative folders was a sizable task. They were provided with a checklist from the principal's office, outlining the items that had to be completed before returning each child's folder to the office files. Miss Baxter received the following checklist:

CHECKLIST FOR FINAL PROCESSING OF CUMULATIVE FOLDERS

Items to be completed by the teacher:

_____Quarterly Pupil-Progress Reports
_____Reports of Parent Conferences
_____School Enrollment Information Sheets
_____Cover Sheets of Group Test Results
_____Individual Test Booklets
_____Health Record
_____Special Reports (Psychologist, Nurse, Therapist)
_____Reading Record
_____Anecdotal Records or notes that contain special information
_____Cumulative Record Card, containing:
    _____Promotion
    _____Attendance Summary
    _____Group Test Results
    _____Individual Test Results
    _____School Citizenship (short summary)
    _____Special Abilities (short summary)
    _____Recommendation for Improvement (short summary)

During their teacher preparation experiences, Miss Baxter and Mr. Bond had not been given responsibility for the final preparation of the pupils' cumulative folders. Their supervising teachers had actually done the major share of the work, because they were the persons responsible for doing so. Both teachers wished that they had been given more opportunities to participate in the process before they were faced with it as beginning teachers.

Preparing the Classroom

Closing the classroom for summer vacation also involved tasks of a special nature. These, too, took time to complete. Each teacher was given the following checklist.

ROOM CHECKLIST

Place a check by each when completed:

____Library books returned to library
____Reading kits returned to library
____Audio-visual materials returned to storeroom
____P. E. Equipment returned to storeroom
____Globes and maps returned to storeroom
____Blackboards and bulletin boards cleared
____First aid box, lesson plan book, building and district handbook returned to principal's office
____Keys returned to principal's office

Miss Baxter and Mr. Bond were able to delegate many of these duties to their pupils. Practically every child in the room hoped to "help out," and nearly everyone had the opportunity.

Final Conference with the School Principal

Both teachers, now flushed with the success of having received a contract for the following year, looked forward to a last talk with their principals before leaving for the summer months. The conferences had been scheduled during the final two weeks of school, and were intended to provide the principal with an opportunity to reflect on the teacher's experiences. For the teacher, the conference presented an opportunity to discuss matters with the principal in a professional and confidential setting. Hopefully, the conference would result in professional improvement for the teacher.

Miss Baxter's Conference

Mrs. Ginsburg had asked each of her teachers to formulate a set of objectives for the following year. These were to be professional objectives for the teacher, as well as those that pertained to pupils. By this time, Miss Baxter felt at ease in Mrs. Ginsburg's office. She, like the other teachers, had profited from several prior conferences.

One of these, at mid-year, had focused on the principal's evaluation of the teacher's performance, and Miss Baxter had benefited greatly from this conference. Mrs. Ginsburg had praised her ability to plan, to relate to children and to parents, and had suggested that Miss Baxter should find the time to get better acquainted with the other teachers and to participate in recreational activities. Mrs. Ginsburg had stressed the importance of relaxation as a "renewal" activity that was especially needed by professional people who are constantly concerned with the welfare of others.

Miss Baxter included these intentions among her objectives:

1. To get additional preparation in music and science.
2. To become more active in the professional association.
3. To provide more creative activities for pupils.
4. To take "time out" occasionally for recreation.

Mrs. Ginsburg commented on the efficacy of Miss Baxter's objectives. Then she said, "Ellen, I have a surprise for you—one that I hope will be inviting." She asked Miss Baxter whether she would like to participate next year in an open-classroom project that would include her own and her neighbor's classroom, in what would become an open space for the children. Mrs. Ginsburg stated that pupils would be selected from the six- to eight-year-old age group. She also said that if Miss Baxter was interested in the offer it would mean she would need to report one month earlier, for an orientation workshop in teaching children in an open-classroom organized on a multiage grouping plan. Mrs. Ginsburg added that it was terribly late to consider doing it, but that only yesterday the superintendent's office had received a state-level funding grant to field-test the plan. Miss Baxter accepted, of course, because she knew she had been invited on the basis of Mrs. Ginsburg's evaluation of her as a qualified and competent teacher. Besides, she realized that it was a golden opportunity to teach in an experimental setting.

Mr. Bond's Conference

Mr. Park had talked to Mr. Bond on several occasions about his teaching performance. Usually these conversations had been brief and to the point. Mr. Bond had grown accustomed to the principal's "dropping in" frequently when he was teaching. It was usually at these times that Mr. Park remarked about what was going on in the room. He had grown to respect Mr. Bond's interest in providing opportunities for learning through social studies activities. He also was impressed with Mr. Bond's ability to plan and organize learning activities. Once Mr. Park remarked, "If everyone planned as well as you do, Jim, there would be more learning going on around here." Mr. Park had been pleased with the results of the achievement tests in Mr. Bond's classroom. At midterm, he had shown Mr. Bond what he had written about him on the district evaluation form. It contained the essence of positive remarks that he had made on earlier occasions.

During the final conference, Mr. Park complimented Mr. Bond on the fact that parents seemed to like and respect him. Mr. Park said he was also very impressed that few "discipline" problems had occurred among Mr. Bond's children. He concluded by telling Mr. Bond he considered him to be an excellent first-year teacher, and was looking forward to working with him again next year. Mr. Bond departed thinking how good it was going to be to return to West School for another year. Now he had even more reason to extend his professional growth through attendance at summer school.

DEVELOPING RELATED COMPETENCIES

It Takes All Kinds of People to Make a World

Mrs. Ginsburg was always pleased with the relaxed atmosphere she found in Ellen Baxter's classroom. The children seemed to enjoy what they were doing. Their enthusiasm showed in their laughter and expressions of appreciation for their classmates. Most impressive of all was the concern her pupils had for one another. They never seemed to be overly critical or cruel, as children can frequently be. Instead, they were supportive of each other. On one occasion, Mrs. Ginsburg remarked to herself, "Those children are very much like Ellen—it just goes to show 'Like teacher, like child.'"

Mr. Park observed much of the same behavior in Jim Bond's classroom. But he couldn't feel completely at ease about what he saw. He had always believed that learning should be difficult and competitive. "The real world out there is hard and cold," he reminded himself. "Competition is much better than cooperation in preparing to deal with the realities of the world." "But," he also wondered, "maybe Jim Bond is more right about it than I am. Time will tell."

1. What does Mrs. Ginsburg's remark suggest about teaching and learning?
2. What criteria do you believe Mr. Park will ultimately apply to determine Mr. Bond's success with pupils?

FOR FURTHER PROFESSIONAL STUDY

Books

Affleck, J., S. Lowenbraun, and A. Archer. *Teaching the Mildly Handicapped in the Regular Classroom,* 2nd ed. Columbus, Ohio: Charles E. Merrill, 1980.

Good, Thomas L., and Jere E. Brophy. *Looking in Classrooms.* 2nd ed. New York: Harper and Row, Publishers, 1978. Chaps. 9, 10.

Orlich, Donald C., *et al. Teaching Strategies: A Guide to Better Instruction.* Lexington, Massachusetts: D. C. Heath and Company, 1980. Chap. 7.

Petreshene, Susan S. *The Complete Guide to Learning Centers.* Palo Alto, California: Pendragon House, 1978.

Ragan, William B., and Gene D. Shepherd. *Modern Elementary Curriculum,* 5th ed. New York: Holt, Rinehart and Winston, 1977. Chap. 6.

Reynolds, Maynard C., and Jack W. Birch. *Teaching Exceptional Children in All America's Schools.* Reston, Virginia: The Council for Exceptional Children, 1977. Chap. 4.

Turnbull, Ann P., and Jane B. Schulz. *Mainstreaming Handicapped Students: A Guide for the Classroom Teacher.* Boston: Allyn and Bacon, Inc., 1979.

Periodicals

Blumenfeld, Phyllis C., V. Lee Hamilton, Kathleen Wessels, and David Falkner. "Teaching Responsibility to First Graders." *Theory Into Practice* (June 1979), 174–180.

Colbert, C. Diane. "Instructional Organization Patterns of Fourth Grade Teachers." *Theory Into Practice* (June 1979), 170–173.

Dunn, Rita, and Robert W. Cole. "Enter Into The World of the Handicapped: P.L. 94-142 Opens the Door." *The Clearing House* (January 1980), 241–243.

Dunn, Rita S., and Kenneth J. Dunn. "Learning Styles/Teaching Styles: Should They . . . Can They . . . Be Matched?" *Educational Leadership* (January 1979), 238–244.

Instructor (March 1980), "Working with Parents"—Special Feature: Eight teachers share their success stories. 52–58.

Peterson, Penelope L., and Terence C. Janicki. "Individual Characteristics and Children's Learning in Large-Group and Small-Group Approaches." *Journal of Educational Psychology* (October 1979), 677–687.

Wattenberg, William W. "The Ecology of Classroom Behavior." *Theory Into Practice* (October 1977), 256–261.

8

Questioning Strategies

THE QUALIFIED AND COMPETENT TEACHER . . .

1. Uses a variety of questions to achieve goals and objectives in teaching.
2. Uses a variety of questions to stimulate pupil learning.
3. Is skillful in framing, stating, sequencing, and pacing questions.

Performance Criteria

As a result of the serious study of this chapter, the student should be able to . . .

1. Write a sample question for a grade of his or her choice for each of the types of questions discussed.
2. Explain the need for different types and levels of questions.
3. Write a series of questions in an appropriate sequence for the development of a learning for a grade of his or her choice.
4. Demonstrate the ability to use questions by teaching a group of children or a peer group; the demonstration to include framing and stating questions, pacing and sequencing questions, and responding to learner responses.

Questioning is among the oldest and most commonly used teaching and learning strategies. Whether in school or out of school, people ask questions when they want to find out something they do not already know. Thus, questioning is a natural way to learn and to satisfy one's curiosity. Questioning can also serve as a teaching strategy in order to draw from the learner specific relevant details, to help learners sense relationships, to facilitate their reasoning processes, to test their knowledge, to challenge their thinking, and for many other purposes. One of the most famous teachers of all times, Socrates, used inductively sequenced questions as a way of deriving and discovering common characteristics of key terms, thereby moving the discussants toward the possibility of arriving at a true and universal definition. Research indicates that classroom teachers today make frequent use of questions; but there has been a considerable amount of criticism of the types of questions asked by teachers, and of the purposes for which questioning strategies have been used.

In recent years, questioning as it relates to teaching and learning has undergone considerable systematic study. This has come about partly because of the increased emphasis on inquiry and partly because thinking has emerged as a high-priority outcome of education. If teachers are to help pupils develop the intellectual skills associated with reflective thought, they will obviously have to ask questions that trigger the use of such skills. Therefore, attention has been focused on so-called *higher level* questions—those that call for application of information, analysis, synthesis, interpretation of data, and so on. In this context, so-called *lower level* questions, those that require the recall of information or the reproduction of information that has been taught, would not be appropriate. Studies of classroom questions asked by teachers, however, have consistently shown that the percentage of factual and recall questions is very high. In some studies the figure reported has been as high as 90 per cent. Questions of this type are not likely to engender thought processes that are consistent with the instructional goals associated with inquiry and reflective thought. It is evident that skillful questioning is crucial to good teaching and learning.

LEVELS OF QUESTIONS

The idea of "levels" of questions, i.e., higher level and lower level, has come from the extensive use of the taxonomy of educational objectives (cognitive domain) by Benjamin Bloom and his associates.[1] This taxonomy classifies educational objectives into six broad groups: Knowledge, Comprehension, Application, Analysis, Synthesis, and Evaluation. There are subcategories within each of the six. Although the taxonomy was designed as a classification scheme for objectives, it serves very well for the classification and study of questions as well. Professor Francis P. Hunkins has conducted extensive research on the use of the Bloom *Taxonomy,* and the reader is referred to his book *Questioning Strategies and Techniques* for many examples of questions in the various taxonomy categories.[2]

It is important to recognize that only one category, the first one, knowledge, deals with the recall or reproduction of information. All of the others have to do with how the individual *processes* the information intellectually. Because it is assumed that the recall of specific information requires less sophisticated intellectual operations than does analysis or synthesis, for example, the idea of higher order and lower order objectives or questions is associated with their position in the taxonomy. This interpretation of the taxonomy is misleading because it implies an ordering of complexity of objectives or questions in accordance with the hierarchy implicit in the taxonomy. Of course, it does not always follow that questions will be simple or complex because of their position in the taxonomy. A complex knowledge question may be much more difficult for a learner than a simple application question. For example, compare the complexity of the two questions:

Knowledge — *Level One*

What events led up to the major outbreaks of civil disobedience in American cities in the late 1960's?

Application — *Level Three*

Show that you know how to use your ruler by measuring the distances between the points shown below:

a. .__________.
b. .___________________________.
c. ._________.
d. .____________________.

It is obvious that the first question is much more complex than

[1] Benjamin S. Bloom, Ed., *Taxonomy of Educational Objectives: Handbook I, The Cognitive Domain* (New York: David McKay Co., Inc., 1956).
[2] Francis P. Hunkins, *Questioning Strategies and Techniques.* Boston: Allyn & Bacon, Inc., 1972. pp. 33–61.

the second one, even though it would be classified as a knowledge-type question and, therefore, lower level. For this reason, one needs to be careful in designating questions as being on lower or higher levels. It makes some difference if one is thinking of *levels* as representing simple or complex intellectual questions, or if one is thinking in terms of levels of difficulty of the questions.

The use of a taxonomy such as the one discussed here has value in reminding the teacher of the many possibilities for types of questions that can be asked. Work with the taxonomy will ensure that several different types of questions, representing various categories of the taxonomy, will become a regular part of work in the classroom. It is always productive for the teacher to think of types of questions in terms of the purposes to be served in the instructional process.

QUESTIONS THAT FOCUS ON THE LEARNING PROCESS

There are many ways to classify the types of questions used by the teacher. One way is to use the taxonomy model previously discussed. Another way is to follow the teaching sequence and analyze the types of questions used by the teacher at each step along the way: motivation, presentation, development, summarization, application. Yet another way to look at questioning strategies is in terms of what effect they have on the *learning process.* That is, what effect does the teacher's question have in triggering certain intellectual operations on the part of the learners? Questions of this type will be discussed in this section.

Determining the Focus

At the beginning of a lesson introducing a new concept, skill, or topic, the teacher wants to establish in the pupils a focus or a mind-set that will bring their attention to the task at hand. The teacher may use a question or a series of questions to establish the focus of the study. These questions may have motivating value as well, but their main purpose is to focus the attention of the learners on what is to be studied.

EXAMPLES:

1. What do the pictures on the bulletin board tell us about the importance of clean air?
2. What important event will be taking place throughout the country three weeks from today?
3. Why do you suppose the story about food received so much attention in the news today?

4. Look at these two plants. Why do you think this one looks perfectly healthy but this one is covered with yellow spots?
5. Where in the world do you suppose this picture was taken?

Concept Formation

Questioning can be an important strategy for the development of concepts. Indeed, appropriate questioning is essential if the teacher uses an inquiry mode that is inductively sequenced for concept development. The kinds of questions a teacher uses for this purpose will be those that help pupils summarize their observations, help identify common properties or criteria for grouping, and ask for labels or definitions of the groups.

EXAMPLES:

1. What did you find in your reading, research, and observation that would be an example of what we have been talking about?
2. Which of these things (pointing to a lengthy list on the chalkboard) should be grouped together?
3. On what basis would you say they should be grouped together? (Referring to question 2.)
4. What would be a good name for each of these groups?
5. What is a common word we use to identify things such as those we have placed in this group?

Generalizing and Making Inferences

To make a generalization requires that the individual put together a declarative statement that expresses a relationship between concepts, situations, or events. Therefore, if pupils are to make generalizations and inferences from data, they must be able to sense common properties in two or more situations or events. Most learning and education specialists encourage teachers to get pupils to arrive at their own generalizations rather than to memorize generalizations developed by someone else. Going through the process of dealing with data, observing similarities and differences, seeing the connection between related concepts, becoming acquainted with the supporting detail that gives meaning to ideas are all prerequisite experiences that lead to learner-generated generalizations. This obviously strengthens learning and enhances transfer possibilities. The types of questions teachers ask can materially assist pupils in their ability to make generalizations and inferences.

EXAMPLES:

1. In what ways would you say these two situations are the same? How are they different?
2. What particular features make these events similar to each other?

3. What conditions are always present when electricity is generated?
4. What does this tell you about how the order in which factors are multiplied affects the product?
5. After seeing these several examples of suffixes, what would you conclude about how they are added to words?
6. What does this suggest about why people are willing to risk their lives?

Valuing

All of the questions we have discussed to this point have dealt with cognitive learning and related skills. But much of school learning should, and does, deal with affective components as well. Almost any topic or subject can be explored in terms of value dimensions. For example, let us say that a class is studying a picture that appears in a science, social studies, or reading book. The picture can be analyzed in terms of what it shows, where it was taken, who the people in it are, and so on. All of this deals with the cognitive messages the picture is conveying. Such questions can be answered as to their correctness by applying objective criteria. That is, the exact number of people in the picture can be established, one can determine what they are doing, and the location of the activity can be established. Now the situation would be quite different if the teacher shifted the discussion to such matters as whether or not the pupils would *enjoy* doing what is being done by the people in the picture, whether or not they would *like* to live in a place like that, or whether they think the people in the picture seem *happy* in what they are doing. These are value questions, and their correctness cannot be established in an objective sense. How the pupils respond to them depends on individual feelings and preferences. They provide an opportunity for pupils to explore their own preferences and values.

EXAMPLES:

1. How do you feel about the decision Chelsea made to return home?
2. Would you like to have been a member of that group? Why or why not?
3. Do you suppose these people lead happy lives? Why do you think so?
4. What decision would you have made in that situation?
5. Which of the attitudes described in the story do you think is the most important?
6. If you had to make the same choices as the heroine, which one would you have given first priority?

Analysis

Questions that call for analysis are those that require the learner to examine a topic, situation, problem, or event by breaking it apart. This "breaking apart" process, or *analysis,* may be done in order to understand component parts, to see relationships between component elements, to understand their function, or to further analyze the nature of these components. For example, a paragraph of prose might be analyzed in order to discover the topic sentence, the supporting detail, and the summary sentence. A mathematical problem might be analyzed in terms of what is given and what is to be solved. An historical event might be analyzed to determine what groups were involved, and what the issues were that led to conflict. A science problem can be analyzed in terms of the relationship among variables, such as temperature, air pressure, and moisture as these relate to weather conditions.

EXAMPLES:

1. What costs are included in the price you pay for a pair of shoes?
2. Read the three paragraphs on page 176. Which sentences are opinions of the author and which ones are based on facts?
3. Suppose you wanted to know in which of these two countries, Yugoslavia or Greece, farming is more important as a way of making a living. What information would you need?
4. Why did the experiment not work the way we expected?
5. You said you became angry when you read this selection. What words did the author use to affect your feelings this way?

Synthesis

Synthesis questions are, of course, the reverse of analysis. In synthesis, the learner is asked to examine various components and fit them into a functioning whole. The idea is to be able to combine parts, functions, or relationships and form a new structure. Synthesis is closely related to processes that involve generalizing, inferring, and coming to conclusions.

It is clear that synthesis requires the learner to engage in creative behavior. In analysis, the learner is seeking out elements or relationships that inhere in the topic, situation, problem, or event. The task is to find them. In synthesis, on the other hand, what is being sought does not exist at all. It is up to the learner to produce a new structure that pulls together the related elements. This obviously requires a high level of innovative thought.

EXAMPLES:

1. Plan and perform a role-playing activity to dramatize the issues that led to the revolt.
2. Write a short summary of the major points made by the speaker.
3. Figure out a way you can show someone the principle of negative numbers.
4. Suppose you were to spend a week in a wilderness all by yourself and could take only ten items with you. What would you include on your list?

5. If you were in a restaurant in a foreign country and no one there could speak English, how would you order breakfast consisting of orange juice, a boiled egg, toast, and milk?
6. If, instead of being settled by people from Western Europe, the United States would have been settled by people from South China, how might the United States be different from what it is today?

Evaluation

Evaluation questions provide feedback for the learner and, therefore, are extremely important in learning. To evaluate means that one must exercise a judgment about the goodness, appropriateness, effectiveness, or worthwhileness of something. It has to do with whether or not things are as they should be. This means that there must be standards or criteria if such judgments are to be made. The Bloom *Taxonomy*[3] discusses evaluation in terms of internal evidence and in terms of external criteria.

Internal evidence has to do with consistency, organization, or structure. For example, the colors used on a map must be consistent with those used in the key; rivers must not run uphill; cities cannot be located in the middle of oceans. The content of paragraphs has to be consistent with the topic discussed. Outlines must follow a similar organization throughout. Titles of essays or of illustrations have to conform to the subject matter discussed or illustrated.

External criteria, on the other hand, have to do with standards that are established by authorities in the field. For example, there are criteria established by musicians, artists, writers, architects, businessmen, professional practitioners, and others that can be applied to the work in their various fields. Thus, a pupil's essay, for example, might be rated high in terms of internal criteria, but might be rated low if judged by the standards that apply to professional writers.

EXAMPLES:

1. As a cultural center, how does New York compare with other American cities? (external criteria)
2. Does the author ever explain the point he introduces in the first paragraph? (internal criteria)
3. Was the slide completely sterile before you placed the specimen on it? (external criteria)
4. Did you have the microscope focused properly? (internal criteria)
5. Are the routes accurately shown on your map? (internal criteria)
6. Is the sentence punctuated properly? (external criteria)
7. Do your points follow one another logically? (internal criteria)

[3] op. cit.

QUESTIONS THAT FOCUS ON SPECIFIC PURPOSES

In our analysis of the types of questions, we now look at questions as they are used for specific purposes by teachers. The teacher must be skillful in selecting appropriate questions in terms of purposes or the results are likely to be disappointing. For example, teachers sometimes report their inability to involve pupils in discussions. An examination of the kinds of questions they are asking often provides clues as to why they are having this problem. If the questions asked require a yes or no answer, or call for the recall of a specific answer from material pupils have read, there is little to discuss. Discussion questions must obviously be those that will allow for some divergence of views, and those that open possibilities for creative interaction. In this section we will discuss several different types of questions in terms of their varying purposes.

Procedural Questions

Teachers ask many questions that have little, if anything, to do with substantive elements of the instructional program. These questions have to do with classroom procedures, the clarification of directions, transitional inquiries, thought pauses, or rhetorical queries. Some of these questions are a necessary part of teaching, of course; but often they amount to little more than time-fillers while the teacher is gathering his or her thoughts. They may even take the form of a threat. ("Do you want me to change your seat?") Frequently no pupil response is given; indeed, none is expected. Teachers usually are not even fully aware of the extent of their use of questions of this type.

EXAMPLES:

1. Does anyone have a question?
2. Are you ready for the next point?
3. How many of you will be having lunch here today?
4. Will someone review for us what we planned to do during our music period today?
5. Do you think we can figure out a better way to return the bats and balls to the storeroom?
6. Is there anyone in the group who has so little to do that he or she wants me to assign additional work?
7. Will someone review what it is we are supposed to do in the event of a fire alarm?

Questions to Motivate

In all subject and skill areas, teachers have a responsibility to develop interest, build readiness for learning, and set the stage for learning to take place. Questions are often useful for this purpose. Such questions would need to be provocative, interest "grabbers"— ones that arouse the curiosity of the pupils. They would probably be open-ended, in the sense that the teacher is not seeking a final answer. The hope is that these questions will stimulate the pupils to discuss the topic and perhaps raise other questions related to it.

EXAMPLES:

1. This metal ball seems to be too large to be passed through this metal ring. Can you think of any magic we might use to get the ball through the ring without damaging either one?
2. Do you think the Indians were as afraid of the white people as the white people were afraid of the Indians?
3. At what kind of an occasion would you imagine this song was first played?
4. Can you think of some ways we can show the rest of the school what we have been doing in this unit?
5. If you had to find five fire-danger spots in your home, where would you look?
6. Why do you suppose the water comes out of the faucet with such force?

Reflective Questions

Reflective questions are those that are open-ended and require higher-level thought processes. Their purpose is to stimulate the creative imaginations of learners. A reflective question should *not* have a right answer, in the sense that one and only one response is acceptable. Reflective questions may be tied to decision making, thereby requiring the consideration of several alternatives and the consequences of each. Reflective thinking is a broader category than any discussed thus far, and includes elements of application, analysis, syntheses, and evaluation.

For generations teachers have been admonishing their pupils to "think." Even today it is fairly common to hear teachers say, "Now think, boys and girls. Think real (sic) hard!" These practices, while performed with commendable intent, are not satisfactory strategies for the development of thinking skills. If teachers are concerned about building those reflective processes we call thinking, questions must be framed that will call those skills into play.

EXAMPLES:

1. In the early years of our country, many people had comfortable homes and a good life in the thirteen states along the Atlantic. Why do you

suppose some chose to leave all that behind and go to the West, which promised a hard and often dangerous life?

2. Scientists think some chemicals are so dangerous to human health that they should not be used for insect and disease control. Can you think of conditions when they might be used even though they are dangerous?
3. What businesses and what kinds of work would be in greater demand if everyone worked only four days a week?
4. How might the story have ended if the family had visited Aunt Sophie and Uncle Charlie one day sooner?
5. Why are some drugs sold only when prescribed by a medical doctor?
6. Do you think it would be wise to protect only those animals that are useful to human beings? Why or why not?
7. Why must the control of air and water pollution go beyond a single community or a single state?

Questions That Probe

The skillful teacher is adept at asking questions that take the learner to some depth intellectually. Such a teacher is not willing

PHOTO FOLIO

Artifacts, models, and bulletin board displays such as those illustrated in this photograph provide the basis for good questions that lead to improved pupil learning. Try to reconstruct what is going on in the teaching episode in the photograph and then frame five questions the pupils might ask.

Do you think the framed poster "THINK," which is so prominently displayed in the classroom, encourages and enhances pupil thinking skills? Why or why not? Provide examples of other strategies the teacher might *also* use to foster thinking skills in pupils.

to accept a general response, but will pursue the matter further with the learners. "What else can you say about urban living?" "Can you think of still another example?" "Why on earth would anyone want to do that?" "Can you think of any possible reason why he would make such a decision?" Questions that probe continue to search out areas of the data or aspects of the topic that have not yet been touched, and bring them to the surface.

The teacher must exercise some judgment as to the extent to which it is wise or even appropriate to probe further. Almost any topic or subject lends itself to endless discussion. All sorts of trivia can be talked about, most of which may be only tangentially related to the study at hand. The teacher's skill lies in intellectually sifting through the subject in order to pursue those aspects of the topic that are relevant and merit meaningful discussion, bypassing those that serve no useful purpose.

EXAMPLES:

1. Can you think of still other forms of pollution?
2. Why would you call that object a "tool?"
3. Yes, but what else might contribute to the formation of the crystals?
4. What happens if you add the same amount to *both* figures?
5. You say that John left home, but *why* did he leave?
6. Is that really what the author is trying to tell the reader? If so, why isn't he more direct in what he says?
7. Where else in the electrical circuit might we look for the difficulty?

Questions That Clarify

It is often of little value to ask a class, "Is that clear?" Not all pupils are secure enough to admit that something is unclear to them if the remainder of the class understands. Besides, the pupil may honestly believe that the material *is* understood, only to discover later that it is not. Everyone at some time has had such an experience in school. It is helpful, therefore, for the teacher to pose questions that clarify not only at the end of a presentation but during the development of the lesson.

Questions that are intended to clarify will ask the pupil to do specific things, such as the following: (1) cite an example; (2) restate something in one's own words; (3) provide a synonym; (4) work an example, as in mathematics; (5) apply what has been learned in the abstract to a concrete situation; (6) indicate the effects of a specific action or decision–for example, symptoms of specific nutritional deficiency; (7) predict effects from certain causes; (8) arrange events in proper sequence.

EXAMPLES:

1. Can you give another example of how we use levers?
2. Are you saying that a condominium and an apartment are the same thing?
3. Can anyone think of another name–a single word–for such foods as fruits, vegetables, milk, eggs, and butter?
4. The author says "the jobs are seasonal." What is an example of a seasonal job?
5. You say the tussock moths in Washington State caused an increase in the price of lumber in California. Will you explain how you came to that conclusion?
6. If inventions of labor-saving machines create less need for workers, which groups of people are likely to be most affected by such changes?
7. In order to conduct the experiment correctly, in what order must the steps take place?

Questions That Verify

In ordinary classroom discourse, there will be times when the teacher will want to challenge pupils to verify something that has been said. It goes without saying that this should be done without embarrassing or threatening the pupil. It is not a good practice to allow unsupported generalizations to be left unchallenged, even if they are true. It is the first mark of scholarship to be able to substantiate what is said. Verification questions get the class in the habit of using authoritative sources to give credence to their responses. They learn to differentiate between fact and opinion. They learn to detect bias in the materials they read and hear. In the middle and upper grades, pupils can consider, in a simple way, the nature of evidence and the meaning of proof.

EXAMPLES:

1. What facts would support such a statement?
2. How do you know when a message has been clearly communicated?
3. Is there a way we could check to know whether or not we have the correct amount of postage?
4. Karen thinks that Upper Michigan was once a part of the Wisconsin Territory. How could we check that?
5. What proof do we have that water is heavier than oil?
6. What is one way we can check to see that our circuit is complete?
7. How can you prove that your answer is correct when you subtract 28 from 72?

Questions That Test

The kinds of questions asked by a teacher to test a pupil depends, of course, on what is to be tested and the purposes for the testing. Most often questions of this type are associated with the recall of specific information. Consequently, testing has developed something of a bad reputation. Perhaps it is true that teachers do too much testing. Nonetheless, testing is an important component of teaching and learning, and therefore it should be done well. Test questions may have to do with the performance of a skill, the use of a form or procedure, or may be aimed at diagnosing weaknesses that need strengthening. These questions differ from many of the others discussed here in that there *should* be right and wrong answers to them. That is to say, it must be possible to establish the correctness or adequacy of the pupil's response, or there would be no test. This means that there must be criteria that serve as the framework within which questions will be asked. The reader is advised to consult a standard work on test construction to ensure that items are technically sound.

EXAMPLES:

1. Arrange the following events in the order in which they took place in the story. (followed by randomly arranged events)

2. Which of the following best explains why objects float? (followed by four options from which to choose, only one of which is correct)
3. Match the causes listed in the left column with their effects listed on the right.
4. From what you have learned about "Batteries and Bulbs," which of the following statements are true? (followed by a series of true-false items)
5. Read this short selection and then draw a circle around all the words that describe, tell about, or explain something.
6. Column A lists some things you might want to know about. Column B lists the places or sources that would give you the answers to the questions in Column A. Match questions in Column A with the sources in Column B.

Questions to Describe

Very often teachers will want pupils to provide a description of an event, of an experience, of something observed, or of something they have read about. The teacher may have a variety of reasons for asking the questions, among them being a desire to stimulate the imaginations of pupils, to check the accuracy of the pupils' perceptions of what is being recalled, or to provide the pupils with an opportunity to enrich their use of language.

Questions that call for a description require the pupil to reproduce verbally something that has been thought about. The description must be accurate and complete enough so that those who are receiving the communication understand precisely what is being described. This means that questions calling for description, and most especially their responses, must be complete in critical detail. They must be elaborate in their use of comparison and contrast. Descriptions may be regarded as word pictures.

It is well known that descriptions are often so poorly presented that they result in misunderstanding. Several witnesses to an identical event, such as a crime, for example, will often provide conflicting descriptions of what occurred. Attorneys in court ask witnesses to tell *exactly* what happened and then proceed to destroy the credibility of the witness by showing that the description was erroneous. Part of the difficulty in faulty descriptions lies in the observation of the event itself, and part of it in the relating of it to someone else. This suggests that pupils need opportunities to develop skills associated with responding to questions calling for description.

EXAMPLES:

1. Describe what you thought was the most important event in the story.
2. How are the Pacific beaches of Oregon different from those of southern California?

3. What feelings does the author convey about the beauty of a cold winter morning?
4. Tell exactly what happened at each of the four stages of the experiment.
5. What words can you use to describe how a boll of cotton feels?
6. Imagine yourself living in the area that was flooded. The river has completely covered the place where you lived. Only the top of your house sticks out of the rushing water. Describe how you think you would feel at such a time.

Questions to Explain

Questions requiring the pupils to explain are, of course, closely related to descriptive questions. In explanations, however, the critical element is that of providing a reason to account for the way things are as they are. In descriptions, the pupils are required to tell *what* happened; in explanations, they must tell *why*. Accurate explanations are essential to instruction in such areas as science, mathematics, social studies, and health.

With increased use of so-called higher-level questions, those that require reflective thought rather than recall, teachers make frequent use of why-type questions. The assumption is that such a question will elicit a creative explanation from the pupil. This does not always happen, because the pupil may simply be repeating an explanation provided by the textbook, encyclopedia, or some other information source. There is nothing particularly wrong with this, providing the pupil understands the explanation. Often pupils do not understand it, and are simply repeating what the information source says; the question, then, is no longer one of explanation but one of recall.

Explanation-type questions provide an opportunity to get into the matter of validity of explanations. How do we know an explanation is a satisfactory and accurate one? What is the nature of the authority that gives the explanation validity? For example, how can we be certain that the earth and other planets actually revolve around the sun instead of the other way around, as was believed for thousands of years? If there are two or more explanations of events, which are we to believe? How can we check on the reliability and validity of various sources of authority? What ways of knowing are there?

EXAMPLES:

1. Explain why the product of two fractions multiplied is smaller than either the multiplier or multiplicand.
2. Explain the conditions that are needed to produce condensation.
3. In what ways is a telephone conversation better than letter writing?
4. Explain why the growth of California was so great after 1849.
5. Tell why the Arctic Circle is located where it is.

6. Explain what is meant by the term "feather bedding."
7. Explain to a foreign visitor why America has daylight saving time.

Questions for Diagnosing Learning Difficulties

At some point along the way, most pupils encounter difficulty in learning. For most, this is usually a simple, short-term problem, and with a little help from the teacher, the pupil is able to proceed. For some pupils, however, the problems are extremely profound and may stubbornly resist the usual remedial procedures. Therefore a substantial amount of the teacher's time is spent diagnosing learning difficulties and prescribing remedial measures. The more accurate the teacher is in the diagnosis of the problem, the more effective he or she is likely to be in helping the pupil overcome it. Insightful questioning is often helpful in pinpointing the difficulty precisely. In diagnosing learning difficulties, the teacher first of all needs to find out which pupils are having difficulty. This can usually be determined by the use of a general achievement test or by careful observation of children on a day to day basis. Having identified those learners who have problems, the teacher will need to find out at what point in the learning sequence the difficulty was encountered. Having pinpointed the location of the problem, the teacher then proceeds to find out why it occurs at that point. Skillful questioning can be helpful in locating pupil errors, and in explaining why they occur. Much of such questioning must be done on an individual basis, for obvious reasons; and it is often helpful to have pupils respond aloud. In this way the teacher can trace the mental operations of the learner as the questioning proceeds and detect errors.

EXAMPLES:

1. Would you please work this problem for me? As you do, say out loud what you are doing at each step.
2. You will notice that the short paragraph I have just given to you has no capital letters. Would you go through with your pencil and put capital letters where they belong?
3. As you read the selection you have just received, would you draw a line under the main idea of each paragraph?
4. Would you please read this page out loud for me? (This is done on an individual basis; the teacher records number of hesitations, mispronunciations, repetitions, omissions, and other errors. Time required to read the passage is also noted.)
5. Show me exactly how you go about finding a book in the library.

Questions to Guide Independent Study

Questions for independent study are ordinarily assigned by the teacher to be used by the pupil during a study period or as homework. It is assumed that the pupil would have a textbook or other information source available. Because the pupils will be on their own while doing the study, questions must be explicit enough to be clearly understood. This is especially important if the independent study is to be done away from school, where the learner cannot get clarification of questions from the teacher. Moreover, the data must be available in order that the pupil is able to answer the questions. That is, questions that should *not* be asked are those that cannot be answered directly, or questions whose answers cannot be inferred by consulting the book or other data sources used by the pupils.

Questions used to guide independent study should be those that encourage good study habits; they should focus on important concepts and ideas rather than on inconsequential detail. For example, if too many fact-type questions are included, the pupil may assume that those facts are all that is important in the material. Perhaps it is best to include a variety of questions—some calling for identification of important facts and ideas, others providing for application of information, others for the use and practice of relevant skills, and still others that require inference and reflection. The guide questions should be constructed in a way that will help the pupils get more from the material than if they simply read it on their own.

EXAMPLES:

1. What terms seem to be the most important for understanding this selection?
2. Can you make a list of the most important events in the story and place them in the order in which they took place?
3. After reading the passage in your science book, make a list of all the pollutants mentioned. Can you divide the list into two groups, one listing *natural* pollutants and the other *man-made* pollutants?
4. Can you draw a diagram to show that you understand the number relationships in a problem of indirect measurement?
5. In each of the paragraphs, can you find the cause and effect relationship between the items?
6. What characteristics of the countries of the Middle East would justify grouping them together as a region?

PUPIL QUESTIONS

It has been said that pupils ask three kinds of questions: (1) to find out how much the teacher knows; (2) to show how much they know; or (3) to find out something they do not know. This of course is a facetious way of saying that there may be a hidden

WHAT'S WRONG HERE?

Young Mr. Jackson had some firm ideas about teaching. Among other things, he believed pupils should develop independent habits of work and that they should learn to think. To achieve these goals he liked to assign homework to pupils. To guide their study he provided pupils with study sheets that contained reflective, open-ended questions. He preferred such questions to informational ones because he did not want pupils to get their answers directly from the book. After a few weeks of this, Mr. Jackson began to get serious complaints from parents of some of the better-achieving children. They said that their child had to be up half the night searching for answers to questions that neither the child nor they could find by reading the book.

1. Are the questions Mr. Jackson selected appropriate for home-study assignments? Why or why not?
2. Do you think that Mr. Jackson's procedures will help him achieve the commendable goals he has set for himself?
3. Under what circumstances is it appropriate to ask pupils questions whose answers are not contained in the learning resources available to them?

reason for questions asked by pupils. Questions are not always asked because something is puzzling the pupil. A pupil may ask a question simply to get attention, to get a laugh from classmates, or to embarrass or irritate the teacher. Pupils may also ask questions for reassurance. Torrance and Myers[4] indicate that most student questions fall into one of these four categories:

1. Questions regarding procedures (for example: May I go to the lavatory? May I have another piece of paper?).
2. Questions regarding tasks (for example: Should we write on both sides of the paper? Should I put my giraffe on the table to dry?).
3. Questions regarding information (for example: How do you spell *train?* Where is the big dictionary?).
4. Questions regarding understanding (for example: What do you mean by *versus?* Why do you invert the fraction?).

The kinds of questions pupils ask should tell the teacher a great deal about the effectiveness of classroom management procedures and about the conduct of instruction. For example, a preponderance

[4]E. Paul Torrance and R. E. Myers, *Creative Learning and Teaching* (New York: Dodd, Mead & Co., 1970), pp. 226–32.

of pupil questions that call for reassurance and teacher approval (e.g., Am I doing this right? Is this what you want us to do? Is it all right if I make my picture sideways?) might indicate the pupils' general feeling of insecurity, a feeling that there is considerable risk in doing things that displease the teacher. It could mean, too, that the teacher has developed a high level of pupil dependence on him or her. It might also mean that the teacher's directions are not clear, and that the pupils do not understand precisely what is expected of them.

Sometimes teachers become annoyed when pupils ask endless procedural and permission questions (e.g., May I sharpen my pencil? Please may I get a book? May I take this book home?). Yet the teacher should recognize that he or she may be contributing to the problem. If pupils are not provided opportunities to develop self-direction, and to assume responsibility for a certain amount of decision making, it can be predicted that they will turn to the teacher to get authority to engage in routine procedures.

Children are likely to model their question-asking behavior after that of the teacher. By listening to the teacher's questions, pupils sense what the teacher believes to be important. Thus, if they hear the teacher asking mainly recall and memory questions, they might naturally assume that such questions are the most important ones. If, on the other hand, the teacher tends to ask provocative questions that enhance higher-level thinking skills, the pupils are likely to follow the teacher's example.

HANDLING PUPIL RESPONSES TO QUESTIONS

How a teacher handles the response of a pupil may be as important as the question itself, in terms of productive pupil learning. As a general guideline, the teacher's comment following a response should be such that it leaves the pupil with the feeling that he or she would like to respond again to another question. Let us examine some of the ways a teacher might deal with the responses of pupils.

Acknowledging a Pupil Response

There are a half-dozen or so common expressions that teachers use to acknowledge pupil responses. Among these are "all right," "uh-huh," "yes," "okay." These are noncommittal, nonevaluative utterances that simply recognize that the pupil has responded. (Of course, these might be accompanied by nonverbal clues that carry very powerful evaluative messages, such as an approving or disapproving facial expression, tone of voice, or body movement.)

Responses of this type, i.e., simple acknowledgments, are often effective if the teacher is encouraging a discussion of the question. When a pupil response is recognized in a noncommittal way, the class knows that the matter is still open and others may contribute their ideas to the discussion.

When listening to tape recordings of their classes, teachers are often surprised—and embarrassed—at how often they use the same expression over and over in acknowledging pupil responses. A teacher may say "all right" a hundred times a day and not even be aware that he or she is using that expression. A teacher needs to strive to develop some variety in the acknowledgement of pupil responses.

Evaluative Statements

Some teachers seem to think they must evaluate every response of the pupils with a "Yes, that's right" or "No, that's not right." Of course teachers need to evaluate the work of pupils, and incorrect responses should not be ignored. But there is much that is wrong with a procedure that necessitates an evaluative comment from the teacher each time a pupil answers a question or makes a comment in class. In the first place, the teacher does not always know whether a response is right or wrong. Moreover, many responses cannot be

categorized as being totally right or wrong. Also, this procedure tends to encourage the kinds of questions for which answers can be evaluated only in this way. Finally, some pupils will not participate in questioning of this type, because they do not want their responses evaluated negatively in front of the whole class. Rather than risking such a contingency, they simply will not participate; and if called on, will say they do not know.

Restating and Clarifying

Not every pupil response needs to be restated and clarified, but this is a good practice from time to time. It is especially appropriate when the response has been spoken so softly that it could not be heard by the entire group. Also, the teacher may know that further clarification will be helpful in either promoting continued thinking about the question or in providing more precision to the response. For example, in a science lesson the teacher may ask, "If I have a gallon of water and I pour in a quart of oil, what happens to the oil?" A child responds by saying, "It goes to the top." The teacher restates and clarifies, "You say it goes to the top. Do you mean that the oil will float on top of the water?" The pupil continues, "Yes, it separates. The oil floats on top of the water." Here, through the

---

PHOTO FOLIO

Should a teacher "call" only on volunteers who raise their hands? Experts disagree on this matter. Some believe a random selection of pupil respondents is best because all must then prepare themselves intellectually to answer the questions. They feel that a fixed pattern of questioning is not effective because pupils prepare themselves to respond only to those questions they know they will be asked to answer. In terms of pupil learning, research studies indicate that the fixed pattern of questioning produces better results because it ensures that all pupils will be involved in the question-answer transactions.

1. Provide anecdotal examples from your own experience that illustrate limitations and advantages of various methods of soliciting pupil responses.
2. Should the teacher be sensitive to the pupil anxiety that is induced through the use of certain questioning procedures? What impact might a fixed pattern of soliciting answers have on a child who is a stutterer, or one who does not speak English well? Discuss.

---

use of another question, the teacher is clarifying in order to verify that the pupil's response has been understood.

Probing

It often happens that a pupil's response is only a partial answer to the question, and the teacher wants to encourage a more complete response. This can be done by probing for additional information. Such responses are often elicited by such statements as these:

1. "Can you say a little bit more about that?"
2. "But why do you suppose he turned back?"
3. "Can you explain why it happened?"
4. "You said 'yes'; now tell why you think so."
5. "That is correct, as far as you have gone, but there is yet another very important point you haven't mentioned."

In probing for a more complete response, there is always the danger that the teacher will press too hard, thereby making the child so anxious and nervous that he or she cannot respond at all. Classrooms should not be conducted as though they are courtrooms; needless stress-producing probing can easily become counterproductive.

Cuing

It may happen that the teacher asks a question and draws a blank—a sea of empty faces. This has happened to all teachers at one time or another. It may mean that the question was poorly stated or it may mean that the pupils simply did not know what it was that the teacher was asking. When this happens, the teacher should not provide the response, but instead should give the pupils a few leads, *cues* that will guide their thinking along the lines being proposed. This involves more than simply repeating the question or even rephrasing it. In cuing, the teacher provides small amounts of additional information.

EXAMPLE:

Teacher: Why is it that the candle went out when we placed a jar over it?
Pupil: It doesn't get any air.
Teacher: (Probing.) Yes, but what is it in the air that is needed to keep the candle burning?
Pupil: (No response.)
Teacher: (Cuing.) Do you remember when we learned about rust . . .
Pupil: (Picking up on the cue.) Oxygen! The candle needs oxygen to burn. It goes out when it has used up the oxygen.

Notice, in this example, that the teacher did not give the answer to

AND YOU SAID . . .

In the following four situations, imagine that you are the teacher. In these situations the teacher asks a question and a pupil responds. The pupil's response, however, is in some way inadequate. You are being asked to supply what you would say next, in order to move the instructional sequence along.

Situation I

Teacher: You enjoyed the poem so much yesterday that I thought we could share another one today. What was it that you liked most about the poem we read yesterday?

Pupil: Rhymes

And YOU said: ____________________

Situation II

Teacher: Now you notice that this line (pointing to a line showing the amount of food produced) on our graph goes up, but this other line (pointing to a line showing number of people living on farms) goes down. What does this tell us about how farming has changed?

Pupil: It tells us that people moved away. They got other jobs.

And YOU said: ____________________

Situation III

Teacher: An electric generator produces electricity by the rotation of a coil in a magnetic field. It needs some source of energy or power to rotate the coil. Thus we see that an electric motor uses electrical energy to produce mechanical energy. A generator, however, uses mechanical energy to produce electrical energy. What forms of mechanical energy do we use to produce electrical energy?

Pupil: (No response; dead silence.)

And YOU said: ____________________

Situation IV

Teacher: In our social studies we have been learning about how people get the things they need to live in our community. You remember we learned two new—and big—words. (Children respond enthusiastically, "consumer" and "producer.") Yes, you remembered well. Now who can tell us something about these words?

Pupil: All consumers are producers.

And YOU said: ____________________

the pupil. The teacher simply provided a small hint that pointed the learner's thinking in the appropriate direction. In this case, the pupil was able to respond even before the teacher completed the cuing sentence.

DEVELOPING SKILL IN USING QUESTIONS

The ability to use questioning strategies effectively is a skill, and as such, will require thoughtful practice if it is to be learned. Teachers who are proficient in using questions have worked at developing this skill. Teachers are not born with the talent to ask good questions; nor will wishing make it so. Three subskills are a part of skillful questioning: framing and stating questions; sequencing of questions; and pacing questions. Let us consider each of these briefly.

Framing and Stating Questions

In this chapter, we have had a great deal to say about the selection of various types of questions, and numerous examples have been provided. But even after the substantive nature of the question is established, a question may be faulted on technical grounds:

1. It may be poorly worded. It may be too long and involved; vocabulary may be too advanced; it may use bookish terms and expressions.
2. It may be ambiguous. The question may not express clearly enough what is wanted in the way of a response.
3. It may contain giveaway cues.
4. It may be stated in an arrogant or even hostile tone of voice.
5. It may be stated in a way that leads the pupil to a response, rather than stimulates his or her thinking.

To avoid these kinds of difficulties, it is recommended that, during the development of a lesson, beginning teachers write out the questions they plan to ask. When the beginner counts on improvising questions while teaching a room full of pupils, the questions are likely to come out badly. After a backlog of successful teaching experience, it is advisable for the teacher to make and listen to a tape recording of his or her teaching in order to self-evaluate questioning skills.

Sequencing of Questions

If ideas are to be *developed* in the course of a lesson, questions must be properly sequenced. Idea development means that the lesson has direction: the questions lead somewhere. One cannot ask a series of questions at random and expect that ideas will build cumulatively. In the sequence of the following questions, notice how each question builds on the one that precedes it. The questions are based on a story of a young man's visit to an abandoned house.

1. Can you give an over-all description of the house Charlie went to visit?
2. What was there about it that made him uneasy?
3. When did he first discover that something was out of the ordinary?
4. Why do you think he did not leave at that time?
5. At what point was he absolutely certain that someone else was in the house?
6. What, exactly, happened that made him know he was not alone?
7. Why could he not go for help then?
8. What can we learn from Charlie's experience about going into strange or unfamiliar surroundings?

Even if the reader is not familiar with the story, essential elements of the story line can be inferred from this sequence of questions. Asked in a random order, the questions would not produce this effect.

Teachers should be conscious of the need for developing a proper sequence in questioning. Perhaps the easiest way to begin is to teach a process that has a fixed sequence, such as following a product through its manufacturing process, or discussing how an item gets from where it is produced to where it is used. Science experiments that necessitate a specific sequence lend themselves well to learning how to sequence questions, as do some operations in mathematics. With increased experience the teacher will become sensitive to whether or not the questions being asked are in an appropriate order. This aspect of questioning is much like building a sequence for programmed instruction. Indeed, the teacher in the classroom *is* the programmer much of the time. Accordingly, if learning is to proceed efficiently, the teacher must provide questions that will deal with small increments of learning in a progressively more complex sequence.

Pacing Questions.

Pacing has to do with the rapidity with which questions are asked. Two problems are commonly associated with pacing. One is that the questions are asked too rapidly. They fly from the teacher like bullets from a machine gun. Little or no time is allowed for the development of ideas associated with a question before another one is asked. Short answers are expected and encouraged, rather than elaborative responses. The second problem has to do with the small amount of time given pupils to respond. Teachers seem to feel that unless pupils respond immediately, the question needs to be restated, clarified, or the learner provided with a cue. Given more time, pupils will often come forth with a thoughtful response.

The position taken here is that teachers should slow the pace of questioning. They should not be hasty in providing cues, nor should they too quickly restate and clarify questions. The atmosphere should encourage reflection rather than quickness of response. Questions are designed to provoke thinking, and thinking requires time. Rapid-fire questioning, with an impatient teacher attitude during the period of silence after the question is asked, usually means that the questions are mainly those requiring recall of information. In that case, most of what we have discussed in this chapter would be of little consequence.

DEVELOPING RELATED COMPETENCIES

How Would You Say It?

The following five questions are badly stated. Identify what is wrong with each one, then restate it correctly.

1. Indian people lived how on the Plains before the coming of the Europeans?
2. At what point in a musical selection does the "finale" come?
3. Can you list the steps in doing the experiment from start to finish beginning with the last step first?
4. I don't think it was a very good idea to use those colors for the picture, do you?
5. What would happen if, but, of course, you would never want to do anything like this, you were hiking along and you suddenly stepped on a rock, twisted your ankle and couldn't walk any further, and you had to get help but there was no one around?

FOR FURTHER PROFESSIONAL STUDY

Books

Anderson, Charlotte C. and Barbara J. Winston. "Acquiring Information by Asking Questions, Using Maps and Graphs, and Making Direct Observations."

Chapter 3. *Developing Decision-Making Skills.* Dana G. Kurfman, Ed. 47th Yearbook. National Council for the Social Studies. Washington, D.C.: The Council, 1977.

Hunkins, Francis P. *Involving Students in Questioning.* Boston: Allyn & Bacon Books, Inc., 1976.

——. *Questioning Strategies and Techniques.* Boston: Allyn & Bacon Books, Inc., 1972.

Periodicals

Banton, Lee. "Broadening the Scope of Classroom Questions." *Virginia Journal of Education* (October 1977), 13–15.

Henson, Kenneth T. "Questioning As A Mode of Instruction." *The Clearing House* (September 1979), 14–16.

Rowe, Mary Budd. "Give Students Time to Respond." *School Science and Mathematics* (March 1978), 207–216.

Sund, R. B. "Growing Through Sensitive Listening and Questioning." *Childhood Education* (November 1971), 68–71.

9

Strategies for Skill Development

THE QUALIFIED AND COMPETENT TEACHER . . .

1. Understands the inseparable relationship among skill, cognitive, and affective learnings in the school curriculum.
2. Is familiar with the many skills for which the elementary-school curriculum is responsible.
3. Is able to design instructional programs to teach and foster skill development, taking into account cognitive and affective dimensions of skill learning.

Performance Criteria

As a result of the serious study of this chapter, the student should be able to . . .

1. Identify the major groups of skills for which the school curriculum is responsible, and provide at least two specific examples of each.
2. Describe basic principles of skills teaching and show by example how each would be applied in a grade and subject area of his or her choice.
3. Show by example how the basic skills (three *R*'s) would be scheduled in a day's instructional program.
4. Select a study skill and provide an example of how it would be taught to a grade of his or her choice.
5. Demonstrate the ability to teach a skill to a group of children or a peer group, applying the principles of skills teaching described in number 2, above.

If one who has never thrown a dart, throws one at a target and scores a bull's eye, we could hardly say that this was a demonstration of the skill of dart-throwing. We would describe such a performance as a lucky shot; what has come to be called "beginner's luck." We would also say that such an experience is an example of chance success rather than of skill behavior. A skill is a physical act or an intellectual process, or a combination of both, that can be performed in a consistently proficient way in repeated performances. Important in this definition are the conditions of *consistency, proficiency,* and *repeated performance.* Let us examine them in greater detail.

Whether something is judged to be done proficiently, that is, whether it is done well or poorly, depends on how well others perform the same act. This means that the norms or standards of performance are developed by observing the same performance by a large number of individuals. If someone were to do something totally new; something that had never been done in the whole history of the human race, there would be no way to judge how well or how poorly it was performed. Standards of performance are also related to the age and maturity of the individual. For example, we would be pleased to see a five-year-old child use his or her fingers to solve a simple mathematics problem, but this would not be acceptable behavior by a student of normal intelligence in a high-school algebra class. In evaluating the proficiency of the performance of a skill, therefore, we must be familiar with the *norms,* the usual levels of expectation that apply to persons of similar age, experience, and cultural background.

The condition of consistency requires that the behavior can be reliably predicted. The individual, for example, does not perform superbly one day and miserably the next. Such a performance would be judged to be too erratic to meet the requirement of consistency. When skills are learned sufficiently well, the individual will be able to perform them consistently over a long period of time, providing the person engages in some amount of maintenance practice. For example, it would be extremely unusual for a child who was an excellent reader in the spring of one year to return to school in the fall having difficulty in reading. In fact, such a circumstance would be so rare that one would suspect that the child had suffered a physical or psychological accident during the summer. Inconsistent performance of a skill usually means that it was not learned well enough in the first place. More thorough learning will increase the reliability of performance.

The requirement of repeated performance eliminates the possibility of chance success. It is possible that almost any Saturday morning duffer can occasionally make a hole-in-one, but it takes a skillful person to play par golf week after week. In school-related skills, a child might by a stroke of chance provide insight that solved a difficult problem, but this does not mean that he or she possesses the intellectual skills necessary to perform similarly in repeated experiences. Obviously, the requirements of consistency and repeated performance are closely related.

SKILL TEACHING

There are general principles and procedures that hold for the teaching of all skills. Of course, these would not be applied in exactly the same way to all skills, but the principle is present nevertheless. Skill teaching must not be allowed to become routine and ritualized. There should be no "steps" to be followed each time a skill is taught. With these precautions in mind, let us examine what is involved in the teaching of a skill.

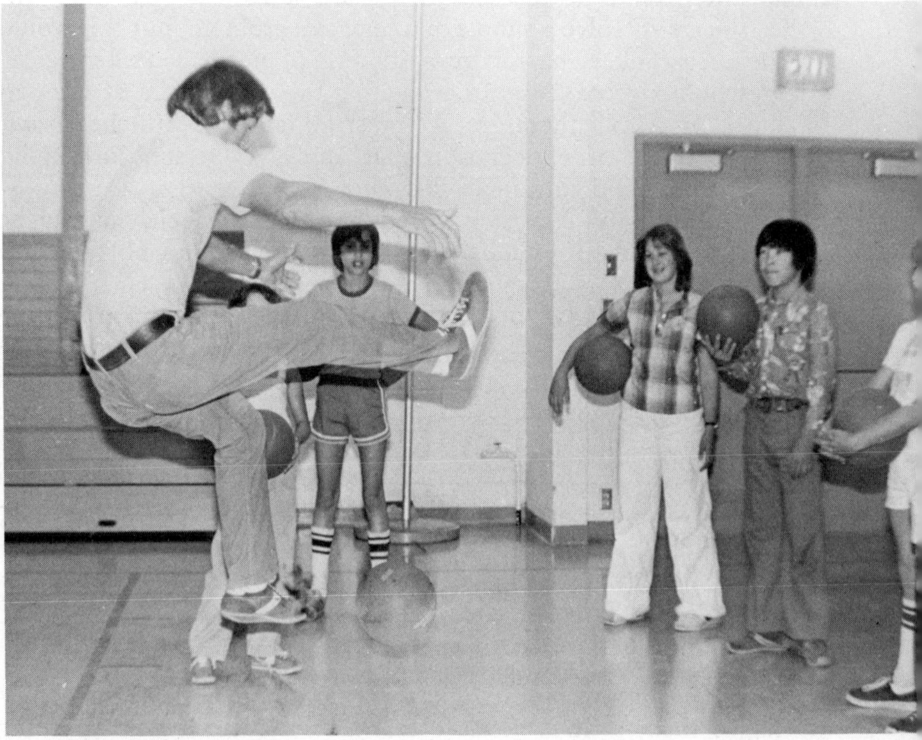

Meaningfulness

As is true with most learning, the process is facilitated if the learner understands what the skill is all about, what is involved in performing it, how it will be used, and "what it's good for." Demonstrations of skills are very effective for showing meaningfulness and for illustrating a good performance. Demonstrations are frequently used in teaching skills that involve physical movement. For example, the music teacher demonstrates how to use the arm in moving the bow in playing the cello. Or the physical education teacher shows how to make a good swing with a golf club. The primary-grade teacher demonstrates how to move the hand and fingers in handwriting. Not all skills are so easily demonstrated. In the case of skills that are mainly intellectual, it is necessary to show the results or effects of skill use, rather than the skill itself. For example, the teacher can show that one can arrive at a correct answer in mathematics, can locate a place on a map, or can find a specific book in the library through the use of certain skills.

PHOTO FOLIO

"Does the trainer have to be able to balance the ball on his or her own nose in order to teach the seal how to do it?" In applying the gist of the foregoing question to school teaching, one could ask, "Does the teacher have to be able to demonstrate everything that pupils are expected to learn?" Do good performers always make good teachers? Does the college all-American football player make the best coach? Does the violin virtuoso make the best violin teacher?

In this photograph, the teacher is obviously demonstrating a complex physical skill for pupils, a skill they will be expected to perform. Why will the pupils' performance be enhanced by watching the teacher do the task?

Suppose this teacher injured his legs in an accident during the summer. To what extent would his teaching of skills such as this be impaired? How important is demonstration in teaching skills?

Establishing meaningfulness serves several purposes that enhance learning. The most important among these is that it helps the learners understand how the skill can be *useful* to them. Unless this happens, the learners are not likely to involve themselves thoroughly enough in the process to learn the skill. Meaningfulness also helps learners know what constitutes a good performance of the skill.

Learner Involvement

If skills are ever to be learned at a high level of proficiency, the learners must involve themselves heavily in the process. Skill learning requires practice and application. When learners invest themselves thoroughly in learning the skill, they constantly seek ways to practice and apply it. Contrast this with other learners; ones who devote only a minimum effort to the skill and give that time grudgingly. One can take any skill as an example—reading, writing, playing a musical instrument, doing physical activities, or learning magic tricks. The individual who is self-directed and highly motivated to learn a skill will proceed much more rapidly and efficiently than one who is not. A key to good skill teaching, therefore, requires that the teacher devise ways to get the learners to involve themselves thoroughly in the learning of it.

Practice

Practice is an absolutely essential requirement in learning a skill. It does not matter how meaningful the teaching has been, or how well the learners understand what they are to do, they are not going to be able to perform proficiently unless they practice the skill. Through practice the learner develops the ability to respond with ease and confidence. There can be no question that lack of practice is a major factor in poorly developed skills. However, if practice is to be a productive exercise, it must take place under certain conditions. Poorly conducted or half-hearted practice sessions can have a detrimental effect on the learner's performance. This would occur if the learner is allowed to practice incorrect responses, or if the practice session encourages poor habits of work.

Although "practice makes perfect" is often used as a guideline for teaching and learning skills, it is *improvement* rather than perfection that is the appropriate outcome of practice. Furthermore, the *desire to improve* is a very important condition of practice. A learner who goes through the motions of a practice exercise but whose heart is not in it will have a difficult time improving performance. It may even produce the reverse effect, because the experience is generating bad feelings, or what is called "negative affect," toward the skill. This means that the learner will not only engage in the practice session in an unproductive manner but will avoid any situation in which the skill is used. This obviously takes the learner farther away from developing proficiency in performance. Thus, highly motivated short practice sessions, with a strong intent to improve, are usually more productive.

The improvement of a skill may mean performing it with greater ease and precision, or it may mean doing it with greater speed. If improvement is sought in the preciseness of the responses, a conscious effort needs to be made to eliminate unnecessary movements and errors. The teacher would need, therefore, to show or tell the learner in what ways the performance is faulty. Exact repetition of the skill is *not* a good format if this type of improvement is sought. Instead, the learner must know how responses can be improved and work on those specific deficiencies in practice sessions. But if the improvement sought is increased speed of response, it would be appropriate for the learner to practice by repeating the performance in more or less the same way, trying to do it with increasing rapidity. In either case, improvement will be enhanced if the learner keeps a record of the improvement made in practice sessions.

In the early stages of skill learning, it is important to have the performance carefully supervised by the teacher. This is to ensure that the pupil is doing it correctly. Left unguided, the pupil may practice incorrect responses, which of course means that these errors will need to be unlearned before progress can be made. Once the pupil is able to do the skill, frequent short practice sessions will promote improvement. When the performance has reached an acceptable level, periodic practice sessions, along with opportunities for application, should be enough to maintain proficiency in the skill.

Feedback

One of the most important elements in skill learning is that the learner be provided evaluative information concerning the performance. This kind of information is called *feedback,* a concept borrowed from systems technology. The feedback phenomenon operates as a self-correcting mechanism in a system. For example, the operation of a system may be monitored continually, and in the event that the system is not functioning properly, the malfunction is immediately detected and corrected. In skill learning, the learner receives feedback on successes and failures, and thereby can make the necessary adjustments in order to improve performance. When the feedback tells the learner of successes, that what he or she is doing is right, that he or she is on the right track, it is referred to as *positive*. When the feedback tells what is being done incorrectly, that the performance is faulty, that the learner is going in the wrong direction, it is referred to as *negative*.

Generally speaking, positive feedback is more productive in maintaining a high level of motivation and promoting successful performance than is negative feedback. Success experiences are positive and predictable in their effect on the individual, whereas individuals are more variable in their response to failure. Some regard failure as a challenge; others are crushed by it, but almost everyone responds positively to success.

Finally, an important difference between the two types of feedback is the extent to which they guide the improvement schedule. Because positive feedback emphasizes what is correct, the performance can be replicated to ensure continued success. In negative feedback, the learner is simply told that what is being done is incorrect but is not provided direction as to how to improve. This can result in a trial-and-error sequence of experiences unless the teacher provides additional guidance and direction. Negative feedback is needed, but it should be coupled with specific suggestions as to how the performance can be improved.

One of the most important sources of feedback is quite obviously the teacher. This is the strongest argument in favor of reduced class size. Fewer pupils make it possible for the teacher to supervise and provide feedback to learners. Besides the teacher, pupils often get feedback on their performances from each other. If handled sensitively, this can be an important means of facilitating skill growth. By using self-correcting materials, and by keeping careful records on trials, the pupil can obtain a considerable amount of feedback on performances. Also, some mechanical devices, such as teaching machines, provide learner feedback.

Application

Essential to skill development is the opportunity to use the skill in a functional setting. Unless this is done, learning the skill will seem to be disassociated from the real world. For example, writing and spelling should not be thought of by the pupils as being used, and useful, only during certain periods in the day or week. Writing, spelling, and reading skills should be applied frequently throughout the day in all other subject areas—excellent settings in which to practice basic skills.

The traditional attitude toward skill development might be described as "learn-now-apply-later." Great emphasis has been given to basic learning skills in the elementary grades, the idea being that they would be used in later grades or in later life. This attitude has a detrimental effect on skill growth in two important ways. First, it separates skill teaching from practical application in the early stages; and second, it shortens the length of time that skill instruction is given. The learning and application of skills must go hand in hand. In reading, for example, we would say that the child should learn to read and read to learn at the same time. These two processes should not be separated.

Whenever it is assumed that skills are taught in the lower grades and applied later, there is a tendency to discontinue, prematurely, systematic instruction of skills. Consequently, many students complete their schooling experience with their basic skills at a functional level of about the fifth or sixth grade. If skills are to be improved and refined, instruction in some skills should be continued into, and in some cases, through high school. The application of skills should begin from the moment they are introduced in the primary grades. In this way a good balance can be maintained between direct instruction and functional application throughout the entire program.

Maintenance

When skills are used and applied regularly, there will be little problem in maintaining them at a satisfactory level. Problems arise, however, when a skill is taught to pupils and then not used for a long period of time. Through disuse the pupil loses whatever proficiency may have been developed. This usually means that the next time the need for the skill is encountered, a considerable amount of re-teaching must take place.

If a skill is taught but not used, one wonders why it was taught in the first place. Should this happen, however, the teacher will need to program regular and systematic practice sessions to regain and maintain the skill at a functional level. In cases where skills are maintained through regular use, the teacher should check from time to time to make sure that the pupils are performing the skill correctly and to provide re-teaching as needed. This will ensure that faulty habits are corrected before they become a permanent part of the pupil's response pattern.

SKILLS IN THE SCHOOL CURRICULUM

A major portion of the elementary-school instructional effort deals with the teaching of skills to children. This is necessary because skills open the doors to other types of learning. Skills represent the tools of learning. Even though it is not clear whether low school

THERE IS NO MYSTERY ABOUT IT . . .

Dr. Ethel Wiggins is a much sought-after speaker for workshops, institutes, inservice programs, and other professional meetings of teachers. She is an articulate and dramatic speaker who has the capacity to greatly inspire her audiences. Besides that she is a competent reading specialist. One day she was visiting with a colleague whose specialty is social studies education.

"Tell me, Ethel," he said, "Which of the new reading programs produce the best results in terms of pupil achievement? There must be differences among them because some schools consistently produce better readers year after year. I'm not talking about differences that are attributable to differing school populations. Schools that serve similar school populations show dramatic differences in reading achievement scores."

"The schools that produce the best readers are the ones that get kids to do a lot of reading," she replied. "Programmatic differences are almost inconsequential except as they differ in getting children and books together. Children who read well do a lot of reading. Those who read poorly do little reading. Of course, instruction is important, too, but it is the actual reading—and a lot of it—that builds genuine independence and skill in reading, and really makes the difference between good readers and so-so readers, barring some psychological, neurological, or physiological impairment.

1. What principles of skills teaching is Dr. Wiggins talking about in this sketch?
2. Is there any reason why every elementary school in the country could not do precisely what Dr. Wiggins says is needed to produce good readers?

achievement is a cause or an effect of inadequately developed skills, the evidence is clear that the two go hand in hand. The school records of poor achievers show a consistent pattern—failure to learn to read, inability to communicate orally or in writing, little or no ability to deal with simple quantitative relationships, inadequately developed work habits, poor social relations.

School learning is often classified as (1) understandings (knowledge), (2) attitudes (values), and (3) skills. These are frequently discussed in terms of (1) cognitive learning, (2) affective learning, and (3) psychomotor learning. This breakdown has merit for purposes of analysis and study, but it is confusing when applied to the realities of classroom teaching and learning. We know, for instance, that not all skills involve psychomotor operations. Some skills are entirely intellectual, with no physical or motor involvement. In almost all cases, skills require some degree of cognitive involvement.

That is to say, the individual needs to have some awareness of what he or she is doing. Finally, skills do have an affective dimension in that the individual has feelings about how well one likes or dislikes what is being done. These relationships can be illustrated through an example from the field of reading.

Tim is a skillful reader. As we watch, his eyes race across the page with obvious interest in what he is reading. With the exception of his eye movements and his turning the page at intervals, we see no movement. When he completes the passage, we ask him detailed questions in order to check the extent to which he has comprehended what he read. We find that Tim answers all of the questions correctly and he also provides some examples of application of ideas that were not included in the passage read. Finally, we ask him how he liked what he had read, and he replies, "Just great! Wow! I could read that stuff all day!" Clearly this skill involved cognitive as well as affective components.

Certain segments of the curriculum are designated as skill areas. For example, reading, spelling, handwriting, oral and written expression, and certain aspects of mathematics are usually thought of as basic skills. They are deemed to be of such importance that a special curriculum sequence is designed to ensure their development. They are "basic" in the sense that most of whatever else children do in school calls on the use of these skills. If the children cannot apply them in functional settings, they are severely limited in the progress that can be made in any field of study.

Another important group of skills are those that are an integral part of the various content fields. Each subject-matter area places demands on the learner to use the specialized skills associated with that field. For instance, one reads social studies content differently from the way one reads directions for conducting a science experiment. Moreover, neither of these situations requires precisely the same reading skills that are needed to read a problem in mathematics. The same could be said for other skills as well. Social studies has its map and globe skills, science its special laboratory equipment, and mathematics has its special signs and symbols. Each has its own peculiar and relatively complex vocabulary. Additionally, each has its own basic study skills requiring the use of particular data sources.

Although the elementary-school curriculum in most cases provides a sequential program of instruction for the basic skills (i.e., the three *R*'s), the special skills related to the separate subject-matter fields are ordinarily not provided with as much systematic attention. More often than not they are treated in a hit-and-miss fashion. This is a major limitation of the skills curriculum in many schools.

The usual assumption is that the basic skills transfer directly to the content fields. Although the professional literature has consistently called attention to the importance of the specialized skills related to each of the subject fields, teachers continue to emphasize content mastery and neglect the content-related skills. This is unfortunate because of the ephemeral nature of content learning as compared to the rather longlasting quality of skills learning. Skills are among the most permanent learnings.

Complex skills such as reading, map reading, using resources, and using oral and written language, consist of many component elements that are themselves subskills. Word recognition is a subskill of the larger skill we call reading. Using phonetic clues is a subskill of word recognition. Using initial consonant blends is a further refinement of the skill of using phonetic clues. In planning a skills curriculum, these component elements must be identified and then programmed to be taught at appropriate times. The performance of the larger skill may be greatly impaired because the pupil is unable to perform adequately one or more of the subskill components. For this reason it is important to have regular checks on the progress of pupils as they move through the skills program. Where deficiencies are apparent, re-teaching or remedial teaching should be instituted. This is particularly important in the case of a child who may have been absent from school at a time when instruction was being provided on a critical subskill.

Ideally, in a skills curriculum, learning experiences will be arranged sequentially, to move the learner from simple variations of the skill to complex ones, over a period of several years. In such sequencing it is essential to provide plenty of opportunities for children to apply their newly acquired skills in functional settings. The basic skills, as well as those taught in the subject areas, should be used frequently. This is the most important way skills can be learned. The teacher should keep in mind that in spite of many different approaches to the teaching of reading, the best readers are always found in those classes and schools where pupils do a lot of reading. While this example uses reading to illustrate the point, the implications clearly apply to any skill. Nothing is as damaging to skill development as the lack of use, or disuse, of the skill.

BASIC SKILLS—THE THREE *R*'s

As we know, the elementary school has had responsibility for teaching the basic skills of reading, writing, and arithmetic from Colonial times to the present day. Great importance is attached

AND YOU SAID . . .

In the following situation, imagine yourself to be the colleague of Mr. Ronald Brooks, and complete the last line:

Mr. Brooks was introduced to the cognitive, affective, and psychomotor "domains" in an Ed. Psych. course during his junior year in college. Later, his methods instructors made frequent references to these categories and in one course the instructor made heavy use of the Bloom Taxonomy.* Now Mr. Brooks is on the job as a beginning teacher and he is thinking about how he will arrange his school day. He thinks it would be a good idea to divide the day into three large blocks of time, one for each of the three "domains." He relates his thoughts to a colleague of a few years teaching experience, over a cup of coffee.

"That's not where it's at, Ron," his colleague responded.

"What do you mean?" asked Mr. Brooks.

And YOU said, "____"

to these skills because they deal so fundamentally with basic literacy. A person who does not have a respectable command of basic literacy skills is greatly handicapped in doing school work, and will obviously be limited in choice-making in life outside of school. Even though these skills are often dubbed "the three *R*'s," they involve a vast array of skills and subskills that make it possible for the child to become a fully communicating human being. If a teacher desires to have a strong program in the basic skills, the following requirements must be met.

1. *The program is organized, structured, systematic, and sequential.* In situations where we find casualties in the learning of basic skills, we often see what might be called a "nonprogram" in basic skills. Instruction is entirely incidental to the informal activities of the classroom. Children write when they express a "need." They read when they have an interest in reading. They learn to write and spell because they want to communicate something in written language. All of this is commendable up to a point. Certainly we want basic

*Benjamin S. Bloom, Ed., *Taxonomy of Educational Objectives: Handbook I, The Cognitive Domain* (New York: David McKay Co., Inc., 1956).

skills to be used in purposeful ways, and no doubt some children can learn basic skills in this way. But for most children, this approach is much too haphazard and opportunistic. It suggests that complex skills can be taught and learned on a catch-as-catch-can basis, with a disregard for the sequence in which the learning occurs. The outcomes of this approach, if widely applied, are predictable—there will be many children who do not learn the basic skills well enough to meet the requirements of school, to say nothing of life outside of school. This is not to say, however, that there are not a few especially talented teachers who, using this approach, can achieve remarkable results with children.

To reduce the risk of having children not learn basic skills, the teacher should plan an organized, systematic, structured, and sequential program of instruction in each of the basic skills. This means that time will be devoted to such instruction on a regular, planned basis. The various components of the skills will be taught sequen-

tially, leading from simple to complex variations of the skill. The teacher will use well-prepared instructional materials produced by a reputable author and publisher. The specific skills to be developed can be and are identified. Pupil achievement is appraised behaviorally. These are qualities that characterize a structured and organized program.

The teacher has a right to expect the school district to provide curriculum documents that detail the structure and sequence of the basic skills program. Such a document should spell out specifically what skills are to be attended to and what level of attainment is expected. If such documents are not available, the teacher should study carefully the teacher's manuals that accompany the reading, language arts, and mathematics texts used in the school. These manuals will acquaint the teacher with the organization and structure of the skills program developed in the children's material. Although the teacher will probably not want to follow such a textbook pro-

PHOTO FOLIO

Teachers sometimes make use of bulletin boards to remind children of the importance of skills. Do you believe that displays such as those in this photograph actually help children learn to perform skills more proficiently? Suggest another idea for a bulletin board display that could be useful in helping develop some important skill.

gram precisely, it will provide an organizing framework around which the teacher can build the basic skills program.

2. *The program is interesting and stimulating to the pupils.*

Instruction in basic skills can easily fall into an uninspiring routine, one that varies little from day to day, and which becomes mindless and dull. For example, each day at the prescribed time, pupils go to their places and the lesson picks up where it was left the day before. And the ritual is repeated day after dreary day. Little wonder the pupils, and their teacher, too, find this type of a program little short of drudgery. It would be unusual to expect any dramatic achievement to result from such uninspired teaching.

What is needed in effective skills instruction is the enthusiasm and interest that children bring with them in their early days of school—the time when learning to read, to write, to spell their names, and to do a little simple arithmetic represents a major success experience for them. How exciting it is for children to learn basic skills at that point in their school life! The child who exclaims, "I can READ!" has discovered whole new worlds opening to him or her. And what wonderful worlds those are! But as the years pass, much of this early enthusiasm wanes. And by the time the child reaches the middle grades, the teacher must conscientiously work at keeping the programs interesting and stimulating.

In order to maintain a consistently high level of pupil interest, the teacher should make use of a variety of practice formats. In addition to the conventional practice exercises, generous use can be made of activities that involve practical application of skills, contests and games, visual and auditory aids, mechanical and electronic devices, and other vehicles that pupils find interesting to use. Variety seems to pay big dividends in keeping the practice sessions spirited and intellectually vigorous.

Experimental programs in skills teaching often report impressive gains in pupil achievement when they are first introduced. Undoubtedly, the novelty of trying something new and different has the effect of making the instruction more interesting and exciting for both the teachers and pupils; consequently this is reflected in improved pupil achievement. This, in turn, has the effect of further inspiring teachers and pupils to work even harder, thereby propelling the multiplier effect. Perhaps *this* is the major contribution of innovative efforts to school programs.

3. *Frequent evaluations are conducted to ensure continuous progress.*

Progress in skill development (increased proficiency of performance), is a continuous, gradual, and cumulative process. It does not take place by stages marked off by grade level, birthdays, levels of schooling, or "stages" of growth. Because progress is continuous and gradual, it is often referred to as "developmental."

The term *developmental,* however, is *not* meant to imply that skill growth occurs as a natural unfolding process, similar to the physical growth and development of a child. Without instruction and/or a conscious intent to learn and improve, skill growth will not occur at all. Skill development can be arrested at any point, for one of any number of reasons. It is essential, therefore, that frequent checks be made of the child's progress, with the results recorded for future reference. We need not be particularly concerned about the amount of improvement in a child's skill from day to day or week to week. But we should be very concerned if we see no progress over a period of a few months or in a school year. Nonetheless, the frequent evaluations–day to day and week to week–will alert the teacher to problems a child might be having. These can be corrected before they seriously impede the child's progress.

Cases are frequently reported where children have advanced to the third or fourth grades before it is discovered that they are having a reading or a writing problem or a problem with arithmetic. There can be little excuse for this kind of oversight. Of course there will be pupils in these grades, and even several grades beyond, who are deficient in basic skills, but they should have been detected early on in the school life of the child. After a child has been in school for a year or more, there should be no surprises for the professional staff regarding a youngster's skill development. When proper attention is given to evaluation, difficulties are diagnosed early and appropriate measures taken to correct them. There are of course children with complex learning difficulties that require highly specialized corrective measures. But the overwhelming number of learning problems of children are relatively simple to diagnose and to remedy.

A few years ago the author encountered a primary-grade child whose school life was coming apart at the seams because he was not "getting" arithmetic. The child, who until this time enjoyed school, was beginning to complain to his parents about school. When it was Tuesday, he wished it would be Friday because that would then be the last day of school. The teacher reported a change in the boy's attitude in school, and that he was having "trouble" with arithmetic.

One evening his father worked with the boy and discovered that he did not grasp the meaning of the equal sign (=). Suddenly, in a flash of insight, the boy made sense out of this concept of number relationships. Repeatedly expressions such as, "Oh, that's what that means!" poured from the child. His entire attitude, not only toward arithmetic but to school itself, reversed dramatically. Left undetected this minor problem might have caused this child many years of serious difficulty in school. It could have been remedied by the teacher in a matter of minutes. Regrettably it was not. It took an interested and concerned parent to diagnose and remedy the difficulty. But what of the thousands of children with similar problems whose parents do not, or cannot help their children? Who will assist them? Can a teacher be considered competent who does not attend to simple learning difficulties of this kind? Teaching means helping children learn, not simply conducting classes.

4. *The program must be individualized.*

There is much about the nature of the school setting that discourages the teacher from individualizing instruction in skills. The teacher has twenty-five or more children with whom to work. Often these children are of the same age and may not be too different from one another in physical appearance or size. This is especially the case in the primary grades. The pupils all look alike to the teacher. Moreover, tradition reinforces the idea that the teacher teaches a *class* rather than *individual pupils* who just happen to be grouped together. It is only when the teacher begins looking at children individually that differences between and among them become apparent.

The range of individual differences between and among children who have been randomly selected for grade groups in the elementary school is well documented. Children of the same chronological age differ in their rate of learning, in their interest in learning, in their learning styles, in their motivation to learn, and in almost every other relevant variable on which we have data. The challenge to the teacher is to devise methods of teaching that will accommodate the individual needs of children in group settings.

Individualizing instruction in skills does not mean that each child is to be shunted off to work alone on a workbook exercise. Individualized instruction can and, most often, does take place in small groups that have been formed to meet specific needs. The groups are temporary and flexible. There is no particular procedure or formula that can be recommended to the teacher, except that instruction probably cannot be individualized if the class is taught as a whole group day after day. The teacher needs to make a careful study of individual children in the class. By so doing, the teacher will get to know the achievement level of each one and will know what special help each requires. Then, by careful grouping of children, the teacher can provide each one with the kind of instruction that best suits him or her. Naturally, there will be many times when there will be a need for a one-on-one relationship between teacher and learner. (This was certainly indicated in the case of the child having problems with arithmetic.) Much of the time, however, instruction in skills can be productively conducted in small groups of five to eight children.

5. *Methods and materials should be used that stress purposeful and functional use of skills.*

The teaching of skills should *not* be separated from situations in which the skills are to be used. A major limitation of many skills programs is that they are isolated not only from life out of school, but from other school learning as well. To be most effective, basic skills must be applied to other school learning and must be an essential component of the child's total school experience. This principle is discussed again in greater detail later in this chapter.

6. *The program encourages habits of independence on the part of learners.*

Several years ago (1948), the late Professor W. S. Gray published a book entitled *On Their Own in Reading.* This is a particularly appropriate title, not only for a book on the teaching of reading, but for any of the basic skills. As soon as possible children should be "on their own" in reading, writing, spelling, arithmetic, and in all of the subskill components that make up these basic skills. If this is to happen, the child will need to be presented with many opportunities for the application and use of newly acquired skills. By using them, the child develops independence in the use of these skills. And as independence is gained he or she is constantly reinforcing and practicing the skill, thereby relying less on the school and the teacher to provide these enriching and extending experiences. The object or ultimate goal of the skills program is, of course, to make all children independent and truly "on their own" in the use of basic skills, and as soon as possible.

STUDY SKILLS

In order to develop some degree of independence as an inquiring and self-instructing human being, the pupil must be able to use skillfully various resources and procedures. We refer here to the work-study, or simply, study skills. They are essential to successful

IS THERE A PREFERRED WAY?

Mr. Barto sets aside specific time periods during the day when he teaches basic skills such as reading, writing, spelling, handwriting, oral and written expression. He feels this is the best way to provide individual assistance to children and keep track of their progress. Beyond that, he does not do much with skills teaching.

Miss West does not provide specific time periods for these skills but lengthens her science and social studies periods and teaches the basic skills as needed in functional settings in connection with these units. She feels skills should not be taught in isolation, but in situations where they are used.

Mrs. Brookover combines what Mr. Barto and Miss West do. She has specific periods of short duration for systematic and sequential instruction, but also makes a big point of having pupils apply these skills in science, social studies and, where appropriate, in all areas of the school curriculum. She feels both types of experiences are needed to ensure the satisfactory development and maintenance of skills.

1. Why does Mrs. Brookover's approach have advantages over those of Mr. Barto and Miss West?
2. Which of the three methods is potentially most vulnerable to the neglect of skills teaching? Which is most vulnerable to meaningless teaching? Why?
3. Assuming all three teachers have the same grade, and that the pupils in all three groups are roughly equivalent in terms of their ability to learn, do you think there would be significant differences in standardized test scores among the three groups on a skills test?

achievement in the subject matter areas of the curriculum, and are central to any type of information gathering and data processing outside of school.

Variations of study skills may be spread along a continuum from simple to complex. The instructional program will introduce simple variations of these skills in the primary grades and spiral toward increasingly complex variations of them as the child moves through school. Thus, when primary-grade children are asked, "What happened first? What happened next? Then what happened?" the teacher is acquainting pupils with the arrangement of ideas in sequence, an important subskill relating to organizing material. Let us examine the study skills more closely.

1. *Finding and acquiring information.*

The deaths of former Presidents Truman and Johnson occurred within a short time of each other; both died during the winter months. Suppose this matter came up in a discussion by a fifth-grade class, and the question arose as to whether or not both former Presidents died during the same calendar year. If no one knew the answer, and it became important for the class to find out, where would they look? What source would be used, and how would they go about finding out what they want to know? Could such information be obtained from the textbook? If so, how would one go about locating it? By using the Table of Contents? The Index? The Appendix, if there is one? Or can this information be obtained in the encyclopedia? If so, how is the best way to go about finding it? Or does one have to use the library, and if so, what special references or reference aids are needed?

This example illustrates that procedures for finding and acquiring relevant information can be time consuming and unproductive unless the individual knows where and how to look for what is wanted. Pupils must be provided instruction, practice, and opportunities for application of skills relating to the use of tables of contents, card catalogs, indices, glossaries, appendicies, tables of maps and illustrations, and others. They must learn what kinds of information are available in each, and how each of the various aids is organized and used. For example, an index is arranged alphabetically but a table of contents is arranged topically.

Skills relating simply to the efficient use of a book are also important in finding and acquiring information. For instance, paging through a chapter and noting the sideheads will often bring the reader quickly to the part containing the information sought. Of course, skimming is an essential subskill relating to the productive search for specific data. Children need to be taught to skim quickly over printed matter in search of specific items of information. This is a subskill of reading having to do with varying the rate of reading in terms of the purposes to be achieved.

Beyond initial instruction, teachers must devise exercises calling for the use of these skills on a regular basis. This will achieve two purposes. One, it will provide maintenance practice for the pupil, and two, it will alert the teacher to any problems pupils are having. That is, it will serve diagnostic and evaluative purposes. For example, the teacher may have pupils use their social studies textbooks to locate a specific fact. If some pupils are observed using the table of contents instead of the index, or worse, if some pupils begin at the front of the book, page through and skim each page, the teacher

knows that these pupils need help in developing more efficient information-search skills.

There are many skills relating to the use of general and special references that are critical in the collection of data relevant to a problem, topic, a question—or other research activity. General and special references are the dictionary, encyclopedia, *World Almanac,* atlases, *Who's Who,* and the *Statesman's Yearbook.* In teaching the use of these sources, pupils need to learn first what the sources are and then, what general or specialized information each will yield. Important in the search for information is knowing what sources are available. Thus, children learn that if they wish to find information on many topics, a general, all-purpose encyclopedia is a helpful reference. But if this source is to be used efficiently, the user must be able to apply such subskills as recognizing alphabetical arrangements, key words, letters on volumes, indexes, and

PHOTO FOLIO

Learning to perform a skill with proficiency requires that the learner engage in a certain amount of practice. The more similar the practice situation is to the conditions under which the skill is used, the more likely the practice is to result in improved performance. Practice sessions should not be "drill" in the traditional sense of simple repetition. Repetition *is* necessary, however, if the objective is to increase the speed and smoothness of responses. Skill teaching should also be individualized for learners. This photograph illustrates one teacher's effort to individualize skill building.

1. Explain how the procedures illustrated in the photograph apply sound principles of skill building.
2. Comment on the validity of the following assertions:
   a. Drill should be a part of a modern elementary school program.
   b. Repetition is the only way one can learn to do anything proficiently.
   c. Meaningfulness is important in concept development but has nothing to do with teaching skills.

cross references. Therefore these specific subskills must be identified, taught, practiced, and used in functional settings.

2. *Reading and interpreting maps, graphs, charts, and other pictorial material.*

The extensive use of illustrative material today makes it imperative that individuals know how to read and interpret these visual devices. They are widely used because of their impact on the reader; they communicate with a minimum amount of effort—even to the reader with limited reading ability. Moreover, visual devices can communicate concepts, relationships, and data that would be extremely difficult, if not impossible, to comprehend in other ways. For example, imagine how difficult it would be to explain world rainfall patterns without the use of a map. A diagram illustrating the concept "chain reaction" is considerably easier to understand than a verbal explanation, and greatly reduces the possibility of misunderstanding.

If pupils are to develop their skills in the use of these devices, a systematic program of instruction is needed throughout the grades. This program would consist of (1) formal and direct instruction on the component subskills and (2) many opportunities for practice and use of them. Too often it is assumed that pupils can learn these skills simply by using them in practical settings. As a result, pupils often learn them in a hit-and-miss way, if at all. The use of each of these visual devices involves skills that can be arranged along a continuum of complexity and instruction should be programmed accordingly. Of course, children in the primary grades cannot read a complicated world map. But they can begin to learn that space can be represented symbolically—through the use of simple layouts and maps of the local area that they themselves make. When the primary-grade teacher uses stick-figure drawings to illustrate a point, the pupils are being provided an opportunity to learn chart-reading skills.

The use of various visual devices often relates to the subject matter of mathematics, science, social studies, health, and the language arts. Therefore, the special skills needed for their use should be taught within the curriculum framework of those subjects. There will be considerable carryover from one subject to the other. For instance, if a pupil learns in the mathematics program basic concepts and skills relating to the use of bar graphs, he or she should have little difficulty in applying these skills to data in science and social studies. Nevertheless, it cannot be assumed that this will happen automatically; the pupils need to be shown how to make specific use of these skills in each of the subject-matter fields.

3. *Organizing information into usable structures.*

Locating and collecting an abundance of information and data is of little consequence unless the individual can organize it in practical ways. There are well-established procedures and skills used for this purpose. Among them are

- outlining
- preparing charts
- making a time line
- classifying pictures
- arranging ideas, events, or facts in a sequence
- making a data-retrieval chart
- identifying a central issue
- placing data in graph form

writing a summary
recognizing trends in data
taking notes
keeping records
evaluating information
processing data through analysis and interpretation

Such a list of skills to be taught presents a formidable challenge to the teacher, who may conclude that the task is overwhelming, impossible. No one could teach all these skills and do much of anything else! But of course, these skills are neither taught nor learned all at one time, or even in one year. The child's growth in the use of these skills is cumulative. The process begins when the child enters school and continues as long as he or she is in school. As is true with most skills, each of these has variants that are arranged in a simple to complex sequence in the curriculum. The primary-grade teacher who asks, "What is the one big idea we should remember from this story?" is helping the child to distinguish relative importance among ideas. This will be helpful to the child later on, when beginning to organize ideas in outline form.

Skills related to the organization of material can frequently be applied throughout the school day. Because this is so, the teacher may assume that direct instruction on them is not necessary. Or perhaps only a minimum level of instruction is provided, again the presumption being that the child will extend and refine these skills through functional use. This can often lead to poorly developed skills or to the restricted growth of them. To ensure that the pupil will move toward more mature and sophisticated use of these operations, some direct instruction should be given on them each year, along with many opportunities for their practical use.

4. *Following directions.*

Following directions is a skill frequently used in life outside of school and, interestingly enough, is one that is either poorly performed or ignored until one gets into difficulty. Who knows how many cakes, cookies, or other delicacies have been disasters because the baker did not follow directions precisely! Postal authorities report that the public is incredibly incapable of following even the simplest directions on mailing procedures. In the use of coin-changing machines, it is not uncommon for users to stuff currency into the coin receptacles! Information accompanying new appliances, toys, and garden equipment always admonishes the buyer to *Read Directions Carefully Before Using,* further reminding us of our general carelessness in following directions.

In school, following directions is a commonly applied skill. There are directions for reading maps, for conducting science experiments, for taking tests and examinations, for constructing models, for using special equipment, and many others. These are times when there is an obvious need to apply the skill; it is at those times that the skill should be taught. Part of the teacher's responsibility is to monitor the behavior of pupils to be sure they *do* follow directions and procedures exactly in those situations where precision is essential. Poor habits in following directions can be reinforced by the teacher's lack of attention. But the teacher must not insist on precision to the point that it overshadows more significant educational outcomes.

THE NEED FOR A SMOOTH TRANSITION

In school, things went quite well for Jimmy until he reached the fourth grade. He was a sensitive, quiet, well-behaved boy and enjoyed the relaxed and informal program in the primary grades. Now the amount of reading he was being asked to do increased considerably from what it was the year before, and Jimmy was not a very good reader. Besides, he had to find things in the encyclopedia and in the library, and he did not know how to find what he was supposed to be looking for. And in social studies there were, in the first part of the textbook, all those maps that he didn't understand. He couldn't pick out a main idea, nor could he write a summary sentence. It just seemed as though nothing in school made much sense to him anymore. He was so discouraged that he would sometimes just sit and stare out the window. One day his teacher said to him, "Jimmy, you will just have to improve your work-study skills." He didn't even know what she was talking about.

1. How might the teacher have been more helpful to this pupil?
2. Why is the fourth grade such a critical year in terms of work-study skills?
3. If Jimmy's problems are left unattended, what would you predict his future in school to be?

INTELLECTUAL SKILLS

The development of children's thinking has been taken seriously as an educational goal by teachers, educators, and curriculum planners. Today much is said and written about "process" outcomes; often the reference is to intellectual processes. Children's textbooks, methods-teaching books, curriculum books, and curriculum guides, especially in the fields of science and social studies, show heavy emphasis on inquiry and other reflective processes. Little wonder, therefore, that intellectual skills are being highlighted in many programs.

Intellectual skills are involved in most of what one does when in a conscious state. As used here, however, the term applies to processes that are included in the application of intelligence to the solution of problems. Some authors have referred to these as *critical thinking skills,* others call them *inquiry skills.* Still other terms have been applied to this cluster of skills—reflective thinking, scientific thinking, creative thinking, reasoning, discovery learning, and investigation-oriented learning. Of course, information-processing skills such as interpretation, comprehension, and analysis are also important intellectual skills. Freedom of inquiry implies a commitment to intelligence and the rational process.

The phases or aspects of reflective thought developed by Dewey have served as the basis for much of the theoretical work in problem-solving and inquiry-teaching strategies.[1] Out of *How We Think* have come the following five basic components of problem solving: (1) recognizing that a problem exists; (2) defining and delimiting the problem; (3) formulating hypotheses concerning the problem; (4) gathering data and drawing conclusions based on those data; (5) testing the conclusions and noting the consequences of the conclusions. In one form or another, these now famous five steps in problem solving have been widely cited in educational literature. Although problem solving and inquiry are not necessarily identical processes, the basic Dewey format is apparent in much of the work associated with inquiry teaching. There is a striking similarity between the familiar problem-solving steps developed years ago and the inquiry models developed by contemporary authors.

The use of structured problem solving and/or inquiry models has often resulted in the formalizing and ritualizing of these processes. Some speakers have amused teacher audiences by ridiculing the structured problem-solving procedure. For example, reference is made to the Nobel award-winning scientist who gets up in the morning and says to himself, "Today I am going to solve a problem. Therefore, I must remember the five steps required in scientific problem solving." This is silly, of course, but it does illustrate the extent to which sound procedures can be distorted through faulty application.

The use of intellectual skills in problem resolution does not mean

[1] John Dewey, *How We Think* (Boston: D. C. Heath & Company, 1933), p. 106.

that one necessarily follows five (or any other number) of formal steps, as is implied by these structured procedures. The individual who develops curiosity and skepticism will develop a system of defining and resolving problems. But if the learner is to develop any discipline in thinking, it is likely that some importance will be attached to such processes as defining and identifying problems, gathering and organizing relevant data, forming hunches and hypotheses, testing these against the reality of the data, coming to conclusions, and behaving in accordance with these conclusions.

The teaching of intellectual skills requires, above all, a low-risk classroom environment, one that encourages and supports diversity of thought, curiosity, and skepticism. This degree of intellectual openness will allow for the free flow of ideas that can be analyzed,

PHOTO FOLIO

Intellectual skills are often referred to as "tools" for learning. They are intended to help pupils learn how to learn. Library-use skills are of that type. The child who knows how to use the library to get needed information has a skill that can be useful for a lifetime in keeping informed. By using present-day storage and retrieval systems, any person has available all the information contained in the world's great libraries and centers of knowledge.

1. What sub-skills are needed in order for pupils to make use of the school library?
2. Discuss how the school librarian can be of assistance to the classroom teacher in helping pupils make good use of the library.

discussed, verified, rejected, or accepted. An environment in which intellectual skills develop and flourish is one that values creativity, flexibility, and inventiveness. It rewards imaginative, unusual, novel responses. It supports and encourages pupils to engage in risk-taking ventures, as opposed to rewarding and praising of pupils for their search for the conventional, accepted, "right" answers. Given a classroom with this kind of intellectual configuration, the teacher may want to use the following suggestions. They have been used with success by classroom teachers:

1. Involve children in decision making in the classroom, dealing with such matters as methods of work, how to allocate time, classroom management procedures, unit activities, and so on.

2. Use role-playing, simulation, and games to provide a setting for firsthand experiences in problem analysis and resolution.
3. Make generous use of "if-then" type questions that necessitate deriving consequences from given antecedent conditions.
4. Provide frequent opportunities for choice making, keeping in mind that choice requires alternatives from which to choose. If there are no alternatives, there can be no choice.
5. Provide instruction and experience for pupils in the use of structured problem solving and inquiry models.
6. Encourage pupils to become independently curious, eager to explore and poke around in things with which they are unfamiliar.
7. Make it easy for pupils to be curious about their surroundings by providing a classroom filled with materials that provoke curiosity.
8. Make frequent use of reflective-type questions, as discussed in Chapter 8.
9. Encourage pupils to explore value dimensions of decision making, i.e., have them learn how their feelings interfere with their judgment.

WHICH IS WHICH?

Which of the following are product outcomes and which ones are process outcomes?

1. Answering all questions correctly on a teacher-made test based on a reading assignment.
2. Writing a friendly letter using the conventional form.
3. Making use of reference books in order to prepare an oral report.
4. Making an oral report to the class.
5. Identifying types of information needed to answer a question or set of questions.
6. Making informed "guesses" (hypotheses) that might explain a problem.
7. Testing informed "guesses" (hypotheses) in question 6 against evidence.
8. Participating in a class discussion.
9. Working on a committee assigned to do a specific task.
10. Playing a musical selection from memory.

Now answer these questions:

1. How might a teacher evaluate each of the ten learning outcomes described above?
2. Are product or process outcomes more easily evaluated? Why? Might this lead to the neglect of one or the other in the instructional program?

SOCIALIZATION SKILLS

When a person learns role behavior that is appropriate to social life in a culture, when one can satisfy one's needs through social discourse and interaction with others, we say that such a person has become *socialized.* In specific terms, this means that one knows how to use the language in communicating with others, behaves in accordance with the mores and folkways of the culture, has internalized the core values and beliefs of the culture and reflects those in his or her behavior, and that the person is able to modify behavior to suit specific social settings. For our purposes, this is an adequate definition of socialization, but it is by no means complete.

There may be specific applications of the socialization concept. For example, we may speak of political socialization as the process that shapes the learner's political belief system. Or we may say that the child has been socialized in the life of the school, meaning that he or she can perform social roles satisfactorily in the school setting. Some authors also write of "sex-role socialization." Sometimes the term *enculturation* is used in place of *socialization* in describing this process of acquiring, incorporating, and internalizing culture.

It is obvious, of course, that the total school program is concerned with socializing the youngster. The socializing process begins early in the child's life in the home and is continued and extended in contacts in the neighborhood, the community, and most especially the school. The forces that shape the socialization of a child are so powerful and pervasive that the process takes place whether or not it is willed and planned. But the nature and extent of this socialization may or may not conform to the expectations of the larger society, and this may make considerable difference with respect to the child's chances for success in the school's social environment. For some children the social environment of the home and the school may be similar; for others the two may be vastly different. In terms of school success, the consequences of these differences are well known.

We deal here with a limited aspect of socialization. Indeed, we are confining our discussion to only three dimensions of socialization skills because it is known that these can be influenced by the school environment. These skills are those involved in (1) social interaction; (2) cooperative group efforts; and (3) conflict resolution. Clearly, these must be considered among the most important skills in the life of a human being because they profoundly affect how one deals with fellow human beings. Learning these social skills is also basic to much of one's personal happiness and stability. The person with deficient social skills is often one whose life is characterized by bitterness, cynicism, loneliness, and distrust.

Skills of Social Interaction

In order to relate effectively to other human beings, one must first of all feel good about oneself. The way one feels about oneself is usually referred to as one's *self-concept.* We think of this in terms of self-esteem or self-image. Helping children build good self-images is probably the single most important thing a teacher can do in terms of the total development of a young human being.

There is overwhelming evidence that those children who have poor images of themselves are not only likely to be low achievers; they show other evidence of maladaptive behavior. It is not altogether clear whether one is the cause or the effect of the other, but it is reasonable to assume that it could be either, depending on individual cases. Be that as it may, there are many cases of improved school achievement and more constructive behavior when the child's self-image has been improved.

Unfortunately, the school itself sometimes contributes to the destruction of a child's self-esteem. A youngster may come to school from a happy home, one that has made the child feel quite good about himself or herself. In school the child may be bullied by other children, or teased; or may encounter difficulty in learning to read; or may experience failure in a variety of ways in the school program. This lack of success in school may cause the child's parents to be disappointed in his or her performance, and this may be conveyed to the child either unintentionally or overtly. Experiences such as these can, and often do, have a devastating effect on the child's sense of personal worth. A child with these experiences is almost certain to have problems in social relations; indeed, it would be remarkable if he or she did not. The importance of successful, confidence-building experiences is stressed repeatedly in educational and psychological literature. For example, Sears and Sherman have the following to say on this matter:

> Through meeting tasks that are challenging to them children learn to cope with the real world. Self-concepts of competence in work emerge gradually, enabling the child to meet subsequent challenges with a calm confidence. Children who do not acquire a sense of competence become dissatisfied with themselves, unfriendly to those around them, resistant to authority, and perhaps rebellious against society. Studies of delinquents have shown that in almost

every case the school was unable to give the individual a sense of competence; he then tried to maintain a sort of self-esteem by antisocial means.[2]

This pattern, so well stated by Sears and Sherman, is documented by a substantial amount of research and by the observations and experiences of untold numbers of teachers. What can the teacher do, then, to build in children this feeling of confidence and competence that is so vital to good self-images?

It is imperative that the teacher establish a social climate and a classroom environment where children learn to feel good about themselves. It should be a place where people are more valued than things, schedules, assignments, or guppies. It must be a place where everyone counts for something. Whether or not they have learning problems, as almost everyone does at some time, is beside the point. This should have nothing to do with making children feel that they are *worthy human beings.* Human beings of any age, but most especially children, should not have to prove their worth.

Healthy self-images develop in *caring* environments that help children build backlogs of success experiences. Self-images are destroyed in environments where children get the impression that no one really cares about them, and where they experience constant failure. Also it is doubtful whether children can perceive of themselves positively if they do not have a personal liking for the teacher, or if they feel the teacher does not like them.

It is the teacher, therefore, who sets the good emotional climate of the classroom, the climate that facilitates social interaction based on trust, respect, and integrity. Although this is achieved mainly by example, children do need to have systematic instruction in social skills. This would include:

1. Ordinary conventions and courtesies associated with social discourse.
2. Sensitivity to the problems and feelings of others; seeing situations from another's point of view.
3. Listening to what others have to say.
4. Developing an awareness of the consequences of large- or small-group behavior on individuals, i.e., the effects of cliques, pressure on individuals to conform to group norms, the excluding of certain children from group activities, and others.

[2] Pauline S. Sears and Vivian S. Sherman, *In Pursuit of Self-Esteem: Case Studies of Eight Elementary School Children* (Belmont, Cal.: Wadsworth Publishing Co., Inc., 1964), p. 3.

5. Achieving an understanding of why people behave the way they do.
6. Becoming aware that social interaction involves decision making and choice, and that the choices one makes often carry with them consequences that affect other people.

Skills of Cooperative Group Efforts

Being able to contribute in a constructive way to a group task is an essential skill in school, and in life outside of school. Most of what the child will do in life will be in cooperation with other people. Consequently, the social values of education are of inestimable importance.

The usual assumption is that people learn group-work skills by experience; that is, by participating in group efforts. Although this of course is true, it overlooks the fact that learning group-work skills can be greatly enhanced through instruction. It is not enough simply to provide the opportunity to work in small groups and committees; the teacher must also instruct children in how to function in those roles associated with group cooperative efforts.

No one ever learned to work cooperatively in a group by working in isolation. If group-work skills are to be developed, there must be many planned classroom activities that involve children working together. Not all of these efforts will be successful; this is to be expected, because in the process of learning, one makes mistakes. The advantage of the school environment is that mistakes can be made without resulting in disastrous consequences. In this respect, in-school experiences are different from those outside of school. Learning to work independently is important, too, but this is not the format in which group-work skills are developed.

The skills that need to be taught and learned in connection with group efforts are these:

1. Contributing to group planning (providing suggestions, evaluating proposals, suggesting alternatives, compromising on points of difference).
2. Defining problems (raising questions, suggesting which questions are relevant, respecting views of others).
3. Organizing to achieve a defined task (deciding on a plan of action, suggesting subtasks, suggesting specific assignments, deciding on what materials will be needed).
4. Working as a committee member (knowing and carrying out specific responsibilities, assisting with planning, cooperating and working with others rather than in isolation, supporting the

leadership of the chairman, working responsibly toward the achievement of group goals).

5. Assuming leadership of groups (developing plans cooperatively with group members, respecting the suggestions and contributions of group members, moving the group toward the achievement of its goals, delegating responsibility as needed, serving as spokesperson for the group, maintaining democratic rather than autocratic relationships with group members).

Instruction in group-work skills needs to take place over a long period of time. The teacher may single out one small subskill and concentrate attention on it when it applies particularly well to the work of the class. Standards for group work can and *should* be developed cooperatively with the children. These can be posted and used as criteria for evaluating the work of the groups. Role-playing is an especially good procedure for teaching children to understand the meaning of group-work skills.

When applying these skills it is usually a mistake to begin by dividing an entire elementary school class into small subgroups. Children are not ready for this degree of independence; they have not developed the maturity to be entirely self-directed. It is better to begin with one small group that is given a specific task—with clear directions. The group should be closely supervised by the teacher. The remainder of the class can be kept intact at this point. Gradually, all of the children can be members of such small groups, at which time two or more small groups can be at work simultaneously. In time, the teacher can have the entire class working productively in small groups. Group-work skills need to be evaluated frequently, and pupils should be provided with generous praise when their efforts have been successful.

Conflict Resolution

Jason is waiting in line at the drinking fountain when Eric comes along and tries to nudge his way ahead of him. Jason tries to close the gap with his body; Eric pushes him out of the way. Jason pushes back; Eric strikes him—and the altercation has escalated into a full-blown fight. A teacher is called. The boys are separated, perhaps led off to the principal's office, and some attempt is made to resolve the matter. It may be that the issue is settled at that point, or it may be that the conflict continues, perhaps resulting in an after-school fight on the way home. Incidents involving two pupils or groups of pupils are fairly common in schools, and are usually unpleasant for all concerned when they happen. Because dominance relationships are so widespread throughout nature, including human beings, there is really no way that conflict can be avoided entirely. There is rarely a social relationship where conflict is wholly absent. This applies whether we are considering national and international issues or examining social relationships on a face-to-face basis within families, in neighborhoods, or on the school playground.

There are three ways the elementary classroom teacher should be prepared to deal with conflict situations. Each is discussed briefly.

1. *Establish classroom conditions that minimize the possibility of conflict and that encourage harmonious social relations.* Why is it that some classrooms are characterized by a higher level of hostility and aggression than others? To answer this question we must examine the conditions within classrooms that give rise to such behaviors.

Perhaps the most powerful force affecting classroom climate are statements made by the teacher. If the teacher uses a preponderance of negative and directive statements, the level of tension and hostility in the classroom will be elevated. This is predictable, and it has been demonstrated in human-relations laboratories hundreds of times. One of the most effective ways to reduce hostility and aggression in groups is to increase the number of positive, constructive statements made by the teacher, and eliminating those that are negative, directive, and critical.

Hostility and aggression also escalate when children are under great pressure to work rapidly, or when they are required to do more than they are able to in the time provided. This can be generalized: Any procedure that continually frustrates pupils is likely to reflect itself in aggression and conflict. Pupils who cannot perform satisfactorily under tension-producing conditions are likely to turn on others when venting their hostilities. A conflict on the playground may be the result of frustrations built up in the classroom. A more comfortable and relaxed instructional pace, coupled with realistically achievable requirements, can go a long way in reducing the possibility of interpersonal conflicts.

The classroom atmosphere can be more conducive to improved human relations if competitive situations are kept in proper perspective. Competition can be wholesome to the productive output of a group, providing it does not get out of hand. Children need to engage in fair competition and to learn the appropriate behavior associated with winning and losing. When children engage in competitive sports and games, the meaning of good sportsmanship is one of the important lessons they should learn. Good sportsmanship is a part of the American tradition. The classroom, of course, is not a sports arena, but it can be a place where competitiveness is always handled with an attitude of fairness and good will. When classroom competition becomes intense, with some pupils lording it over others, there is likely to be hostility leading to conflict. Cooperative group efforts by the class can do much to reduce the ill-effects of competition, and can teach children values associated with consideration for others.

2. *Resolve interpersonal conflicts immediately, but plan for longer range solutions to the problem.* When there are conflicts between individual children or between groups of children, the teacher must intervene immediately. That may take care of the problem for the moment, but some type of longer-range corrective measures should be undertaken. When a fight is stopped in the lunchroom, the teacher may be treating the symptoms rather than the causes of conflict. Very often the teacher begins by asking who is responsible. Of course, the children blame each other. ("He hit me first," says one. "But he started it by swiping the ball," says the other.) After some discussion the children apologize to each other, shake hands, and the matter seems to be settled. When there have been injured feelings, however, this is not a satisfactory settlement of the issue. It does little good to force an apology from a youngster, or to have them shake hands, unless something is done about the conditions that brought about the conflict in the first place. An exploration of these conflicts will often show that both children are contending for something of value, whether it is approval by classmates, peer leadership roles, positions on athletic teams, or the favor of a high-status classmate.

3. *Provide instruction on conflict and conflict resolution.* Much of our work with conflict in the elementary school might be described as little more than *moral injunctions* against conflict. "Good" children do not fight, quarrel, or bully others. They show proper respect and consideration for others. They are kind to each other. They are admonished to "turn the other cheek" rather than to strike back at someone who has offended them. Although there may be some need for this kind of instruction at early levels, over-all these approaches have not proven to be effective strategies for dealing with conflict. Children and adults continue to fight, quarrel, and bully each other; they do not show respect and consideration for others—in spite of valiant efforts by the home, church, and school. We still read about ill-tempered persons who hurt or even kill others as a result of conflicts over trivial matters:—someone honks his horn because the car ahead did not move quickly enough when the light turned green; someone makes an obscene gesture

at someone else; or someone tries to bypass others while standing in line with a child waiting to see Santa Claus. In each of these three cases an individual was killed as a result of the ensuing altercation. The six to seven hours a day that American children spent watching television undoubtedly adds little to their desire, or ability, to resolve conflicts rationally.

Perhaps more productive strategies should involve analysis of conflict situations, an exploration of the values that are at issue, and the development of an appreciation of the affective dimension of conflicts. An important part of this teaching must concern itself with *coping* behavior. One must learn that it is not always possible to have one's own way; neither can an individual always allow himself or herself to be trampled on. Moreover, pupils need to learn what constitutes appropriate behavior when confronted with conflict situations.

Instruction in conflict resolution involves three important elements. The first is the identification of all the *facts* of the case. Who did what to whom, when, how many times, with what consequences? The second is the identification of the *issues* involved. Why is there a problem? What is the source of the conflict? How, and why, are the facts perceived and interpreted differently? And the third is the definition of all *possible decisions* that can be made regarding a resolution of the situation, along with the ensuing consequences of each decision. By using this model in studying cases of conflict, pupils will learn that usually one party is not wholly wrong and the other wholly right; the issue involves value choices between options, both of which may be right.

In applying this model to the study of conflict resolution, cases may be devised by the teacher, relying on real-life conflict experiences of children. Simulation games, role-playing, and value-clarification experiences are particularly well-suited for instruction in conflict resolution.

DEVELOPING RELATED COMPETENCIES

What Do You Think About This?

Mr. Willitz is conducting the first meeting of the year with the faculty of the elementary school of which he is principal. He is concerned about improving the handwriting of children in the school. Accordingly, he is asking that once a day the middle-grade teachers (grades four through six) write a short paragraph on the chalkboard and have all children copy it. In this way, he believes children will be getting regular practice in developing their handwriting skills.

1. Do you think the plan Mr. Willitz is presenting will result in improved handwriting skills?
2. Can you think of an alternative plan a school might adopt if it were interested in improving handwriting of pupils?

Using Machines . . .

Situation I

In special classes for intellectually gifted pupils, occasionally one will find the room equipped with typewriters. Do you think typing is a skill that demands superior intellect?

Situation II

Some educators think that in the near future it will be common practice to provide each child with a hand calculator, just as they are provided with textbooks today. If that happens, what present skills would receive less attention and what new skills would have to be added? Do you think it would be a good idea to provide pupils with hand calculators?

What Is "Perfect" Performance?

Miss Bell uses behavioral objectives in connection with the teaching of important skills and subskills. Pupils keep practicing until they are able to achieve the criterion-level of performance Miss Bell has set as minimally acceptable. Therefore, the program is individualized to the extent that pupils may vary the amount of time they need to complete each of the objectives. Miss Bell likes to think of such completions as "perfect" performance. "You can't go on to the next lesson until you get a perfect score on the one you have now," she tells her pupils. "Practice makes perfect, you know!"

1. What is your assessment of this approach to skills teaching in terms of the ideas discussed in this chapter?
2. What is wrong with using the concept of *perfection* in this way?

The Point of Diminishing Returns . . .

Through the years, some curriculum writers have made reference to an idea called "diminishing returns" as a criterion for the selection of content and skills. This means that the more proficient one is in a skill, the more time will need to be spent practicing it to get even small increments of improvement. Some believe that once a pupil has learned certain skills at a level of proficiency adequate for ordinary use, the huge investment of practice time needed to get additional improvement might more profitably be spent on something else.

1. Can you think of examples of skills taught in the elementary school that should be thought of in terms of the diminishing returns concept?
2. Can you provide examples of "something else on which such practice time might be more profitably spent?"
3. Provide examples of skills that require such a high level of achievement that the diminishing-returns criterion should not be applied to them.

FOR FURTHER PROFESSIONAL STUDY

Books

Armstrong, David G., Jon J. Denton and Tom V. Savage, Jr. *Instructional Skills Handbook.* Englewood Cliffs, New Jersey: Educational Technology Publications, Inc., 1978.

Bauer, Caroline Feller. *Handbook for Storytellers.* Chicago: American Library Association, 1977.

Casteel, J. Doyle. *Learning to Think and Choose: Decision-Making Episodes for the Middle Grades.* Santa Monica, California: Goodyear Publishing Company, Inc., 1978.

Chapin, June R. and Richard E. Gross. *Teaching Social Studies Skills.* Boston: Little, Brown and Company, 1973.

Kurfman, Dana G., Ed. *Developing Decision-Making Skills.* 47th Yearbook. Washington, D.C.: National Council for the Social Studies, 1977.

Periodicals

Indrisano, Roselmina. "Putting Research to Work." *Instructor* (December 1978), 98–100.

Levenson, Dorothy. "Minimum Competency Testing." *Instructor* (January 1979), 83–88.

Miller, Etta. "First Grade Reading Instruction and Modality Preferences." *The Elementary School Journal* (November 1979), 99–104.

Suid, Murray. "How to Take Copying Out of Report Writing." *Learning* (November 1979), 46, 51.

10

Strategies for Cognitive Learning

THE QUALIFIED AND COMPETENT TEACHER . . .

1. Understands the nature of concepts and generalizations and their importance in human learning.
2. Is able to apply appropriate strategies in teaching conceptual learning to pupils.
3. Uses conceptual approaches in organizing his or her teaching of substantive material in the content fields.

Performance Criteria

As a result of the serious study of this chapter, the student should be able to . . .

1. Provide examples of basic concepts and generalizations from various school subjects.
2. Describe basic principles of conceptual teaching and show by example how each would be applied in a subject and grade level of his or her choice.
3. Show by an example the difference between inductive and deductive approaches to the teaching of concepts.
4. Show by an example how cognitive, affective, and skills learning are interrelated.
5. Demonstrate the ability to teach a concept to a group of children or a peer group, applying the principles of conceptual teaching described in #2, above.

As you read the following short selection, consciously try to visualize what is being described:

> From the 10,000 foot level, the valley below presented a landscape of incomparable beauty. After a few inches of newly fallen powder on a crisp winter morning, the mountains were magnificent in their splendor. The ski valley itself was really the shape of a rectangle, rather than the more typical bowl. And right in the center of it, as if diagonal lines were drawn to mark the spot, was the community that claimed an international reputation as the "Ski Capital of the World." Originally a wild mining town, it nearly died from its dissipated youth only to regain its life from those who sought it out each winter to test their skill on the mighty slopes nearby. Indeed, so great are their numbers that the village needs the summer months to hibernate in restful sleep in order to awaken refreshed with the first snowfall of a new season.

Now answer these questions:

1. Where in the world would you say this place is located? Why would you place it there?
2. What mental pictures do you form when you read the phrase "wild mining town?"
3. What would you estimate the population of this community to be during the summer months? What word provides you with a clue as to its size?

This is an interesting exercise because it illustrates so well the human capacity to engage in problem solving, conceptual thought. In reading the selection, one can construct in one's mind the reality being described. The example illustrates very well the fact that one does not, in all cases, need to work directly with real objects in solving problems. That is, one is able to manipulate reality intellectually. This remarkable ability of human beings separates them from the rest of creation.

In the life of each individual who has just read the description, there was a time when it would not have been possible to respond correctly to the questions asked about the example. As a young child, one would not have been able to visualize the reality that was described. The young child would not know the meaning of "10,000 foot level," "diagonal lines," "hibernate," "powder," "landscape," and several other concepts used in the paragraph. It is doubtful that many who read this passage have experienced on a firsthand basis a place exactly like the one described. Yet most adults would have no problem visualizing the reality depicted, knowing that it is probably located somewhere in the western part of the United States. This is so because the reader is familiar with the basic ideas necessary to construct the situation in his or her mind. Many prior firsthand and vicarious life experiences have contributed to one's ability to derive meaning from a passage such as this. Human beings have the capacity to reconstruct imaginatively situations previously encountered, as well as to invent new ones, by using intellectual processes and conceptual tools.

THE RELATIONSHIP AMONG FACTS, CONCEPTS, AND GENERALIZATIONS

The relationship among facts, concepts, and generalizations is often represented by using a pyramid-shaped diagram. Facts, being the most numerous, are placed at the base of the pyramid, concepts at midrange, and generalizations at the apex. The logic of this abstraction is that facts (i.e., individually experienced perceptions of

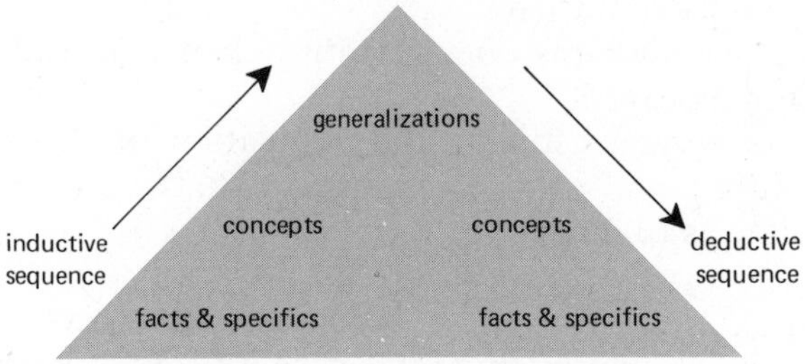

reality) are combined into categories of related meaning to form concepts. Concepts, then, are used to form generalizations that show the relationship between and among related concepts. To a point, there is merit in representing the structural relationship among facts, concepts, and generalizations in this way.

Much of the literature on teaching and learning of cognitive components regards facts and specifics disdainfully. Such expressions as "mere facts" or "facts simply require recall" appear frequently in professional books and in journal articles. Presumably the reason for such comments is to encourage the teacher to be concerned with broader, more significant learning outcomes. Unfortunately, such references may be construed to mean that facts and specifics are unimportant, and this can lead to ineffective teaching of concepts and generalizations. Facts and specifics are not only important, they are essential requirements for the development of meaningful concepts and generalizations. None of the various strategies for concept development claims that facts and specifics are unimportant.

Without exception, these strategies urge that specifics, growing out of direct, firsthand experiences, be incorporated into some type of larger conceptual framework.

It is often stated that facts are soon forgotten, whereas concepts and generalizations are remembered longer. This is only partly true. Many facts and specifics are quickly forgotten, but *some* are remembered for a lifetime. It is further claimed that where facts are remembered for a long period of time, there is opportunity for frequent review and reinforcement. This also is only partly true. For example, it is not uncommon for veterans to recall their military service numbers fifty years or more after they were in the service, with hardly any review of this learning in the interim. Persons in their seventies can often recite poems they memorized when they were in the elementary school. It is claimed, further, that such facts are remembered for a long period of time when they are *overlearned,* but this is not necessarily the case either. Sometimes a single experience or exposure to a specific bit of information will be remembered for a lifetime. For instance, an individual might remember the exact day and hour that he shook the hand of the then President John F. Kennedy. We must conclude, therefore, that there are many exceptions to commonly accepted easy generalizations about how facts are learned and how long they are retained.

We do not discourage overemphasis on facts because they are unimportant or cannot be remembered, but because of their *limited* usefulness and their overwhelming number. Very simply, there is just too much specific information to be able to remember it all. Also, there is little need to remember vast amounts of specific information for a lifetime. Reference works, and now sophisticated information-retrieval devices, can provide adequate data storage for us. Naturally those specifics and facts that we need and use frequently ought to be learned so they can be instantly recalled. One should not have to consult a science reference book each time one needs to know that water freezes at 32° F. and boils at 212° F.

Facts and specifics are more functional and more easily recalled if they are learned in relationship to some overarching concept. The concept becomes a category in which specific facts can be placed. This may not always be practical and feasible, in which case facts deemed to be important must simply be taught directly and learned. For example, a young child does not need to have a well-developed understanding of such concepts as voltage, electrical current, circuits, and conduction to learn the fact that if one places a metal object into the receptacle of an electric outlet one is likely to be severely injured or even killed.

Conceptual teaching means teaching for meaning. Therefore any

teaching strategy selected must be one that promotes meaningful learning. Herein lies the chief difference between factual learning and conceptual learning. Factual learning is sharply limited in the extent to which it can or even needs to be given depth of meaning. Factual learning can be and often is achieved by associating a specific bit of information with the verbal symbol used to label it. For example, the symbol × in mathematics is the symbol indicating that two values are to be multiplied as, 4 × 5. How much time needs to be spent making such a fact (×) meaningful? Hardly any at all; it is simply memorized as a fact.[1] Obviously, some facts can and should be made meaningful whenever possible, as for example, in

[1]We are here talking only about the sign ×; *not* the relationship 4 × 5, which, of course, should be learned meaningfully.

PHOTO FOLIO

Why would a teacher want a child to do something such as this in an elementary school classroom? How would you justify the educational value of this activity to a parent and/or taxpayer?

learning the symbol for hundredweight, cwt. Mathematical facts such as those of multiplication, addition, subtraction, and division can and should be made meaningful. Comment on the extent of meaning that could be developed in connection with the teaching of the following facts:

There are four cardinal directions.
Seven times six is forty-two.
Columbus made his first famous voyage in 1492.
Washington State is a major producer of apples.
The distance from the earth to the moon is approximately 280,000 miles.
The earth rotates from west to east.
The United States entered World War II on December 7, 1941.

Combining the colors red and blue will produce green.
Combustible materials are those that will burn.
The Fourth of July is a national holiday in the United States.

These examples clearly illustrate that facts vary in the extent to which they can be made meaningful, but in any case, the amount of informative "cargo" they carry, so to speak, is limited; restricted to the specific situations to which they refer. Quite the reverse applies to concepts and generalizations.

THE NATURE OF CONCEPTS

Mental images, which are identified by terms such as "diagonal," "landscape," "village," "rectangle," "center," "straight line" are referred to as *concepts.* One does not know their full meaning by learning a definition of them, because their meanings are expansive, open-ended. Understanding concepts depends to a large extent on one's experience, and therefore it is not ever possible to learn all there is to know about many concepts. There are always new variations, new horizons, additional refinements that extend the meaning with increased experience.

Specific concepts have qualities, or *attributes,* that distinguish them from other concepts. A rectangle has attributes that are different from those of a triangle or a circle. The attributes give a rectangle its "rectangle-ness." For example, in order to have "rectangle-ness" a figure must be an enclosed plane figure having four sides, and the sides must connect to form four right angles. It does not matter whether it is large or small, whether it is drawn on colored paper or plain white, whether the lines are wide or narrow—none of these qualities has anything to do with making a figure a rectangle. Moreover, what this figure is *called* has nothing to do with altering its attributes. It could just as well be called an "oogaloo" and still be "an enclosed plane figure having four sides that connect to form four right angles." It just happens that long ago it was decided that such a figure would be called a rectangle—not an altogether illogical choice of labels.

Labels simplify discourse in that one does not have to recite all of the attributes of a concept each time one refers to it. We simply use the word label, in this case "rectangle," and we understand that what is meant is "an enclosed plane figure having four sides that connect to form four right angles." Concepts and the word labels used to identify them are sometimes confused. The story is told of the child who said, "'Pig' is a good name for a pig because it is such a dirty animal!" This amusing confusion illustrates the substitution of a label for a concept.

Just because a youngster is able to use the word or phrase that represents a concept, it cannot be assumed that communication is complete or that he or she understands the concept. Obviously, there is little problem with a simple concept such as "rectangle." A rectangle has few attributes, and it is a concept that can easily be made concrete. We could, for example, have the child draw one. But when in social studies we deal with abstract concepts such as authority, justice, and culture; or transpiration, photosynthesis, and life cycle in science, the matter of differentiating between knowledge of the concept and using its label is not so simple.

Concepts are important in teaching and learning because they constitute the basic structure of a field of knowledge. Concepts are used to form theories and generalizations in fields of knowledge and, therefore, serve as the keystones to the understanding of these broad principles and laws. In recent years programs in mathematics, science, and social studies have, almost without exception, organized their curricula around key concepts in those fields. Examples of key concepts from each of these fields are given on page 322.

CONCEPT DEVELOPMENT

Concepts, as we have already noted, are ideas that are heavily loaded with meaning and are expressed as words or phrases. Concepts are often referred to as having *depth* and *dimensions,* underscoring their potential for meaning. Strategies for teaching concepts, therefore, must take these characteristics into account.

Strategy One

One way to develop concepts is to use a listing-grouping-labeling sequence. This strategy was elaborated by the late Hilda Taba in connection with concept attainment in social studies.[2] Imagine a primary-grade class engaged in a unit on their local community. The teacher might ask the question, "If we went on a walk through the community, what would we find there?" Pupils would respond with such items as these: houses, supermarket, barber shop, buses, cars, bicycles, trucks, bakery, bank, insurance office, drug store, beauty shop, gasoline station, fire station, police station, churches,

[2] Hilda Taba, Mary C. Durkin, Jack R. Fraenkel, and Anthony H. McNaughton, *A Teachers' Handbook to Elementary Social Studies: An Inductive Approach,* 2nd ed. (Reading, Mass.: Addison-Wesley Publishing Co. Inc., 1971).

A Sampling of Basic Concepts from Various School Subjects

	Mathematics	
Set	Factor	Ratio
Decimal	Per Cent	Place Value
Scales	Regrouping	Natural Numbers
Numeral	Zero	Common Denominator
Area	Subset	Measurement
Volume	Prime Number	Whole Numbers
Fraction	Point	Rational Number
Cardinal Number	Average	Number System
	Science	
Air	Ecosystem	Energy
Atmosphere	Gases	Adaptation
Force	Soil	Climate
Atom	Motion	Living Things
Liquid	Inertia	Life Cycle
Friction	Matter	Magnetism
Electricity	Molecules	Plant Kingdom
Gravity	Light Year	Boiling Point
	Social Studies	
Justice	Resources	Power
Responsibility	Production	Social Change
Social Class	Conflict	Modernization
Division of Labor	Money	Culture
Imperialism	Urban Life	Needs and Wants
Labor	Freedom	Colonization
Authority	Distribution	Habitat
Property	Institutions	Exchange

park, jewelry store, motorcycle, telephone booth, newspaper stand, clothing store, Five and Dime store, parking lot, department store, library, post office, apartment houses, doctors' offices, hospital, school, playground.

After having listed as many specific items as possible, pupils are asked to see if they can group them. That is, the things that seem to go together should be placed together. This involves identification of some common elements that serve as the basis for the grouping. It is in this process that conceptual formation takes place. The items might be grouped as follows:

cars	bakery	insurance office
buses	drug store	fire station
bicycles	jewelry store	police station
gasoline stations	clothing store	hospital
motorcycle	Five and Dime	doctor's office
parking lot	department store	
trucks	supermarket	

barber shop beauty shop bank church	houses apartment houses	post office telephone booth newspaper stand
school library	park playground	

The next step in the process is to have the pupils give a name or a label to each of the groups. For example, the following names might be appropriate for the groups defined.

transportation *personal services* *education*	*retail stores* *homes* *recreation*	*protective services* *communication*

This example is a good illustration of what happens in concept formation. We make countless numbers of individual perceptions of reality in our day-to-day living. We group these perceptions in ways that place related ones together, and we give these categories labels. The object of concept teaching, therefore, is to get related specific *instances* or *examples* of concepts together in categories, and to get nonrelated ones out. For example, placing "gasoline stations" in the "homes" group would be incorrect and, therefore, a *misconception.*

In the foregoing example, the following procedures were employed:

1. The teacher had the pupils *enumerate* and *list* as many items as they could think of that were associated with the subject. They were responding to the question, "If we went on a walk through the community, what would we find there?" They had to be able to *differentiate* what they would see on a walk through the community as opposed to what they would see on a walk in the forest.

2. They were then asked to *group* those items that seemed to belong together. This necessitated *identifying common properties.* They had to respond to the question, "What belongs together?" They had to decide on criteria to apply in deciding what items belong together.

3. They then had to *label* each group. Here they were responding to the question, "What would you call these groups?"

RECOGNIZING CONCEPTS

Read the following selection and identify as many concepts as you can.

All winter and spring you trudged on without a vacation. You are ready for a different environment. You decide to leave the city and spend a week in the desert. You get in your car, drive to a large interchange, and take the freeway east.

As you travel east the freeway signs remind you that you are passing near or through several communities, but they seem to merge one into the other. You conclude that this is what the professor meant when he talked about urban sprawl in your ecology class last quarter. One of the signs directs you to a reservoir. Soon you see on your right a large airport and a sign that tells you it is an international airport.

You travel along and observe that the region is less densely populated than it was a few miles back. There are more open spaces and cultivated fields between the cities. You seem to be leaving the metropolitan area. You also notice that the terrain is changing, and you recognize foothills on either side of the highway. Soon you know you are at a higher elevation because you can feel the difference in air pressure affecting your ears.

Now you see high mountains on either side of the freeway. Just ahead you go through a mountain pass. A sign identifies an Indian Reservation to your left. You now find yourself descending the eastern slopes of the mountains. Although you see mountains in the distance, you recognize this as a desert landscape. You stop here, check your odometer and find that you have driven about 130 miles.

1. Were you able to form mental images as you read this passage? Does this tell you something about the importance of concepts?
2. What part of the country is being described in this passage? How do you know?

The first paragraph contains the following concepts: winter, spring, vacation, environment, city, week, desert, car, interchange, freeway, east. Now identify the concepts in the remaining three paragraphs.

Strategy Two

The procedure just explained is only one of several ways that concepts can be developed. Let us examine another procedure that represents a somewhat different approach. We will select an example from science: *the lever.* This concept is related to a larger concept, *simple machines.* These concepts are almost always a part of the elementary-school science program.

In everyday life the lever is one of the most commonly used devices. The handle of a claw hammer, baseball bat, golf club, tennis racket, and a wrench are used as levers. Our arms are levers. Tools such as nutcrackers, pliers, scissors, crossbars, can openers, and nail pullers are levers. A see-saw is a lever. Any device used for prying something is probably a lever.

A lever consists of a rigid bar that can be turned about a fixed point. The point is called the *fulcrum.* In the operation of the lever there is a *weight* to be moved and a *force* applied to do the moving. The *distance* between the weight to be moved and the fulcrum is called the *weight arm.* The distance between the fulcrum and the force to be applied is called the *force arm.* Thus, *weight, force, weight arm* and *force arm* are subconcepts of the main concept, *lever.*

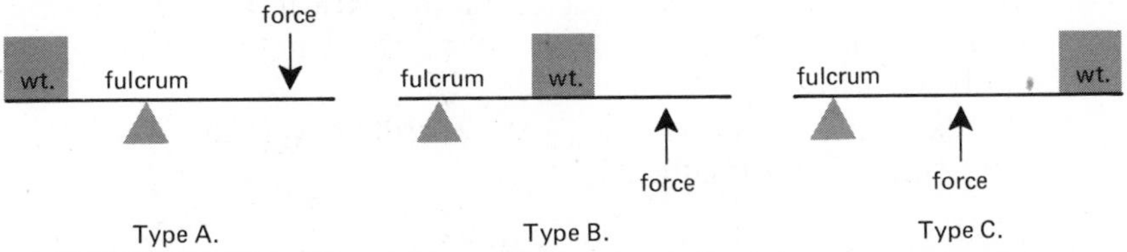

Figure 1. Essential parts of a lever in three different configurations.

In developing the concept *lever* and its related subconcepts, the teacher provides the learners with numerous direct experiences with levers. For example, with a 1″ × 4″ board three or four feet long to serve as a lever, and a brick to serve as a fulcrum, the learners can experience directly the principles involved in the operation of a lever. With a stack of books as the weight, it can be demonstrated that the amount of force needed varies with the length of the weight arm and the force arm. If the playground has a teeter-totter, the teacher can demonstrate how one child can lift two or more children simply by placing them at the right position on opposite sides of the fulcrum. A small child can lift the teacher, who is much heavier, by using a short weight arm and a longer force arm in a Type A lever. (See Figure 1, above.) As children are involved in these activities, they begin to identify certain ideas and principles relating to levers. These statements made by the pupils can be used as working hypotheses to be tested in other settings. For example, children may conclude that "the longer the lever, the less force is needed." The teacher can help clarify this generalization by having children explore further to learn that what they really mean is that in a Type A lever, "when the distance from the fulcrum to the force is longer than the distance from the fulcrum to the weight, the amount of force needed is reduced." This can be refined further by noting that "force needed is reduced when the force arm is longer than the weight arm in levers where the weight and force are on opposite sides of the fulcrum."

After some of the basic terminology, subconcepts, and elementary principles of levers are introduced through direct experiences, the teacher extends the experience base of pupils by providing other examples. For instance, the teacher might bring to class—or have pupils bring to class—ice tongs, nutcrackers, pliers, scissors, a shovel, a wrench, a claw hammer, a can opener, and similar lever devices. On each of these, the pupils could be asked to identify the fulcrum, the weight arm, and the force arm. They could be asked to explain how the lever principle operates in each case. Depending on the maturity of the learners, the teacher might even refine the lever concept by developing the precise mathematical relationship between the weight and force as related to the length of the weight arm and force arm.

As we examine the procedure just described, we find that it involves the following principles:

1. Learners are provided extended, direct, firsthand exploratory experiences with the concept.
2. Essential terms and subconcepts are defined and their meanings developed as the need for such definitions and meanings emerge in the learner's process of study.
3. Learners are encouraged to make statements of principles that seem to explain the main concept, based on their observations and firsthand experiences.
4. These statements are then tested, rejected, and/or confirmed by observing new examples of the concept in operation.
5. The statements are refined through extended firsthand experiences, thereby expanding the meaning of the main concept.

The procedure as outlined is widely used in the development of science, mathematics, and social studies concepts. It involves back and forth intellectual movement, from direct observation to hypothesis-making, to hypothesis-testing back to direct observation. A concept such as *lever* has no meaning unless it is used in some type of descriptive or functional statement. Such statements are really generalizations. Pupils should be encouraged to make such statements and then use them as hypotheses to be tested. We see, therefore, that in the development of substantive meanings, concepts and generalizations are very closely related.

WHAT WOULD YOU DO?

Mr. Hendricks was conducting a unit entitled "Healthful Living" with his fourth-grade class. In the process he wanted to develop the concept *nutrition.* He remembered two principles of concept development discussed in his methods class in college.

"Learners are provided extended, firsthand exploratory experiences with the concept."

and . . .

"Learners are encouraged to make statements of principles that seem to explain the main concept, based on their observations and firsthand experiences."

1. If you were Mr. Hendricks, what "firsthand exploratory experiences" would you provide these fourth graders?
2. What statements of principles can you think of that would "seem to explain the main concept?"
3. What subconcepts would be important to develop in connection with the main concept *nutrition*?

Strategy Three

The two examples of concept development cited are both based on inquiry procedures. The pupils were to a considerable extent involved in discovering the meaning of the concepts. Although the meaning of concepts is never *given* to the learner by the teacher, there are more direct ways of teaching concepts than the two examples just discussed. These more direct approaches also make use of inquiry, but rely less on the discovery of meanings by pupils. Let us examine one such procedure.

Let us say that a middle-grade class was studying a science unit on animal life, and the teacher wanted to introduce and teach the concept *crustaceans.* The teacher might explain that there is one group of animals called crustaceans, write the word (concept label) on the chalkboard, and explain that the class was now going to learn how to identify crustaceans. The teacher goes on to say that in order to be a crustacean, an animal must have these characteristics:

1. a hard outer shell
2. jointed legs
3. antennae that serve as feelers

The teacher then shows the class a plastic model of a lobster and tells them that it is a typical crustacean. The class is shown that this animal meets the requirements of having (1) a hard outer shell, (2) jointed legs, and (3) antennae that serve as feelers. The teacher points these out to the pupils and lets them touch and feel the model crustacean themselves. They tap the outer shell lightly with their pencils, confirming the fact that it is, indeed, hard. They move the plastic legs to see what "jointed" legs mean and how the legs work. They touch the huge pincers that are formed by one pair of legs. They are amazed at the length of the antennae. As this is taking place, the teacher has the pupils contrast the characteristics of this animal with animals they are familiar with in everyday living, such as dogs, cats, and horses. In this way nonexamples of crustaceans are presented. The pupils have now experienced both examples and nonexamples of the concept.

The teacher proceeds to use other visual aids. A plastic crab is displayed, and the class is asked if it is a crustacean. It is established that the crab has all the attributes, and is indeed a crustacean. They then examine a plastic turtle. Although the turtle has a hard outer shell, it does not meet the other requirements. The same applies to an armadillo. A shrimp, however, does meet the requirements. A sand dollar does not. At this point the teacher asks the pupils to identify one example and one nonexample of a crustacean for the next day's lesson, and be able to tell why it is or is not a crustacean. Following this series of lessons, the teacher will want to evaluate the class's understanding of the concept. They should be able to identify instances and noninstances of crustaceans from pictures, models, or live specimens.

In this last example of concept development, the following procedures were employed:

The teacher

1. identified the symbol for the concept.
2. provided the major attributes of the concept.
3. provided an example that illustrated the specific attributes of the concept.

4. provided a nonexample of the concept.
5. presented examples and nonexamples, had the learners identify major attributes, and explain why each was or was not an example of the concept.
6. encouraged pupils to find examples and nonexamples on their own, as a follow-up exercise.
7. evaluated whether or not pupils could identify examples and nonexamples.

THE NATURE OF GENERALIZATIONS

Elementary-school teachers often ask pupils questions such as these.

1. Can you tell us in one sentence what we have learned about a shopping center today? (grade 2)
2. Who can think of a sentence that explains how goods and people move in and out of a community? (grade 3)
3. Who can think of a statement that tells what characteristics are important in defining a region? (grade 4)
4. Will someone make a statement that tells how farming practices changed during this period? (grade 5)
5. What would you say is the relationship between an individual and the culture in which the person lives? (grade 6)

When questions of this type are asked, the teacher expects the pupil to respond by making a summarizing or concluding statement. One-word answers will not be adequate. In each case the question calls for a statement that explains a *relationship* of some type. Let us examine some possible responses to the foregoing questions.

1. A shopping center helps people get the goods and services they need.
2. Goods and people are moved in and out of a community by a connected transportation system.
3. In any region there must be one characteristic that is found in the whole area.
4. During this period the use of horses decreased, the use of power machinery increased, farm population decreased, and production increased.
5. An individual learns his or her way of life from his or her culture.

Notice that in each case the response consists of (1) a declarative statement that (2) expresses a relationship between two or more concepts. We refer to such statements as *generalizations.* Along with concepts, generalizations have become important in recent years in planning and implementing conceptual approaches to teaching and learning.

As is apparent from the foregoing response examples, generalizations vary in their degree of abstraction and complexity. To further illustrate this characteristic, notice the difference in abstractness and complexity of these two generalizations from science:

Objects made of iron are attracted by magnets.

The magnetism of a substance is due to the magnetic qualities of the electrons in its atoms and to the arrangement of its atoms.

Because concepts are combined to form generalizations, it is sometimes mistakenly presumed that generalizations are more difficult to understand than concepts. The illustration presented here clearly shows this *not* to be the case. There are simple and complex generalizations, just as there are simple and complex concepts. At early levels in school, children will be learning the meaning of relatively simple variations of concepts and will be making concluding statements that represent simple generalizations. As the youngsters grow in maturity the concepts and generalization with which they work will correspondingly increase in abstractness and complexity. A few examples of generalizations from social studies, science, mathematics, and language arts follow.

A Sampling of Representative Generalizations from Various School Subjects

Social Studies

The physical environment affects the way people live.

People fulfill most of their common needs and desires in the community in which they live.

The unequal distribution of natural resources makes trade between states, regions, and nations necessary.

Successive or continuing occupance by groups of people, as well as natural processes and forces, have resulted in a changed and changing landscape in our state.

Many tools and new equipment make work in the home easier.

Places on the earth have a distinctiveness about them that makes them different from any other place.

The global location of a nation or a region contributes to its importance in international affairs.

Science

Life exists almost everywhere on earth.

Living things are built of basic units called cells.

Air is a mixture of nitrogen, oxygen, water vapor, carbon dioxide, other gases, and dust.

Air is essential for life.

Animals and plants depend on each other in many different ways.

Some resources such as soil, vegetation, animal life, and fresh water are renewable.

Machines make work easier.

A fuse is the weakest link in the electrical circuit.

Mathematics

A set is a collection or group of objects that are known as the members, or elements, of the set.

A given symbol must have a name, a design, an order, and a value.

The area of a rectangular plane surface can be found by multiplying the length by the width.

When the same quantity is added or subtracted to both quantities of an equation, the equality of the quantities remains the same.

In order to add or subtract fractions, each must be reduced to a common denominator.

Language Arts

Language consists of a sound pattern, words, structure, and a system of word arrangement.

Many words are formed by combining other words.

Capital letters are used at the beginning of sentences, for all proper nouns, and for each line of poetry.

In forming the plural of most nouns, add *s* or *es*.

In contracted words, the apostrophe is placed where letters are omitted.

DEVELOPING GENERALIZATIONS

As has already been indicated, a generalization is a relationship between two or more concepts. A declarative statement is the most common form of expressing a generalization, although other forms may be used, too, as for example, a formula, $a + b = b + a$. Actually,

SENSING RELATIONSHIPS

For each of the following sets of concepts, form a generalization that expresses a relationship among them.

Set I river, heat, light, generator, electricity
Set II fiction, characters, life styles, modern times
Set III human groups, families, basic needs, survival
Set IV web of life, living things, animals, plants
Set V holidays, seasonal, culture, social roles
Set VI tools, workers, unemployment, production

it is not the *statement* but the *relationship* that constitutes the generalization. This is an important distinction in teaching because a learner may be able to verbalize a generalization without understanding the relationship it expresses. Nor is the ability to express a generalization necessarily an indication that the individual will behave in accordance with the content of the generalization. Every teacher knows that pupils are often able to cite rules of grammar without being able to speak or write correctly. Examples of generalizations are listed on pages 330–331.

Because the statement of a generalization asserts an existing relationship between and among concepts, in order to teach generalizations one must (1) understand the concepts involved and (2) discover anew or verify the asserted relationships between and among them. This can only be accomplished by having learners experience the relationships in several instances. No one has ever been able to develop an understanding of a generalization on the basis of a single case. This would be logically impossible.

There are four types of generalizations commonly taught in the elementary school. They can be illustrated by the following examples:

1. A primary-grade class has been studying the movement of goods and people in their community. The teacher asks them to think of a concluding sentence that tells something about the need for different kinds of transportation in the community. After some cuing by the teacher, the group concludes that "The community needs many different kinds of transportation to move goods and people."

This is an example of a *descriptive* generalization. It simply describes in summary form a relationship that has evolved as a part of the instructional process. Other examples of descriptive generalizations are these:

Everyone is a consumer, but only some persons are producers.
Our environment consists of both living and nonliving things.
There is a constant ratio between the radius of a circle and its circumference.
People spend their lives in some type of society.

2. A class has been conducting a series of experiments on plant life. They have controlled variables such as heat, light, moisture, and soil. They have worked with several plants. Some plants have lived; others have died. Their concluding generalization is that "A plant needs a proper amount of heat, sunlight, air, water, and good soil in order to grow."

This is an example of a *cause and effect* generalization. If something happens in one part of the relationship, it will have an effect on something else. Other examples of cause and effect generalizations are these:

Improved tools can make possible increased production.
When people do not buy goods, the workers who produce them may become unemployed.
Metals expand when they are heated.

3. A news article spurred the class discussion of equality of opportunity. It came just at the time when the class was studying American ideals and the great documents of freedom. References were made to specific provisions of the Bill of Rights and to other Amendments to the Constitution. The class concluded that "Practices that discriminate because of race and religious beliefs go against what we believe is right in this country."

This is an example of a *value principle* expressed as a generalization. Most ethical-guidelines statements are of this type. Other examples are these:

One should place the general welfare over one's own when a choice between them is necessary.
Business and professional affairs must be conducted in accordance with ethical principles.
Freedom, as expressed in the Bill of Rights, is a cherished value in the United States.
Everyone is required by conscience to treat fellow human beings with compassion and humaneness.

4. A sixth-grade class has been engaged in a study of ways of living in various cultures around the world. In each case they see how people have built

their cultures, and at the same time they see how profoundly these people are affected by their cultures. This leads them, with careful teacher guidance, to the generalization that "Human beings build their culture, but culture builds human beings."

This is an example of a *law* or *principle* based on a vast amount of research and abstract knowledge. Curriculum directors and textbook authors have used generalizations of this level of abstraction as their organizing frameworks for social studies, science, and mathematics curriculum documents and textbooks. Other examples are these:

All languages have a grammatical structure, but few grammatical relations are common to all languages.

Matter is not destroyed; it changes in form.

The art, music, architecture, food, clothing, sports, and customs of a people help to produce a national identity.

PHOTO FOLIO

We see here a group of pupils and their teacher involved in an activity of considerable interest to them. They are preparing Mexican food in connection with a social studies unit on that country. Besides being interesting and enjoyable, activities of this type provide learners with backgrounds of experience out of which they fashion their understanding of concepts. Experience is essential to the development of cognitive abilities. It is, of course, not necessary for us to learn everything by doing. Nonetheless, the acquisition of new knowledge, or the elaboration of concepts and generalizations already familiar to us, must somehow relate to what we already know.

1. Provide examples from your own life to illustrate the importance of first-hand experiences in understanding something.
2. Should the extensiveness—or paucity—of life experiences by children affect the school's curriculum? Why or why not? Provide specific examples of your points.

Language is a system of arbitrary vocal symbols that permits human communication.

In any society, consumers outnumber producers of goods and services.

These examples of the four types of generalizations emerged in settings that should be familiar to most adults, because they are so commonly used in schools. In each case the pupils had extensive experience with the basic concepts involved, and were already mindful of many of the relationships that prevailed. All that was needed was the formal statement concluding or summarizing the relationship. In most cases, relationships are not suddenly perceived in a brilliant flash of insight. Quite the contrary. A great deal of preliminary goundwork was prepared by the teacher to make it possible for the pupils to "see" the relationship. To allow pupils to just muddle around on their own, hoping they will stumble on a complex relationship, is not the way generalizations are developed. A better procedure would be to have the teacher do the following:

1. Make sure the pupils understand the major concepts involved in the relationship.
2. Encourage pupils to make statements or propositions linking two or more concepts.
3. Encourage pupils to combine statements into ever larger, more encompassing propositions that relate the concepts to each other.
4. Test the validity of the assertions by relating them to experiences and observations.
5. Test the validity of the assertions by applying them to new situations.

The procedures described thus far follow what amounts to an *inductive sequence* of instruction. The generalizations emerged as a natural extension of the inquiry into concepts and their relationships. It is of course possible to develop an understanding of generalizations by using them as working hypotheses that can be verified, confirmed, or rejected. When the validity of generalizations is developed through a *deductive process,* two approaches may be used, demonstration or verification.

In teaching a generalization through demonstration, the object is to show the learner the validity of the assertion. Neither the learner nor the teacher sets out to test the truthfulness of the statement. For example, take the generalization, "The earth along with its moon revolves around the sun every 365 days, while the earth rotates on its axis every 24 hours." The motions of these heavenly bodies are well documented and must be accepted on the basis of sound scientific evidence. A generalization such as this one can, therefore, be demonstrated without questioning its validity. A piece of equipment, such as a planetarium, is helpful in demonstrating the relationships expressed in this generalization. Similarly, the generalization, "The volume of a rectangular figure can be found by multiplying its length by its width by its height," can be demonstrated through the manipulation of one-inch size cubes. These can be arranged in layers and counted, thus showing the relationship embodied in the generalization. This could, and probably should, be followed with the learners demonstrating the generalization themselves. In using demonstration procedures to teach generalizations, it is important to observe the following:

1. The generalization should be stated and the basic concepts understood.
2. The nature of the relationship expressed by the statement should be made explicit.
3. The application of the generalization in operation should be presented. If possible several different applications (cases or instances) should be presented.
4. The learners should replicate the demonstration, explaining the relationship involved.
5. The learners should provide additional examples or instances of generalizations.

A somewhat different procedure is involved if the generalization is regarded as an hypothesis to be verified or rejected. It should be emphasized that both options—verification and/or rejection—can and should be used. For example, superstitious beliefs are forms of generalizations that can be tested and will probably be rejected.

The verification of generalizations for school purposes relies on scientific procedures. This means that the assertion is stated and a search is begun to find examples that show the statement to be true or false. Examples must be of so high a calibre that independent, objective observers would agree that what is observed is, indeed, an instance or case of the relationship. The evidence supporting many generalizations has to come from secondary sources. It is not possible for learners to personally verify many generalizations; historical and some scientific principles being obvious examples.

INDUCTIVE AND DEDUCTIVE SEQUENCING

The serious study of teaching and learning has always concerned itself with the question of whether it is more productive to provide instruction that goes from the specific to the general or from the general to the specific. Whatever mode of teaching is selected, the teacher will be making important decisions concerning the sequence to be followed. Let us examine each of these briefly.

Inductive Sequencing

This term refers to a process of going from specific examples to a rule, a generalization, or a broad principle. For example, suppose in a social studies lesson the teacher wanted to develop the idea that "money (a medium of exchange) serves as a convenient way of exchanging goods and services." The idea as expressed here is a generalization. In inductive teaching it would come near the *end* of the teaching or presentation sequence. In other words, the teacher would engage the pupils in a series of activities and experiences that would provide them with a broad exposure to the exchange of goods and services. Perhaps this would begin with examples of bartering. The pupils would see the difficulty in establishing a standard of value that would be acceptable to everyone. That is, if one person has goat skins and another has a horse, and they want to exchange these goods, who decides how many goat skins are equal to the value of a horse? One way to do this would be to convert both to a third item, whose value is established and acceptable to both parties. Suppose such an item were bushels of wheat. Then, if a goat skin is worth one bushel of wheat and a horse one hundred bushels, it would require one hundred goat skins to effect an exchange for the horse. But bushels of wheat as a medium of exchange have obvious disadvantages. These could be discussed by the class and other alternatives suggested. Without going into all the details of a lesson of this type, it is clear that the discussion of specific examples will lead to the use of money, and that pupils can thus be brought to the idea that "money serves as a convenient way of exchanging goods and services."

Examples from other areas of the curriculum could be cited to show the inductive or example-rule sequence. In mathematics a child can be shown several groups of similar items and be led to the principle that "a set can be thought of as a group of things or ideas that are precisely defined." In science, the teacher can provide several examples of the interdependent relationships between plants and animals in the cycle of life, and have pupils conclude from this exploration that "animals and plants depend on each other in many different ways." In spelling, the teacher can show several instances of adding the *ing* suffix to words ending with the letter *e*, such as bite–biting, strike–striking, write–writing. Children then learn the rule: the use of this suffix with words ending with *e,* when preceded by a single consonant, necessitates dropping the *e* before adding the *ing*.

It is clear that inductive sequences favor discovery learning by the pupils. Often teachers are advised to provide a sufficient number of examples so that learners can discover the relationship for themselves. Partly for this reason, it is sometimes mistakenly assumed that discovery learning and inquiry learning must involve inductive sequencing of teaching. This is not necessarily the case. As a matter of fact, a conclusion based on an inductive search might quite properly be considered a *tentative* hypothesis, subject to further testing by a deductive process, as we shall see.

Deductive Sequencing

This process reverses the procedure described under inductive sequencing. In this case, the teaching sequence moves from a rule, generalization, or principle to specific examples. Teaching is planned in a way that introduces learners directly to the rule, generalization, or principle. They are then expected to search for examples or instances of it. It can provide inquiry or discovery aspects if the given rule, generalization, or principle is accepted as a *working* hypothesis. Pupils can then gather data to prove or disprove it.

Deductive sequencing is a common form of teaching. It has been subjected to a fair amount of criticism in recent years because it is associated with traditional telling and recitation teaching procedures. An obvious limitation of deductive sequencing is that the learner may commit the rule or generalization to memory and be able to reproduce it for examination purposes, yet have no familiarity with the basic concepts and supporting details that give depth of meaning to such statements. For example, a child may be able to recite "money is a convenient means of exchanging goods and services," but may not be able to support such a statement with examples and nonexamples.

Commentary

Great claims have been made for the values of inductive sequencing; and as already noted, much criticism has been leveled against deductive sequencing. Because the development of thinking has emerged as a major goal of instruction, it is believed that inductive sequencing is more consistent with the use of intellectual processes associated with reflective thought. Such claims, however, most often represent beliefs or opinions rather than research-based findings. After an extensive review of the literature on this subject, Branch concluded that "Research on the effect of inductive or deductive sequencing of instruction while voluminous, has failed to produce consistent results favoring either sequencing."[3] The research does suggest, however, that deductively sequenced instruction facilitates immediate retention and inductively sequenced instruction enhances greater transfer of learning and delayed retention. The tentative nature of these findings is indicated by the caution exercised by researchers in reporting them. The use of qualifiers such as "there may be a tendency," "it seems to be that," and "there appears to be relatively" characterizes much of the literature dealing with this subject.

[3] Robert C. Branch. *The Interaction of Cognitive Style with the Instructional Variables of Sequencing and Manipulation to Effect Achievement of Elementary Mathematics.* Unpublished doctoral dissertation, University of Washington, Seattle, 1973, p. 1.

Because of the equivocal findings relating to these processes, the teacher is well advised to develop teaching strategies that involve both deductive and inductive sequencing. Although traditional teaching may have relied too heavily on deductive procedures, perhaps present-day strategies give more credence to inductive sequencing than can be justified on the basis of research evidence. The two sequences involve different thought processes, and for this reason alone the child should have experience with both. Inductive procedures tend to be more time consuming than deductive strategies. Consequently, where efficiency of instruction is an important consideration, perhaps deductive strategies should be used.

WHICH IS WHICH?

The following sketches suggest that the teacher may be using either an inductive or a deductive sequence in teaching. Study each one and tell whether you think inductive or deductive sequencing is being employed.

1. The teacher explains the rules of a game about to be played by the pupils in a P.E. class.
2. In a reading lesson, pupils have learned about key sentences in paragraph reading. Now the teacher has them read new material to identify key sentences.
3. The class has been studying "Batteries and Bulbs" in a science lesson. The pupils have had extended firsthand experiences with bulbs, batteries, wires, and switches. Near the end of the lesson, the teacher asks, "What conditions have to be present for us to have a complete electrical circuit?"
4. In the social studies unit on the supermarket, the teacher says to the class, "Suppose we took a walk through a supermarket, what would we see? You tell me and I will write what you say on the board."
5. The teacher says, "Be sure you study carefully the part called 'Hints for Better Spelling,' on page 23. Those rules will be helpful to you in spelling words correctly."
6. In a lesson on safety, the teachers says, "This large study print shows people doing fifteen things that are unsafe. How many can you find?"
7. Each pupil has written a short news story and the teacher says, "I will write two standards for your papers on the chalkboard. Before handing in your news story, please check to see that it meets these two standards.
8. "We have talked about several examples," says the teacher. "Now who can state a rule that summarizes what we have said?"

DEVELOPING RELATED COMPETENCIES

Selecting concepts

1. Select five concepts that would be appropriately incorporated in the study of each of these topics:

Seasonal Changes	Moving with Music
Caring for Our Bodies	Living Things
Preventing Pollution	Communicable Diseases
Comparing Quantities	Indian Arts and Crafts
Big Sky Country	Using Common Fractions

Stating Generalizations

2. Using the concepts you have identified above, form a generalization that expresses a valid relationship central to the topic being studied.

Developing Hierarchies of Concepts

3. The concepts in the groups listed below are related to each other but are scrambled in terms of their degree of abstractness. Rearrange each group, placing the most abstract at the top and the least abstract at the bottom of each group.

mountain	urban area	fish
peak	city	living things
landform	village	animal
landscape	metropolitan region	trout

city council	symphony orchestra
government	orchestra
kingdom	soloist
state legislature	ensemble

Concepts Are Where You Find Them

4. Miss Wakefield was a firm believer in providing firsthand experiences for her pupils in developing concepts. "Opportunities to enrich the meanings of concepts for children are all around us," she told a colleague one day in the teachers' lounge. What concepts

might have their meanings enlarged for pupils in situations such as these?

a. tasting various foods
b. listening to a recording of "city sounds"
c. listening to a recording of "night noises"
d. engaging in role-playing
e. planting a tree
f. assembling a model of a human figure
g. conducting a mock trial
h. feeling objects and materials such as wool, ice, cotton, sandpaper, glass
i. visiting a museum
j. visiting a factory
k. watching carpenters at work
l. spending a week at school camp
m. role-playing safety rules
n. digging a hole in the ground for no reason in particular

FOR FURTHER PROFESSIONAL STUDY

Books

Blank, Marion, Susan A. Rose, and Laura J. Berlin. *The Language of Learning: The Preschool Years*. New York: Grune and Stratton, Inc., 1979.

Bloom, Benjamin S. *Human Characteristics and School Learning.* New York: McGraw-Hill Book Company, Inc., 1976.

Castañeda, Alfredo and Manuel Ramírez III. *Cultural Democracy, Bicognitive Development, and Education.* New York: Academic Press, Inc., 1974.

Kaltsounis, Theodore. "Developing Concepts and Generalizations Through Inquiry." Chapter 4 of *Teaching Social Studies in the Elementary School.* Englewood Cliffs, New Jersey: Prentice-Hall, Inc., 1979.

Martorella, Peter H. *Concept Learning: Design for Instruction.* Scranton, Pennsylvania: Intext Educational Publishers, 1972.

Periodicals

Barbe, Walter B. and Michael N. Milone, Jr. "Modality." *Instructor* (January 1980), 44–47.

Klein, Marvin L. "How Well Do Children Reason? Some Suggestions for Language Arts Programs." *The Elementary School Journal* (January 1979), 147–155.

Martorella, Peter H. "Research in Social Studies Education: Implications for Teaching in the Cognitive Domain." *Social Education* (November–December 1979), 599–601.

Wasserman, Selma and Meguido Zola. "Promoting Thinking in Your Classroom." *Childhood Education* (October 1977), 24E ff.

11

Strategies for Affective Learning

THE QUALIFIED AND COMPETENT TEACHER . . .

1. Has a sensitivity to the affective dimension of all learning.
2. Is able to assist pupils in clarifying values, and involves pupils in choice making and decision making.
3. Establishes a classroom environment that reflects the general values embraced by this society.

Performance Criteria

As a result of the serious study of this chapter, the student should be able to . . .

1. Provide specific examples of general values and be able to explain how these differ from personal values.
2. Describe characteristics of a classroom that enhance affective learnings.
3. Describe basic principles of affective learning and show by example how each would be applied to a grade of his or her choice.
4. Demonstrate the ability to conduct a valuing strategy by doing so with a group of children or with a peer group.

"Michael is studying, but his heart is not in it." This statement illustrates the interdependent relationship between the cognitive and the affective—the affairs of the head and those of the heart. The fact of the matter is that as long as "Michael's heart is not in it" his studying and learning will not be as productive as they might otherwise be. The school experience is a powerful force in shaping the affective development of children. They learn to like school or dislike it. They develop and extend their value system in school. They grow to feel good about certain encounters and certain people, or they are repulsed by them. Most of these feelings they will carry around with them as part of their affective baggage, so to speak, for the rest of their lives.

There has been a tendency in recent years to speak of learning as being either cognitive or affective. We see such terms as "noncognitive" or "neocognitive" used in educational literature. And the concept "domain" is applied to the cognitive and affective, as if they were completely independent of each other. In the writing of objectives for curricula and courses of study, authors will often group them into affective and cognitive categories, thereby stressing the separateness rather than the interdependence of cognitive and affective learning.

Cognitive learning, as we have seen in Chapter 10, is that which deals with knowledge and knowing, and focuses on the substantive content of the curriculum. Affective learning deals with attitudes, values, and feelings, and focuses on the aesthetics, arts, and humanities aspects of the curriculum. For purposes of study and analysis, this dichotomy between cognitive and affective is a convenient one. In reality, however, the two go hand in hand, and must be considered together. It is difficult to imagine, for instance, how a pupil could learn mathematics without developing some feelings about that subject. The same could be said about any subject or skill studied. In the discussion that follows, therefore, the reader should keep in mind that the emphasis is on learning that is characteristically more affectively toned—*not* that it is lacking in cognitive elements.

The curriculum reform movement of the recent past placed heavy emphasis on the cognitive and on content-related skills. Much of this was desirable, for a re-examination of content and skills was long overdue. One of the side effects of this emphasis, however, was a diminishing of the importance and the attention given to the aesthetic components of the curriculum. This is unfortunate, especially at the elementary-school level, because it is at this time in the child's life when it is particularly appropriate to develop the sensitivities and to build the technical skills that the arts and humanities require.

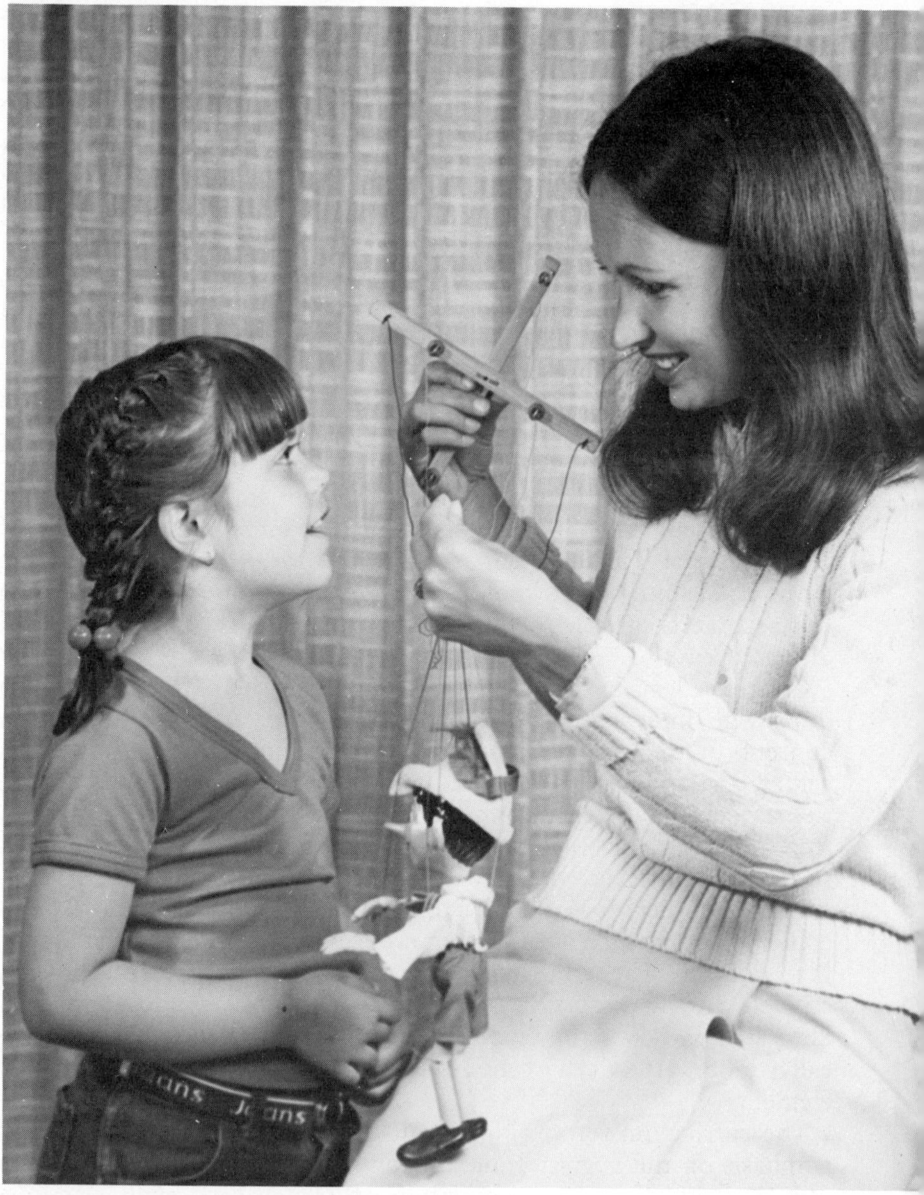

It is easy to interest a primary-grade child in a poem, a play, a dance, or a piece of art. Moreover, such an interest, if well-established early in life, stays with the child, becoming a permanent part of his or her intellectual and cultural equipment. If young children are deprived

PHOTO FOLIO

Children's book and stories, creative dramatics, puppetry, music, and other creative art activities provide good vehicles for building an environment in which affective learnings can flourish. The arts program in a school is sometimes criticized because it is thought to encourage permissiveness and a lack of discipline. Yet successful artists and performers are among the most disciplined persons in society. They must engage in endless hours of practice if they are musicians or dancers, and must exercise great patience, care, and attention to minute detail if they are painters, sculptors, or weavers.

1. What reasons can you give for the erosion of the arts in the school curriculum in recent years?
2. Should education in the arts in the elementary school consist only of pleasurable, "do your own thing" activities, or should they involve disciplined approaches similar to those of artists? Provide a rationale for your response.
3. What class activities might have preceded and followed the exchange between the child and teacher in the accompanying photograph?
4. What are some of the educational values that can be derived through the use of children's literature? Dramatics? Puppets and marionettes?

of this learning, one has little reason to be optimistic about the level of aesthetic sensitivities of adult society.

The need to redress the balance of emphasis in favor of affective learning has long been recognized by many educators and lay persons. Now being questioned are the effects of an emphasis on basic skills at the expense of the arts and affective education. The practice is especially questionable when this learning is projected into the lower grades of the elementary school where aesthetic sensitivities are most easily nurtured. This problem cannot be resolved without serious attention to priorities in education, questioning what education is all about, and what it should do for young children.

It is easy to understand why some components of the curriculum are regarded as more important than others. To strive, to work hard for a better standard of living, for a good income, and for material advantages is an important part of the American tradition, one that runs deep in the character of Americans. In a great many ways, this quality has reflected itself in what Americans value. They usually admire one who has overcome great obstacles to achieve material and economic success. This quality also expresses itself in what is valued in the school curriculum. Typically, those subjects and skills that are related to, or instrumental in, achieving economic advantage are the ones most highly prized. Thus, it is clear why reading, writing, mathematics, and science are assigned high priority in the curriculum. These are "useful" subjects and skills. They help the learner to become a productive person. The arts, literature, drama, and aesthetics are not "useful" in this framework of values. It is not surprising, therefore, that these components of the curriculum are given a low priority. Indeed, in many schools very little is done with them at all.

The industrial technology in the second half of the twentieth century is changing economic and social conditions to the extent that this traditional set of priorities must be challenged. People do not have to spend most of their waking hours earning a living. It appears that such concepts as the four-day week and a guaranteed annual wage will become realities in the near future. Retirement ages are being reduced and are likely to be reduced even more in the next decade. Increasingly, machines are doing the work. Consequently, people now have and will continue to have more and more time for themselves. But what are they to do with this leisure time? Serious questions are being asked as to whether people can actually cope with an environment of affluence over a long period of time. This can be a more serious problem than is often thought. Dr. Lefebre, for example, writes of it as follows:

> Time forces us back on ourselves. The more time we have, the more dangerous time becomes and the more means we must invent to kill it. Unfortunately those engaged in the battle with time must fight it constantly, lest they be

brought face to face with themselves after all. There are still those unavoidable moments when the hangover has lifted but a bottle is not handy; when sexual passion has spent itself and one wonders whether the partner is not a stranger; when one has reluctantly returned from a grass or acid trip; when our mechanical partners, radio and TV, have been turned off but the Nembutal has not taken effect yet—moments of utter and complete loneliness.

These moments are beyond soothing by any human agency, be it lover, wife, husband, parents or children. They cannot be bridged for long by pets, charitable activities, causes, nature, drugs, or art. These moments force us to realize that we are individuals first of all and give us a taste of what it must be like to die.[1]

Many believe that loneliness is the overwhelming problem of modern life.

WHAT'S WRONG HERE?

American art and culture have no shortage of critics. Elitists are willing to acknowledge the unquestioned leadership of this nation in such fields as science, industry, technology, and medicine. But in the arts the attitude is widespread that we occupy a position of something considerably less than third rate. Yet, *Newsweek* magazine had this to say on the subject in its December 24, 1973, issue:

> The arts in America have produced more world records than any other society can boast—more creators, more packagers, more distributors, more consumers than anywhere else; more money and more need for money than anywhere else; more lust for art, more fear of art, more confusion about art than anywhere else; more brilliant insight into what art is all about—and more balderdash on the same subject than anywhere else.

1. With such an obviously heavy investment in art, not only in money but in creative talent as well, why do American arts enjoy such low estate?
2. What implications do you see in this for the elementary school's work in the field of arts?

---

[1] Ludwig B. Lefebre, "Human and Extrahuman Partnership," *Psychology Today* 2:48 (November 1968).

THE AFFECTIVE ENVIRONMENT

The areas of the curriculum that have the heaviest affective loadings are art, music, literature, and drama. There is little to be gained, however, in providing a formal curriculum in these subjects unless the total classroom and school reflect a sensitive concern for affective learning. What is required, first of all, is an environment in which people are more highly valued than things and procedures. Any practice that contributes to the erosion of the self-image and self-esteem of individuals must be open to question. This is of vital importance in promoting affective learning because self-esteem is so easily threatened whenever creative self-expression is involved. A thoughtless remark by a teacher may do permanent damage to a child's willingness to participate in any form of creative art—be it music, drama, literature, painting and art, or creative writing.

Pupil growth in the affective area requires, above all, a risk-free environment.

In addition to the concern for affect in human relations, the physical environment of the classroom must be conducive to affective growth. Regrettably, American schools do not always provide the pupil with aesthetically pleasing surroundings. Sometimes the child in school is surrounded by ugliness. Old rundown buildings, dark hallways, exposed heating pipes and electrical conduits, and drab classroom interiors—broken only by old portraits of Washington and Lincoln—still characterize many American elementary schools. There are of course numerous exceptions to this traditional institutional stereotype. Many of the newer schools, particularly in the suburban areas, do reflect a sensitivity to aesthetics. All schools need to follow the lead of those areas that have been pace-setters in planning educational facilities that are not only functional but aesthetically pleasing as well.

PHOTO FOLIO

What experiences do adults remember of their elementary school years? The reading groups? The math lessons? Science experiments? Plays? Pageants? Holiday programs? Or would it be those fictional characters, Ismail, Omak, Juanita, and Juan, who graced the pages of the social studies texts? One can speculate only that what is remembered are experiences that are heavily weighted with affect. Experiences that were particularly enjoyed or those that were especially disliked have a better chance of remaining on long-term deposit in one's memory bank than those that were affectively neutral.

1. What activities and experiences of your own elementary school days stand out in your memory? Were they affectively toned?
2. What is there about the photograph that suggests a positive affective setting?

There is a great deal that individual teachers can do, and *do* do, to enhance the aesthetic quality of their classrooms. Bulletin boards and display areas can be used to exhibit materials conveying affective messages. Often paintings and reproductions are available to the teacher on a rental basis, perhaps through the school district's instructional services center. Books, visual materials, periodicals, and recordings can be made available for pupil use within the classroom, where appropriate. These suggestions are presented simply to indicate that a teacher who is concerned about the affective quality of the physical environment can often do much to improve it, at little cost or effort. Imagination and a willingness to be concerned pay big dividends here.

THE ARTS CURRICULUM

In thinking about the arts curriculum, the teacher may find concepts developed in the Krathwohl taxonomy to be useful.[2] This document suggests an hierarchal system of categories suitable for classifying educational objectives that deal specifically with the affective domain. The major categories of the taxonomy are (1) Receiving, (2) Responding, (3) Valuing, (4) Organization, and (5) Characterization by a value or value complex. There are subcategories within each of the five groups.

In the elementary school much of the learning of art, music, drama, literature, and other aesthetic areas consists of experiences that are in the receiving and responding categories of the taxonomy. To illustrate how this occurs let us follow a sequence of affective learning, using the enjoyment of poetry as an example. Let us assume that the goal we are seeking to achieve is to get children to read poetry—on their own, simply because they enjoy doing so. We might roughly divide this process into two parts. The first, listening to poetry read by the teacher; the second, poetry that the children read independently. These two stages would extend over a period of several years.

The affective learning sequence might begin in the primary grades, perhaps as early as kindergarten, if teachers familiarize children with poetry by reading selections to them. Such experiences make children *aware* that there is such a thing as poetry. Typically, young children find listening to poems and rhymes pleasurable and look

[2] David R. Krathwohl, Benjamin S. Bloom, and Bertram B. Masia, *Taxonomy of Educational Objectives: Handbook II, Affective Domain* (New York: David McKay Co., Inc., 1964).

forward to having selections read to them. Such behavior indicates, obviously, a *willingness* to listen. The next step in the sequence would be represented by a situation in which a child, if given a choice of a few activities, would freely select listening to poetry in preference to doing something else. The teacher could at this point sharpen perception by having children do selected listening, i.e., identifying rhyming words, action words, words that describe, color words, and so on.

As children learn to do independent reading, the teacher may assign poems to them to read. Pupils will respond to such an assignment with varying degrees of enthusiasm. Undoubtedly many children, if given a choice, would want to do something else, but at the same time, they may not be openly hostile to the idea of reading poetry. If doing the reading, even somewhat reluctantly, produces a satisfying effect for the children, they might on subsequent occasions even express a preference for poetry reading over some other activity. The time may come when the teacher notices that a child has checked out a book of poems from the school library. The librarian has reported to the teacher that the child commented that reading poetry, and even writing it, is fun.

In the two foregoing paragraphs we have sketched briefly the early phases of the affective sequence from awareness building to public affirmation of a value, to freely selected participation in an affective related learning activity. All of these early experiences that deal mainly with *receiving* and *responding* activities take place, of course, under the direction and guiding hand of a sensitive teacher.

Poetry was used in this example, but one could substitute almost any one of the arts and, in like manner, follow its development through the various stages. It would be a mistake, of course, to apply this sequence (in such a structured and rigid fashion) to all affective learnings. One does not learn things in quite so orderly a way. But this format does provide the teacher with clues as to how instructional sequences should be developed in providing learning experiences in the affective area. It should also remind the teacher that affective learning is not likely to be achieved in a few easy lessons, or over a short period of time.

The sequence represented by the foregoing example emphasizes the need for continuity in affective learning. It is easy to bypass lead-up or lead-in experiences that are critical to the long-term response involvement of children. For example, we may be asking pupils to show satisfaction in response when they are hardly at the awareness level in their own development. It takes a great deal of contact, extended over a long period of time, to get to the point where one is able or even willing to respond musically, artistically, or dramatically—to say nothing of gaining satisfaction from such responses. It often takes many years of supervised and required practice on the piano before the learner is willing to turn to the instrument on his or her own, just for the fun of it.

As pupils move to higher levels of sophistication in their affective growth there is a shuttling back and forth between developing sensitivity and responding through art media. As the pupil responds, the teacher helps heighten awareness; thus subsequent responses become more refined. For example, in creative drawing the child may represent houses with windows but no doors, and the teacher builds awareness of the importance of doors. As the child grows to maturity, perception becomes more keen—visually, aurally, tactilly. Accordingly an increased awareness of the world is developed and it is possible, then, to make ever increasingly finer discriminations in responses. The teacher must be sensitive to this development and provide the child with appropriate encouragement and guidance as needed.

DO THINGS LIKE THIS STILL HAPPEN IN SCHOOLS?

Cora was a sensitive child, seven years of age and in the second grade. Her year and a half in school had gone well for her. She was learning how to read and write, and she participated in class projects as actively as most children. She liked being in school. In "singing" she belted out her songs with a good, loud voice. One day during the singing lesson her teacher said, "Cora, please don't sing so loudly. We can hardly hear the other boys and girls." Cora was embarrassed and hurt by the teacher's insensitive remark. It was at that point that Cora stopped singing. She is now a woman more than sixty years of age, and to this day does not sing.

1. Would every child have reacted to the teacher's remark in this same way?
2. Can you provide examples from your own experiences of children being "put down" by a teacher? Does such teacher behavior contribute anything at all to enhance children's learning?

VALUES AND VALUING

Values are elements in the human personality that determine what an individual perceives as important and unimportant, what he or she thinks is worth striving for, what is believed to be right and wrong. One's values may be inferred from what the individual does and how he or she behaves—what motivates a person, what his or her attitudes are, what interests and aspirations are apparent, what concerns are expressed, and what one believes. Values may be defined as internalized guides to human behavior.

From early Colonial times to the present, it has been understood that elementary schools have a shared responsibility for the moral development of pupils. This being the case, it can be said that values education must be an essential component of the school program because (1) one's value orientation is basic to choice making and decision making; (2) harmonious social life requires commitment to a common core set of values shared by individuals in society; and (3) the behavior of individuals is ultimately determined not only by what they *know* but perhaps more importantly by what they *believe.*

Whenever society experiences a breakdown in social control—such as a riot, a demonstration that got out of hand, an unauthorized work stoppage, a student walkout, or a violent crime, we are reminded once again how much we rely on individual citizens to conduct themselves in responsible ways. We go about the business of ordinary living in our neighborhoods, communities, at our places of employment, at recreational centers, and in other social settings with the full expectation that the persons with whom we associate will conduct themselves in predictable and, for the most part, trustworthy and honorable ways. Although we take reasonable precautions, we really do not expect to be mugged, robbed, raped, cheated, or lied to, or to have our homes burglarized or our reputations slandered. We assume that most people will do what we perceive to be "right."

It is often said that one cannot legislate morality, and that a law that is perceived to be unjust cannot be enforced. These observations, based on centuries of experience, tell us that in the matter of personal and group behavior, there must be a willingness to comply with whatever standards are established. External force and police power may be effective in keeping a few unwilling offenders in line, or even large numbers of people for short periods of time, but in the long run, external measures to force compliance are not effective in enforcing behavior that is not acceptable to the group. Consequently, societies get willing compliance by socializing their members into behavior patterns that cause most people to believe that they *should* behave the way the group expects them to behave. This means that individuals must internalize the values that are important to that society, and as a result, they will conduct their lives in accordance with those values.

All indications are that one's value orientations take shape fairly early in life. Children learn the values that guide their lives from the adults who are close to them in their childhood. Their parents and family, of course, are prime sources of personal values, as are other significant adult figures in their lives. This might include neighbors, religious leaders, authority figures in the community, and certainly teachers in the elementary grades.

The child does not learn personal values entirely from human beings with whom he or she is closely associated. The media encountered are also important mechanisms in values education. Children may be involved in several hours of television viewing each week, and what they see and hear shapes their values. Magazines, newspapers, pictures, and advertisements help tell what is important and what is not; what is good and what is bad. Very significantly, in this cluster of value transmitters are also instructional materials the children use in school, particularly the textbooks studied. The content and illustrations of textbooks have a profound effect on children's values, if we are to believe the research that has been done on this subject.

Textbook content and illustrations can have an impact on the values of readers in numerous direct, as well as subtle, ways. Does it make any difference if males are always shown in positions of greater prestige than females? In the case of social studies texts, does it make any difference that some books deal with controversial issues as if there really *is* consensus on these issues? Does it make any difference if important aspects of our nation's history are not included in the text, such as sensitive matters dealing with racism? Does it make any difference if a child is never required to consider various conflicting aspects of a problem, never required to do creative thinking on problems, or is always asked to search for the "right" answer? Many authorities think all of these issues, and many more like them, *do* make a very great difference in the value orientation of the child. Moreover, the research tends to support this view.

But what right does the school or the textbook author have to promote certain values? Besides, assuming they have such a right, *what* values are to be promoted? These are complex and difficult questions. The issues suggested by these questions are often the cause of much controversy between parents and schools. Either the schools are promoting values not shared by the parents, or the school is failing to promote certain values deemed to be important by the parents. This has caused cautious (and often fainthearted) school teachers to assume an alleged neutral position on the values question.

To claim neutrality on the teaching of values is not a realistic way to deal with it. For example, even a decision to *avoid* a sensitive, controversial issue in the classroom is an expression of a value. By so doing, the teacher is valuing social harmony, possibly even his or her job, more highly than value placed on the educational outcomes of the controversial lesson. This is not meant to suggest that the teacher should or should not make one choice or the other in such a case. We mention this only to show that value preferences are always present in teaching, and cannot be avoided. A hundred times a day the teacher makes decisions that are values-based—what questions to ask, what questions to avoid, who should be called on to respond, what is to be read, how much time is to be spent on a topic, what films to use, who to invite as a resource person, what materials to avoid. Similarly, the textbook author makes hundreds of decisions about what topics to include, which ones to emphasize, what study questions to ask, how many pages to devote to certain historical periods, and so on. Whether or not the school and the textbook author have the *right* to promote certain values is really beside the point, because the promotion of values cannot be avoided in either schools or textbooks.

The question, therefore, comes down to *which* values are to be promoted. In order to deal with this issue, it is necessary to differentiate between *general* values and *personal* values. General values may be defined as the ethical and moral guidelines that are embraced by this society. They are identified in the great historical documents of the republic. They are defined in the laws of the land. They have been clarified by court decisions. They are a part of our religious heritages. They are universally accepted as the keystones of social morality, and the woof and warp of the fabric of our national character. They are sometimes alluded to in a humorous way as representing "God, country, and motherhood"—meaning that they are so generally pervasive and so abstract that they are acceptable to everyone. Freedom, equality, the right to life, liberty, and the pursuit of happiness, honesty, truthfulness, fair play, good sportsmanship are a few examples of *general* values.

Ordinarily the school and the textbook author encounter few if any problems in promoting general values. Indeed, they are required to do so by the education codes of most states. For example, a recent study by the Robert A. Taft Institute of Government found that forty-seven of the fifty states had legislative requirements calling for instruction in citizenship. It is important for the teacher to recognize the presence of general values in the curriculum, and to understand that communities throughout this country expect citizens to know and to embrace them.

As we move from *general* values to *personal* values, we encounter quite different conditions for teaching and learning. Personal values are those ethical and moral guidelines that an individual internalizes to guide his or her own personal life. In this society, where freedom of conscience is a highly prized general value, personal values must be individually derived. Personal values are the interpretations and applications of general values that each individual human being makes. For example, the school may promote honesty as a general abstract value, but precisely how an individual behaves in situations that involve honesty is for the person alone to decide. Thus, what may be interpreted as honest behavior by one individual might be viewed as social insensitivity by someone else. What one individual may perceive as a consuming and rewarding hobby may be seen as a total waste of time by someone else. One person's interpretation of freedom is what the next sees as soft-headed liberalism.

What often happens is that personal values are taught as if they were general values, or even as if they were cognitive learnings. For example, the value *loyalty* (a general value) may be taught as though there is only one way to behave if one is loyal: being totally and unquestioningly obedient. The concept of "loyal opposition" would be unacceptable to this interpretation of loyalty, yet it is a well-established principle in both American and British political life. Or, to take another example. Suppose fourth graders were studying city life. A great deal of substantive content about cities and city life may be included. Several general values may also be included, such as the need for sanitation, concern for the environment, the pleasure of aesthetically pleasing surroundings, and others. But the child may be asked, "Do you like the idea of a Megalopolis?" Or the child may be shown a city dwelling of the future and be asked, "How do you like it?" These are good examples of questions that help pupils clarify their own personal values. How can one tell someone else what he or she should like or dislike? How can one claim that there is a "right" answer to such questions? Yet these are important questions, because sooner or later everyone will need to sort out the things one likes and those one dislikes. Children need to be thinking about their preferences—not only what they are, but why they choose them.

Children need frequent opportunities to clarify their value choices in a nonthreatening environment such as the classroom. They need to try their ideas out on each other. Of course, none of this will get very far if the teacher is looking for "correct" answers from the children to questions dealing with personal values, or allows the responses of children to be ridiculed because they happen to be different from others in the group. Personal values are just that—very personal, private matters. Teachers need to be careful not to pry. One does not read another's personal diary. Some personal values should only be thought about, not shared with anyone else, least of all one's classmates.

With children in the primary grades, it is difficult to distinguish between general and personal values. The examples used to explain a general value are likely to be personalized by the youngster in developing his or her own value framework. For example, in the first grade such general values associated with family life as affection, security, and caring for others are often apparent. The child will interpret these in terms of his or her own family. How the child personalizes these values will, of course, depend on how consistent they are with the realities of his or her own life. At these early levels children need many examples of behavior based on general values. Otherwise, they would have no way of knowing what behavior society expects, i.e., behavior that results in reward, and that which results in punishment. Even at this level, however, the teacher should allow generously for simple choice making, because this provides children with opportunities for expressing value preferences.

As children move into the middle and upper grades, more can be done in differentiating between general and personal value development. At this level, children should become more actively involved in the *valuing* process. This process involves the identification and analysis of value components of problems and issues, making personal choices and commitments, understanding the consequences of value choices, and acting in accordance with value preferences. Professor Sidney Simon has developed a number of interesting valuing exercises that can be used for this purpose. Take the following as an example:

> The teacher obtains blank Western Union telegram blanks. Or simply has students head a piece of paper with the word *Telegram.* He then says, "Each of you should think of someone in your real life to whom you would send a telegram which begins with these words: I URGE YOU TO . . . Then finish the telegram and we'll hear some of them."[3]

Valuing exercises of this type, when properly handled by the teacher, may provide the pupils with opportunities to think about and clarify their own values, and to explore the extent of their own commitment to particular values.[4]

[3]Sidney B. Simon, "Values-Clarification vs. Indoctrination," *Social Education* 35: 903 (December 1971).

[4]The following source contains many specific value-clarification exercises useful to the classroom teacher: Sidney B. Simon, Leland Howe, and Howard Kirschenbaum, *Values Clarification: A Handbook of Practical Strategies for Teachers and Students* (New York: Hart Publishing Company, 1972).

The teacher is cautioned against the indiscriminate use of value-clarification exercises. The procedures are deceptively simple but may carry a powerful emotional and psychological impact. For instance, using the I URGE YOU . . . exercise described in the foregoing paragraph, suppose a ten-year-old child sends the following "telegram" and posts it on the bulletin board for all to see:

Dear Mommy and Daddy,

I urge you to stop drinking and arguing and fighting every night after I go to bed. I can hear the mean things you say to each other, and they make me cry. I hate you for it.

Your daughter

Debbie

One can only speculate on the potential psychological damage that could result from such a public statement about one's parents, but it would have to be great. The child is bound to recall this public disclosure later in life, and be embarrassed and disturbed by it.

ACTIONS SPEAK LOUDER THAN WORDS

The following is a list of values that to some degree are embraced by large numbers of Americans:

Justice	Individual liberty
Competitiveness	Industriousness
Independence (personal)	Consideration for others
Productive output	Time conservation

1. Can you think of examples of specific classroom practices that support and reinforce these values?
2. Can you think of examples of classroom and administrative practices that contradict these values?
3. Which of these values most frequently reflect themselves in classroom practices? Is this consistent with what schools claim to be emphasizing?

Valuing strategies that explore the child's interior psychological space may be defended on the basis of value clarification but may in fact be violating the person's privacy. Responsible advocates of value clarification go to great lengths in explaining to teachers that participants in value clarification must always have the choice of participating or not. Yet with all of us, and with young children in particular, the social pressure to participate is often so compelling that the individual is not really able to exercise a choice. A teacher who is exercising responsible judgment will not place a child in a position of having to make such a difficult decision.

Value clarification gets into difficulty when it takes on the characteristics of group therapy. In the process, children are involved in "exploring" basic beliefs that guide their lives. This almost certainly leads the discussion in the direction of religious values, precepts, and beliefs that children have learned at home or in their church. Of course, this results in parental objection, as it properly should. When value clarification enters the private lives of pupils to the extent described here, the teacher has far exceeded the ethical, and perhaps even the legal, parameters of the curriculum of the public school classroom.

Conventional approaches to moral and value education have defined moral behavior in terms of specific and discrete traits. That is, one is honest or not, responsible or irresponsible, truthful or deceitful, self-directed or dependent, self-controlled or impulsive, and so on. Moreover, the strategies used to teach these fixed traits have been largely authoritarian, impositionist, exhortative–preaching, punishment, reward, example, expository, catechetical. The assumption is, of course, that verbal behavior is a correlate of action; that knowing means doing.

The research of Professor Lawrence Kohlberg suggests some new directions for moral education that may prove to be more efficacious than the traditional ones have been. Kohlberg rejects the definition of moral character in terms of "fixed traits" such as honesty, responsibility, and selflessness. Instead he conceives of moral judgment as being developmental, proceeding through a series of three levels divided into six stages. His conclusions are based on several studies, the most significant being a longitudinal study of seventy-five boys extending over a period of eighteen years. The Kohlberg stages of moral development are summarized in Table 1.[5]

[5] Kohlberg's ideas are elaborated on in: "Stages of Moral Development As a Basis for Moral Education," Clive Beck, Brian Critterdon, and Edward Sullivan, Eds., *Moral Education* (Toronto: University of Toronto Press, 1970); See also Lawrence Kohlberg, "Moral Development and the New Social Studies," *Social Education* 37 (May 1973), 369–75; Lawrence Kohlberg and Phillip Whitten, "Understanding the Hidden Curriculum," *Learning* 1 (December 1972), 10–14; Lawrence Kohlberg, "Moral Education in the Schools: A Developmental View," *School Review* (Spring 1966), 1–30.

TABLE 1
Kohlberg's Stages of Moral Development

Preconventional Level

Stage 1. *Punishment and obedience orientation*
(The physical consequences of behavior are of central concern; avoidance of punishment directs right behavior.)

Stage 2. *Instrumental relativistic orientation*
(Pragmatic approach to right actions; doing right things because such action satisfies one's needs.)

Conventional Level

Stage 3. *Interpersonal concordance or "good boy-nice girl" orientation*
(Conformity to role stereotypes; good behavior is that which pleases others and is approved by them.)

Stage 4. *"Law and order" orientation*
(Right behavior is doing one's duty; authority, fixed rules and maintenance of social order are valued.)

Postconventional Level

Stage 5. *Social contract legalistic orientation*
(Right action defined in terms of individual rights and standards that have been critically examined and accepted by the whole society. Emphasis on procedural rules for arriving at consensus. The official morality of the U.S. government and Constitution.)

Stage 6. *Universal-ethical-principle orientation*
(Right action defined by one's conscience consistent with self-chosen ethical principles. These are universal principles of justice, of reciprocity, and equality of human rights, and of respect for the dignity of human beings as individual persons.)

These six stages are arranged in such a way that each level leads into the next higher one:

Consider how each level of judgment leads into the next higher one. A young child growing up is punished or rebuked (stage 1) but soon realizes that these punishments coincide with his own best interests (stage 2). Unpunished activities are not only more pleasurable, but they anticipate role expectations encountered at home and in school (state 3). Conformity to such role expectations over a period of time enables the child to understand the role he plays in a larger constellation of roles organized by legal authorities (stage 4). The child uses his awareness of lawfulness as the basis for his own contracts and interpersonal commitments (stage 5). After repeated formation of such volun-

WHAT CAN YOU DO ABOUT IT?

To what extent do classroom situations contribute to stealing, lying, cheating, aggression, hostility, and lack of consideration for others? Many think they contribute very substantially. Consider the following situations:

1. A teacher leaves loose change lying around on her desk during the school day.
2. A teacher stores her purse containing money in an unlocked and easily accessible closet in the classroom.
3. Assignments are unreasonably excessive, with embarrassing consequences for noncompletion.
4. Testing situations are poorly or carelessly supervised.
5. A child or children fear drastic consequences if it is found that they have been involved in an infraction of school rules.
6. The classroom atmosphere is one of high tension and anxiety; pupils are constantly edgy, easily irritated.
7. There are many competitive situations, where children are pitted against each other, and are such that pupils enjoy excelling or "beating" their classmates.
8. The teacher makes an excessive number of negative and destructively critical statements.
9. There are few opportunities to relax and enjoy social interaction.
10. The pupils fail to establish attitudes of respect for the belongings of others, or careless storage of personal items, making it easy for pupils to use and take things (innocently or intentionally) that belong to others.

1. What would you predict to be the consequences of each of the situations described?
2. Do situations of the type described encourage dishonest or inconsiderate behavior even at the college level?

tary commitments, he is able to abstract and apply those principles of conscience (stage 6) that render mutual relationships valuable and satisfying.[6]

If the Kohlberg ideas are sound—and not all authorities agree that they are—they have obvious implications for a program of

[6] Lawrence Kohlberg and Phillip Whitten, "Understanding the Hidden Curriculum," *Learning* 1 (December 1972), 12-14.

moral education in schools. First of all his analysis recognizes that individuals may be at different stages in their moral development. The stages do not correspond to the age of individuals. Adults may be at stage 3 or stage 4, and doubtless many of them are. School children may equal or exceed the moral development level of persons who are much older. This scheme also has the advantage of dealing with traits in terms of *development* rather than as fixed traits. This means that one does not approach learners as if they were honest or dishonest, for example, but rather, how they are able to deal with a moral dilemma in which honesty is involved.

An important guideline to moral education would seem to be to present moral issues at the appropriate level for learners. Kohlberg and Whitten point out that "A series of carefully duplicated experimental studies demonstrates that children seldom comprehend (moral) messages more than one stage above their own."[7] Thus, it is possible to gear moral teachings at either too high or too low a level. When geared too low, children are apt to perceive the instruction as inappropriate, that they are being treated as though they are less mature than they are; in short, the moral message does not have their respect. This is undoubtedly a major shortcoming of moral education of the past. If, on the other hand, the message is too high, the learner will not understand what is involved. It would seem that the most appropriate level is just above the present developmental level of the learner.

DEVELOPING RELATED COMPETENCIES

"And He Rested on the Seventh Day . . ." (Genesis 2:2)

Explain how you would have responded had you been the teacher in the following situation based on an actual classroom incident:

The class had been studying the solar system in their sixth-grade science. The children were fascinated by it, especially so because their teacher took full advantage of the publicity concerning a meteor shower in progress at the time. Their teacher was well-informed on the subject and responded authoritatively to the children's questions. The lively discussion proceeded into the realm of the origin of the universe. Their teacher explained in simple terms that a current theory that many scientists support is the "Big Bang Theory."

[7] Ibid., p. 14.

She also pointed out that not all scientists support this theory and that there are other views on the subject. She further explained that no one really knows how the universe came into being. At this point one of the girls in the class said, "Miss Gormley, why are we talking about this when everyone knows that God made the world and everything in the universe?"

The Missing Persons List

Mrs. Fong often reads children's biographies of great Americans to her second- and third-grade combination class. She feels that through the lives of these outstanding persons the pupils will develop an attachment to ideals and values that can be useful in guiding their own lives. Her list of biographies includes George Washington, Abraham Lincoln, Thomas Edison, John C. Fremont, Charles Lindbergh, Mark Twain, Meriwether Lewis, and Andrew Carnegie.

1. What are your views regarding Mrs. Fong's selection in terms of the purpose of this activity?
2. If you were to compile such a list, what names would you include?

"Keep Those Cards and Letters Coming"

The following excerpt from a letter to the editor appeared in a local newspaper:

> I am tired of seeing our tax dollars spent on public schools that teach social and moral attitudes that are foreign to everything God-fearing and patriotic Americans fought and died for. Children should be forced to learn those principles that made America the great democracy that it is. Unquestioning obedience of the law and respect for authority are absolutely essential to the preservation of a free society. Teachers should be summarily discharged who fail to instill these values in children.

1. Does this sound ludicrous to you? Letters similar to this one appear in American newspapers each day. How would you respond to such a letter?
2. How can a teacher guard against being intimidated by such broadsides?
3. What recourse does a teacher have if he or she should be "summarily discharged" for the reasons cited in the letter—or for any other reason?

FOR FURTHER PROFESSIONAL STUDY

Books

Berman, Louise M. and Jessie A. Roderick, Eds. *Feeling, Valuing, and the Art of Growing: Insight into the Affective.* Washington, D.C.: Association for Supervision and Curriculum Development, 1977.

Gilbert, Anne Green. *Teaching the Three Rs Through Movement Experiences.* Minneapolis, Minnesota: Burgess Publishing Company, 1977.

Raths, Louis E., Merrill Harmin, and Sidney B. Simon. *Values and Teaching*, 2nd ed. Columbus, Ohio: Charles E. Merrill, Inc., 1978.

Rockefeller, David, Jr., Chairman. The American Council for the Arts in Education: Special Project Panel. *Coming to Our Senses: The Significance of Art for American Education.* New York: McGraw-Hill Book Company, Inc., 1977.

Samples, Bob, Cheryl Charles, and Dick Barnhart. *The Wholeschool Book.* Reading, Massachusetts: Addison-Wesley Publishing Co., 1977.

Periodicals

Allen, Elizabeth G. and Jone P. Wright. "Just for Fun: Creative Dramatics Learning Center." *Childhood Education* (February 1978), 169-175.

Bloom, Benjamin S. "Affective Outcomes of School Learning." *Phi Delta Kappan* (November 1977), 193-198.

d'Heurle, Adma. "Play and the Development of the Person." *The Elementary School Journal* (March 1979), 225-234.

Leming, James S. "Research in Social Studies Education: Implications for Teaching Values." *Social Education* (November-December 1979), 597-601+.

Joseph, Pamela B. "Parents and Teachers: Partners in Values Education." *Social Education* (October 1979), 477-478+.

Thomas, Donald and Margaret Richards. "Ethics Education Is Possible!" *Phi Delta Kappan* (April 1979), 579-582.

12

Professional Development of the Elementary School Teacher

THE QUALIFIED AND COMPETENT TEACHER . . .

1. Recognizes the importance of professional development throughout a career.
2. Is knowledgeable about the societal and professional impacts on the teaching profession.
3. Takes advantages of the opportunities for professional development.
4. Participates in activities that promote personal growth.

Performance Criteria

As a result of the serious study of this chapter, the student should be able to . . .

1. Analyze the role of teacher organizations in the professional development of teachers.
2. Describe the opportunities for professional development that result from membership in professional associations.
3. Describe the opportunities for professional development programs for inservice education, certification, advanced degrees, continued education, and career-branching specializations.
4. Provide examples of activities that enrich personal growth.

Some believe that the life of a teacher is a relatively easy one, and until recent years, the occupational restraints felt by teachers were somewhat less rigorous than those imposed on members of most other occupations. The reasons for this belief—many would prefer to call it a myth—seem to bear up rather well when certain facts are considered. These facts show that (1) admission to teacher education, in terms of entry requirements, is easier than that of most other professions; (2) the amount of coursework devoted exclusively to professional education is very low—a national average of about thirteen percent of the total coursework required for a baccalaureate degree; (3) reentry into the profession usually requires no special preparation other than locating and securing a teaching position; (4) requirements for keeping current in professional knowledge and attendant skills are loosely coordinated; (5) performance evaluation of teachers is frequently opposed by teacher associations; and (6) fringe benefits, including a work year of approximately 185 days, are provided.

Many would argue that these advantages are more than offset by several counterbalancing factors: (1) teaching, psychologically speaking, is a high stress occupation; (2) possibilities for professional promotion within the teaching ranks are limited and are usually confined to "advancement" to an administrative position; and (3) the teaching profession is subject to the caprice and whims of a voting public in so far as decision making and job security are concerned.

These pros and cons relative to the merits of the profession are sufficient to suggest that perhaps teaching does not qualify as a true profession; however, the vast majority of educators insist that teaching is a profession and should be so designated. They frequently base their claim for this distinction on the fact that education has certain characteristics that are similar to those associated with the medical profession. Both provide essential service to society, and each group requires a specialized body of knowledge for its practitioners. Both have governing structures—the American Medical Association and the National Education Association. A training period followed by a certification or licensing requirement are imposed on practitioners of each group. Both groups also promote professional standards and protect the welfare of their members.

Although these claims are reassuring, most educators would probably agree that education has much to accomplish before it can match the uniformity of standards and professional rewards enjoyed by the medical profession.

We believe the teaching profession must make a serious effort to establish its professional image. This can best be done by recognizing the teaching profession as a long-term career that requires continual development on the teacher's part. We also believe that preservice teachers need to give serious thought to the teaching profession as an enduring career at the onset of their program. The selection of the teaching level, academic field, and other aspects of the preparatory phase become choices that, when made early, with a long-term career in mind, can serve to make teaching a fulfilling occupation.

Professional development has many dimensions that can be explored and enjoyed by the elementary teacher. Chief among these are opportunities provided by participation in teacher organizations and professional associations, pursuit of a continued education, and a variety of career-branching opportunities within the profession. All of these opportunities will be discussed in this chapter.

THE IMPACT OF TEACHER ORGANIZATIONS ON PROFESSIONAL DEVELOPMENT

Political power in a democracy is developed and applied largely through organized groups. The concept of teacher involvement in politics is viewed in certain quarters as unethical. Teachers, however, tend to view political activity as a legitimate means to achieve their objectives. Since World War II they have turned in ever-increasing numbers to teacher organizations as the vehicle for the realization of their goals. They view a strong professional organization as a necessity for their professional advancement and as a vital linkage between the profession and the public.

For a professional organization to have credibility it must be well organized and have the majority of the group it represents as its members. In the field of medicine such an organization is the American Medical Association. The American Bar Association is the prime organization for lawyers. Dentists recognize the American Dental Association as their professional organization. Thus, in the major professions, the majority delegate their individual authority to the organized parent group whose leaders exert a collective authority on their behalf.

Elementary and secondary teachers have two major teacher organizations that represent their interests and that exert political power on their behalf. These are the National Education Association (NEA) and the American Federation of Teachers (AFT). Each of these teacher organizations has associations at the national, state, and local levels.

The National Education Association

This is the larger of the two teacher organizations with approximately 1,800,000 members in 1979. The NEA grew out of the National Teachers Association established in 1857. The name of this organization was changed to NEA in 1879. The organization serves members who are located largely in suburban and rural areas. Its membership constitutes about one-half of the nation's teachers.

The NEA offers numerous services to teachers. In addition to working toward better salaries and improved working conditions the NEA has established:

1. a code of ethics and a bill of rights for teachers.
2. a national liability program.
3. a legal services program for defense.
4. a research program.
5. a political action program.[1]

The organization has a constitution and a set of bylaws for the governance of its activities. NEA governance offers numerous possibilities for teacher participation at the local, state, and national levels.[2] The Representative Assembly is the primary legislative body. Policy making is conducted by this group of nearly 8,000 members. The assembly meets annually and acts on resolutions and proposals that have originated at the local level and in most instances have received endorsement at state-level representative assemblies. Leadership of the NEA is conducted by the board of directors, the president, and the executive committee, all of whom have been elected by the members of the association. A professional career-type staff is employed to conduct the daily affairs of the association. The Executive Director is responsible for the organization and management of the professional staff.

At the close of the 1970's NEA was very active in the support of national policies that affect the profession. Principal among these policy-endorsements were:

1. one-third federal funding of public education as a means to provide relief from the various types of local taxes and as a guarantee of stability in the support of schools.

[1]Adapted from the *NEA Handbook*, 1978-79. (Washington, D.C.: National Education Association, 1201 Sixteenth St. N.W., 1978). pp. 8-9.
[2]See *Ibid.* for the various types of NEA Teacher Organization activities.

2. a cabinet-level Department of Education to insure increased funding, provide a fair allocation of funds, bring together all federal education programs into one agency, and give teachers a strong voice on the federal level of government. (A cabinet-level Department of Education was approved by Congress and the President in 1979).
3. ratification of the Equal Rights Amendment.
4. elimination of discrimination in society.

The NEA has grown away from its once close affiliation with school administrator members. There are various reasons for this estrangement; however, the NEA's adoption of militant strategies, such as teacher strikes as a means to obtain benefits for teachers, has widened the gap between administrators and teachers.

The National Education Association's programs directly reflect its goals and objectives. The goal "Professional Excellence," one of six adopted for 1978–79, includes objectives that provide excellent examples of career enrichment possibilities for teachers.[3] One of these objectives is to make preservice and inservice education relevant to teaching as defined by Association policies. To accomplish this the NEA participates in the National Council for Accreditation of Teacher Education (NCATE) toward the improvement of the accreditation system, disseminates information relative to federal teacher center legislation, and provides technical assistance for establishing those centers, assists local and state affiliates in enacting standards and licensing statutes that comply with NEA policy, and provides an organized response to matters that relate to the preservice and inservice preparation of teachers. Another objective promotes research that responds to classroom teachers' problems, and a third objective provides information systems that support the individual teacher's professional practice. To this end two publications are provided each member. *Today's Education* addresses curriculum and instruction topics, and the *NEA Reporter* covers professional and association developments. Additional publications, such as various research reports and topic-specific memoranda, are available for sale to members. Direct services of a professional nature are also available to members on request. Additional personal benefits for members include computer job location service, educational travel opportunities, low cost medical plans, group insurance, annuities, and reduced cost purchase plans.

For preservice teachers the NEA sponsors the Student NEA found

[3] *Ibid.*, pp. 44–45.

on numerous college campuses. It offers student members many of the benefits available to members of the parent organization.

The American Federation of Teachers (AFT)

The AFT was founded in 1916 and was granted affiliation with the American Federation of Labor that year. Today it is an affiliate of the American Federation of Labor and Congress of Industrial Organizations (AFL–CIO). Most of its around 500,000 members reside in large cities where labor unions are strong. The AFT led the way in more militant forms of political action to obtain teacher rights, largely through teacher strikes and collective bargaining tactics.

The AFT parallels the NEA in many aspects of its organization, purposes, and services. It has a constitution and bylaws for the governance and conduct of its business. It operates through local affiliate groups, area councils, and state federations. The AFT conducts an annual national meeting of its delegates. Its administrative organization includes a president, various vice-presidents, and an executive council. It has eight departments and several councils. These departments and councils offer a variety of services to members as well as helping them to improve their salaries and working conditions. These services parallel, in general, the kinds of services provided by the NEA, including legal counsel and defense and protection against unfair disciplinary or dismissal actions. The AFT publishes the journal, *Changing Education,* and the *American Teacher* that provides members with congressional news.

IMPACT OF PROFESSIONAL ASSOCIATIONS ON PROFESSIONAL DEVELOPMENT

The professional development of the elementary teacher is greatly enhanced as a result of enrichment opportunities offered by numerous professional associations. These associations are devoted to the promotion of excellence in teaching and to improvement of curriculum. They have a scholarly orientation, a characteristic that sets them apart from the larger, politically-oriented teacher organizations such as the AFT and the NEA. We believe that the career teacher should be aware of these associations and participate in one that is relevant to his/her teaching interest. These groups conduct a variety of professional activities as well as publish journals, yearbooks, bulletins, and miscellaneous reports that enable the teacher to keep abreast of developments in academic areas.

THE TEACHER AS A SCHOLAR . . .

William Bradshaw believes that teaching is a fulfilling profession. Early in his career he became active in the local activities of the National Council for the Social Studies. As a result of this involvement, he was selected for membership on a major social studies curriculum development committee in his school district. Recently, Mr. Bradshaw began working on a master's degree in social studies education. Through a contact at the university he was asked by a major publishing company to be a contributing author for a teacher's manual in an elementary school textbook series. Mr. Bradshaw has discovered that even though these activities are time-consuming, his teaching has been enriched as a result.

1. As you read the following section, identify the professional association(s) that offer possibilities for your development.
2. Visit a library and examine several of the professional publications identified in the following section.

Professional association conventions/meetings bring teachers together from across the nation. At these meetings recognized leaders speak and report on research and development. Publishers display books and materials in attractive exhibits. Teachers have opportunities to make new acquaintances, share ideas, serve on committees that meet at convention time, and to mingle with persons who have a high level of professional commitment. All of these activities create a rich atmosphere for professional development.

A sampling of several professional associations that offer career enrichment possibilities for elementary teachers includes:

1. *Association for Supervision and Curriculum Development* (ASCD), 1701 K Street N.W., Suite 1100, Washington, D.C. 20006. An association for professionals who are interested in curriculum and supervision. Membership includes supervisors, curriculum coordinators, curriculum consultants, curriculum directors, professors of education, classroom teachers, school administrators and others who are interested in curriculum. The association has approximately 23,000 members. Publications include a journal, *Educational Leadership,* a yearbook, and miscellaneous monographs. Annual convention/meetings are held.

2. *International Reading Association* (IRA), 800 Barksdale Road, Newark, Delaware 19711. Purpose of the association is to stimulate research and to disseminate knowledge about reading. The membership is comprised of individuals who teach or supervise reading at all school levels. Publications include the *Journal of Reading, Reading Teacher, Reading Today,* and the *Reading Research Quarterly.* There are approximately 70,000 members. An annual convention is held.
3. *Phi Delta Kappa* (PDK), Eighth Street and Union Avenue, Bloomington, Indiana 47401. A professional, honorary fraternity in education. Publications include the journal, *Phi Delta Kappan.* Membership is approximately 111,000 professionals. The association conducts biennial conventions.
4. *Pi Lambda Theta,* P.O. Box A850, 4101 E. Third Street, Bloomington, Indiana 47401. A professional honorary association in education. Publications include a quarterly journal, *Educational Horizons.* Committees include one on status of women. There are approximately 18,500 members. A biennial convention is held.
5. *National Council for the Social Studies* (NCSS), 3615 Wisconsin Ave., N.W., Washington, D.C. 20016. Purpose of the association is to promote the study of the problems of teaching social studies and related issues. Publications include the journal, *Social Education,* and numerous monographs. Approximately 19,140 members belong to the association. Annual conventions are conducted.
6. *National Council of Teachers of English* (NCTE), 1111 Kenyon Road, Urbana, Illinois 61801. Association is for teachers of English at all levels. Publications include the *English Journal* and *College English.* There are approximately 100,000 members. An annual convention is held.
7. *National Council of Teachers of Mathematics* (NCTM), 1906 Association Drive, Reston, Virginia 22091. Association is for teachers of mathematics at all levels. Publications include the journals, *Mathematics Teacher, Arithmetic Teacher,* a yearbook, and other monographs. The association has approximately 47,000 members. The association meets in an annual convention.
8. *National Science Teachers Association* (NSTA), 1742 Connecticut Avenue, N.W., Washington, D.C. 20009. Association is for science teachers at all levels. Publications include the journals, *The Science Teacher, Science and Children,* and other monographs. There are approximately 42,000 members. An annual convention is conducted.

Many professional associations have a student membership fee for preservice teachers. This courtesy offers preservice teachers an excellent opportunity to affiliate with a professional group early in their career.[4]

TEACHING WAS NOT FOR HIM . . .

Edward Taylor is an example of "teacher burnout." Early in his career he discovered that teaching was a stressful occupation. Mr. Taylor found classroom management difficult, especially whenever disciplinary action was required. He spent most of his time away from school worrying about facing his class the next day. Mr. Taylor also found parent confrontations to be threatening.

The annual achievement testing program caused Mr. Taylor anxiety for days on end as he fretted about how well his pupils would score on the tests. This worry was unnecessary, however, because his pupils usually compared favorably with other classes on their grade level.

Mr. Taylor found that preoccupation with his concerns about teaching was preventing him from taking advantage of opportunities for professional development. Summer vacation was not long enough to renew him, and he returned to school in the fall in a state of fatigue. At the end of his fifth year of teaching, he resigned from his position.

1. Have you given some thought to your ability to cope with the stress that teaching produces?
2. Most teachers are successful in developing coping behaviors that enable them to live with stress. Discuss this aspect of teaching with several successful teachers.

OPPORTUNITIES FOR PROFESSIONAL DEVELOPMENT AT THE LOCAL LEVEL

The certification of teachers usually occurs upon completion of a four-year professional training program and a baccalaureate degree. As a consequence of such a tightly packed program, the education of teachers is considered to be only partially completed on receiving the degree and an initial teaching certificate. The majority of

[4] For a comprehensive list and description of professional associations see: Mary Wilson Pair, Editor, *12 Edition, Encyclopedia of Associations, Volume 1: National Organizations of the U.S.* (Detroit: Gale Research Company, 1978), 1434 pp.

states recognize this limitation by requiring teachers to take post-baccalaureate work prior to receiving a permanent or continuing certificate.[5] In many instances this additional course work is completed as part of a fifth-year requirement. This is a common practice in many states and is usually based on the condition that the fifth-year of training is to be completed only after the teacher has demonstrated successful teaching experience.

The beginning teacher should acquire a clear understanding of the state requirements for coursework beyond the baccalaureate degree. These requirements differ from state to state. The Teacher Education Office or the Graduate Advisory Office in Colleges of Education has this information. It can also be obtained from any state Department of Education certification office. The information is also usually available in the certification or personnel offices of local school districts.

Certification requirements are often misunderstood by teachers, resulting in course work taken that is not relevant for certification purposes or, even worse, failure to take courses that are required. The beginning teacher should seek responsible advice at the outset, before any coursework for certification is undertaken. It is advisable for the teacher to obtain a written evaluation of needed coursework in order to have an official documentation.

The combination of coursework for permanent certification and advanced degree attainment is an attractive possibility that is overlooked by many beginning teachers. The number of credits required for both of these goals is usually only slightly greater, if at all, than that required for only one of them. Forty-five quarter credits[6] are generally required for both. Frequently teachers who have completed required coursework for the permanent certificate discover, too late, they could have been pursuing work for a master's degree at the same time. Teachers should recognize that they must be admitted to a graduate program prior to taking courses that are to be applied to an advanced degree. Usually coursework taken before admittance to a graduate program is not approved for inclusion in such a program. For these reasons, as well as to insure proper guidance, the beginning teacher should seek official advice at the earliest possible time.

The professional development of teachers is thus assured, up to a point, following the preservice training period. After the receipt

[5] These certificates are variously referred to as Standard Certificates, Continuing Certificates, Life Certificates, and Permanent Certificates.

[6] Quarter credits can be converted to semester credits by reducing them by one-third, e.g. 45 quarter credits equal 30 semester credits.

of the permanent certificate, however, subsequent professional development of the teacher is an individual matter. The successful career teacher is knowledgeable about the many opportunities for professional development and has the dedication to participate in activities that are available.

The possibility for professional development of teachers has never been as good as it is today. This fortunate situation is the result of various impacts on the profession, including those created by the changing role of social institutions, the increasing intervention by governmental agencies, the growing power of teacher organizations, and the programs and activities offered by professional associations. Thus, dramatic changes have occurred in the expectations and demands on the teacher's time and energy.

Prior to the 1950's teachers were simply expected to do a competent job in teaching the pupils assigned to their classrooms. School administrators, by and large, were expected to take care of the management and conduct of the school, as well as the larger questions concerning teacher welfare. As a consequence, salary policies, working conditions, curriculum development, evaluation of teaching, and inservice education were administrative prerogatives. Today teacher decision making and participation are common in all those activities. With this ever-growing number of teacher activities has come a corresponding increase in opportunities for professional development for teachers. The career teacher should recognize these activities as opportunities not only for professional development but as possibilities that contribute to a fuller personal life as well.

Inservice Education Activities

The 1970's was the decade of "inservice education." The decline of public school enrollments along with the resulting oversupply of teachers caused a shift in attention from preservice education to education at the inservice level. As a result, elementary teachers as well as their colleagues in the secondary schools were confronted with a puzzling array of offerings designed to provide inservice education. The inservice movement, however, suffered as a result of the confusion surrounding the governance of the various offerings and the wide divergence of quality control that was applied. Anything from a course in back-packing to a scholarly college offering in "Recent Interpretations of the American Revolution," was thus considered to be appropriate inservice education.

The situation was confused even more by the competitive atmosphere in which various agencies and institutions offered inservice courses for college credit. Private corporations entered the picture with "packaged courses" in various aspects of curriculum and instruction. These courses were sometimes sponsored by institutions of higher education for college credit. Nonaccredited educational agencies also offered course credits in activities based on "effective ways to teach" or "newer ways to discipline," adding to an already confused situation. The National Education Association, through its state associations, endorsed inservice courses for teachers—a development that represented a sharp break from its historical dependence on teacher education institutions to select and provide courses for career teachers.

The career teacher in many instances was caught in the middle of a growing confrontation between teacher organizations and teacher education institutions in a struggle for control in the governance of inservice education. This dilemma sometimes manifested itself in the teacher's frustration in discovering that credits he/she had earned in an inservice course offered by an agency on the district level was not acceptable in his/her master's degree program at the university. The confrontation between teacher organizations and teacher education institutions also produced a propaganda campaign to confuse the teacher still further. Teachers received circulars advertising a given teacher organization inservice course as being "practical" rather than "theoretical." The unfortunate result of this labeling was an acceptance on the part of many teachers of the belief that college courses were too theoretical to have any value for the inservice teacher. This power struggle with its negative consequences shows few signs of abatement at the present time. As a result a promising avenue for professional development is weakened.

Any attempt to create divisiveness in the teaching profession is unfortunate. The responsibility for the competitive climate that exists at the inservice education level between teacher organizations and teacher education institutions must be addressed by both groups in an honest effort to build better relationships. A workable definition of inservice education must be provided in order for professional unity to occur. We believe that the vast array of activities now being lumped together under the inservice umbrella needs to be sorted out in order to distinguish between (1) those courses that represent continuation and extension of the teacher's development in the study of teaching and learning, and (2) those courses that are intended to enable the teacher to fulfill a job-specific requirement. Konecki and Stein[7] refer to the first type as an example of "continued education"—an organized program of courses or experiences

[7] Loretta Konecki and Alida Stein, "A Taxonomy of Professional Education." *Journal of Teacher Education,* Volume XXIX, No. 4, July–August, 1978, p. 43.

leading toward a professional goal or a graduate degree, and the second type as "inservice education"—courses or experiences that meet the need of the employer and employee on the district level. This classification serves a useful purpose in providing the teacher with a rationale for understanding the purpose of a given course or experience. Thus, a teacher might pursue course work or experiences that contribute to both objectives—inservice education as well as continued education activities—at various times throughout a career.

The Teacher Center represents an approach designed to promote inservice education. Centers exist at various locations throughout the nation, usually supported by federal funds. The NEA has supported the teacher-center concept for several years as a mode of inservice education that is controlled by the profession rather than by teacher education institutions. The teacher-center rationale is essentially based on the notion inservice education is more effective

when teachers determine its content and are active in providing instruction to their peers.

Whatever the type of professional development—inservice education or continued education—the career teacher should utilize the opportunities that each offers. The teacher who has developed a specialty in a teaching technique such as role playing, questioning, creative dramatics, story telling, or creative writing should take advantage of opportunities to instruct others in that particular skill. Such opportunities are increasing as a result of expanding inservice education programs.

Staff development programs offered by school districts as a form of inservice education also offer professional development opportunities. Teachers can enroll in staff development courses designed to improve skills in such areas as communication, problem-solving, and human relations.

The teacher who has completed a graduate degree should be alert

---

PHOTO FOLIO

Professional associations offer teachers opportunities to participate in activities that enhance their development. These groups are devoted to the promotion of excellence in education. The teachers in this photograph are members of a professional association committee that is working on the development of a curriculum guide for mathematics in the elementary school. The teachers on this committee have an important responsibility as they represent a large number of elementary teachers who are depending on their good judgment.

1. Select one of the professional associations listed in this chapter that conforms with your professional interest. Locate the nearest local chapter and inquire about its activities.
2. Also inquire about the curriculum guides that have been developed by teachers in the school district in which you plan to do your student teaching.

---

to opportunities to teach in the evening or summer school programs offered by teacher education institutions. Many of these institutions encourage local teachers to assist in their instructional programs and the practice contributes to the teacher's professional status as well as to the professional enrichment of his/her colleagues.

Continued Education Activities

Teachers who live near a college or university have an excellent opportunity to pursue advanced degree course work during the school year by taking late afternoon or Saturday classes. Most institutions schedule their offerings at times that make it possible for teachers to pursue their studies while teaching full-time. Summer school sessions offer teachers a chance for full-time study. For teachers who wish to enroll for summer school work only, colleges and universities usually make it possible for them to enroll without the admission procedures that apply to regular year programs. Most professional educators agree that the teaching profession needs to encourage its practitioners to continue their pursuit of knowledge beyond the baccalaureate years. Colleges and universities offer academic and education courses that make it possible for the teacher to complete an advanced degree or to satisfy requirements for an advanced certificate. In each case, the teacher is usually encouraged to continue the pursuit of knowledge beyond the baccalaureate degree.

Many educators believe that too much emphasis has been placed on the vocational aspects of teaching at the expense of scholarship. The concept of the *teacher as a scholar* has its place at all levels of education. Recent public clamor about the school's failure to teach literacy reflects a growing concern that teachers do not place sufficient value on preparing pupils with the knowledge and skills necessary for participation in a literate society. For teachers to do so they must provide role models for pupils that encourage scholarship and literacy.

School districts provide incentives for teachers to complete advanced degree work through the awarding of salary increases for completion of advanced degrees. Advancement on the salary schedule is also frequently attached to the number of credit hours the teacher accumulates. As a result of the recent explosion in the kinds of courses and credits being offered by outside agencies in the name of inservice education, many school districts have decided to grant salary increments only for those courses offered by colleges and universities.

In any case, continued education in the pursuit of an advanced degree, or for the completion of advanced certification requirements, or that satisfies both requirements, remains a highly respected avenue for professional development.

Teacher Organization Activities

At the local school district level, teacher organizations provide teachers with numerous opportunities to serve their colleagues. At the same time, these activities stimulate the professional development of teachers who participate in them. The Shoreline Education Association,[8] affiliated with the Washington Education Association and the National Education Association, provides an excellent example of these activities.

The constitution of the Shoreline Education Association establishes a governance structure that includes:

1. The President, Vice-President, immediate past President, Secretary, and Treasurer. Each of these officers has prescribed responsibilities and duties required by the constitution.
2. The Executive Board, composed of the officers and designated organization members.
3. The Representative Council, consisting of the elected officers and at least one representative from each school and the Instructional Services Center. The Council is the governing body of the organization and its duties include the authorizing of the organization's bargaining team to negotiate with the school district on matters relating to salaries and working conditions.

The Bylaws of the Shoreline Education Association establish additional groups that assist in the governance of the organization.

1. The Certificated Cabinet consists of six members appointed by the President and the Representative Council and six members appointed by the school Superintendent. The body serves in an advisory capacity and its goal is to improve communication between the school district and the teacher organization.
2. The Standing Committees/Commissions. There are five standing committees and three commissions. These meet at least once each month and are responsible to the Representative Council. Members are appointed by the President and are sub-

[8]Shoreline Education Association, 17505 68th. Ave. N.E., Suite 204, Bothell, Washington, 98011.

ject to ratification by the Representative Council. (These are detailed in the following eight descriptions.)

3. The Instructional and Professional Development Committee is responsible for recommending proposals involving class size, preparation time for teachers, departmentalization, curriculum and instruction, and other related concerns.
4. The Welfare Committee is responsible for the development of recommendations concerning school district personnel policies and practices.
5. The Salary Committee is responsible for studying and making recommendations for salary improvement.
6. The Public Relations Committee is responsible for recommending proposals related to community and pupil relations.
7. The Legislative Committee is responsible for informing members about legislative matters at the local, state, and national levels. It also is responsible for mobilizing members for political action.
8. The Bargaining Commission consists of ten members who have trained for the bargaining process. It is charged with the responsibility of bargaining with the school board.
9. The Teacher Education and Professional Standards Commission is responsible for supervising and promoting standards of teachers through various activities that enhance teacher education conditions, improved teacher certification standards, and staff evaluation procedures.
10. The Grievance Commission studies and prepares action programs for obtaining satisfactory policies and procedures for the redress of grievances brought by its members.

Many teachers extend their teaching careers in a meaningful way through participation in activities such as the foregoing. They require the talents of the very best teachers, those who have the professional knowledge, human relations skills, and selfless dedication to serve their profession. These qualities are essential for the intelligent leadership of the teaching profession.

Teacher Promotion

Promotion of teachers within the ranks is virtually nonexistent. The only avenue to advancement for a teacher is promotion *out of teaching* and into an administrative or supervisory position. This is unfortunate because frequently an outstanding teacher is rewarded through promotion to a principalship, only to become an average or even a mediocre administrator. The temptation of a higher salary structure is a powerful incentive for a teacher to aspire to an administrative position. The qualifications for each position are obviously quite different; however, the traditional practice of promoting a teacher to an administrative position continues to flourish on the assumption that "a good teacher should be a good administrator."

The absence of a promotion system for teachers also removes what could be a powerful incentive for professional development. Attempts to establish a promotion system have usually been resisted by teacher organizations on the grounds that a hierarchy would be created within the teaching ranks which in turn would result in discrimination and divisiveness.

Efforts to establish a promotion system have tended to follow three approaches: (1) recognition of master teachers, (2) merit pay, and (3) differentiated staffing. The Master Teacher plan is based on an evaluation system that includes criteria for outstanding teaching. A panel of judges, including teachers, evaluates each candidate. The master teacher recognition usually results in a higher salary for the teacher, and, may sometimes entail additional responsibilities.

The Merit Pay plan provides for salary increases for teachers who meet specific criteria such as leadership and teaching effectiveness. The granting of merit pay is usually determined by a panel or a committee.

Differentiated staffing has been attempted more frequently in secondary education than at the elementary level. Even so the concept is appropriate for the elementary school. Team teaching is the common mechanism for implementing the differentiated staffing plan. The team is usually led by a master teacher who receives a higher salary than the other team members. Sometimes the team also includes teacher-aides who are on a lower salary schedule than those team members who are certificated teachers. The plan has many advantages, one of which is the assignment of teachers to perform in those areas where they are strongest and where their specific interests lie. The major disadvantage of the plan lies in the staffing of schools with personnel who have the diversity of competencies and interests necessary to establish balanced teaching teams. Screening, selection, and classification of teachers for assignment also present problems that school district administrators are reluctant to assume.

The absence of teacher promotion constitutes a serious deficit in professional development opportunities. The promotion of teachers to administrative positions is also characterized by still another problem in our society—sexism. The number of women teachers who are promoted to administrative positions is very small. Recent federal legislation, such as the provisions contained in Title

IX, may correct this situation through the opening of additional administrative positions to women. Until the profession is willing to reward the qualified and competent teacher through some kind of recognition within the ranks, teachers will continue to be regarded as underlings in a hierarchical system headed by administrators. This can only contribute to the already wide gap of understanding existing between the two groups.

CAREER OPPORTUNITIES IN EDUCATION

Career-branching opportunities for teachers are increasing. They are the result of the growing complexity of our social and political structure that is demanding a diversity of professional roles in education. These roles frequently are attractive opportunities for elementary teachers who wish to specialize in an educational role that provides an essential service for classroom teachers.

The following are examples of professional roles that offer possibilities for career branching for the elementary teacher.

1. *School Administrator*

The elementary school principal is the most frequent example of this role. Urban school districts, however, often employ assistant principals for the larger elementary schools. Administrative positions, of course, exist on higher levels, such as the Superintendent, Assistant Superintendent, Personnel Manager, Business Manager, or Research Director. Many excellent administrators have come from the ranks of elementary school principals.

2. *Librarian*

This is an important position at all levels of instruction in local school districts. The larger elementary schools frequently have a school librarian assigned on a full-time basis.

3. *Learning Resources Specialist*

This position often includes responsibilities for the coordination of learning resources for the K–12 program. Possibilities for the learning resources specialist to produce instructional programs that are disseminated via school television are available in some school districts.

4. *Subject Area or Grade-Level Consultant*

The large school districts frequently have full-time consultant positions in various subject areas, such as art, music, physical education, mathematics, science, social studies, language arts, or reading. Many smaller districts employ part-time consultants for this purpose.

These persons ordinarily teach part time in order to fill a full-time assignment.

Consultants are sometimes classified according to Elementary or Secondary Education, and in such instances have a comprehensive responsibility for various school subjects. In certain instances, the consultant also supervises teachers in the various subject areas or grade levels.

In addition to the foregoing professional roles, there are also career-branching possibilities contained in the various specialized referral services that are made available to elementary teachers. These include:[9]

1. *Communication Disorders Specialist*
This specialist provides diagnostic, therapeutic, and consultant services for pupils who are handicapped by language, speech and/or hearing disorders. He/she is usually assigned to several elementary schools and serves pupils on a rotating basis.
2. *School Counselor*
The counselor provides individual and group guidance services for pupils with personal, social, or educational concerns. The role also requires that the counselor have knowledge of career development information and educational assessment and testing.
3. *Occupational Therapist*
The school occupational therapist works with pupils who have disabilities that impair their ability to cope with ordinary tasks of living. These disabilities may be caused by deficits in development, physical injury or illness, or other psychological or social problems. The occupational therapist receives pupils for diagnosis and possible treatment.
4. *Physical Therapist*
The physical therapist serves pupils who require relief from a physical disability or pain, and/or restoration of motor function. The specialist seeks to assist the pupil to achieve maximum performance within the limits of the disability. Assessment and diagnosis of the pupil's disability and prescription of treatment are primary responsibilities of this role.
5. *School Psychologist*
This role requires the specialist to conduct academic and intellec-

[9]Descriptions of the responsibilities of these specialized roles are adapted from *Washington Administrative Code: Professional Preparation Certification Requirements,* Chapter 180-79. Olympia, Washington: Office of State Superintendent of Public Instruction, 1979.

tual assessment and diagnosis (including administration and interpretation of individual intelligence tests); make behavioral observations and analyses; counsel pupils and interview parents, teachers, and others relevant to the situation; develop remedial programs for pupils; and conduct research and evaluation relative to pupil-related matters.

6. *Reading Resource Specialist*

The reading resource specialist provides numerous services for pupils and school personnel. These include serving as a diagnostician, advisor, consultant, and trainer of school personnel who work with the reading program. Specifically, the specialist must be able to demonstrate knowledge and techniques of teaching reading; compare various approaches to teaching reading; interpret research data; conduct diagnosis of pupils' reading difficulties; plan and implement reading programs; and conduct staff development training programs.

7. *School Nurse*

The school nurse works with pupils and their families on health matters. He/she develops a school health program and responds to the individual pupil's health problems. A major responsibility is the development of a school atmosphere that promotes sound health practices.

8. *Social Worker*

The social worker assigned to schools assists pupils and their families in resolving social adjustment problems. Knowledge of human development and the social structure are necessary for the successful performance of this role. The social worker also must have knowledge and skill in interviewing pupils in an individual or family setting; working with family members; and in providing assistance to family, educational, and other personnel related to the problem. Knowledge and use of referral agencies for the pupil and/or the family are necessary in order to accommodate the problems that are frequently encountered.

The enactment of PL 94–142, the *Education for All Handicapped Children Act,* will necessitate additional professional roles necessary for the assistance of teachers who are to provide for mildly handicapped pupils in their classroom instruction. These are yet to be defined in most instances beyond the utilization of teacher aides and the various specialists who work with handicapped pupils. We believe, however, that there will be a need for additional support persons once the mainstreaming of mildly handicapped pupils in regular classrooms becomes a reality across the nation.

There is obviously an abundance of career-branching opportunities for the elementary teacher who wishes to become a specialist. On the other hand, those beginning teachers who plan to devote a career to classroom teaching should be encouraged to do so because the foundation of elementary education would be destroyed without a solid group of dedicated teachers. It is hoped the ideas presented in this chapter will contribute substantially to the professional development of the career teacher as well as the teacher who wishes to serve the profession in a specialized role.

PERSONAL DEVELOPMENT

Our discussion of the professional development of teachers focused on opportunities available in those activities that are necessary to the conduct and development of the profession itself. Teachers must also take advantage of opportunities that contribute to their personal development if they expect to pursue teaching as a career. We have emphasized that the growing complexity of the social structure is imposing more and more demands on the teacher's time and energy; consequently, the level of teacher stress is also increasing. "Teacher survival" in the face of these pressures is becoming much less certain than it used to be.

Teachers must serve many audiences, each with its own agenda of demands and expectations. The very same examples presented as sources of opportunities for professional development also represent audiences that teachers must satisfy in one way or another. To satisfy each and every one frequently creates "role conflicts" for the teachers. The school bureaucracy, for example, expects the teacher to be loyal to school administrators while, at the same time, the teacher organization demands the teacher's support in a salary-issue confrontation with the school administration.

Parents are becoming more militant in their expectations for teachers. There is a growing number of law suits against teachers who "failed to teach a child properly." State legislatures are increasing their surveillance of teachers by enacting laws that require competency testing of pupils. Frequently the result of such legislation is an intense pressure on teachers "to produce." Test scores are often compared on a school-to-school basis resulting in a comparison of teachers within a school.

These pressures, coupled with such social problems as inflation, threats of war, family conflicts, segregation, sexism, petroleum shortages, pollution, fear of nuclear energy and a host of others, confront the teacher. The fact that teaching itself is a high-stress occupation intensifies problems already complicated by pressures, role-conflicts, and fears.

We believe, therefore, teachers must develop a life style that is personally rewarding if they are to survive the struggle between the "self" and "social structure."[10] The constraints on teachers imposed by the school and the larger society must be ameliorated by activities that are renewing and personally satisfying.

Opportunities for personal development are numerous and, in the main, similar to those enjoyed by persons in related professions. Many teachers take advantage of summer months to participate in recreational or avocational pursuits. Travel, including study abroad, is an attractive summer possibility for many. Teachers in increasing numbers are active in social and civic groups. Doors to the outside

[10] For an excellent discussion of this concept as well as other sources of teacher conflict, see Chapter 10 in Phillip C. Schlechty, *Teaching and Social Behavior: Toward an Organizational Theory of Instruction.* (Boston: Allyn and Bacon, Inc., 1976). pp. 187-214.

PHOTO FOLIO

Professional associations conduct conventions that are attended by teachers from across the nation. Many of these groups also sponsor regional, statewide, and local meetings. These conventions offer numerous professional rewards to teachers who attend them. The latest textbooks and supplementary materials are displayed in exhibits at the convention center. Nationally recognized leaders and researchers make presentations. Teachers are also provided opportunities to make new acquaintances and to exchange ideas. Committee meetings are held to conduct the business of the association. All of these activities create a rich professional atmosphere for the teacher.

1. What additional resources are available to teachers for becoming acquainted with the latest educational materials?
2. Begin consulting the publications listed for the various professional associations cited in this chapter. These contain valuable information about teaching and the profession in general.

world are being opened by these teachers and the profession is the better for it.

Personal development must accompany professional growth in order for teachers to enrich their lives in a satisfactory manner. The qualified and competent teacher who lives life to its fullest provides pupils with an excellent role model for an abundant and productive existence.

DEVELOPING RELATED COMPETENCIES

A Success Story

Rita Hernandez is an example of a career-minded teacher. She began her career with several professional goals in mind. One of these was to become active in the teacher organization and to develop skills that would enable her to achieve a leadership role. Another goal was to pursue work toward a graduate degree while completing requirements for a permanent teaching certificate. During her fifth year of teaching, Ms. Hernandez was elected vice president of her teacher organization and the following summer she completed requirements for her permanent teaching certificate. In one more year the course requirements for a master's degree in school counseling should be completed. Ms. Hernandez is an example of a teacher who has made the most of opportunities for professional development.

1. Obtain a copy of a local teachers' organization handbook. Identify the possibilities for leadership roles and committee participation it contains.
2. Discuss the advantages and disadvantages of membership in a teachers' organization with a teacher who is a member.
3. During your student teaching experience, discuss with teachers their goals for professional development and the arrangements they have made for realizing them.

A Misplaced Priority

Adam Thomas is an example of a teacher who failed to grow professionally. During his fourth year of teaching he made a decision to accept a job for the following summer, working with a colleague in a business venture. He discovered, too late, that he had devoted more attention to his business affairs than to his teaching position. He failed to complete requirements for his permanent certificate within the stipulated time limit. His petition to the state certification office for an extension of time was denied and, as a result, he was forced to leave the teaching profession.

1. Many teachers have avocations. Some of these individuals find it necessary to work during summers for financial reasons. Unlike Adam Thomas most of these teachers manage to balance their priorities to enable themselves to be successful in their chosen profession and to continue their professional growth. What qualities do you believe a teacher should have in order to be successful in this kind of situation?
2. Prepare a list of avocations that are complimentary to the professional and/or personal growth of the teacher.

FOR FURTHER PROFESSIONAL STUDY

Books

Jarolimek, John. *The Schools in Contemporary Society: An Analysis of Social Currents, Issues, and Forces.* New York: Macmillan Publishing Company, Inc., 1981. Chap. 10.

Lortie, Dan C. *School Teacher: A Sociological Study.* Chicago: The University of Chicago Press, 1975.

Ornstein, Allan C. *Education and Social Inquiry.* Itasca, Illinois: F. E. Peacock Publishers, Inc., 1978. Chap. 8.

Schlechty, Phillip C. *Teaching and Social Behavior: Toward an Organizational Theory of Instruction.* Boston: Allyn and Bacon, Inc., 1976. Chap. 10.

Periodicals

Aiello, Barbara. "Am I Being Paid What I'm Worth?" *Teacher* (October 1979), 66–70.

Bardo, Pamela. "The Pain of Teacher Burnout: A Case History." *Phi Delta Kappan* (December 1979), 252–254.

Corrigan, Gary J. "Corporate Training: A Career for Teachers?" *Phi Delta Kappan* (January 1980) 328–331.

Freeman, Jayne. "The Joy of Teaching: Another Case History." *Phi Delta Kappan* (December 1979), 254–256.

Gehrke, Nathalie J. "Renewing Teachers' Enthusiasm: A Professional Dilemma." *Theory Into Practice* (June 1979), 188–193.

Newman, Katherine K. "Teachers' Lounge Talk: Hidden Messages." *The Clearing House* (October 1979), 69–71.

INDEX

D

E